Over and Back

Brian J. Cudahy

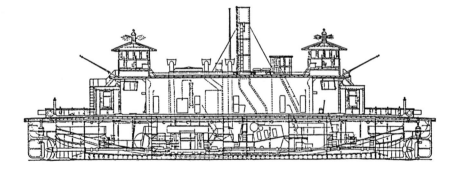

Over and Back

The History of Ferryboats in New York Harbor

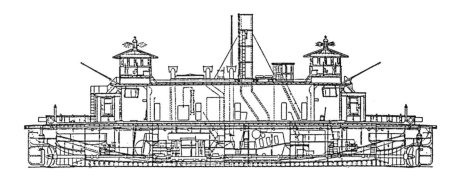

Fordham University Press *New York*

© Copyright 1990 by
Fordham University
All rights reserved
LC 89-84357—ISBN 0-8232-1245-9

Designed by Richard Hendel
Printed in the United States
of America

Publication of this book

was aided by a grant from

The Henry and Ida Wissmann

Fund

Contents

Contemporary action on the ferryboat route that links lower Manhattan with Staten Island; the 1982-built Samuel I. Newhouse *eases into one of the slips at Saint George.* [author]

Introduction

This is a book about the ferryboats of New York Harbor – their past, their present, their future. But it will treat present and future only briefly. Not that the future is bleak for such vessels; it isn't, *it isn't*. It's just that there is such interesting and largely unknown information from the early days of ferryboating in New York, material that helps add color and dimension to the story of the city itself, that more time will be spent talking about what's already happened than what's happening now or might happen in days yet to come.

Much, of course, has been written about other aspects of New York and its harbor – its general history, its role in national and even world economic developments, its immigrants, its ocean-going ships, its railroads, its politicians. And New York has even recently begun to revive a once-more-common willingness to celebrate events and anniversaries related to its port: Operation Sail in 1976, the centenary of the Brooklyn Bridge in 1983, the re-dedication of the Statue of Liberty in 1986. (All of these, it should be noted, being very much in the tradition of the grandest party the port ever staged, the Hudson–Fulton Centennial of 1909!) But the doughty little double-ended ferryboats that were once the only, then the principal, and now just a vestigial means for people and their vehicles to travel over and back across the area's rivers and bays – why, they've been largely ignored, and haven't been properly celebrated since the middle of the last century when Walt Whitman put pen to paper. For it was Whitman who confessed "I have always had a passion for ferries." It was a passion he rendered most artistically in Book VII of *Leaves of Grass* with a poem entitled "Crossing Brooklyn Ferry":

> *Cross from shore to shore, countless crowds of passengers!*
> *Stand up, tall masts of Manhattan! stand up, beautiful hills of*
> *Brooklyn!*

But that was Whitman in the years before the Civil War. By the time a later New York writer, O. Henry, happened on the local scene in the early 1900s, any passion for ferries had decidedly cooled. In his story "The Ferry of Unfulfilment" the heroine, Miss Claribel Colby, is identified as belonging to that "sad company of mariners," commuters from New Jersey, who must perforce cross the Hudson River twice each day on a smoke-spewing ferryboat to the foot of Manhattan's West 23 Street. And what O. Henry said in fiction H. L. Mencken later put in essay form. He felt the most dejected people he ever saw were Manhattan workers who daily had to march "up from the ferries" to their day's toil. Small wonder, then, that ferryboats have lacked the glamor and appeal of tall ships, ocean liners, paddlewheel river boats, and 12-meter yachts.

New York ferryboats are also an elusive lot. When one manages to run across the occasional technical or historical or social commentary on them in some more general work, one finds the treatment at very best limited, and often quite wrong. Indeed, the altogether pleasant prospect that new ferry services will soon be inaugurated in New York makes it all the more important that the harbor's original ferryboat operations be known and understood correctly. The advent of the new should not generate misinformation about the old.

Now as to techniques and proce-dures: the book is divided into two different and unequal portions, the first a narrative story of ferryboat development in New York, the second tables of data and information – including an attempt to present a roster of *every single ferryboat* ever to operate in New York. There is documentation included with the narrative text by way of footnotes to indicate sources of further information and so forth.

In the pages that follow, the term "ferryboat" will have a quite specialized and precise meaning. It will be understood to mean a double-ended and mechanically-powered vessel that hauls passengers and/or vehicles on short trips over and back across rivers and bays. "Double-ended" may cause some head-scratching by those unfamiliar with transportation idiom; it refers to a vehicle that can operate equally well in either direction and doesn't really have a front and a back but two fronts, one of which becomes the back when the other is functioning as the front. (This is much easier than it sounds: an automobile is single-ended, a railroad box car is double-ended.) In any event, in this book when we talk about ferryboats we'll be talking only about double-ended vessels – double-ended vessels with engines.

As with many other New York institutions, precision of linguistic behavior is difficult to enforce. Thus one hears talk today of the Circle Line "ferryboats" that run to Liberty Island – except they're not, according to the above definition. Liberty Island is now, and always has been, served by conventional "single-ended" vessels – that is to say, boats with a bow in the front and a stern in the back and the twain never changing places. Likewise, while some mention will be made of early sailing vessels that preceded ferryboats, properly speaking, on several key routes, the story that follows can be said to have its beginnings only after Robert Fulton demonstrated for all the practicality of powered navigation in the year 1807. Some books, though, shamelessly persist in calling pre-Fulton vessels "ferryboats." They may well have "ferried" their passengers across rivers, and they were likely authorized by "ferry leases" awarded by various local governments. But, damn it, they weren't "ferryboats."

Ferryboats are boats, incidentally, not ships; the terms "vessel" and "craft" are also correct. On the other hand, something that isn't a ferryboat may very likely have been a *steamboat*. That's the proper term for a single-ended vessel that plies inland waterways, the very same places ferryboats are normally found. A steam*ship*, on the other hand, is something that's bigger and goes out to sea, and this altogether useful distinction might very well have held to this day had not a Parisian-born German engineer by the name of Rudolph Diesel come along and invented a different kind of power-plant that fouls everything up, no pun intended. ("Motorship" and "motorboat" do not convey at all the same distinction as "steamship" and "steamboat," and more's the pity they don't.) Since a good deal of our story predates the widespread adoption of Herr Diesel's engine for marine purposes, these considerations are important, even if they entail a touch of ambiguity.

Speaking of Diesel, both man and engine: our story spans the time when his creation evolved from being identified with a capital letter to a small one. In this and other instances, our contemporary spelling, capitalization, and punctuation shall be used throughout, save in direct quotations and citations.

The identification of particular New York ferryboat routes can also be a confusing and perplexing exercise, and while a lexicon of sorts has developed over the years, we shall make a studious attempt to avoid its use entirely. For example: "the Staten Island Ferry" usually refers to the route between the foot of Whitehall Street at the southern tip of Manhattan Island and Saint George on Staten Island, five miles or so down the bay. This presents no particular problem or confusion for contemporary travelers since there is but one ferryboat service for those bound for Staten Island. But, as we shall see, at one time or another there were in the range of a dozen routes serving the island from various points, each being semi-popularly known by its own designation – e.g., the 39 Street Ferry, the Carteret Ferry, and so forth. But through it all only Whitehall Street–Saint George was *the* Staten Island Ferry. Hoboken service likewise involved a case of preferential terminology: there were many ferries to and from Hoboken, only one of which was *the* Hoboken Ferry.

In the pages that follow, an effort has been made to correct this imprecision, and all routes will be identified by both of their terminals; in the case of lines that serve Manhattan, the Manhattan terminal will always be mentioned first. Thus we will speak of the Whitehall Street–Saint George line, the Barclay Street–Hoboken line, and so forth. The older terminology, which some may find more comfortable, is all listed and catalogued in Appendix B.

Many ferryboat operators owned more than one vessel with the same name, one typically replacing the other. (The record in this regard would appear to be the name *Hoboken*, of which one company, and its successors, owned five.) Such names do not include numerical designations in the formal enrollment, so for clarity's sake *within a given fleet* vessels that bore the same name will be identified by sequential Roman numerals set inside parentheses. Thus *Hoboken* (i), *Hoboken* (ii), etc. These numerals are not, it must again be noted, part of the vessel's official name.

Now, in a book about the ferryboats of New York Harbor just what geographical boundaries are being established for New York Harbor? In general, *but not absolutely*, the book will restrict itself to ferryboat services that operated to or from at least one terminal located within what is today the City of New York. The exceptions to this rule will be those services that are simply too interesting to ignore!

The advantages and limitations of various source materials will be noted and discussed throughout the book, as well as in Appendix A. A preliminary and very special word, however, is in order on the central importance that will be placed on a venerable publication of the United States Government, *Merchant Vessels of the United States*, or *MVUS* for short. Under the terms of Federal legislation first passed in the year 1868 and renewed with the establishment of the Bureau of Navigation in 1884, the government each year issued a register of all vessels formally enrolled in a given year and, therefore, entitled to fly the American flag, navigate Federally-controlled waterways, and so forth. If building and launching a vessel is equivalent to birth, enrollment in *MVUS* is the parallel of recording that birth in the county court house.

Over the years the format of *MVUS* has evolved; at various intervals new information items have been added. The name of a vessel's owner, as one example, has been shown in the annual publication only since 1926. But one important constant has been the use of an *official number* for each enrolled vessel, a number that never changes over the life of a vessel, even if its name does. This is quite helpful, not to say invaluable, in tracking a given vessel through a complex history of multiple owners, different names, and even structural changes in registered dimensions, style of power plant, and so forth – not uncommon happenings. A ferryboat that burns to the waterline in 1908 and is rebuilt with a different engine and a totally different profile in 1909 is the *same vessel* if it carries the *same number*. If it doesn't, it isn't; then it's a new vessel built with a second-hand hull.

Sad to report, *Merchant Vessels of the United States* may have become a casualty of Federal spending reductions in the 1980s. The most recently issued edition is that of 1981 (see Appendix A for details).

Two other parallel resources need also to be mentioned. The first is a work of recent scholarship that has attempted, over several editions, to bridge the gap from the onset of American steam navigation ca. 1800 and the first publication of *MVUS* in 1868. Popularly known as The Lytle–Holdcamper List, the most recent edition calls itself *Merchant Steam Vessels of the United States, 1790–1868* (Staten Island, N.Y.: The Steamship Historical Society of America, 1975). Further details about this work, including supplements to the 1975 edition, are to be found in the bibliography (Appendix A).

The final source of vessel information deserving special mention here is the National Archives of the United States, located on Pennsylvania Avenue and 7th Street, N.W., in Washington, D.C. Here are to be found the original enrollment certificates of all U.S. merchant vessels no longer in service, including considerable information not captured by *MVUS*. These certificates are, of course, the primary documents upon which *MVUS* was based, and from which the scholars who compiled the Lytle–Holdcamper List also drew. This is a marvelous national treasure trove. As will be noted from time to time in the pages that follow, one often gets a special sense of contact with the owners and operators of some long-forgotten ferryboat by holding a large, parchment-like document in one's hands and examining the notations, signatures, seals, and stampings that were affixed to it periodically over the years, including, sometimes, quite unofficial marginal notations in pencil.

But it gives one pause. Some day in the future all of these materials may be reduced to "bits and bytes" and one will be able to sit at a computer terminal, perhaps in one's home, and learn, in seconds no doubt, the full documentation history of a particular vessel – or even a whole fleet. Fortunately that day is not yet at hand. Tracking down old ferryboats is still good fun.

I must thank many people for their assistance and their patience in helping make this book possible. George Fletcher, the Director of Fordham University Press, who approached me with the idea that this book now has become, is first on the list. But a virtually countless number of librarians, archivists, curators, friends, steamboat enthusiasts, and, if I might coin a phrase, professional New Yorkers all seemed to come forward at just the right moment with a needed service, or reference, or suggestion, or photograph . . . or even challenge. To all I profess my sincerest thanks.

My family and friends and coworkers have shown forbearance beyond the call over the past months; they, too, have earned my deepest thanks.

A very special word of appreciation is reserved for the many total strangers who responded to published queries I made for recollections and information about New York ferryboats. Many of the letters I received have helped provide form and color to the narrative, but I would like to cite two special responses here.

One was from a woman in New Jersey who told a story – a very sad story – that I must share. She was telling of her family's annual vacation trips to the New Jersey shore back in the 1920s, the car all loaded down with a summer's worth of belongings, and headed out of the city by ferryboat. On one such trip they had driven aboard a vessel and were getting out of the car to enjoy the short voyage. Ahead of them was an ambulance, and in the ambulance was a hopelessly insane woman being taken to a facility out in the country someplace. But inside the ambulance the woman was singing joyfully, and the ambulance driver explained why. The woman realized she was aboard a boat, and was thus convinced she must be returning to her native Italy and the peace and tranquillity she once knew . . . or thought she knew.

Then there was the former captain of a Jersey Central ferryboat who now lives, in retirement, in Portland, Oregon. I would write to the captain after his initial reply to my query and ask all manner of questions. How were the boats fueled? Why, by horse carts full of coal being driven aboard at the New Jersey side several times a day, he patiently explained, until the boats were converted to oil fuel after the Second World War. Once I was attempting to learn how the C.N.J. ferryboat service was suspended when heavy fog gripped the harbor. Who made the decision, I wanted to know. Was it a supervisor on the scene? Did an executive have to be reached, possibly at his home, late on a foggy evening? Or what?

I will quote the captain's terse answer, pointing out that it was written with a firm hand and in larger letters than the rest of his response. "The ferry service was never shut down." The Jersey Central R.R.'s ferryboats quit running in 1967, and it was surely a sad day for my friend, the captain. But in a larger sense his proud claim has proved to be wonderfully prophetic. May it ever remain so.

Burke, Virginia
April 1989

Prologue
"All right, Bunt, You May Go Ahead."

Alice Austen *class, City of New York,*
1986 –

Emblem currently used by the City of
New York to identify the ferryboat
service between Manhattan and
Staten Island. [author]

On Thursday, October 25, three men who were contending with each other for the right to be mayor of the City of New York were bringing their respective electoral campaigns down to the inevitable first Tuesday after the first Monday. The incumbent Democrat, a 39-year-old former Congressman from Manhattan whose father once sat in the United States Senate, remained confident; on October 25 odds-makers were saying he was a four-to-one favorite. The Republican challenger, at best a bland non-entity, was standing poised for his one-time leap into that bottomless abyss to which New York Republicans often seem compelled to consign their mayoral aspirants. The pepper in the stew, this time around, and the man who would give the incumbent Democrat a race for his money a few days hence, was a third-party candidate. He was a man whom many decried as brash, reckless, irresponsible, and a threat to the stability of the Republic itself, but whom others saw as their lone salvation. The year? It was A.D. 1905.

George B. McClellan was the Democrat. The candidate's father had been not only a United States Senator but also a famous Civil War general, and 1905 was a time when many voters could personally remember that awful agony. It was also General McClellan who unsuccessfully ran against Lincoln in war-weary 1864 when the latter sought re-election. McClellan-the-younger had succeeded a man by the name of Seth Low two years earlier and was now running for re-election to a four-year term in City Hall. Endorsed by most New York newspapers, McClellan would eventually win, but not with anything like the kind of margin four-to-one odds on October 25 suggested.

A man by the name of William M. Ivins, a Manhattan attorney, was the inconsequential Republican. The far-from-inconsequential third-party candidate was someone who in 1905 was on the second leg of a frustrating hat trick that will likely never be equaled in American politics. In three consecutive years he ran, unsuccessfully in each case, for President of the United States, Mayor of the City of New York, and Governor of New York State. And as if this weren't enough, throughout all of his campaigns he continued to publish the brashest newspapers in New York City – plus a few elsewhere – and served as a sitting member of the United

Wheelhouse of the Ferryboat Brooklyn, *a sister ship of* Manhattan, *the boat that handled the first official trip from Whitehall St. to Saint George under municipal auspices on October 27, 1905. [Staten Island Historical Society]*

States House of Representatives as well. He was California-born William Randolph Hearst, "Citizen Kane" in the flesh.[1] (He was a bona-fide election-day candidate for mayor and governor, but Hearst's presidential campaign never took him beyond the Democratic convention in 1904, a conclave that nominated Alton B. Parker to run against, and be beaten by, Republican incumbent Theodore Roosevelt.)

Hearst appeared on the city ballot in 1905 under the heading of something called the Municipal Ownership League, and the name suggests his principal concerns. He and the league wanted the city government, and not profit-seeking corporations – "interests," he called them, and always with a sneer – to own and operate such necessary public services as local transportation and the supplying of illuminating gas to households. Needless to say, it was not a platform universally supported. *The New York Times* contended that "every phase and every kind of dissatisfaction have been marshalled under the leadership of Mr. Hearst." And while this is certainly strong language, it is rational and measured in comparison to the lurid and unrestrained prose one finds in Hearst's own *New York American*, where basic distinctions between news reporting, editorial writing, and paid political advertising were non-existent most of the time and all the more so when the boss was in the fray himself. People conditioned today to such election-time restraints in the media as equal time, fairness doctrines, and limits on advocacy journalism can scarcely imagine the kind of non-stop gang warfare that passed for political reportage in 1905. It was, in short, a glorious election.

But it was an election that was still twelve days away on the morning of Thursday, October 25, 1905, and on this day McClellan and his incumbent apparatus had a priceless opportunity to demonstrate their concern for the city's masses and steal a little thunder from the challenger's ideology while doing so. For at eleven-thirty in the morning a brand-new and sparklingly white 246-foot-long ferryboat called the *Manhattan* was to steam away from the foot of Whitehall Street on Manhattan Island and sail down New York Bay to Saint George, Staten Island. Ferryboats had been making this run more or less regularly for almost a hundred years, but what would make 11:30 A.M. on October 25, 1905, different was that for the very first time the service would be run with a city-owned boat manned by municipal workers, and this was to be the new dispensation henceforth. After protracted negotiations to extend the lease of the company that had run the service since 1884 had failed, and when another proposal from a rival company was found wanting, the city made plans in 1903 to take over the operation itself.

But consider this very important fact, please. Today, from sea to shining sea in America, virtually all urban mass transit services – that is to say, subways and buses and trolley cars and what few ferryboats are still to be found – are all publicly owned and publicly operated, and the very

---

1. I have called Hearst a "third party" candidate in the 1905 mayoral election, but the usage bears qualification. The ballot that year bore the names of six candidates for mayor, the three mentioned in the text plus these: Algernon Lee, Socialist Party; James G. Crawford, Prohibition Party; John J. Kinneally, Socialist Labor Party.

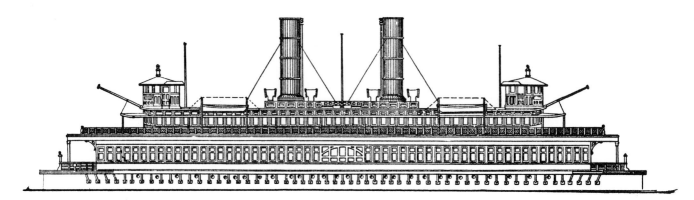

Profile of Borough-class ferryboats purchased by the City of New York for Staten Island service in 1905. [author's collection]

notion is the epitome of conventionality. But in October 1905 the "Staten Island Ferry" became the very first urban passenger conveyance of any consequence to leave the private domain of risk and profit and move into the public domain of subsidy and service. And it wasn't radical, bombastic William Randolph Hearst and his Municipal Ownership League that would make the change and sweep out the old order. It was Tammany Hall's George McClellan, orderly and methodical to a fault, who tooted the new ferryboat's whistle, so to speak, that October morning.

The weather was not auspicious. At ten-thirty storm warnings were ordered posted along the Atlantic Seaboard from Baltimore to New York and later in the day driving rain would drench the mayor to the skin at a campaign stop in Richmond Hill. A storm centered over western Tennessee early in the morning was rapidly moving east, but as eleven-thirty approached it was merely cloudy and overcast at the ferry slip where the 1954-ton and flag-bedecked *Manhattan* was ready for her ceremonial departure. Some 2000 invited guests were on board as the mayor's cavalcade wheeled into the plaza in front of the ferry building adjacent to the South Ferry terminal of Manhattan's four elevated railway lines.[2] His Honor quickly

2. Throughout, I will refer to the ferry terminal at this location as Whitehall Street, and Whitehall Street only. When I use the expression "South Ferry," I will be talking about adjacent subway and el stations, or the general neighborhood surrounding the ferry terminal.

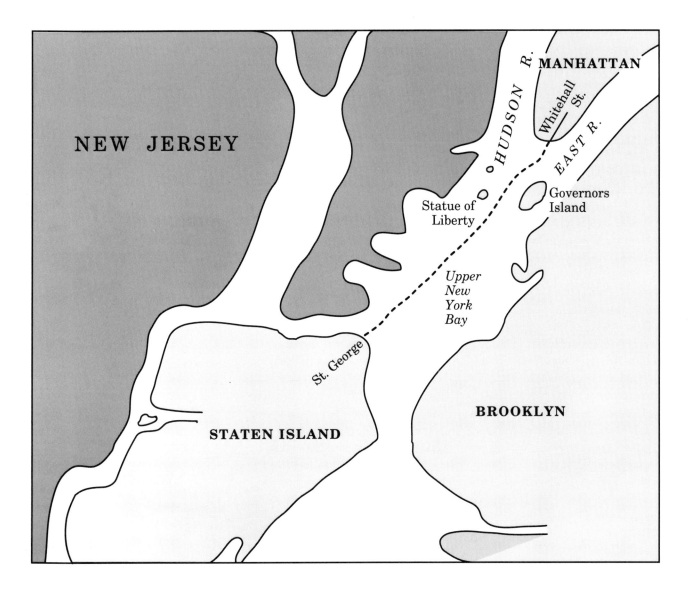

1. Route of the Municipal Inaugural, October 25, 1905

boarded the new vessel and was escorted to the pilot house above the hurricane deck for the inaugural. Captain M. N. Bunt was to be *Manhattan*'s master for the trip, and after a dutiful round of handshakes McClellan turned to Bunt, who was decked out in his new municipal blue serge ferry captain's uniform with shiny brass buttons, and said, "All right, Bunt, you may go ahead."

Captain Bunt, incidentally, was identified in *The New York Herald* as "Bunce," and the paper even included a photograph of the man standing smartly on *Manhattan*'s top deck with all the aplomb of a North Atlantic mailboat captain about to depart New York for the channel ports of Europe. But the man's name was Morris N. Bunt, and he lived at 150 West Street in Manhattan, and furthermore no "Bunce" appears either on the payroll records of the city's Bureau of Ferries in 1905 or as the holder of a Federal certificate to serve as the master of inland steam vessels at the port of New York. Incidentally, too, before joining the municipal service Bunt skippered ferryboats for the Jersey Central Railroad. Indeed, his Fed-

eral license was suspended for thirty days in 1903 when he was found to be at fault in a minor collision while in command of that railroad's *Lakewood.*

Bunt called for power from *Manhattan*'s twin 2-cylinder steam engines, and down below the main deck Chief Engineer Lawrence Oliver pulled the levers and turned the handles that fed hot steam into *Manhattan*'s four cylinders. With mighty salutes from the ferry's steam whistle to mark the occasion, *Manhattan* began to move out. Just as she was clearing Whitehall Street an inbound boat from Staten Island was arriving in the adjacent slip. She was the 41-year-old *Middletown*, one of the private ferryboats whose tenure on the line was coming to an end; the contrast between the two was extreme. *Manhattan*'s white superstructure was glossy and new, *Middletown*'s was old and dirty; the new vessel had a steel hull, the old one a hull made out of wood; *Manhattan* was propelled by screw propellers, *Middletown* by old-fashioned sidewheels.

As *Manhattan* made her way toward Staten Island, harbor craft of all sorts greeted the newcomer

with lusty whistle salutes. The flagship of the city's fireboat fleet, *The New Yorker*, moved out from her berth at the Battery and added a piercing siren to the general din, a cacophony that many aboard *Manhattan* felt was getting downright painful.[3] Reporters noted that women, especially, found the noise objectionable.

No sooner was *Manhattan* clear of her Whitehall Street slip than passengers began to take notice of

---

3. Save only its ferryboats, the city's most colorful and interesting maritime operation over the years has been its fleet of fireboats, and I will try to identify as many of the latter as convenient during the narrative story of the former. *The New Yorker*, for instance, was a 112-foot-long vessel that was built in 1890 as *New Yorker* – yes, it was a formal name-change to add the definite article – and she served for many years as the flagship of the Fire Department fleet, a nominal honor given to the vessel assigned to the post near the Battery. The current flagship, Marine Company Number One in today's F.D.N.Y. argot, is the *John D. McKean*, built in 1954 in Camden, N.J. In earlier years, before the current terminology was adopted, the flagship designation was "Engine 57."

Since municipal operation was begun on the Whitehall St.–Saint George line in 1905, every trip has included a pass-by of the famed Statue of Liberty. Here in 1987, just days after the city and the nation celebrated the statue's centenary, the municipal ferryboat The Gov. Herbert H. Lehman *repeats the ritual.* [*author*]

four identical twin-stack ferry-boats that were laying-to off the Statue of Liberty, steam up. These were *Manhattan*'s sister ships; they were named, all five of them, for the five boroughs of the City of New York. As the inaugural boat made her way down the bay to Staten Island, the other four fell in behind to form a convoy. One of the four, identity unknown, had been officially accepted from the builder only that very day!

Eye witnesses are not of one mind as to *Manhattan*'s precise departure time; one said it was 11:38, another 11:40, and one re-porter even said the trip left on schedule at 11:30. There is no dis-agreement on the running time to Saint George, though. It was uni-versally reported as being 21 min-utes and 40 seconds – suggesting, perhaps, that the various report-ers simply accepted an official fig-ure the city announced at the end of the voyage.

Once *Manhattan* was secure in her slip at Saint George, the mayor and his party went ashore and from a flag-bedecked platform in front of the ferry house the ex-pected political oratory flowed in great abundance. "Two years ago I promised that before the expira-tion of my term in office Staten Is-land should have the best ferry service on earth," said the man who was then trying to secure an extension of his term in office. Entoned Maurice Featherson, McClellan's appointed commis-sioner of the Department of Docks and Ferries, the city agency given the task of running the ferry and whose proud new emblem decorated each vessel's smoke-stacks: ". . . the present admin-istration has made a reality the thing which agitators have used as a play thing." Few misunderstood

It's 1954 and the Cornelius G. Kolff *is nearing St. George, Staten Island, on a trip from Whitehall St., Manhattan. Give or take a few buildings on the Staten Island shore, this is the same view passengers and crew had as the* Manhattan *made the first approach under municipal operation in 1905.* [*author*]

whom Featherson had in mind when he talked about "agitators."

The only discordant oratorical notes sounded at Saint George came when Richmond Borough President George Cromwell, in his speech, tried to say that some of the credit for the day's accomplishments must be shared with former mayor Seth Low. The Tammany

types on the platform registered visible annoyance at the reference. Another less-than-festive aspect of the Saint George ceremony was the sight of twelve black women standing tearfully together on the edge of the celebration. They were former matrons whom the private company had employed to tend the "Women's Cabin" on each ferryboat, and who were paid the sum of a dollar a day for their toil. One woman, Quetta Williams, had worked for the company for over thirty years. When asked why she and the others even bothered to attend the Tammany ceremony, she simply remarked that they had no place else to go. The city had discharged scores of the former company's workers as part of its take-over, and hired an even larger cadre in their stead. The new workers were perhaps skilled and competent, but despite the rigors of the municipal civil service system they were also people with political connections. "[T]welve old colored women" – the language is that of *The New York World* – lacked such connections and so found themselves out of work.

Then it was back aboard *Manhattan* for the official return to Whitehall Street, a slightly slower 26-minute trip because of unfavorable wind and tide conditions. Three of the other four Borough-class ferryboats again fell in behind the leader, but *Richmond* moved into the Staten Island slip vacated by *Manhattan*. After the celebrants had been let ashore back at the north end of the line, *Manhattan* was given a final once-

over and then the first regular cash customers were let aboard. She left Whitehall Street in early afternoon on her first revenue trip under municipal auspices and *Richmond* handled the inaugural out of Saint George. Others of the new boats were then phased into service as needed, and the older side-wheelers were laid up.

The first cash-paying passenger to board the new municipal ferryboat service, unfortunately, did not have his or her name memorialized for posterity. On the day before the municipal inaugural, October 24, 1905, the Honorable Lester L. Clark, a justice of the Richmond County Supreme Court, purchased the first passenger ticket for the ferry to be issued by the city; the little one-by-two–inch pasteboard bore number 1000001. It's unlikely in the extreme, however, that Clark was also the first passenger. What is known is that the very first vehicle to be loaded aboard *Manhattan*'s twin main-deck gangways designed for such traffic was a wagon load of fresh vegetables hauled by a single horse.

The early hours of municipal operation had their moments, especially later in the evening as the

Flag and stack-marking of the City of New York's Department of Docks & Ferries, operator of the municipal ferryboat fleet in 1905. [author's collection]

storm worsened, although the inexperience of new crews operating new boats surely contributed. The boats "worked stiff," many said. On a 7:15 P.M. trip out of Saint George the ferryboat *Richmond* lost her steering for a short time; instead of the scheduled twenty-five-minute trip, the vessel didn't tie up at Whitehall Street until 8:35, causing many theater-bound Staten Islanders to miss the first act. *Manhattan*, on a following trip out of Saint George at 7:45, also had trouble. The captain – not Bunt, incidentally; he had been spelled by another man – made a poor approach to the sole Whitehall Street slip that had thus far been deepened adequately to berth the new city boats, and after reversing his engines and pulling away from the shore he found it easier to circumnavigate Governors Island before making his second, and successful, approach.

The city's newspapers treated the onset of municipal operation of the Whitehall Street–Saint George ferryboat service with less rather than more interest. Hearst's *American* put the story on page one the next day, but devoted fully the first half of the account to the embarrassing problems *Richmond*

and *Manhattan* experienced the night before, not the novelty of municipal operation itself. "City Opens New Ferry; One Is Lost an Hour" was the headline. McClellan's place in the wheelhouse on the inaugural trip went quite unnoted once the story even got around to talking about the first trip, as did the fact that the mayor was among the speakers during the Staten Island ceremony. McClellan was only mentioned in the *American*, for that matter, in the last paragraph as the man who reluctantly put Seth Low's municipal-operation plan into effect, who missed all the key deadlines along the way, and who helplessly permitted a shipyard in far-away Baltimore to win the contract for the construction of *Manhattan* and her sisters when local yards, and local workers, were perfectly ready and able.[4]

But even in the 'papers that

supported McClellan in his upcoming re-election bid, the story was not big news. It wound up on some front pages, true, but not with banner headlines, and was more typically tucked away on an inside page. Clearly the event wasn't even slightly the vast celebration that greeted the onset of subway service in New York on October 27, 1904, 363 days earlier.[5] It was something, of course, of vital importance to and for Staten Islanders, but Staten Island's population was but 60,000 or so out of the city's total 3.4 million (U.S. Census numbers from 1900), and

---

4. We shall see in detail in chapter 6 how the Maryland Steel Company of Sparrows Point (Baltimore) was awarded a contract for the construction of the five ferryboats, although one of them, the vessel that was eventually named *Richmond*, was subcontracted to a yard in Staten Island.

5. On October 27, 1904, the same Mayor McClellan was in the motorman's cab for the inaugural trip on the city's first subway. Built with public funds, the subway was leased to a private firm, the Interborough Rapid Transit Company, for operation. Onward from the 1870s, however, privately built (and operated) elevated rapid transit lines were running in New York. Private operation of city-owned subways ended in 1940, and since that time they have been publicly operated. I have written of the subways elsewhere: see my *Under the Sidewalks of New York*, rev. ed. (Lexington, Mass.: Stephen Greene Press, 1988).

the demise of private ferryboat operation and its replacement by a municipal service just wasn't that big a story, city-wide. For that matter five new ferryboats in the harbor, whoever owned and operated them, were statistically insignificant. In the previous year, 1904, *Merchant Vessels of the United States* shows 147 ferryboats registered with New York as home port. *Manhattan* and the four other Borough-class vessels were the biggest ferryboats in New York, true; but they weren't that big a deal because ferryboats weren't that big a deal; they were just ordinary. Why, before the day was out, Mayor McClellan and his campaign caravan would have occasion to ride yet another ferryboat or two![6]

On Tuesday, November 6, 1905,

George McClellan beat William Randolph Hearst 222,795 to 219,708; Ivins received 133,043 votes. The mayor's margin over Hearst was a mere 3087 votes, or one-half of one per cent of the total cast for the three men.

On election night *The New York Times* planned a special signal to tell all who cared which man was elected. In addition to the usual street-level scoreboards set up by most newspapers outside their office buildings, the *Times* had placed a huge and powerful searchlight atop its new headquarters building at Broadway and West 42 Street – the very same building where, for decades, the descent of a lighted ball would signal the start of each new year to crowds gathered below in Times Square. As to the searchlight: it would be

turned on when the results were known, and from the direction it was pointed, by prearrangement, people could tell who won. At exactly 7:00 P.M. the beacon began to shine to the north: it was McClellan! In their next day's editions the newspaper's editors proudly boasted that they had announced the winner seventeen minutes ahead of the closest competition. Something about a sampling procedure from key wards . . .

The *Times* also felt duty-bound to applaud the city's voters, editorially, for their election preference, but more for the repudiation of Hearst than the selection of McClellan. "Their votes have spared the city the humiliation, the trials, and the dangers of a four years' management of its affairs by a peculiarly reckless, unschooled, and unsteady group of experimenters and adventurers." Had Hearst won, reflected the newspaper, it would have sent "a shiver of apprehension over the entire nation."

Neither Hearst nor his critics were through, of course. During his 1906 run for the New York State governorship a year later, President Roosevelt instructed his Secretary of State, Elihu Root, to

---

6. In 1905 there were but two bridges, and no tunnels, connecting Manhattan with Long Island: the Brooklyn (opened in 1883) and the Williamsburg (opened in 1903). At 7:30 P.M. on October 25 McClellan and his campaign entourage crossed the East River to Hunter's Point on a Long Island R.R. ferryboat and then traveled to Richmond Hill on a special L.I.R.R. train. How or when he returned to Manhat-

tan I was unable to determine. Spoke the mayor at a campaign rally that evening, with newspaperman and social reformer Jacob Riis sharing the platform to indicate his support of the incumbent: "It was one of the gladdest moments of my life when the service was inaugurated [this morning], for it is the grandest exhibit in municipal ownership in the world."

refer to Hearst in public as "an insincere, self-seeking demagogue," and suggest that somehow or other his rabble-rousing newspapers bore some share of responsibility for the assassination of President William McKinley in 1901. Hearst, for his part, never seemed to weary, and while his attention would never be wanting for causes and crusades of more immediate concern, the man until the day he died in 1951 insisted that he had really won that mayoral election back in 1905 and that it was actually stolen from him by corrupt politicians of the Democrat persuasion.

The world of October 1905 sometimes seems remote and distant – but, then again, sometimes it doesn't. For consider:

– the subway in New York had been open but a year. Still there were constant demands being made to expand the system and to do something about its terrible overcrowding.

– John McGraw's New York Giants provided the city with its very first World Series championship that month when they beat the American league's Philadelphia entry, under Connie Mack, four games to one. Christy Matthewson topped off his 31 regular season victories by pitching three complete-game shutouts in the World Series, a feat that has been equaled in no October since. (A gentleman by the name of Robert Brown Thomson, who would make his home on Staten Island for a period of time and achieve just as much October fame in a Giants uniform as either McGraw or Matthewson, was actually born on the eighteenth anniversary of the onset of municipal ferryboat operation, October 25, 1923!)

– Roosevelt-the-Republican was the nation's president. One day some years later a city-owned ferryboat would be named in his honor. (The only other U.S. president to be so honored was a Democrat, John F. Kennedy.)

– the man around whom Orson Welles would one day create a fictional legend on the screen was out roaming the land and creating a legend of his own. (Welles himself wouldn't be born for ten more years.)

– the very same editions of the city's newspapers that reported *Manhattan*'s 1905 inaugural also carried cable dispatches from the Russian capital city of Saint Petersburg on their front pages telling of street riots against Nicholas II and speculation that a new constitution being prepared by the Czar would not quell the demands of the populace. (It just wasn't a good year for the Russian leader. The previous month his government was compelled to sign the Treaty of Portsmouth ending the Russo-Japanese War, a conflict in which Russia was soundly defeated and which set critical parameters for the design – and role – of warships on into the new century.)

In any event, ferryboat service between the foot of Whitehall Street at the southern tip of Manhattan Island and the place called Saint George on Staten Island became a municipal responsibility in the fall of 1905 and has remained so ever since. Exactly how this state of affairs developed and why it became public policy in New York will be explored in subsequent chapters, as will the "municipalization" – an awkward-sounding term that later became popular – of other ferryboat services in the harbor. Also still to be discussed are technical details about *Manhattan* and her four sister ships,

not to mention her predecessors, her contemporaries on other lines, her successors, and the many other ferryboat services that operated over and back throughout the harbor. Why, there's even an interesting yarn about how the ferry landing at Saint George came to be called Saint George! But all of this in due course; the onset of public operation of ferryboat service on October 25, 1905, is a proper and useful point of departure for the story to follow – the history of ferryboating in the greatest port in the world.

What could possibly be more symbolic of frequent over and back ferryboat service in New York than the two simple words used to tell waiting passengers which slip in a terminal they should use to catch the "NEXT BOAT"? [author]

1. How It All Got Started

1812–1824

Had there been an Associated Press or a United Press International in the long-ago summer of 1812, the following is a story one or another of them might very well have moved over its news wire – granted, of course, that Samuel Morse wouldn't come along and invent the magnetic telegraph for another quarter-century.

NEW YORK, N.Y. – July 12, 1812: A new steam-propelled boat bearing the name *Jersey* today entered service across the mighty Hudson River, linking this city with Paulus Hook on the New Jersey shore, a location whereat travelers can readily obtain carriages bound for Newark, Elizabethtown, Trenton, and Philadelphia.

Hundreds of curious spectators watched intently from the banks of their respective shores as the large machine safely crossed the broad river in less than twenty minutes' time and in a seemingly effortless manner. So thoroughly delighted with the accomplishments of the day were the men from New Jersey state that they hosted a lavish banquet for the members of the New York Common Council in celebration of the momentous event, at the tavern located in Paulus Hook. It was New Jersey interests that subscribed the funds for construction of the vessel while it was New York City officials who awarded the lease to navigate.

Jersey was built and is operated under the supervision and auspices of Mr. Fulton of New York, a gentleman singularly renowned for novel introductions in the maritime field. It was but five years ago that he caused to be operated a steam-boat called *Claremont* between here and Albany, a service that has since become an accepted institution between the two cities, as well as way landings along the river.

Unlike *Claremont* and other of Mr. Fulton's several steam-boats intended for journeys of great distances, *Jersey* is built to accomplish more modest intervals. Hence this ferry-boat is made to operate equally well in whatever direction it might be traveling, ahead or back, it not having a fore and an aft but two similar ends that alternately serve as either. Because steam propelling wheels would be

151-foot class, City of New York, 1925–1967

A hundred-and-ninety or so years after the world's first ferryboat carried passengers across the Hudson River between lower Manhattan and Paulus Hook, New Jersey, the scene looked like this; tall buildings define the Manhattan skyline, and while the river itself lacks any evidence of cross-river surface travel, beneath the river rapid-transit trains and automobiles move swiftly through trans-Hudson tunnels. Route of Jersey's inaugural trip is indicated by the dotted line. [Port Authority of NY & NJ]

subject to extreme and frequent danger during *Jersey*'s many landings and sailings, they have not been positioned along the vessel's outer sides as Mr. Fulton has commonly done heretofore. Rather there is but one propelling wheel and it is to be found between two distinct hulls, which gives this uncommon vessel an even more remarkable appearance. The hulls are joined together at their topmost level by timbers firm and sturdy upon which the powering machinery is securely affixed. The propelling wheel is thus hidden from casual view between the two hulls and causes the unknowing observer to ask how the vessel is able to make way at all since it appears to have no means for doing so, the sole clues to the contrary being, one, a tall black smoke pipe which harmlessly wafts the sky with the noxious combustions of the vessel's boiler, and, two, a trail of frothy water that is left behind as *Jersey* proceeds toward her destination.

So easily and swiftly does this new ferry-boat provide a superior means for crossing the river than common periaugers, sloops, and row boats normally to be found between Cortlandt Street and Paulus Hook by those whose commerce compels such trips that one seems secure in saying that Mr. Fulton's new vessel, and others that surely will be built to its general plan and specification, will soon become the common rule for river crossing rather than its current novelty.[1]

The news account is, of course, contrived; but the facts are not. On Thursday, July 2, 1812, Robert Fulton inaugurated steam-powered ferryboat service in New York Harbor. *Jersey* developed mechanical problems soon afterward and was withdrawn for repairs, but she was back in business on July 18, 1812, and continuous mechanically-powered ferryboat service in New York dates from then.

Fulton, born in 1765 of Irish descendants in Lancaster County, Pennsylvania, was not, as is often assumed, the true *inventor* of the steamboat. He was, rather, a clever, talented, and exceedingly resourceful fellow whose trip to Albany aboard the *Claremont* on August 17–18, 1807, represented more the successful bringing-together and orchestrating of available techniques and technologies than the creation of something completely new. The *Claremont*, it is important to stress, was a commercial as well as a technical success, and Fulton is to be seen rather as a high-risk entrepreneur anxious to deploy a new idea in the marketplace more than as a lonely inventor quietly working in his machine shop out behind the barn.[2]

Earlier, Fulton had established a partnership, of sorts, with Robert R. Livingston – Chancellor Livingston, a landed Husdon Valley aristocrat whose up-river estate, Claremont, provided Fulton's most famous steamboat not only with its name but also with a landing to lay over the night on its historic two-day voyage. Livingston was quite a celebrity in his own right: member of the Continental Congress, negotiator of the Louisiana Purchase while serving as the U.S. minister to France, and the man who swore in George Washington as the nation's first president in New York City on April 30, 1789 – there not being a Chief Justice of the United States to do the job until the first president later got around to appointing one.

In 1798 Livingston had managed to have himself awarded a state franchise making him the exclusive operator of steam-powered vessels serving New York ports for a term of twenty years, provided that he, and no one else, put a first such vessel in service within a year's time and the vessel performed up to certain established specifications. This, of course, was quite prior to Fulton's "invention" of the steamboat, the point being that talk of, and experiments with, such vessels were quite the rage.

---

1. A periauger was a distinctive one- or two-masted flat-bottom vessel used for local transportation around New York since the days of Dutch rule, although the name is of Spanish origin. It was especially adept at handling wagons, teams, and livestock. While primarily a sailing craft, periaugers could be supplemented by oar power.

2. For further discussion, see John H. Morrison, *History of American Steam Navigation* (New York: Sametz, 1903; repr. New York: Stephen Daye Press, 1958). Also George Henry Preble, *A Chronological History of the Origin and Development of Steam Navigation* (Philadelphia: Hamersley, 1883). A more recent biography of Fulton is Cynthia Owen Philip, *Robert Fulton: A Biography* (New York: Franklin Watts, 1985).

At first Livingston wasn't able to succeed. But what he was able to do was to secure renewals of his franchise from the New York legislature until an encounter with Fulton in Paris in 1803 led to his claiming the prize on the basis of *Claremont*'s 1807 voyage. Indeed, the legislature even extended the term of the franchise on the basis of how many additional steamers Livingston (and Fulton) might put in service: five years per extra boat to a maximum of 30 years – which is to say, ten extra years for two extra boats.

This produced, of course, a monopoly, pure and simple – an exclusive franchise that prohibited anybody but Fulton and Livingston, or any person or firm they might see fit to license, from operating steamboats in New York waters. The state law – and there were similar statutes in other states governing endeavors other than steamboating; the New York legislation was not that unique – was motivated by a wholly understandable desire to give an inventor some proper period of exclusive benefit from an invention. The Federal Patent Law enacted in 1800 was also designed to do as much, but in the beginning days of

industrialization and experience with newly-developed technical products, not to mention the nation's early testing and probing of the kind of political and economic life provided by a still-new Federal Constitution, the limits of such protections were uncertain and anti-trust legislation was still in the future.

The state-granted monopoly was eventually judged to be illegal and unconstitutional by Chief Justice John Marshall's Supreme Court in the famous *Gibbons vs. Ogden* decision. One of the key factors that led to this litigation was New York's assumption that the multi-year monopoly it had granted Fulton–Livingston extended, not merely to steamboat service wholly between New York ports of call, but also to operations between New York and other states. Indeed, not because of the monopoly per se but on the strength of documents of political incorporation issued by the British Crown, New York even regarded its borders as extending all the way to the New Jersey shore. When the ferryboat *Jersey* entered cross-Hudson service in 1812, therefore, New York officials felt content that her route was en-

tirely within their jurisdiction, even though they also felt that the monopoly they had awarded Fulton–Livingston protected service linking Manhattan and, say, points inland on the Raritan River in the New Brunswick area – i.e., unarguably New Jersey territory. By the end of 1812, after five years of monopoly protection, Fulton had placed six steamboats in service; *Jersey* was the only double-ended ferryboat of the lot.[3]

What kind of vessel was New York's very first ferryboat? She was 118 tons, 80 feet long, all wood of course save her machinery, and was built for Fulton at the Charles Brown yard in New York, builder of *Claremont* and most of Fulton's other early vessels. *Claremont*'s engine was imported by Fulton from the Boulton and Watt people in England, but by the time *Jersey* was built Fulton had his own facility for doing machine work near the Paulus Hook ferry landing,

---

3. Preble lists (p. 51) the six, and their respective services, as these: *Claremont* (1806), *Car of Neptune* (1807), *Paragon* (1811), and *Fire Fly* (1812) in operation up and down the Hudson River; *Raritan* (1807) on the Raritan River; *Jersey* (1812) in trans-Hudson ferryboat service.

roughly where Greene and Morgan streets intersect in Jersey City today. *Jersey*'s engine was, to borrow a phrase, made in the U.S.A.

Jersey's twin-hull design, while different, was not that novel in 1812 New York. The final style of pre-steam ferries to serve the harbor was similarly constructed, right down, in most cases, to the center paddlewheel. On these boats the wheel was turned not by machine power but by horse power – two words, in this case, not one. Draft animals were harnessed to treadmills, or capstans, and thus did the paddlewheel go around.

These horse boats, or team boats as they were sometimes called, made something of a valiant stand against *Jersey* and the new concept she introduced. For one thing they allowed a non-monopoly ferry operator to avoid the litigation, prosecution, and even seizing of vessels that the Fulton–Livingston people were sure to initiate at the first whisp of smoke, and yet to upgrade service. For the team boats equaled the early steam ferryboats in size and carrying capacity – although hardly in speed – and were gener-

ally much superior to sailing craft. In addition they utilized a style of propulsion – horses and a kind of crude gearing common for centuries in the fabrication of water mills and the like – that did not demand the hard-to-find technical skills needed with exotic new steam engines. It was easier, and considerably cheaper, to hire a man who could mend harness and pitch feed than one who could correctly diagnose a problem with a balky steam valve. Needless to say, a horse boat cost far less to build than its steam equivalent.

Some popular history books suggest that horse boats were developed in reaction to and after the onset of steam ferryboats. This does not appear to be correct, although it is clear that they enjoyed their greatest popularity in the period between *Jersey*'s inaugural and John Marshall's ending of the Fulton–Livingston monopoly in 1824.

But this is to digress, if not retrogress, from what happened in July of 1812. *Jersey* had a wide beam; each of her twin hulls measured ten feet across, thus giving her an overall width of 30 feet. Her length was 80 feet. On her in-

tended Hudson River service the current runs perpendicular to her route, so Fulton said: "I found a great breadth of beam absolutely necessary to prevent the boat rolling in the trough of the sea."[4] Wagons and teams were accommodated on *Jersey*'s open main deck on one side of the engine – over one of the twin hulls, in other words – and passengers, on the opposite side. Here an awning was provided for protection from the elements and a below-deck cabin was also available for truly severe weather. The cabin was 50 feet long, but a mere five feet high. The engine was on the main deck in the area between the hulls, together with connecting rods to the paddlewheel.

Fulton was quite proud of *Jersey*'s double-ended design, the horse boats being not necessarily so constructed. Some of them had to come around 180 degrees before or after each landing, and Fulton made much of the fact that considerable time and effort were to be saved when wagons were able to

---

4. From a letter written by Fulton in 1812 to one Dr. David Hosack and quoted by Morrison, p. 518.

disembark from his ferryboat in the same direction they boarded.

Fulton also devoted considerable attention to the two ferry landings so traffic and passengers could easily and quickly board *Jersey*, the key being a floating platform connected to a fixed wharf by a gangway. He devised a system of heavy floating logs to guide and funnel the vessel up to the floating platform – a ferry slip, in other words – as well as another system that used buffers, pulleys, and huge buckets filled with river water to absorb a ferryboat's momentum "without the aid of boat hooks or any pushing or pulling or loss of time or shock, the latter being the most material to guard against."[5] The shock-absorbing buckets had holes in them and were positioned in the river below water level. When the ferryboat hit the buffer momentum began to transfer from the moving vessel to the task of raising the water-laden buckets. When the process was concluded and the ferryboat was secure to her landing the now largely-empty buckets dropped back into the river to re-fill and

await the next arrival. The whole apparatus – that is to say, the float, the ferry slip, and the shock absorbers – was positioned at the end of a wharf that extended out into the river from the shoreline on each side of the Hudson.

Speaking of shorelines, it is interesting to note that in the year 1812 the Hudson River had a slightly different shape to it than it does today. On the Manhattan side the Hudson met Cortlandt Street at West Street, but this was land that had only recently been reclaimed from the river. The famous "Ratzer Map" of Manhattan that was produced in 1767, for instance, puts the river's edge closer to Greenwich Street, two blocks to the east, although even on this map at the foot of Cortlandt Street was to be found the "P. Hook Ferry," *Jersey*'s windjammer predecessor whose Manhattan terminal was smack in the middle of the parcel of land on which today sits the World Trade Center. Across the Hudson on the Jersey side, though, the river's 1812 profile was considerably different than it is today. Where now the Hudson River shoreline opposite Manhattan is relatively

straight in a north–south orientation, then, just below Hoboken, the river widened considerably to the west and cut inland, and Paulus Hook was just that, a hook-shaped piece of land jutting out into the stream. (See map, page 35.) Over the years acre upon acre of the river has been filled in and Paulus Hook was absorbed, in a manner of speaking, as the shoreline extended out to its current alignment.

Robert Fulton, practical man that he was, voiced an important caution as *Jersey* entered service. It might well have been engraved in large letters and posted at the pilot station not only of *Jersey* but of every single ferryboat ever to operate in New York from 1812 to the present day. Said the man who started it all: ". . . to prevent shocks it is necessary the men should be attentive to stop the engine in time."[6]

In due course, which is to say the next year, Fulton supplemented *Jersey* with a running mate, a virtual sister ship called *York*.[7] (One can sometimes find

5. Ibid., p. 521.

6. Ibid., p. 522.
7. *York* was also built in New York by Charles Brown. Of her Fulton said:

this vessel identified as *Little York*, but the Lytle–Holdcamper List shows only the shorter name.) The state-granted monopoly aside, before operating a ferry service in New York City one had to obtain a lease, or franchise, from the local government, and the authorization Fulton and his corporate backers had obtained from the City of New York in 1811 specified that two steamers were to be placed in service. For the Cortlandt Street–Paulus Hook venture, Chancellor Livingston was not an active business participant, although Fulton himself was able to claim full monopoly protection for the service. Newark interests were quite active in the project as Paulus Hook was their "port of embarcation" en route to New York City, and Fulton raised much of the capital for the construction of the two ferryboats there. The operating company came to be called the Associates of the New Jersey Com-

pany, or Jersey Association for short, and the route survived. In due course this ferryboat operation was absorbed into the transportation system of the mighty Pennsylvania Railroad and the Cortlandt Street–Paulus Hook line was to be as important a single route as one will find in the harbor – anywhere, or any time. But it will also always and ever stand as the very first over and back service in New York – or anyplace else in the world, for that matter – to operate mechanically-powered, double-ended ferryboats. It began doing so on July 2, 1812, during the presidential administration of James Madison and a mere 36 years, almost to the day, from the adoption of the Declaration of Independence by the Continental Congress. King George III, against whose rule that same Declaration had been directed, was still on the British throne in 1812, but only technically so. The poor man had gone totally mad and from 1811 until his death in 1820 England was ruled under a regency by the Prince of Wales, the man who eventually became George IV and who, as regent, had to deal with the declaration of war against

his country that was declared by America on June 18, 1812, two weeks before *Jersey*'s inaugural.

And what of the rest of the world on the day the first ferryboat steamed across the Hudson River? Well, Napoleon's armies had just crossed into Russia with dreams of conquest; his infamous retreat from Moscow would begin before the year was out. Ludwig van Beethoven completed his Seventh and Eighth Symphonies in 1812, and 1812 was also the year both Charles Dickens and Robert Browning were born. Back in America Abraham Lincoln, a later-day passenger on the very same Cortlandt Street–Paulus Hook line as shall be seen in chapter 4, was a little boy of three years old on the day *Jersey* first crossed the Hudson River, and George Washington was dead a mere thirteen-and-a-half years.

Jersey operated from a New York City whose population was fewer than 100,000 people – a village, really, where crops were grown, livestock raised, and wild game hunted within the city limits, city limits that were located just below where 34 Street crosses Manhattan Island today. But New

------

"The boat which I am now constructing will have some important improvements, particularly in the power of the engine to overcome strong ebb tides" (quoted by Morrison, p. 521).

One of the newest ferryboats operating in New York Harbor in the late 1980s, a vessel of the two-boat Barberi *class, passes in front of the Statue of Liberty on a trip from Manhattan to Staten Island. Liberty's torch is regarded as an old and venerable part of New York's maritime heritage; yet when Robert Fulton's* Jersey *inaugurated trans-Hudson ferryboat service in 1812, the Statue of Liberty was still seventy-five years in the harbor's future.* [author]

York was, surely, a very important city in the new American republic. It had served as the national capital until 1790, twenty-two years earlier, and *Jersey* symbolizes an important first step for New York into an important new era of machines and corporations and other kinds of bigness. Regular ferry leases to operate trans-Hudson service pre-date the Revolutionary War, but July 2, 1812, marked the first time that the same engine that would power and make possible the whole In-dustrial Revolution, the reciprocating steam engine, was successfully deployed for such an ordinary task as a ferryboat crossing of the river.

And consider this, too: *Jersey*'s advent pre-dates the construction of *any* railroad in America or the world, she was one of but six steamboats legally operating in New York waters per the terms of the Fulton–Livingston monopoly, and her Cortlandt Street–Paulus Hook route was the sole place in all of 1812 New York where pow-ered machines were available for local travel.[8] Fulton's other five boats were deployed on services to distant cities; for getting around "town" all else was on foot, at the whim of the wind, or by animal power from an agricultural era that was on the verge of being mechanized, industrialized, and urbanized out of existence. In the

8. There is one important exception to this claim, a small steamboat named *Juliana* (ii) that will be discussed later in this chapter.

wake of *Jersey*'s first trip an industry would soon form – a ferryboat industry providing new mobility for New Yorkers, and yet an industry whose growth will closely parallel industrial, economic, and social developments in the area, in the country, and in the world.

One final and whimsical thought about *Jersey*. The difference between the first deployment of a new transportation concept, be it the railroad train, the airplane, or the automobile, and later evolutions of the same notion, are normally extreme in design, and even more so in performance: Kitty Hawk *vs.* the 727, "Tom Thumb" *vs.* "The Super Chief," the horseless carriage *vs.* the BMW. But *Jersey*'s voyage across the Hudson River in 1812 wasn't all *that* different from *Manhattan*'s to Staten Island in 1905 – or even the *Andrew J. Barberi*'s on the same route today. It was certainly not of the same order that separates Orville and Wilbur from the Boeing Company or Messrs. Daimler and Benz from Lee Iacocca. *Jersey*'s cabin wasn't electrically lighted and was a little short of headroom, and her pilot had no access to a radar scope on foggy mornings. But her under-

twenty-minute crossing time and the stability provided by an 80-foot length and a 30-foot beam say that, were shipwrights to replicate her design today, she would be looked upon as an industrial curiosity, true; if the need ever developed, though, this imaginary *Jersey* (ii) could also be fired up and put to work in perfectly ordinary trans-Hudson service and carry a couple of hundred commuters across the river virtually as well and almost as swiftly as a contemporary vessel.

Not too many people know about *Jersey* and July 2, 1812. Too bad, because together they represent an important national milestone.[9]

---

9. It is not known how long *Jersey* remained in operation, but when she was eventually dismantled some of her timbers are reported to have been used to construct a stable on Greene Street in Jersey City by one Isaac Edge. As late as 1909 the Edge family still owned two souvenir canes made from wood of the world's first steam ferryboat. See *Sail and Steam: An Historical Sketch Showing New Jersey's Connection with the Event Commemorated by the Hudson–Fulton Celebration, September 25–October 9, 1909* (Jersey City, N.J.: Free Library, 1909), p. 13.

Robert Fulton himself died in 1815, soon after *Jersey*'s first trip, although as will be discussed later he did inaugurate a second New York ferryboat service after Cortlandt Street–Paulus Hook. His was a tragic and unexpected death, and the man was but fifty years old. Fulton died of pulmonary complications that developed after spending a cold winter day in wet clothing in a drafty hallway waiting to see a New Jersey official in Trenton on steamboat business. He was buried in the yard of New York's Trinity Church and was genuinely mourned in New York; his name was given to streets and vessels, and monuments were built in his honor.[10] But it was the monopoly that he and Livingston enforced and that lasted until 1824 which perhaps even more than Fulton's technical legacy served to color the early years of New York steamboating – and New York ferryboating.

One person whose own water-

---

10. The U.S. Navy's first steam-powered vessel, designed by Fulton and under construction when he passed away, was renamed *Fulton the First* in his honor. Her original name was *Demologos*.

borne plans were being constantly thwarted by the Fulton–Livingston combine was an extraordinary gentleman whose descendants continued to have an impact on the development of ferryboats in the harbor well into the twentieth century. His name was Colonel John L. Stevens, and while he will spend much energy contesting with Livingston, he and the chancellor were brothers-in-law. If there is one family name that stands out among all others in the history of New York ferryboating, it is Stevens – Colonel John and his progeny.

Stevens was born in New York of wealthy parents in the year 1749, but he is associated more with neighboring New Jersey. After the Revolutionary War he purchased certain tracts of waterfront property along the west bank of the Hudson River opposite Manhattan, and for a time in the waning years of the eighteenth century the man owned outright what is today the city of Hoboken.[11] For several

years Stevens' winter residence was at Number Seven Broadway in lower Manhattan, but he spent his summers across the river in Hoboken in a near-palatial manor house whose construction was completed in 1787.

Hoboken, though, would not remain a private family preserve. In 1804 Stevens laid out the rudiments of a street grid and at high noon on April 9, in the famous Tontine Coffee House on Broadway near Rector Street, he proceeded to auction off building lots to people described by Stevens' biographer Archibald Douglas Turnbull as "gentlemen of leisure and fortune."[12] Stevens, obviously, hired no advertising agency to promote this sale and he issued no four-color brochures to encourage people to buy his land. But his efforts with the written word to

pursuade those "gentlemen of leisure and fortune" to part with their money and buy Hoboken real estate, while stated in the prose style of another era, sound terribly like the offers to buy land that arrive in one's mailbox today from time to time. Wrote the colonel:

As many persons are desirous of obtaining situations, where they may transact business free from the dangers of yellow fever, the restrictions of quarantine, the duty of auctions, and the heavy taxes on incorporated cities; the subscriber offers for sale the most advantageously situated parts of his estate, laid out in the form of a town and subdivided into full lots for the convenience of purchasers. . . .[13]

Stevens had eleven children, but it was two of his sons – Robert Livingston Stevens, born in 1787 and named for Chancellor Livingston, and Edwin Augustus Stevens, born in 1795 – who joined him in creating a dynasty that will perfect ferryboat technology into an industrial art form in the years

---

11. During the Revolutionary War, what is now the City of Hoboken was owned by a man named William Bayard. Bayard was a patriot early on, but shifted his support to the Crown during the war. As a result his lands

were confiscated at war's end and on March 16, 1784, Stevens purchased them for £18,360. For additional details, see Harry J. Smith, *Romance of the Hoboken Ferry* (New York: Prentice-Hall, 1931).

12. Archibald Douglas Turnbull, *John Stevens: An American Record* (New York and London: The Century Company, 1927), p. 180.

13. Quoted by Turnbull, p. 180. Hoboken became a town in 1849, a city in 1855.

leading up to the American Civil War. As will be seen in chapter 2, the clan was also much involved with the construction of New Jersey's early railroads, but even earlier efforts to inaugurate steam-powered ferry service between Manhattan and Hoboken in the face of the Fulton–Livingston monopoly are interesting and must be included as part of the first era of New York ferryboating.

(Colonel Stevens' own imagination knew virtually no bounds, and the man could be called an American Leonardo da Vinci. He worked up designs for pontoon bridges, a floating battery across the Narrows to repel enemy ships, and even a trans-Hudson tunnel, the latter fully a century before such a facility was ever built.)

The earliest lease to operate pre-steam ferry service to the land Stevens would one day own dates to 1775. Prior to that, persons wishing to reach Hoboken from New York had to negotiate their passage individually with owners of appropriate sailing craft. In later years Stevens, exasperated at poor-quality service that would often thwart his desire to visit his Hoboken home for days at a time,

secured the lease himself. This was sometime around 1790, and onward from then Stevens added to his list of technical objectives – not to say obsessions – that of mechanizing the ferry service, probably with steam power. The word "probably" is a necessary qualifier here, though, because believe it or not Stevens was also enamoured of powering vessels with engines utilizing ". . . a piston working in a cylinder and put in motion by the explosion of an inflammable gas."[14] As with subaqueous tunnels, the man was generations ahead of his time. His mind was thinking about internal-combustion engines fifty or more years before others would actually invent them!

Steam, however, turned out to be the energy source Stevens deployed. His first steamboat – little more than an experimental launch, actually – was the *Juliana* of 1804, named for one of his daugh-

---

14. This quotation describing Stevens' notion is taken from correspondence written to him in 1798 by Marc Isambard Brunel, another of the towering engineering figures from the early days of industrialization; quoted by Turnbull, p. 139.

ters. *Juliana* steamed across the Hudson that year but was not regarded as terribly successful. She was, though, three years ahead of Fulton's *Claremont* and one aspect of her design is worth noting: she was propelled not by paddle-wheels but by a crude kind of twin screws – thirty years or so before propellers were perfected to the point of being conventional, to repeat again the common Stevens refrain.

The second Stevens steamer was called *Phoenix*. Built in Hoboken in 1808, she was fully a product of Stevens' own inventive genius and facilities. Unlike *Claremont* with her British-built engine, *Phoenix* was entirely homemade. It has been claimed that in the year 1807 Stevens' Hoboken facilities alone in America had the capacity for fabricating and building steam engines.

Phoenix was intended for Manhattan–Hoboken operation. Single-ended and sidewheel-propelled, she ran for a time in such service, but neither regularly nor as a public ferry sanctioned by lease or franchise. She is also known to have run between New York and points in New Jersey on the Raritan River, a critical route in the nineteenth century in that it permitted mechanically-powered transport to replace horse-drawn carriages on a portion of the heavily traveled New York–Philadelphia corridor. But *Phoenix* could not survive in New York under the terms of the Fulton–Livingston monopoly. Stevens had no choice, so he decided to send his steamboat south for service on the Delaware River between Philadelphia and Trenton, another portion of the New York–Philadelphia route but one not subject to monopoly protection; and that's where *Phoenix* spent the rest of her career. But one note: in traveling to Philadelphia and her new home port, John Stevens' *Phoenix* became the very first steam-powered vessel ever to navigate in open ocean waters.[15]

With the departure of *Phoenix* Stevens turned to team boats for Hoboken service. He himself, while continuing his interest in, and even influence on, the trans-Hudson operation, was no longer the formal lease-holder of the ferry. But on February 8, 1811, the New York City Council executed a new lease with Stevens himself, specifying under its terms and conditions that ". . . One steamboat (to be built on such construction as Mr. Stevens may judge best but of capacity and dimensions sufficient to transport horses, chairs and passengers) must be placed on said ferry and kept there plying as a ferryboat within two years from and after the commencement of the said term. . . ."[16]

That this lease was possible, given the Fulton–Livingston monopoly, is explained by the fact that Stevens felt that he would be able to negotiate a satisfactory agreement with Fulton to permit steam on the Hoboken run. On February 28, 1811, Stevens wrote to Fulton:

I have obtained a lease from the Corporation [of the City of New York] for the Hoboken Ferry for the term of fourteen years on condition of putting a steamboat on the ferry in two years. I am ready to make you any compensation you desire for your patent, right, etc. I therefore trust you will not put it in the power of any Company to defeat the good intentions of the Corporation for the public accommodations, besides involving me in a litigation which, terminate as it may, cannot benefit you but may prove ultimately injurious to the establishment of your rights. It is unquestionably in our power to settle this business ourselves.[17]

Nuance of language from the year 1811 is difficult to interpret over a century-and-three-quarters later, but Stevens' letter appears to come on rather strong and might even be said to contain a note of threat. Whether or not this

15. *Phoenix* was under the command of Robert Livingston Stevens, the colonel's son, when she put to sea for the trip down the New Jersey Coast to the mouth of the Delaware River at Cape May, N.J. It was not a calm and uneventful voyage, and severe weather caused young Stevens to seek shelter for a time at Barnegat Inlet.

16. Taken from a December 10, 1810, committee report of the Common Council of the City of New York which led to the February 8, 1811, lease; quoted by Smith, p. 23.

17. Quoted by Smith, p. 26.

reading is correct is a moot point; but what isn't is that Stevens proceeded to build another steamboat to carry out the terms of his 1811 lease on the assumption he would be able to settle with Fulton. The only trouble is, he didn't.

Stevens called his new vessel *Juliana* (ii). She was an open boat some 62 feet long and 12 feet abeam (considerably smaller than *Jersey*, for instance), and on October 11, 1811, she entered formal ferry service between the foot of Vesey Street in Manhattan and Hoboken. But she was withdrawn when negotiations with the Fulton–Livingston monopoly failed to reach an accommodation. She ran through the fall of 1811 but not during the dead of winter months, apparently came out again for all or part of the 1812 navigation season, but in 1813, after a protracted lay-up, she sailed off to the more hospitable waters of Connecticut.

But note the dates. *Juliana* (ii) initiated lease-sanctioned and steam-powered service across the Hudson River almost a year before Robert Fulton's *Jersey*, and there are those who therefore claim that she was the harbor's first mechanically-powered ferry-boat. But *Juliana* (ii) was not a true double-ended ferryboat; she was a steamboat – single-ended and propelled by side-mounted paddlewheels. Thus her inaugural in 1811, while interesting and surely important, may not be referenced to fault the claim that *Jersey* was the first ferryboat.

Onward from July 2, 1812, of course, *Juliana* (ii) and *Jersey* were simultaneously – and to an extent competitively – engaged in trans-Hudson service. And it was during this time that Fulton and Stevens engaged in some spirited correspondence, not about the monopoly *per se*, but about other things; however, the monopoly protection Fulton enjoyed was never very far from either man's mind. Wrote Fulton to Stevens on October 27, 1812, for instance:

I have just been informed by Mr. Stoudenger that your foreman, and with your knowledge, has been endeavoring to entice some of my workmen, who have gained experience in our shop, to go to work for you at Hoboken. I hope this is not true. But if so, and one man moves from my shop, even by his own voluntary act, I shall instantly insist on all the rights to which I am entitled in law & justice, and which have been encroached on in a manner that cannot be maintained.[18]

Replied the colonel by, in essence, return mail: "Your letter of this date is couched in terms so offensive that I should not have deemed it incumbent upon me to have returned an answer, were it not that it is necessary and proper I should be informed explicitly what you mean when you say 'I shall instantly insist on all the rights to which I am entitled'. . . ."[19]

Two serious men were dealing with serious issues, but two serious men were also getting angry. And while Fulton's ire may have been raised by his suspicion that Stevens was pirating skilled craftsmen from his shop, he soon fell back on his more general concern that Stevens and *Juliana* (ii) were violating his state-sanctioned monopoly. On this score Stevens was unable to prevail.

Again it was back to the horse boats for a period of years, but

18. Quoted by Turnbull, p. 331.
19. Ibid.

there is one story from this steamless era that is worth recounting. In 1819 the lease passed into the hands of Philip Hone, but, sad to say, Hone's management of the service left a good deal to be desired. Barclay Street–Hoboken trips would routinely take hours – and not just one or two, but four, five, and more! Hone fell into the practice of leaving an exhausted team of over-worked horses harnessed to the treadmill for day-long stints. On East River horse boats, by contrast, fresh teams were brought aboard several times a day. But there may have been an ulterior motive to Hone's tactics – that is, even more ulterior than running a ferry service for which one held an exclusive franchise in the least costly way possible. For Hone had installed facilities aboard his boats for the sale of beverages – brewed and distilled and aged, as appropriate – to help travelers while away the hours as an overworked team of horses fought the Hudson's tides and currents. What galled Stevens perhaps even more than the terrible-quality service Hone was providing was the fact that ferry passengers would have their fill of spirits dur-

ing their prolonged voyage and thus have no need for a post-voyage brace in Stevens' own "public house" in Hoboken. Suits were filed; Hone was served a "Declaration of Ejectment" in 1821 by Stevens, and later that year the parties settled their differences and the ferry lease reverted to the Stevens family.[20]

Shortly afterward steam returned to Hoboken and this time banished the horse boats for good and all. In late 1821 a new firm called the Hoboken Steamboat Ferry Company was incorporated

---

20. Philip Hone (1780–1851), born of an old New York family, is a distinguished person in the city's history, even if his career as a ferry operator appears to be less than distinguished. He was elected mayor of New York in 1826, served on many boards of trustees, and provides, through his diaries, a fascinating view of city and national life in the early nineteenth century. His criticisms of the policies of President James Polk as they relate to the Mexican War of 1846–1848 and the admission of new "slave states" to the Union are especially interesting. See Philip Hone, *Diary, 1828–1851*, ed. Allan Nevins, 2 vols. (New York: Dodd, Mead, 1927).

by Stevens, and on May 1, 1822, the 98-foot, steam-powered, and double-ended *Hoboken – Hoboken* (i), actually – began running under the aegis of a lease then held jointly by Stevens and his son, Robert Livingston. *Hoboken* (i) was the first double-ended New York ferryboat to eschew Fulton's original twin-hull design and utilize a conventional single hull. Her route was Barclay Street–Hoboken, and thenceforward that service would remain the principal operation between Manhattan and the land once owned outright by John Stevens. (In the fall of 1822 the New York terminal had to be shifted to Hulbert Street for two months because the area around the Barclay Street landing was rife with yellow fever.)

The Hoboken Steamboat Ferry Company will grow into one of the harbor's major ferryboat operations: lots of boats, many different trans-Hudson services, a strong tradition of technical innovation, and a lengthy and colorful history. Of course, that *Hoboken* (i) came out in 1822, two years before the Fulton–Livingston monopoly was struck down by Chief Justice John Marshall's Supreme Court, does not mean that an agreement was reached between Stevens and the monopoly. It was just that pressure was building, litigation was starting, and people were less fearful of challenging the exclusivity growing out of *Claremont*'s 1807 voyage than they had been in the days of *Phoenix* and *Juliana* (ii) just a decade or so earlier. Before a recounting of the end of the Fulton–Livingston monopoly, though, a word is in order on the second ferryboat service instituted by Robert Fulton himself.

Prior to steam navigation there were many ferry services operating on the East River connecting Manhattan with Brooklyn. Sloops and row boats and periaugers dated back to the days of the Dutch, and horse boats came along at about the time the eighteenth century was giving way to the nineteenth. The lower portion of the East River also saw *more* ferry routes than any comparable stretch of waterfront in the harbor, although perhaps it would be more accurate to say that no other portion of the harbor should even be compared to the East River between the Battery and the place where the Williamsburg Bridge now stands

on the question of the quantity of ferryboat service operated. Precisely because these ferries were so many and so heavily trafficked they became the first group of lines, collectively, to be supplemented with bridges and tunnels in New York, and also the first to fade from the scene entirely when they proved unable to compete with these newer modes of transport.[21]

In any event, the days of heavy passenger traffic, much less the days of bridge and tunnel replacements, were quite in the future when the East River's very first steam-powered ferry, *Nassau*, was built by Robert Fulton to the

---

21. The early years of ferry service on the lower East River, both before and after the introduction of steam-powered vessels, are painstakingly chronicled in a marvelous book that was written in 1879. Unfortunately the volume was privately published and is anything but easy to find, although it has recently been made available on microfilm by the Library of Congress (No. 17958): Henry E. Pierrepont, *Historical Sketch of the Fulton Ferry and its Associated Ferries* (Brooklyn: Union Ferry Company, 1879).

same general plan as *Jersey* and *York*. She, too, was turned out by the Charles Brown yard.

For this East River venture Fulton formed a new partnership with William Cutting of Brooklyn, a man who was also Fulton's brother-in-law – or, more precisely, his wife's brother-in-law. Fulton, of course, retained the monopoly rights accorded him by state law, and thus the new firm, the New York and Brooklyn Steamboat Ferry Association, enjoyed the same legal protection as did the Jersey Association, operator of the Cortlandt Street–Paulus Hook line. *Nassau*'s inaugural trip was on Saturday, May 10, 1814, and the speed of her crossing – between four and eight minutes – plus the comfort of her appointments were warmly praised in the press. In addition to her regular ferry crossings, *Nassau* was often used for moonlight cruises as charter parties sought to relax after a day's work. Sometime after her introduction, deck houses of sorts were installed for the benefit of *Nassau*'s passengers, but perhaps the most startling thing that can be said of her is this: sixty years later *Nassau* was still in

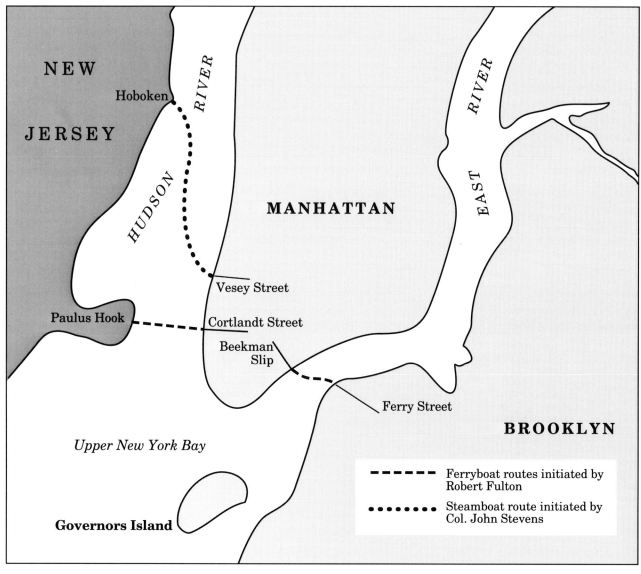

NEW
JERSEY

Hoboken

HUDSON RIVER

MANHATTAN

EAST RIVER

Vesey Street

Paulus Hook

Cortlandt Street

Beekman
Slip

Ferry Street

BROOKLYN

Upper New York Bay

Governors Island

- - - - - Ferryboat routes initiated by
Robert Fulton

•••••• Steamboat route initiated by
Col. John Stevens

2. The Initial Ferryboat Routes

business! Not as an operating ferryboat, true, but as a floating chapel tied to a New York wharf.

To comply with service-level requirements set forth in the lease Fulton and Cutting had received from New York City, *Nassau's* trips were supplemented by horse boats. The company tried to duck out of a requirement specified in the lease that they add a second steamer to the route, and they were successful for some time; *Nassau* remained the line's only powered vessel until 1827 when another twin-hull ferryboat was delivered. Cutting had assumed control of things after Fulton died in 1815, but the company did not prosper under his charge. He himself died in 1821, and the second steamer in 1827 was named *William Cutting* in his honor.

Nassau ran from Beekman Slip on the Manhattan side of the East River to Old Ferry Street on the Brooklyn side. Both Beekman Slip and Old Ferry Street were later re-named Fulton Street in memory of the man who inaugurated steamboat service in New York, and the ferry service then became one of a handfull, over the years,

to connect landing terminals with the same name.[22]

As to the origin of the *vessel's* name: Nassau Island, in 1800 and earlier, was the common designation for what is today Long Island. In 1814 Brooklyn was but a town within Kings County, a small enclave at the edge of the East River, and the entire county had a population of just over 8000 residents. A village of Brooklyn would be established in 1816, and the City of Brooklyn dates its beginnings to 1834, each new political incorporation involving an expansion of territory from the preceding entity. In 1898 Brooklyn was absorbed into the City of New York as a borough, details of which will be discussed in chapter 5.

Brooklyn – town, village, city, and borough – has often seen itself as being put upon by the older metropolis, which is to say, New York

City. Onward from 1730 New York regarded itself as deriving its authority from something issued under George II in that year and called the Montgomery Charter. The document was most explicit in giving the city ". . . sole, full, and whole power and authority of settling, appointing, establishing, ordering and directing . . . such and so many ferries around Manhattan's Island, alias New York Island, for the carrying and transporting people, horses, cattle, goods and chattels from the said Island of Manhattan to any of the opposite shores all around the same island. . . ."[23] And if it weren't enough that New York City could

---

22. My desire to refer to all New York ferryboat routes by both their terminals will be put to the test in later chapters when this route will be rendered Fulton Street–Fulton Street. Understandably, the service is more routinely identified as "the Fulton Ferry."

23. Excerpts from the Montgomery Charter are quoted in *A Compilation of the Existing Ferry Leases and Railroad Grants Made by the Corporation of the City of New York*, comp. David T. Valentine (New York: Jones, 1866), pp. v–vii. Valentine is a man whose work we will see much of in the ferryboat story. In the middle years of the nineteenth century he was the "official compiler" of actions taken by the City of New York, and his many volumes of published data and information are invaluable.

cite such an enabling instrument to control exclusively all ferries between Brooklyn and Manhattan, it was also able to use the same document to claim that its own territory extended all the way to the limit of high tide on the Brooklyn shore. Brooklynites strolling along the water's edge at low tide, in other words, were legally in Manhattan. Ferry houses built on piles below the limit of high water were likewise on Manhattan real estate.

Brooklyn interests, always unhappy with this state of affairs, brought suit against this portion of the Montgomery Charter and in 1775 won a provisional ruling. New York then appealed to the King's Bench but American independence ended the Crown's jurisdiction and matters reverted to their former state – and stayed there. At one point before the Revolutionary War, agitated Brooklynites burned down one of those New York ferry houses on the Brooklyn side of the East River to express their strongly-held feelings on the whole matter.

Soon enough the principal ferryboat operations on the lower East River would be consolidated into a single firm, the Union Ferry Company of Brooklyn, one of the harbor's truly premiere operators. The corporate evolution that brought this about will be a topic for subsequent chapters, as will the take-over of certain key Union routes by the City of New York in the twentieth century when the company reached the end of its corporate tether. But the more than fifty steamers that operated over the years under the Union house flag – plus a dozen or so ferryboats provided by the City of New York during the final years of East River ferry service – can all trace their lineage to Robert Fulton's *Nassau* of 1814.

And now, finally, the downfall of the Fulton–Livingston monopoly.

Few commentators would today argue that the monopoly served any constructive purpose at all. A. D. Turnbull, Stevens' biographer, said it quite well in 1927: "Intentionally or not, the monopoly was well designed to cut the young [steamboat and ferryboat] enterprise off from the breath of life – open competition."[24] Stevens himself, viewing the monopoly in legal terms, felt it was ". . . passed in contravention of the Spirit and Letter of the Federal Constitution. . . ."[25]

Two sovereign states, New York and New Jersey, squared off over this issue in deadly earnest. When New York passed legislation in April 1808 empowering the Fulton–Livingston combine to seize any vessel violating their rights, New Jersey countered with a retaliatory legislative strike in 1811 that authorized New Jersey steamboaters whose vessels were seized in New York waters to reciprocate against appropriate monopoly steamers when they visited New Jersey ports.

Perhaps the steamboat service against which the Fulton–Livingston monopoly proved to be most restrictive, and drew New Jersey's most intense ire, was not trans-Hudson ferry service but sailings between New York City and ports along the Raritan River such as the Amboys and New Brunswick, often with way landings at various Staten Island points or at places

24. Turnbull, p. 231.

25. Quoted by Turnbull, ibid.

like Elizabethport, N.J. This was, as noted earlier, a most important service in the early years of the nineteenth century. It permitted new mechanically-powered steamboats to be used, in pre-railroad and even pre-canal days, on at least a portion of the important New York–Philadelphia route. Other steamboats beyond the monopoly's control – like John Stevens' *Phoenix* – operated on the Delaware River between Philadelphia and the headwaters of navigation near Trenton, leaving but a 25-or-so-mile ride across the narrow "waist" of New Jersey to be made by horse-drawn carriage. Prior to the arrival of the steamboats the whole 90-mile trip from the banks of the Hudson to Philadelphia was by overland coach, a journey the very thought of which makes today's New Jersey Turnpike seem gentle and benign.

Enter Messrs. Gibbons and Ogden: Thomas Gibbons, a former mayor of Savannah, Georgia, who owned a summer home near Elizabethport, N.J., and Aaron Ogden, Revolutionary War hero from the Battle of Yorktown. At first they had worked cooperatively. Ogden held a bona-fide franchise from the

monopoly and he ran a steamboat from New York to Elizabethport. Here he connected with Gibbons' *Bellona*, a vessel lacking monopoly authorization, but not needing it since it sailed from Elizabethport beyond to the Raritan and served only New Jersey ports. (The Fulton–Livingston monopoly continued to exist as a legal entity after Fulton died in 1815 and Livingston in 1813.)

But Gibbons and Ogden had a parting of the ways. Some say it began on personal grounds, Ogden attempting to settle a nasty quarrel between Gibbons and a family member but only managing, as so often happens, to make matters infinitely worse. The matter quickly spilled over into business and in 1818 Gibbons decided he would eliminate the Elizabethport connection and sail *Bellona* all the way through to New York City in direct competition with Ogden's steamboat, *Atlanta*, but more importantly in open defiance of the monopoly.

Exciting days followed. The captain of Gibbons' steamer was a brash young Staten Islander by the name of Vanderbilt – sometimes rendered "Van der Bilt" in

contemporary accounts. The man's first name was Cornelius and he would later come to be called "the Commodore" in deference to his maritime beginnings as he became, arguably, the nation's premier railroad baron of the nineteenth century.

Vanderbilt's tactics and exploits were legendary. He would land *Bellona* at a different place in New York each day to thwart the monopoly's efforts to seize the steamer, and/or arrest its master. How New Jersey–bound passengers were ever able to find *Bellona* is quite another matter, but it is clear that this was a fight over a long-standing principle and not at all a short-term competition to carry the heavier passenger loads. Other accounts tell of Vanderbilt hiding from warrant-bearing New York officials in secret compartments aboard *Bellona* while the vessel was tied up in Manhattan.

Ogden sued his former friend Gibbons in New York, and the litigation must have been remarkable as it proceeded from court to court and eventually to a decision from the highest court in the land in February 1824. The defense, who emerged victorious, was represented by a legal team headed by no less than Daniel Webster, then in the early days of his remarkable career. The plaintiff, Ogden and the monopoly, included among its attorneys Thomas Emmet, whose brother, Robert, the Irish patriot and orator, was hanged – *and then beheaded* – by British justice in Dublin on Thursday, September 20, 1803, and whose name is to this day memorialized in Irish stories and songs.

The Supreme Court's finding for Gibbons was momentous. It helped the young nation define the relationship of the states with each other by vesting in the central government the sole right to regulate commerce between the states. The decision was based on Article I, Section 8, of the United States Constitution: "Congress shall have the right . . . to regulate commerce with foreign nations, and among the several states. . . ." The Fulton–Livingston monopoly was illegal and New York could no longer keep selected steamboats from its ports. The Marshall court let the monopoly stand as a valid regulatory instrument governing *intra*-state commerce, but shortly afterward New York State courts

stepped in and overturned this as well.[26]

Gibbons vs. Ogden brings to a close the earliest era in the New York ferryboat story. New York now stands poised for decades of growth that will make it nothing less than the premier seaport – and premier city – in the world, and how the descendants of *Jersey* and *Nassau* and *Juliana* (ii) contributed to that growth will be the subject of the chapters to follow.

Before leaving the 1812–1824 era, though, let us sample a quaint little bit of verse. The story of steam ferryboats has now begun and horse boats will quickly become obsolete. But the spirit of the early 1800s in New York Harbor is surely captured by these lines, including their fearful assessment of the new order.

---

26. For additional discussion of *Gibbons vs. Ogden* in the practical world of nineteenth-century New York steamboating, see Robert Greenhalgh Albion, *The Rise of New York Port, 1815–1860* (New York: Scribners, 1939), esp. pp. 145–53. (Albion's work has frequently been reprinted – most recently, New York: South Street Seaport Museum, 1984.)

How well I can remember the
    horse-boats that paddled
'Cross the East River ere the
    advent of steam;
Sometimes the old driver the
    horses would straddle,
And sometimes ride round on
    the circling beam.

The old wheel would creak, and
    the driver would whistle
To force the blind horses to pull
    the wheel round;
And their backs were all scarr'd
    and stuck out in bristles,
For the driver's fierce stick their
    old bones would pound.

The man at the gate, in fair
    weather or rainy,
Stood out in the storm by the
    cold river-side,
With pockets capacious, to hold
    all the pennies;
It took just four coppers to
    cross o'er the tide.

The pilot, he, too, took the wind
    and the weather,
Perched o'er the horses, with
    his tiller in hand;
Sometimes would the wind and
    the tide fierce together
Delay him in getting his boat to
    the land.

Though four-horse was the
    power that plowed the fierce
    river,
Yet oft in his hurry would the
    passenger curse,
Though no thought would come
    to make a man shiver
About the dread danger of a
    boiler to burst.[27]

27. The poet's name was Banvard, and these lines were composed sometime, and perhaps even a long time, after horse boats had passed from the scene. Banvard apparently enjoyed a lengthy life; in 1881 he was interviewed by a reporter and claimed to have "crossed this Fulton Ferry . . . on this first steam ferry-boat." That would be, of course, Robert Fulton's *Nassau*, a vessel introduced 67 years earlier. Banvard's verse is quoted by Preble, pp. 60–61.

In the late 1960s a passenger gazes at the receding Manhattan skyline as an Erie Lackawanna R.R. ferryboat heads across the Hudson River to Hoboken. Vessels have evolved since the day of Robert Fulton's inaugural trip in 1812, as have the buildings along both shorelines; but the mighty Hudson River creates a strong bond between this lone passenger and the people who rode Fulton's Jersey. *[Howard W. Serig, Jr.]*

Passengers aboard Robert Fulton's Jersey *in 1812 rode largely out of doors, although they did have access to a low-headroom cabin when the weather turned foul. In later years, as ferryboat cabins grew larger, this distinctive perspective became a sight frequent passengers quickly recognized: the graceful curving of the cabin to conform with the lines of the vessel. [Howard W. Serig, Jr.]*

2. Years of Growth   1824–1860

I. The Hudson River

Mary Murray *class, City of New York,*
1937–1982

1. From the fleet roster in Appendix
C, I have calculated the following
numbers of ferryboats in service
in New York in 1860: cross-Hudson
routes, 15; East River operations, 52;
Staten Island and other, 6; total, 73.
Using the Lytle–Holdcamper List,
one can count 78 ferryboats as poten-
tially in service in New York in 1860.
Both of these calculations are approxi-
mations. Cf. chapter 7, for example,
where the number of ferryboats operating in New York in the year 1866
has been established as 69 using better-
quality information sources not available for 1860.

I f the period from the maiden voyage of Robert Fulton's *Jersey* in
the year 1812 to the United States Supreme Court's decision in *Gibbons vs. Ogden* in 1824 can be called the first era of steam-powered
ferryboating in New York Harbor, then the second era begins in
1824 and runs up to the start of the American Civil War in 1861. It was a
time of virtually unrestrained growth – growth for the nascent New York
ferryboat industry, growth for the City of New York in general, and
growth for the whole country.

Consider some statistics: on the day *Gibbons vs. Ogden* was rendered
there were fewer than a half-dozen individual ferryboats plying New
York waters; in 1860 there were over 70.[1] Furthermore the 1824–1860
interval was a period of explosive growth for New York at large. Population increased from 200,000 residents to 1,176,000; import and export activity through the harbor soared. In 1824 imports and exports were each
in the range of 100,000 tons annually; by 1860 almost two million tons of
products and goods were being imported through New York, and over a
million-and-a-half were being exported. The nation was shifting from a
small and somewhat self-contained agricultural economy to the early
stages of an industrialized trading economy.

Statistics at the national level tell a different side of the same story. In
1824 the country's population was 8.5 million and the Union contained 24
states, less than half today's total. The 1860 U.S. Census counted 63 million people and the Union had grown to 33 states. In 1860 the nation
fronted two oceans; in 1824 the westernmost state was Missouri.

Immigration is another barometer of America's growth. In the decade
of *Gibbons vs. Ogden,* 1820–1830, just over 150,000 people landed on
America's shore to seek the opportunities promised by a New World. In
the decade before the Civil War that figure was over two-and-a-half million. In 1824 there were *no railroads* whatsoever in America; by 1860 national mileage was 30,000. Indeed even the great era of canal transportation was still in the nation's future in 1824, the Erie Canal not opening
until 1825. But by 1860 canals were no longer regarded as the key to fu-

ture intercity transportation needs and were on their way to becoming a dated relic from the past. That's how much change was encompassed in the interval between *Gibbons vs. Ogden* and the Civil War!

There are other contrasts worth noting, as well. In 1824 there were no fixed-route omnibus services in New York City, and no horse-drawn streetcars, either; in 1860 they were such a commonplace that the requisitioning of horses by the military during the Civil War produced widespread inconveniences for the city's population, not at all unlike the rationing of gasoline during the Second World War.

And consider, too, the range of some of the differences just discussed. A population increase from 200,000 to 1,176,000 is 488% – and it happened over an interval of but thirty-five years, the term of a person's worklife, perhaps. In 1824 New York City was today's Dayton, Ohio; by 1860 it had become Detroit, Michigan. This, then, is the context within which the growth of New York's ferryboat fleets must be viewed. The chart in Table II-1 displays some

of these statistics in graphic form.

For purposes of discussion here and henceforth it is useful to cluster the harbor's various ferryboat services into three geographical groupings. First are the interstate services across the Hudson River linking Manhattan with Jersey City, Hoboken, and other communities – the routes pioneered by Fulton's *Jersey* and Stevens' *Juliana* (ii), and *Hoboken* (i). The great majority of these will eventually come under the ownership and management of various overland railroad companies whose Manhattan-bound lines terminated on the west bank of the Hudson. The second cluster of services are the many East River lines, largely operated by small and independent companies – descendants, in one way or another, of Fulton and Cutting's *Nassau*. Ferryboat service to and from Staten Island represents category three. This chapter will discuss the first category, Hudson River ferryboat lines, as well as some general notions and developments from the 1824–1860 period; chapter 3 will treat clusters two and three.

Hudson River ferryboat services often tended to have an aura

of long-distance adventure to them, at least when contrasted with the normally more locally-oriented East River lines. One crossed the East River from Manhattan to go to Brooklyn, Greenpoint, and Long Island City — and possibly beyond to some point on Long Island. One crossed the Hudson River to close-by Jersey City and Hoboken, true, but also on the first leg of a journey to Philadelphia, Pittsburgh, or Chicago. (This generalization is limited, of course. As will be seen in the next chapter, for a few years a ferryboat ride across the East River was the first leg of a trip to Boston!)

The Hudson River is also wider than the East River in the New York City area. Without being too precise about it: the Hudson is roughly a mile across, give or take a little, as it flows past the west side of Manhattan Island; the East River is about a half-mile across. This bit of distinction is also interesting; the Hudson is a true and classic river, rising in Lake Tear in the Adirondack Mountains 300 or so miles north of New York City and 4000 feet above sea level. But what's called the East

One of the key design features of the typical American harbor ferryboat is illustrated in this 1897 photograph of Hackensack *(originally of the Hoboken Ferry Company but sold to the New York & College Point Ferry Company in 1893), aground on the rocks at Sunken Meadows, Long Island. One can see how the paddle-wheel guards, so called (see text), gave the vessel considerable deck space in areas outboard of the hull. Note the paddlewheel extending down from the main deck past the vessel's normal waterline, indicated where dark paint gives way to white.* [Steamship Historical Society of America]

River isn't really a "river" at all; properly, it's a tidal strait that connects Upper New York Bay with Long Island Sound. At any point along the East River one can reach the Atlantic Ocean by going in either direction![2]

Cortlandt Street–Paulus Hook and Barclay Street–Hoboken

were, of course, the Hudson River's first steam-powered ferry services. While the line to Paulus Hook was in business earlier than the one to Hoboken, it was on the latter that one can best trace the evolution of the basic design of the American harbor ferryboat in the years after *Gibbons vs. Ogden*: the

2. The Hudson is affected by tidal action as far inland as Albany, 150 miles upriver from New York City, prompting some to say that the downriver portions are more of a fjord than a river. Since we're dealing here with terminology it's appropriate to men-

tion that the Hudson is often called the North River, despite the fact that it runs parallel with a river that's called East. The usage dates to the days of the Dutch and it serves to distinguish the Hudson from the Delaware, to the south.

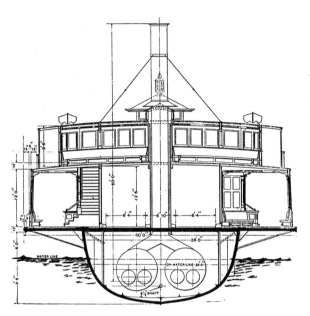

The relationship of deck area to hull size is seen in this cross-sectional diagram of an early twentieth-century ferryboat, Edgewater *of the Riverside & Fort Lee Ferry Company. At the vessel's middle, fully forty per cent of the deck space is in areas beyond the limits of the hull.* [author's collection]

process was largely managed by Colonel Stevens' son, Robert Livingston Stevens.

First, Stevens adopted a single-hull design for his ferryboats and he propelled his vessels with conventional side-mounted paddlewheels—one on each side—common to the rest of the early steamboat industry. Then, to protect the paddlewheels from damage, Stevens extended the main deck of his ferryboats outward from the hull in such a way that the paddlewheels were encompassed within the boat's outer dimensions, a de-

sign that also served to create more deck room – usable, load-carrying deck room. Observing such a vessel head-on and from a low angle one might see that the vessel's overall width was considerably greater than its hull width. That portion of the boat extending out beyond the hull came to be called the paddlewheel guard; "width over guards" and "hull width" are the appropriate measurements of these differing dimensions and the photograph on page 44 illustrates the point. Indeed, even after screw propellers later

replaced paddlewheels on both ferryboats and steamboats this style of construction was generally retained for vessels plying sheltered inland waters. It was not, of course, a desirable feature on ocean-going ships: heavy seas often induced rolling, and an extended main deck down close to the waterline would be downright dangerous. But on calmer inland waterways it was, and still is, a design efficiency to build a vessel whose hull width is less than the width of the vessel's cabin.

Stevens was not the only person

so to design sidewheel-propelled steamboats in the nineteenth century. But he did early work on the concept and clearly popularized its use on double-ended ferryboats.

The engine on early ferryboats was low in the hull, but not so low as to be fully below the main deck; two vehicle gangways on the main deck thus had to pass around the engine room, one to each side. Since the engine had to transmit power to side-mounted paddle-wheels, the gangways would normally crest at midship to clear a power shaft. Boilers were usually deep in the hull, although on some early designs they were placed on the main deck out on the paddle-wheel guards; such an arrangement can easily be detected in photographs and drawings by virtue of the fact that the smoke-stacks are to be found away from the vessel's center in the same area, it being an almost universal truth that smokestacks rise vertically from the boilers they serve, to ensure proper draft and combustion. While *Jersey* and her contemporaries were wood-burners, coal quickly became the universal ferryboat fuel – not to mention the basic fuel that was powering and

making possible the entire Industrial Revolution. Indeed, even into the post–Second World War era many steam-powered New York ferryboats tended to eschew oil-fired boilers and remained coal-burners.

What became the conventional power plant on nineteenth-century steamboats and ferryboats was a big and primitive engine mounted vertically amidships. Stress the word big: a typical cylinder, of which each vessel had but one, might be 50 inches in diameter and have a stroke of ten feet. The "cylinder head" was at the bottom – that's an automotive expression which may not be technically correct, but provides a convenient analogy – and the piston rod drove upward and was connected to one end of a huge, pivoting iron parallelogram mounted above the top deck of the boat to an "A" frame that was itself anchored at the very bottom of the vessel's hull. As the piston rose and fell from the force of steam in the cylinder, the parallelogram pivoted at its center on the "A" frame and a crank arm mounted to the opposite end turned the paddlewheel shaft back down in the hull just

above the waterline. The photograph on page 47, while showing a steamboat and not a ferryboat, depicts the relationship of parallelogram and paddle wheel.

The motion was slow and captivating – 25 revolutions per minute was a typical engine speed – and, given the visual relationship of the rocking parallelogram to the forward motion of the boat, the arrangement came to be called a "walking beam." The *parallelogram* was the walking beam; the whole engine with its transmission system was called a "beam engine," or a "vertical-beam engine." An especially fascinating aspect of the operation of such an engine was getting it started.

On receiving a bell signal from the pilot house to get underway, the chief engineer essentially had to urge the mighty beam engine into motion manually. He did this with a long pole-like device called a starting bar; using a pump-like motion on the starting bar, the engineer manipulated the engine's valve until sufficient speed and momentum was attained so the valve could function automatically. The valve was the all-important sliding element that ran in a small

This broadside view of a typical late nineteenth-century steamboat shows the basic propulsion system used on most New York ferryboats of the era; the dark-colored parallelogram atop the vessel is the "walking beam" and it transmits energy from a large vertical single-cylinder engine located beneath its left side to a crankshaft connected to the paddlewheels at its right. The heavily decorated semi-circular structure is the "paddle box," within which one of two circular paddlewheels rotates; the smokestack off to the left designates the location of the boilers that generate steam for the engine. In this view of the steamboat Cygnus, *the vessel is proceeding from right to left; but her captain has just called for "reverse power," and so frothy water can be seen forward of the paddlebox as the engine begins to bring the vessel to a stop. [author's collection]*

chamber parallel to the cylinder and fed steam first to one side of the piston, then on its reverse stroke to the other, and allowed exhausted steam to be expelled as well. Unlike automobile engines where force is applied to but one face of a piston, steam engines generate power on both strokes by feeding steam into the cylinder, alternately, on either side of the piston.

The transition from "manual" to "automatic" operation was called "dropping the hooks," or "hooking up," and it had to be performed deftly and quickly for there was one ever-present possibility that could spell disaster – allowing the huge piston to stall at either the very top or the very bottom of the cylinder before it had gained sufficient momentum to continue running past these dead spots, so to speak, in the power cycle. Should the piston get so stalled the vessel was totally without power and helplessly adrift. Short bursts of steam from the valve by a skillful engineer could sometimes correct the problem, but more often a stalled piston was a major problem that required extraordinary action by the whole crew to correct – "general quarters," after a fash-

ion.[3] Add to this already complex equation the attention the engineer had to pay as well during these critical moments to injecting water into the condenser and running the air pump and one begins to get some appreciation of the travails involved simply in getting a vertical-beam engine underway. In addition, in ferryboat service there was this added peril from an untimely response to engine commands: with a boat heading into a ferry slip, the reverse-engine order simply *had* to be executed smartly lest the vessel smash headlong into the shore facility, thus inflicting serious damage to slip or

3. What happened when a piston was truly stalled at the top or bottom of the cylinder? Crewmen would rush to a point in the boat near the paddle boxes – which is what the housing of the paddlewheels was called – and open an access door. "Then they grabbed a long, stout lever kept on a rack for this purpose, inserted one end of it through the open door, and hooked it under any convenient part of the paddlewheel. Then they bore down on it hard, to ease the wheel around a bit and get the piston off dead center" (Bob Whittier, *Paddle Wheel Steamers and their Giant Engines* [Duxbury, Mass.: Seamaster, 1983], p. 21).

vessel, and probably to both. With a vertical-beam engine, a command to reverse the engine called for another round of manual work with the starting bar, again the engineer having to be mindful to keep the piston from stalling at the top or bottom of the cylinder.

As a ferryboat was easing into a slip, all of this risk was focused on those few critical seconds after the captain rang for back power and the ferryboat continued farther into the slip. Would the engineer execute the command promptly? The ferry keeps moving forward. Has the piston stalled? The end of the slip is little more than a boat-length away. Then a reassuring vibration throughout the entire boat from keel to wheelhouse as the paddlewheels start to turn in reverse and the mighty vessel is brought to a controlled stop. Adventure? Yes, but it also became the day-to-day routine repeated hundreds of times each day in New York as ferryboats steamed over and back across the harbor's rivers and bays in the middle years of the nineteenth century.

While big in size, beam engines worked off relatively low-pressure steam, between 25 and 30 pounds per square inch being common boiler ratings. In the twentieth century when smaller (but more powerful) multi-cylinder engines were developed, steam pressure rose to a hundred and even two hundred pounds per square inch. Of course, in the early days of steam power it was not appropriate to regard 25 or 30 pounds as "low" pressure – it was simply "the" pressure generated by a new technology, a technology whose limits and dangers were learned only through awful experience. Boiler explosions were the ultimate tragedy in the early days until standards, practices, and inspection programs were developed – and regulatory jurisdiction established. The worst tragedy ever to befall a New York ferryboat will involve a boiler explosion and it will be discussed in chapter 5. Full details are lacking, but it is also thought that Robert Fulton's second ferryboat on the Cortlandt Street–Paulus Hook route, *York*, suffered such a tragedy in her early months of operation, killing her pilot as well as one or more passengers.

Thus powered by a vertical-beam engine, the typical New York ferryboat in the pre–Civil War period came to be a vessel with a non-compartmentalized wooden hull and a wooden superstructure. Length could range from 100 to 200 feet, width over guards might extend to 50 or 60 feet, and the "floor plan" of the main deck usually included twin vehicle gangways the length of the vessel and passenger cabins outboard of these on the paddlewheel guards. The passenger cabins, of course, had to allow room for the paddlewheels.

On certain early designs the passenger cabins and engine room were enclosed, but the vehicle gangways were exposed to the elements. (Curiously, some present-day ferryboats feature this same concept.) But the more common design eventually called for the whole main deck to be enclosed, cabins as well as gangways.

The next step was to turn the top of the main-deck cabin into a second deck for passenger use, and eventually a separate passenger cabin was added to this upper deck, particularly by those operators for whom vessel capacity was critical. It was usually possible to arrange a full outdoor promenade around the entire second deck of these vessels, and long before "jogging" became the craze

it is today, commuters en route to work would often demand of themselves a certain number of brisk circuits of the upper deck as their ferryboats made their way from Staten Island to Whitehall Street, or Hoboken to West 23 Street.

The very first two-deck ferryboat to work in New York Harbor bore the peculiar name *Hunchback*. Her walking beam was encapsuled inside a protruding structure atop her second deck, thus generating a rationale for the less-than-stately name. *Hunchback* was built in 1852, spent the next decade working for the Staten Island and New York Ferry company, played a strange and unusual role in the Civil War, and ended her working days in Boston Harbor – developments that will be treated in subsequent chapters.[4]

In any event, wooden ferryboats and big walking-beam engines were the rule, and the extremes of

4. Victor Hugo's 1831 novel *Notre-Dame de Paris* was translated into English in 1833 as *The Hunchback of Notre Dame*, perhaps giving some popular coin to the term. One wonders if literary-minded Staten Islanders would have preferred calling the vessel *Quasimodo*?

As ferryboats grew larger than Robert Fulton's Jersey, Nassau, *et al., heftier ferry slips were needed than the simple floating logs Fulton used. Here, in a contemporary view of the municipal terminal at the foot of Whitehall St. in Manhattan, one can gauge the size of the cluster of pilings at the slip's end by comparing it with the three-deck* Andrew J. Barberi, *loading for a trip down the bay to Staten Island. Inland from these pilings will be found "racks," so called, large vertically-positioned planks that are periodicaly treated with grease, and designed to absorb momentum as a ferryboat eases into its berth.* [author]

these construction materials were never more apparent than when a vessel would catch fire. "Morning after" photographs routinely show a boat destroyed down to its water line with only the beam engine and the smokestack remaining, an apparent total loss. But not always. Sometimes if the blaze had been a quick flash fire and the engine components weren't twisted and damaged, a vessel that by some standards didn't seem to exist any more could often be fully "re-built,"

and in a rather short time at that. Indeed, drawings and even photographs of a given vessel at different stages of its career that bear virtually no resemblance to each other can often be explained on this account.

A tradition and practice that quickly developed once ferryboats came to be equipped with two separate and symmetrical passenger cabins on the paddlewheel guards of the main deck was the designation of one cabin for men and the

other for women. The Stevenses had installed a cabin exclusively for women on their *Pioneer* of 1823, but it was below deck. According to Smith it was ". . . carpeted and warmed by open fireplaces . . . and a further temptation to the ladies was the installation of two large looking glasses."[5] But *Pioneer* was too early to be called a typical harbor

5. Smith, *Romance of the Hoboken Ferry*, p. 57.

The racks and pilings of a typical ferry slip are shown in this latter-day view of the Barclay St. terminal, long *a Manhattan landing for the Hoboken Ferry Company. Timbers along the sides of the slips were designed to flex* *and absorb momentum as ferryboats eased their way into the berth. [Howard W. Serig, Jr.]*

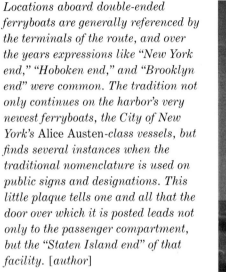

Locations aboard double-ended ferryboats are generally referenced by the terminals of the route, and over the years expressions like "New York end," "Hoboken end," and "Brooklyn end" were common. The tradition not only continues on the harbor's very newest ferryboats, the City of New York's Alice Austen-class vessels, but finds several instances when the traditional nomenclature is used on public signs and designations. This little plaque tells one and all that the door over which it is posted leads not only to the passenger compartment, but the "Staten Island end" of that facility. [author]

ferryboat, one, that is to say, with twin main-deck cabins flanking twin vehicle gangways. She had a fully open main deck, her cabin was below deck, and she was a pioneer ferryboat in fact as well as in name.

The practice of providing one cabin for men and one for women surely grew out of a proper early Victorian concern for manners and morals. Some ferryboat companies even hired uniformed women attendants to be available for assistance to travelers with small children, and such. But it must be noted that some ferryboats operating in New York into the 1960s continued to have such designations posted on their lower cabins. There was no practical difference between the two save that appropriate rest rooms were usually to be found inside each and often the women's cabin was designated a "no smoking" area as well. But few, in later years, paid any mind to the designations and men and women traveled in either cabin quite indiscriminately. Indeed there is some question if the dual cabin notion was *ever* accorded any overwhelming observance. It's quite difficult, for instance, to imagine traveling parties in the 1850s rigidly following the custom and as a ten-minute Hudson River crossing was ending one of a group standing up and saying: "Gentlemen, shall we join the ladies on shore?"

People traveling alone were, perhaps, another matter, but there is reason to believe that the intended segregation by gender never happened with any frequency. Consider, for example, the following "Letter to the Editor" that appeared in *The New York Times* on March 10, 1858. Indeed, consider this letter very carefully.

To the Editor of the New York Times:

The ferries between this city and Brooklyn are established, as everybody knows, for the express and exclusive accommodation of male passengers. Yet instances are not wanting of those who claim the title of ladies, crossing the river in the company's boats. Nor can any excuse be offered for this improper conduct on their part, except the palpably absurd one that their business or social engagements call them from one city to the other. They do not even attempt to palliate their misconduct by conforming to the known ferry-boat useage of using tobbaco, and expectorating the juice thereof in amber-colored pools upon the cabin floor or over each other's dresses.

The indignation which this persistent wrong-headedness of theirs excites in the minds of men whose rights they invade, is seriously aggravated by their invariable practice of occupying the wrong side of the boat when once they are on board. A common share of female modesty, it should seem, ought to prompt them to take the cabin which they almost always find unoccupied, for here they might be by themselves, instead of being mingled with a promiscuous mass of men. Instead, however, of occupying this proper apartment, they universally enter the saloon in which almost every seat is occupied by a man or boy. They cannot plead that this is done by mistake, for the throng of men entering and leaving this apartment would suggest to any one of common sense that the place was not intended for ladies. The only excuse they ever offer for thus intruding themselves into the men's apartment is a merely technical one, which some shrewd special-pleader must have put in their heads. It is, absurdly enough, the fact, that over the door is placed in raised letters the inscription, "Ladies' Cabin."

Can anything be more preposterous than their pretended ignorance that this is a mere form adopted in a musty period of antiquity, when the primitive state of human enlightenment tolerated the idea that a woman had any real claim to a share of the privileges that men enjoy? As well might they attempt to excuse their neglect to eject tobacco juice about the floor, by reference to the little printed slips tacked to the walls of the saloon, high up above the reach of eyesight, setting forth the dogma that gentlemen ought to regard the foolish prejudice of ladies against indulging in a wholesome foot bath of tobacco juice, spirited in indiscriminate puddles on the floor beside the seats they are to occupy.

Such abstractions as these might well enough engage the fancy of visionary metaphysicians. But ordinary observation would show any one of the least practical sense, that they have no more to do with the real practice of every-day life than the first principles of moral philosophy have with the practical politics of the day. Some of the young gentlemen, passengers in the boats, have taken in charge the task of correcting this female impropriety which we have described. If the ladies themselves have the least spark of modesty left, the means taken ought to accomplish a reform. The plan adopted is, first, to occupy every seat in the "Ladies' Cabin," if possible, before a lady can have time to seat herself. If this doesn't succeed, all the young gentlemen who wear shiny hats, spangled vests, and galvanized watch-guards, are to pass back and forth through the cabin, staring impudently into every lady's face, and to deposit a tobacco decoction with such force and proximity to her as to bespatter her apparel. If all these experiments fail, perhaps the boat proprietors themselves can step in and make some arrangement to check this impudent infringement on the rights of Creation's lords.

Yours, Anti-Woman's
Rights.

The question this letter raises concerns its unknown author. Was he the hopeless woman-hater the letter tries to suggest? Or was he – and more likely she – a marvelous satirist whose identity will remain forever unknown? In either case it serves as appropriate evidence that passengers tended to disregard the ferryboat companies' efforts to segregate passengers by sex.

Returning to matters technical: Robert Stevens upgraded Fulton's original "floating log" ferry slip by the use of pilings driven into the river bottom and flexible vertical plankings – usually called racks – attached to them to define the slip and absorb vessel momentum. In place of a floating platform for boarding and alighting, Stevens developed a gallows-like gangway that was raised and lowered from a fixed frame by cables and pulleys. The gangway was also designed with considerable ability to absorb "shocks," as Robert Fulton would say, for while an

Nowadays it's all done with automatic controls located in the pilot house, but for many years a crude but effective system was used to disengage the forward rudder while a double-ended vessel was operating in that direction. This "pin," located on the main deck directly over one of the rudders, allows its rudder to operate freely when it is in the raised position, as shown; the rudder is disengaged and held steady when the pin is lowered flush with the deck. Front rudder is always held secure; aft rudder steers the boat. [author]

The typical ferry slip from the mid-nineteenth century included a ramp that was raised and lowered on a gallows-like frame to allow level loading for both passengers and vehicles. Here a ferryboat is pulling away from such a ramp; when a vessel is berthed, the extending girders on the ramp rest on the vessel's deck, thus precluding momentary disruptions in the boarding process. Such ramps typically had three separate gangways – a middle one for vehicles and two outer ones for foot passengers – and were also designed to accommodate the shape of the given operator's fleet. Often when a vessel was sold from one ferryboat company to another, alterations were required in the configuration of the end of the vessel's deck to ensure proper alignment with the new company's ferry slips. [author]

ideal berthing saw a ferryboat reduce its forward momentum by a skillful captain's reversing his engine and sliding his boat against the side of the slip and then coming to a gentle halt with the boat just nudging up against the gangway, now and again a vessel would hit the gangway with a bit more force. The design was forgiving of such performance, at least up to a point. Stevens' ferryslip is, for all intents and purposes, the design still in use today; the man also perfected other aspects of ferryboat technology, including a number of subtle enhancements in the area of engine operation.

Turning now away from matters of general ferryboat design and examining actual operations in a particular sector, the Hudson River, one can see that during the 1824–1860 interval the original two trans-Hudson lines began to be supplemented by others. The major period of Hudson River expansion did not get underway until after 1860, but in 1838 Stevens initiated a second line out of Hoboken; it crossed the river directly to the foot of Christopher Street in Manhattan. On January 1, 1859, a service was begun from a point well north on Manhattan Island,

linking what is today the foot of West 42 Street and the Slough's Meadow section of Weehawken, across the Hudson and still farther north. This service, provided by a firm called the Weehawken Ferry Company, did not prove to be a robust venture as Weehawken was hardly a heavily settled area. The company's two ferryboats, the *Lydia* and the *Abbie*, were purchased second-hand from an operator on the East River. This service was eventually taken over by and combined with a later and larger ferryboat operation to and from a major rail-passenger depot elsewhere in Weehawken, a development that will be explored in chapter 5.

Before the end of the nineteenth century five major rail-passenger depots will be built along the Hudson's west bank; all will have ferryboat service for passengers to cross the river and reach Manhattan. Each depot will primarily be identified with a single railroad – that is to say, each depot will be owned by a railroad whose own trains will constitute the principal services operating out of the terminal. But each of the five will also host the trains of other companies at one time or another. The full

complement of five will not be in place and operational until after the Civil War – i.e., beyond the scope of this chapter – but for the sake of perspective it is well to identify all of them at this time before discussing in detail the one depot that was in full service before 1860.

Weehawken, just mentioned, was the northernmost of the five, and the railroad most identified with this depot was the New York Central. Moving southward one next comes to Hoboken, once Colonel Stevens' private estate but in later years better known as the eastern terminal of the Delaware, Lackawanna and Western Railroad. Stevens' Hoboken Steamboat Ferry Company, later rendered more crisply as the Hoboken Ferry Company, was formally absorbed by the D. L. & W. in 1903, but even before this formal corporate link, railroad passengers used the Barclay Street–Hoboken and the Christopher Street–Hoboken ferryboat services as part of their journey to Manhattan.[6]

---

6. The Hoboken Steamboat Ferry Company was incorporated in November 1821 when the Stevens family restored steam-powered vessels to the

The land south of Hoboken that was incorporated as Jersey City in 1855 was home to three separate rail depots. The northernmost was the Erie's; the one farthest to the south belonged to the Central Railroad of New Jersey. In between was Paulus Hook, and it was here that the Pennsylvania Railroad had its original New York passenger terminal. Just as Paulus Hook was the site of the Hudson River's very first ferryboat landing, so too it was the place where the first riverside rail terminal was constructed and the first ferryboat-to-train connections were made by a predecessor company of the Pennsylvania. It happened in September 1834, ten years after *Gibbons vs. Ogden*, and deserves a somewhat more detailed examination. The rail depot at Paulus Hook, then, was the only one of the five to be in operation before the Civil War.[7]

In later years under the auspices of the Pennsylvania Railroad, passenger trains steaming west from Paulus Hook were fast-stepping limiteds bound for Washington, Saint Louis, and Chicago. The inaugural rail service in the autumn of 1834 was slightly less auspicious; it involved horse-drawn rail cars operating over a line between the Hudson River and Newark, a mere five miles inland. The company's first locomotive didn't arrive until 1835; service was extended to Rahway, N.J., in January of 1836 and to New Brunswick

---

Barclay St.–Hoboken line in spite of the Fulton–Livingston monopoly. In 1838 the company was reincorporated as the Hoboken Land and Improvement Company. It wasn't until 1889 that the ferry operation was separated from other real estate interests and the name Hoboken Ferry Company became official. In 1896–1897 the Stevens family sold the company to another famous New York ferryboat clan, the Eldridges – Roswell and Lewis – who had earlier gained fame with various East River ferryboat operations. The new firm under Eldridge management was formally the New York and Hoboken Ferry Company, but it was still popularly called the Hoboken Ferry Company. Eldridge ownership continued until the year 1903 when the Delaware, Lackawanna and Western R.R. acquired all of the company's capital stock and assumed direct operation of the various ferryboat services under lease. The D. L. & W. merged with the Erie Railroad to form the Erie Lackawanna in 1960 and the ferry service was abandoned in 1967. See Smith, *Romance of the Hoboken Ferry*, passim; Graham T. Wilson, "The Hoboken Ferries," *Steamboat Bill*, No. 149 (Spring 1979), 3–10 and No. 150 (Summer 1979), 90–101. For information on the corporate evolution of the D. L. & W. Railroad, see Carl W. Condit, *The Port of New York* (Chicago: University of Chicago Press, 1980), esp. pp. 64ff.; also, Robert J. Casey and W. A. S. Douglas, *The Lackawanna Story* (New York: McGraw-Hill, 1951), passim.

7. To clear up some details left over from chapter 1 but having a bearing here as well: the first settlements at Paulus Hook, or "Powles Hoeck," date to 1633. There was a fort on the site during the Revolutionary War; it was captured from the British in 1779 by the famous Major Henry ("Light-Horse Harry") Lee. A town was established in 1804, eight years before Robert Fulton's *Jersey* made her first trip. The "City of Jersey" was established as part of Bergen Township in 1820 and the area became a city in its own right, Jersey City, in 1855. "Light Horse Harry" Lee had a college classmate at the College of New Jersey (now Princeton, from which he graduated in 1773, incidentally) who has played a key role in our story thus far, and will make another appearance presently – Aaron Ogden.

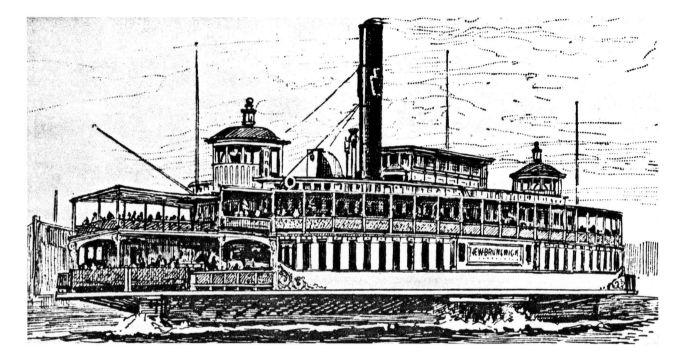

Not among the very earliest of the trans-Hudson ferryboats, but an old-timer in any event, is New Brunswick, *built in 1866 for the New Jersey R.R. and Transportation Company. In this sketch the vessel is shown in the livery of the Pennsylvania R.R., eventual operator of the Cortlandt St.–Paulus Hook service.* [author's collection]

in 1839, thus encompassing a main line distance a small fraction under 34 miles and the limit of the original company's ambitions. The organization called itself the New Jersey Railroad and Transportation Company; a major engineering feature of its line – and one whose execution involved an overrun of cost estimates for its construction by over a hundred per cent – was a mile-long cut through the forty-foot-high rock formation

known as Bergen Hill. Bergen Hill is the southernmost extremity of the geological perturbation called the New Jersey Palisades, a common rock barrier all Hudson-bound railroads will have to confront save the Central of New Jersey, which will later make its approach over filled-in swampland south of where the Palisades begin. Indeed, the New Jersey Railroad and Transportation Company had an easier time of it with the Palisades than later neighbors to the north. The others had to build tunnels; Bergen Hill was conquered by the New Jersey R.R. with an open cut, unofficially known ever since as Shanley's Cut in honor of the engineer responsible for its construction – and, presumably, the cost overrun as well.

The new railroad amalgamated itself with the older Cortlandt Street–Paulus Hook ferryboat company in a series of maneuvers. Sometime after Fulton's death the ferry lease had passed into the hands of Aaron Ogden and Samuel Swartwout; in late 1826, after the overturning of the Fulton–Livingston monopoly, these two transferred the line to a gentleman with the marvelously euphonic name of Cadwallader D. Colden. With Colden the ferry did not prosper, however, and while under other circumstances – i.e., absent the new rail line westward from Paulus Hook – such a state of affairs might have been of lesser consequence, investors in the New Jersey R.R. could hardly risk losing their critical trans-Hudson link. Thus on January 1, 1836, the railroad leased the ferry, and in 1853 they purchased it outright.

But the state charter that gave life to the New Jersey Railroad and Transportation Company established it as a local Jersey City–New Brunswick line, not as the first leg of a long-distance enterprise.

To understand how this 34-mile local railroad built in the mid-1830s later hooked up with connecting lines and eventually became part of what many would unhesitatingly call the most powerful railway system the world has ever known, it is necessary to roll the clock back to 1811, four years after *Claremont* and one before *Jersey*. That was the year a thoroughly extraordinary gentleman petitioned the New Jersey legislature for a charter to construct and operate a railroad between Trenton (on the Delaware) and New Brunswick (on the Raritan). The line's purpose was not to link Rutgers University with the state capital; it was to provide that crucial and middle overland portion of a transportation enterprise connecting two of the nation's major cities, New York and Philadelphia. From New York passengers would sail down the bay and up the Raritan on a steamboat, transfer there for the 25-mile trip across the tight

"waist" of New Jersey by carriage, and then continue on down the Delaware on a second steamboat.

But consider the year in which this petition was made. It was 1811 – *and there wasn't a railroad anyplace on the face of the earth.* So who was this daring pioneer who fearlessly was asking the State of New Jersey that he be allowed to do something never done before? Colonel John Stevens, that's who!

In 1815 Stevens was finally issued his charter, the first for a U.S. railroad, but while state legislators may have been willing to give the colonel his chance, potential investors were not, and it wasn't until December 1832, 21 years after Stevens first petitioned the legislature, that construction was completed on the first leg of the first "trans-Jersey" railroad. During this interval other rail lines, in both America and Great Britain, became the actual pioneers of the new transport mode Stevens wanted to inaugurate back in 1811. Between first proposal and actual execution the route of Stevens' railroad shifted a bit; instead of running New Brunswick–Trenton his line traveled a parallel course five miles or so to the southeast and linked South Amboy on the Raritan with Bordentown on the Delaware, but the concept was the same – New York to Philadelphia by boat–train–boat.

The company was called the Camden and Amboy Railroad and Transportation Company, and while trains only ran as far as Bordentown in 1832, by September 1834 the line had pushed southward along the east bank of the Delaware River to Camden, across from Philadelphia. It was still a boat–train–boat trip, but the boat on the Philadelphia end was now a cross-river ferryboat and not an upriver steamboat.

The colonel's son, Robert Livingston Stevens, was largely in charge of building the Camden and Amboy, and, just as he would later use his inventive talents to develop much of the basic equipment for the ferryboat industry, so did his genius help form and shape the American railway industry. It was he, for example, who developed the "T"-rail design of railway track that is today standard the world wide. The idea supposedly came to young Stevens while on board ship en route to Great Britain to purchase equipment and supplies for

the C. & A., an idea he quickly whittled into a prototype with a block of wood.[8]

Now the plot begins to thicken, because Stevens' Camden and Amboy R.R. wasn't the only trans-Jersey transport enterprise of the early 1830s. The Delaware and

Raritan Canal was chartered at the same time as the C. & A. and it opened in May 1834. Thus by the end of that year the Camden and Amboy was up and running between the Raritan and Camden, the Delaware and Raritan canal was open for business, albeit sea-

8. Stevens sailed for England in the fall of 1830 aboard Cunard's *Hibernia*. When he landed in Britain he sought out Robert Stephenson, the foremost locomotive builder in the world. Together they drew up specifications for the Camden and Amboy's first steam locomotive, which was called the "John Bull." Stephenson's people then built "John Bull," disassembled her and shipped her off to Philadelphia, where she was hauled north to Bordentown for re-assembly by the Camden and Amboy. Thus in the fall of 1831 "John Bull" became the C. & A.'s first locomotive; but progress is progress and she was soon overshadowed by more modern designs. Hold on, though, the story's just getting started! The old locomotive managed to avoid the scrap heap and be preserved, and in the course of events she found herself on static display in the halls of the Smithsonian Institution's Museum of American History in Washington; and now it gets even better. In September 1981 the people from the Smithsonian took

"John Bull" out to a branch line of the Baltimore and Ohio R.R. in Washington, put a fire in her boiler, and celebrated her 150th anniversary by letting "John Bull" do what she was built to do back in 1831 – steam up and down a railroad. And what happened next is probably even more remarkable, although old Colonel John Stevens would surely have taken it all in stride. "John Bull" was hauled out to Dulles Airport, put aboard a Boeing 747, and flown off to Dallas, Texas, for a year-long exhibit there. She's back in the Smithsonian now, proudly identified as the oldest self-propelled anything that's still in operating condition, and patiently awaiting her next assignment.

For further details on this remarkable locomotive including the extraordinary 1981 anniversary, plus historical information on the Camden and Amboy R.R., see John H. White, Jr., *John Bull: 150 Years a Locomotive* (Washington: Smithsonian Institution Press, 1981).

sonally, and the Hudson River–Newark segment of the New Jersey Railroad and Transportation Company was also in operation, with active plans to push beyond to New Brunswick.

The next ingredient came from the Pennsylvania side of the Delaware River; the Philadelphia and Trenton Railroad was incorporated under state law there in early 1832 and by late 1834 was operating between Philadelphia and Trenton. The railroad reached the New Jersey capital city by bridge, although until it was strengthened in 1839 to bear the weight of locomotives the company's passenger cars were hauled across the river by horses, even though locomotives were used elsewhere on the line.

Naturally enough the Philadelphia and Trenton R.R. began to look beyond Trenton. Two dozen or so miles away across flat New Jersey countryside at New Brunswick there was – or would soon be – the New Jersey Railroad and Transportation Company's line out of Jersey City, and closing this gap would permit through-rail service from Philadelphia to the banks of the Hudson; indeed, the P. & T. had been thinking in such terms

even before its line was completed to Trenton.

In retrospect from the frantic days of the 1980s the Camden and Amboy's style of doing business certainly seems pleasant, and can even elicit envy – a day-long trip between New York and Philadelphia involving leisurely cruises at both ends and overland railroad trains only when necessary. (One could even be inclined to wonder if there might be commercial potential for such an operation today!) But in the 1830s faster travel times were uppermost in mind. Thus Jersey City–Philadelphia through trains on a rival network would pose a serious competitive threat for the C. & A., would likely have an equally serious impact on the Delaware and Raritan Canal, and do very bad things to the earning power of each.

But good old-fashioned American competition was addressed in an equally old-fashioned American way. The New Jersey legislature created an old-fashioned American monopoly. Between their being chartered and the completion of their construction, Stevens' Camden and Amboy R.R. and the Delaware and Raritan Canal were

allowed to amalgamate into something called the United Railroads and Canal Companies of New Jersey, more commonly called the Joint Companies. Once the Philadelphia and Trenton R.R. reached New Jersey it, too, was absorbed into the monopoly, and construction of the obvious Trenton–New Brunswick link-up was then handled by the newly combined entity free from competitive threats to or by anybody. The Trenton–New Brunswick line was formally part of the Camden and Amboy R.R., and the very first train from Paulus Hook to Kensington Station in North Philadelphia ran on January 1, 1839, after the New Jersey Railroad and Transportation Company and the Joint Companies executed a cooperative operating agreement, although not a formal merger at this point. Eventually there was such a merger, but not without a degree of acrimony. Stevens, at one time, threatened to break the connection at New Brunswick, isolate the New Jersey R.R., and construct a new connecting line that would funnel the Joint Companies' trains to his own Hoboken ferry terminal. The matter was eventually resolved by the state legislature, and in 1861 the New Jersey Railroad and Transportation Company became part of the United Railroads and Canal Companies of New Jersey by dint of law.

But the biggest development of them all happened in 1871. That was when the Joint Companies became more than a group of legislatively interlocked transport companies dealing with traffic between Philadelphia, New York, and intermediate points. That was when the various railroad companies, including the ferryboats crossing the Hudson River from Paulus Hook, were secured by the Pennsylvania Railroad under long-term lease. (The lease was converted into an out-and-out purchase in 1917.) This development was part of a much larger pattern, a truly national play-out of economic, political, and transport policy. While it clearly involves developments well beyond the time frame of this chapter, 1824–1860, they are important to understand.

In the years before the Civil War the major national railroad systems that linked the East Coast and its seaports with the nation's growing agricultural and industrial centers beyond the Allegheny Mountains were restricted to a single gateway: one railroad, one seaport, so to speak. Commodore Vanderbilt's New York Central and Hudson River Railroad prevailed in New York, reaching the coast from the north through the Hudson and Mohawk valleys – "the water level route you can sleep," as it would later be called in advertisements for the company's overnight passenger trains. In Philadelphia the principal railroad was the Pennsylvania; its main line aggressively assaulted the mountains due west, in essence, from the city's Delaware River piers. And finally in Baltimore the nation's very first common-carrier railroad, the Baltimore and Ohio, brought people and goods to the Atlantic Coast through the Cumberland Gap.

New York's share of the country's imports and exports kept growing, though; the city was bigger, the harbor was better, and trans-Atlantic freight rates were cheaper. Thus, despite heroic efforts to promote their respective "home ports," both the Baltimore and Ohio and the Pennsylvania quickly realized that they had better make arrangements to get themselves to New York. Each of these corporate decisions will have a significant impact on the New York ferryboat story. Indeed, their significance on New York ferryboating cannot possibly be understated.

For a railroad funneling its traffic into Philadelphia as did the early-day Pennsylvania, the United Railroads and Canal Companies of New Jersey, whose southern extremity was also in Philadelphia, was tailor-made. Thus in 1871 the Pennsy absorbed the Joint Companies. Interestingly, though, in the complicated world of stocks and bonds and contracts and other pieces of paper that help give form and shape to a major industrial corporation, this could be said of the Pennsylvania Railroad for many years: the oldest formal charter among its many constituent elements authorizing the performance of a transport function was an 1804 document issued to the Jersey Associates for the Cortlandt Street–Paulus Hook ferry line. This was the same formal instrument Robert Fulton made use of when he brought steam to the service in 1812. The charter was still an active and valid document a century and more later when the

Pennsylvania Railroad was running 100-car freight trains and 100 m.p.h. passenger trains.[9]

Returning, now, to the years before 1860: the New Jersey R.R. invested a good deal of its capital in improvements to the ferry terminals on both sides of the Hudson River. On Wednesday, August 4, 1852, a new ferryhouse was opened in Manhattan at the foot of Cortlandt Street. "It is by far the most capacious and best planned ferry-house in New York or vicinity, and is worthy to be commended to all other Ferry Companies as a model house," noted *The New York Times*. A novelty of the design, but something that would soon become standard in New York on the major ferry services, was separation of inbound from outbound passengers by means of gates, passageways, and walls.

In the late 1850s the railroad reclaimed almost 20 acres on the New Jersey side and built a new terminal on land that had previously been the Hudson River. Five ferry slips were included in the complex, as well as a large shed under which passengers might board and alight from their trains with no fear of inclement weather. Newer and larger ferryboats were also designed and built by the New Jersey R.R., with a common practice being, for a period of years, naming vessels in honor of corporate officials of the company. Thus there was the *John S. Darcy*, a 772-ton ferryboat built in Brooklyn in 1857, the *D. S. Gregory* of 1853, and the *John P. Jackson* of 1860.[10] Why, even old Cadwallader Colden, who owned the ferryboat line before it was taken over by the railroad, had a

boat named in his honor. Sad to say, though, she was called, simply, the *Colden*, and thus isn't even in the running for the title of the most colorful name ever to grace the

shipyard in the Red Hook section of Brooklyn where she was built to the New Jersey R.R.'s facilities at Jersey City the day after she was launched for further fitting out. On Monday, July 27, 1857, she unlimbered her big 400-h.p. vertical-beam engine during a trial trip with 400 invited guests aboard. She sailed down the bay almost all the way to Sandy Hook, and then back up the Hudson River. The eleven-foot stroke and 42-inch diameter cylinder of her engine was the largest of any ferryboat in the harbor, and she was equipped with a portable apparatus for the on-board manufacture of illuminating gas. *John S. Darcy* entered revenue service between Cortlandt St. and Paulus Hook on Friday, August 14, 1857. I examined her final enrollment certificate in the National Archives; her gross tonnage had been increased to 772 from the 614 it was when she was built. The Pennsylvania R.R., her final owner, surrendered her papers on January 5, 1903, and they contain this hand-written notation: "unfit for service." John S. Darcy, the man, was the president of the New Jersey Railroad and Transportation Company in 1857.

---

9. For further details on the Pennsylvania Railroad's lease of the Joint Companies and its entry into New York, see Condit, pp. 46–53; George H. Burgess and Miles C. Kennedy, *Centennial History of the Pennsylvania Railroad* (Philadelphia: Pennsylvania Railroad, 1949), esp. pp. 241–70.

10. When the ferryboat *John S. Darcy* was launched in Brooklyn on the afternoon of Wednesday, April 22, 1857, she became the largest ferryboat in the harbor. Her measurements of 191 × 33 × 11.3 were four feet longer than the previous record-holders, the *D. S. Gregory* and the *Colden*. *John S. Darcy* was towed from the Burtis

Hudson River ferryboating began in 1812 with the voyage of Robert Fulton's Jersey *and continued steadily for over 150 years. The days are running out, though; it's the fall of 1967 and the Erie Lackawanna R.R.'s* Elmira *is one of but two ferryboats still in lower Hudson River service.* [*Howard W. Serig, Jr.*]

letterboards of a New York Harbor ferryboat. Now, had Mr. Colden's first name been made part of the 1851-built ferryboat's title, she would have been a very legitimate claimant for that honor.[11]

Shortly after 1860 what will become a near-universal custom among railroad ferryboat operators began to establish itself on the New Jersey R.R. when vessels started to be named after on-line cities served by the railroad – *Jersey City* of 1862, *Newark* of 1865, and *New York* of 1865, for example. Two New Jersey R.R. ferryboats, *John P. Jackson* and *Jersey City*, will play important and even poignant roles during the third era of the New York ferryboat story, the Civil War years. Before turning to this period, though, some discussion is appropriate about ferryboat service on the East River as well as to and from Staten Island, and this will be the subject of the next chapter.

---

11. Cadwallader David Colden (1769–1834) is one of a host of individuals who played a minor role in the story of New York ferryboats, but who achieved renown in some other facet of life. Colden was mayor of New York from 1818 to 1820; he was elected to the U.S. Congress in 1821 where he delivered a ringing speech in 1822 at-tacking the Fugitive Slave Law. Following his term in the House of Representatives he was elected to the New York state senate, and there became identified with all manner of progressive legislative causes. He was especially interested in improvements for marine navigation and was also active in the construction of the Erie Canal. He was an author, too, and published a *Life of Robert Fulton* in 1817. His grandfather, Cadwallader Colden (1688–1776), was also involved in political affairs, but achieved more lasting fame for his work as a naturalist in classification of various flora in upstate New York.

Welfare *was one of the single-ended steamboats used by the City of New York for service to various East River health and penal institutions.*
[*author*]

Erie R.R.'s Youngstown, *1956.*
[*author*]

Jersey Central R.R.'s Elizabeth *(ii),*
1956. [*author*]

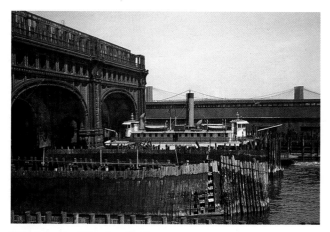

Ellis Island, *1954.* [*author*]

Jersey Central R.R's Wilkes-Barre,
1956 [*author*]

U.S. Coast Guard's The Tides *at*
Governors Island, 1988. [*author*]

City of New York's John F. Kennedy, *1987.* [*author*]

Erie R.R.'s Youngstown, *1955.* [*author*]

U.S. Army's Sgt. Cornelius H. Charlton, *1954* [*author*]

City of New York's Pvt. Joseph F. Merrell, *1979.* [*author*]

Delaware, Lackawanna & Western R.R.'s Binghampton, *1957.* [*author*]

U.S. Coast Guard's Pvt. Nicholas Minue, *1979.* [*author*]

New York Central R.R.'s Stony Point, *1954.* [*author*]

Delaware, Lackawanna & Western R.R.'s Pocono, *1957.* [*author*]

New York Central R.R.'s Rochester, *1957.* [*author*]

Jersey Central R.R.'s Somerville, *1956*
[*author*]

New York Central R.R.'s Stony Point,
1957. [*author*]

*Baltimore & Ohio R.R. train-
connection bus aboard Jersey Central
R.R. ferryboat, 1956.* [*author*]

Rockaway Boat Line's Columbia,
1956. [author]

City of New York's Jamestown, *1966.*
[Roger J. Cudahy]

City of New York Kennedy-*class*
ferryboats, 1972. [*author*]

City of New York's John A. Noble *at*
Williamsburg, 1988. [*author*]

City of New York's Cornelius G. Kolff, *1957.* [*author*]

City of New York Dongan Hills-*class ferryboat, 1957.* [*author*]

U.S. Coast Guard's Pvt. Nicholas Minue, *1979.* [*author*]

Jersey Central R.R.'s Elizabeth *(ii), 1956.* [*author*]

Jersey Central and New York Central ferryboats at lower Manhattan slips, 1956. [*author*]

Jersey Central R.R.'s Wilkes-Barre.
[*author*]

New York Central's Niagara, *1957.*
[*author*]

New York Central's Albany, *1957.*
[*author*]

U.S. Army's Colonel Robert E. Shannon, *1954.* [*author*]

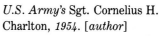

U.S. Army's Sgt. Cornelius H. Charlton, *1954.* [*author*]

U.S. Army service to Governors Island, 1954. [author]

A Kennedy-class ferryboat and a Circle Line excursion boat from the Statue of Liberty head back to Manhattan. [author]

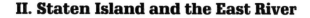

II. Staten Island and the East River

Just about anyplace in America today, if one were to play a word-association game and say "Staten Island," the response would very likely be "ferry." The service that now operates between the foot of Whitehall Street in Manhattan and Saint George five miles or so down the bay is remarkable because, one, it's still in operation, two, it has purchased four marvelous new ferryboats in the 1980s, and, three, it has its best days yet to come – or at least some would so maintain, and not without some pretty good arguments to support their case.

The future aside, though, the service has its roots deep in the nineteenth century and saw important growth in the days after the *Gibbons vs. Ogden* decision of 1824. Sloops and other sailing craft began regular service between Staten Island and Manhattan under the terms of formal ferry leases even earlier, of course, fifty years or more before the Revolutionary War. Steam power came to the service in 1817 in open defiance of the state monopoly held by the Fulton–Livingston organization, although the first powered craft were single-ended steamboats, not ferryboats.

During the early nineteenth century Staten Island was a remote and bucolic outpost whose residents were interested in farming and fishing; it was removed from New York City and its concerns by the waters of Upper New York Bay and had a population of 5347 people according to the 1810 Federal census. Indeed, glancing at a map of the metropolitan area even today, one might be inclined to wonder why Staten Island belongs to New York State at all. It is separated from New Jersey on several sides by only narrow tidal straits, while any other New York point is across open water. The most amateur geologist would readily concede that at one time not all that long ago Staten Island must have been joined to the New Jersey mainland. On a map Staten Island just *looks like* it should be part of New Jersey!

Except it isn't Staten Island, N.J., it's Staten Island, N.Y. Territorial claims for off-shore islands that seem as though they should belong to somebody else have always been among the more stoutly and emotionally defended – e.g., Quemoy and Matsu, Jersey and Guernsey, the Falklands,

Governor Moore class, *Electric Ferries, Inc., 1926–1968*

or the Pescadores. There's a legend that in the 1680s the Duke of York did Solomon one better and mediated the rival claims of New York and New Jersey to the island by offering it to whichever jurisdiction could first circumnavigate Staten Island in less than twenty-four hours. (New York supposedly won.) As to the dual names by which the place is still known: Henry Hudson is credited with first using the name Staten Island, still the popular designation, while Richmond, the island's official name as a county of New York State and, since 1898, a borough of the City of New York, was imposed by the British at the end of Dutch rule in 1664 in honor of the Duke of Richmond. "Staten Island" had a decidedly Dutch ring to it, especially in its original rendition, Staaten Eylandt, and the British were intent on Anglicizing their new territory as much as possible. Their success, in this case, was less than complete.

Returning to the final years of the Fulton–Livingston monopoly: the entrepreneur who introduced steam-powered vessels to the Manhattan–Staten Island service was young Cornelius Vanderbilt. Vanderbilt, it will be recalled, was a principal actor in the monopoly's demise when he piloted Thomas Gibbons' *Bellona*, the vessel whose disregard of the monopoly led directly to *Gibbons vs. Ogden.* Vanderbilt's pioneer steamer on the Staten Island route was a vessel named *Nautilus* – a steamboat, however, not a ferryboat.[1]

Three different steamboat companies soon emerged, each linking a different section of Staten Island with Manhattan. The direct corporate descendant of Vanderbilt's initial service, known originally as the Richmond Turnpike Ferry and later, simply, as the Staten Island Ferry, ran from Whitehall Street in Manhattan to Clifton, a section sometimes called Vanderbilt's Landing. A second company, the Tompkins and Staple Ferry, ran between Manhattan – presumably Whitehall Street – and Tompkinsville. The New York and Staten Island Steam Ferry Company, sometimes known as the Peoples' Ferry, connected the foot of Liberty Street in Manhattan and Stapleton, although in 1851 the company experimented for a year's time and used a landing at Clifton. All of these communities, separate towns or villages in the 1800s although today just neighborhoods, are located along Staten Island's eastern shore, the waterfront area that faces out on the Narrows with

---

1. Cornelius Vanderbilt was born on Staten Island in 1794 and with money borrowed from his mother instituted a wind-jammer ferry between his home and Manhattan as a boy of sixteen in the year 1810. He was 23 when his steamboat *Nautilus* first navigated the bay, in defiance of the Fulton–Livingston monopoly incidentally, and through the years leading up to the Civil War he expanded his steamboat holdings.

In 1862 Vanderbilt sold these maritime interests and invested in railroads; soon he controlled the New York Central and Hudson River R.R., a powerful line whose name would later be rendered more simply as New York Central. The Commodore, as he was called in deference to his business beginnings and not to any naval title that he formally earned, died in 1877 at the age of 83 having amassed a personal fortune estimated at $100,000,000. He endowed Vanderbilt University, and his son, his grand-

A view of the various ferry terminals at the foot of Whitehall St. in Manhattan ca. 1840. Ferryboats bound for Brooklyn and Long Island used slips in the middle; Staten Island service operated out of the building (and ferry slip) to the right. Horse-drawn omnibuses were available for debarking ferry passengers. [*author's collection*]

what is now the Bay Ridge section of Brooklyn on the other side. (See map, page 225.) It's also common to speak of a North Shore of Staten

sons, and even a great-grandnephew continued family control of the New York Central for many decades. When Cornelius Vanderbilt died in 1877, the cortège that bore his remains to their Staten Island resting place steamed down New York Bay aboard two ferryboats of the Staten Island service, *Westfield* (ii) and *Northfield*, descendants of Vanderbilt's own *Nautilus* of seventy years previous.

Island, the east–west shoreline along the Kill Van Kull opposite the Bayonne section of New Jersey and Newark Bay. Staten Island, shaped something like an upside-down pear, has an area of 36,600 acres; its longest north–south dimension is 13.9 miles, and its east–west is 7.3.

In 1853 the three Eastern Shore ferry companies merged into one; Whitehall Street became the exclusive Manhattan landing – and has remained so ever since – and service was operated from there to all three Staten Island landings previously served by the separate companies: Clifton, Tompkinsville,

and Stapleton. Saint George, the current terminal, not only wasn't a ferry landing in 1853, it was a rather undeveloped and even unpleasant piece of real estate not particularly conducive to berthing ferryboats since it wasn't a place people had any particular reason to go. (What's now called Saint George was once known as Ducksberry Point.) The resultant entity of this three-way merger was called the Staten Island and New York Ferry Company.

One thing that gets a little murky as one looks back almost 150 years is which of the early powered vessels were double-ended ferryboats and which were single-ended steamboats. This tends to be a problem on the Staten Island service more than on the cross-river lines because of the greater length of trip involved – it's over five miles from the southern tip of Manhattan Island to the closest point on Staten Island, a journey that understandably could be seen as more like the "long distance" trips normally made by single-ended steamboats than the kind of short over and back operation typically made by ferryboats. In addition, vessels operating *between* Manhattan and Staten Island often continued *beyond* Staten Island to places like Elizabeth, Perth Amboy, and New Brunswick in New Jersey, or Bath Beach and Coney Island in Brooklyn, services very clearly more of a "long distance" steamboat style of operation than a ferryboat service. This was especially true for a number of services that operated between Manhattan and points along Staten Island's North Shore, landings, that is to say, on the Kill Van Kull at such Staten Island points as Port Richmond, West Brighton, and Mariners' Harbor. These operations are distinct from the three companies that merged to form the Staten Island and New York Ferry Company in 1853 and appear to have been run exclusively with single-ended vessels. But single-ended boats also worked Eastern Shore landings in the early years, for the S.I. & N.Y. Fy. Co. as well as for incidental operators whose vessels' final destinations were ports beyond Staten Island.[2]

The earliest Staten Island double-ender may well have been the 252-ton *Samson*, built in 1837 for Vanderbilt's company. Other possible double-enders were *Columbus*, a 369-tonner that came out in 1838, and *Staten Islander*, 222 tons and built in 1839. The *Hunchback* of 1852, the harbor's first twin-deck ferryboat discussed in chapter 2, was obviously a true ferryboat.[3] Precision in these determinations can often be thwarted by the fact that a vessel might be converted, during its lifetime, from double- to single-ended, or from single- to double-ended. One thing clear is that by the early 1860s the Staten Island and New York Ferry Company was operating both single-enders and double-enders but replacing the former only with new bona-fide ferryboats as they were retired. *Josephine*, for example, a 552-ton single-

---

2. Steamboat operations to North Shore points on Staten Island have been treated by B. C. Betacourt, Jr., "The Staten Island Ferry," *Steamboat Bill of Facts*, No. 27 (September 1948), 54–56. Betacourt's work is actually a fine three-part series covering all aspects of Staten Island ferry service, all of which appeared in the same journal. See also No. 26 (June 1948), 25–29, and No. 28 (December 1948), 83–86. Betacourt's work was revised and re-published some years later: see "The Staten Island Steam Ferries," *The Staten Island Historian*, 16 (April–June 1955), 9–13; 16 (July–September 1955), 17–19.

3. I am relying here on the Lytle–Holdcamper List which identifies these four vessels as ferryboats from among a dozen vessels, all the rest surely single-ended steamboats, known to have operated for the three companies and their single successor in the years before, roughly, 1860. An 1856 woodcut of *Columbus*, however, which is reproduced in Betacourt's series of articles (see No. 26: 26) shows what is clearly a single-ended vessel. The full dozen are as follows:

ender, was built in 1852, the year before the three companies merged into one, and operated for the new 1853-formed company for a decade side-by-side with steamboats and ferryboats until she was replaced by double-ender *Northfield* in 1863. *Northfield* will then serve for 38 years before ending her career in ignominy and tragedy on Flag Day in the year 1901 – but that's to get quite a bit ahead of things. *Josephine*, however, was quite likely the last single-ender to serve regularly on the route, and thus did the ferryboat service that

continues to operate today between Whitehall Street and Saint George have its beginnings in the pre–Civil War period.

Ferryboat service across the East River in the years between 1824 and 1860 represents the harbor's most intense concentration of such transport. The routes were many and the vessels darted swiftly back and forth with people and vehicles going about their daily activities. Three major operators eventually came to dominate the East River; each was identified with a particular geographic area.

Up river and steaming out of a terminal at Hunter's Point in what is today the Long Island City section of the Borough of Queens came the boats of the Long Island R.R. This service was something of a late addition to the East River, at least in comparison with the other two of the "big three," initiating operations in 1859 as the East River Ferry Company. Trains of several railroads that eventually were unified into the L.I.R.R. terminated here, although it wasn't until well after the Civil War, in 1892, that the ferry company was formally taken over by the railroad.

The Long Island R.R. is itself a major curiosity, shadowed through much of its history by failed dreams and bad luck. As with the Whitehall Street–Saint George ferry service, though, the Long Island is still in business today; like the ferry it, too, is now a public agency.[4]

VESSEL	TONNAGE	BUILT	DISPOSITION
Nautilus	n/a	n/a	n/a
Bolivar	153	1825	abandoned; 1850
Herculus	192	1832	abandoned; 1856
Telegraph	243	1836	lost; 1870
Samson (f)	252	1837	lost; 1853
Columbus (f)	369	1838	abandoned; 1865
Staten Islander (f)	222	1839	abandoned; 1865
Gazelle	216	1841	abandoned; 1844
Sylph	290	1844	lost; 1868
C. Durant	128	1851	abandoned; 1858
Hunchback (f)	517	1852	abandoned; 1880
Josephine	552	1853	lost; 1898

(f) = Lytle–Holdcamper notation for ferryboat

Of the four "potential" ferryboats, I have included only *Hunchback* in the roster in Appendix C.

4. Among the components of today's Long Island R.R. that operated independently out of Hunter's Point at one time or another were the New York and Flushing R.R. (portions of which are today's Port Washington branch of the L.I.R.R) and the Long Island City and Manhattan Beach R.R. (portions

The early steam-powered vessels that the likes of Cornelius Vanderbilt once sailed between Manhattan and Staten Island saw the ultimate evolution of steam propulsion in the three-boat class of triple-deck ferryboats designed and built for the City of New York in 1951. Here one of the trio, Verrazzano, *awaits a call to duty for the evening rush hour at a lay-up slip west of the Saint George passenger terminal.* [author]

The ferry slips at the foot of Whitehall St. have dispatched double-ended vessels to Staten Island for many years. Here is a view in the early 1970s; on the left is the steam-powered Cornelius G. Kolff *and to the right is the* John F. Kennedy, *a diesel-powered vessel.* [author]

of which are today's lightly-used and freight-only Bay Ridge branch). Unraveling and understanding the history of the Long Island's many lines, branches, and predecessor companies is not a task undertaken lightly. For some help, see Mildred H. Smith, *Early History of the Long Island Railroad* (Uniondale, N.Y.: Salisbury, 1958); Elizur Brace Hinsdale, *History of the Long Island Railroad Company, 1834–1989* (New York: Evening Post Job Printing House, 1989), and, by far the most complete study, Vincent F. Seyfried, *The Long Island Rail Road: A Comprehensive History*, 7 parts (Garden City, N.Y.: Seyfried, 1961–75). Also useful, particularly in that it contains a full roster of all ferryboats and steamboats owned by the Long Island R.R., is Ron Ziel and George H. Foster, *Steel Rails to the Sunrise* (New York: Duell, Sloan and Pearce, 1965).

A somewhat later view of the Whitehall St. ferry complex than the drawing shown on page 67; now ferry passengers can transfer to steam-powered elevated trains, and horse-drawn streetcars have replaced the stagecoach-like omnibuses. This tranquil scene is ca. 1890. [Library of Congress]

This photograph was taken shortly after 1883 when the newly opened Brooklyn Bridge provided nineteenth-century photographs with a new perspective on the city's waterfront.

Most of the action is provided by steamboats, not ferryboats, and the docks along South Street – today the site of the South Street Seaport – are filled with the masts of sailing ships. But look closely: there's a ferryboat or two amid all the clutter. [Steamship Historical Society of America]

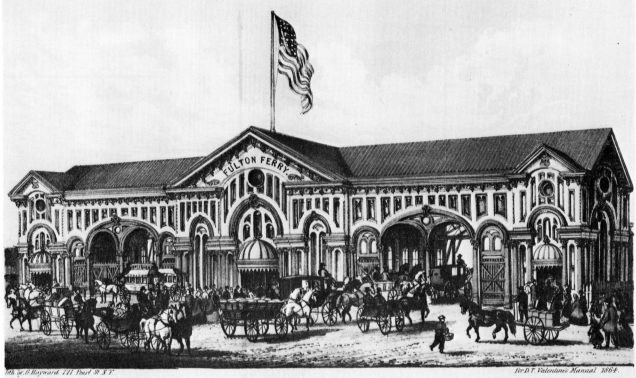

lith. by G. Hayward 171 Pearl St N.Y.   *for D.T. Valentine's Manual 1864.*

FULTON FERRY, NEW-YORK.
Built of Iron 1863.

This handsome cast-iron ferry house was built in 1863 at the foot of Manhattan's Fulton St. to serve what was then the Union Ferry Company's premier East River crossing – Fulton St., Manhattan, to Fulton St., Brooklyn. [Library of Congress]

In 1834 the railroad's early backers were enamored of the idea of using Long Island's flat midland as a cheap and fast right-of-way which might become the first leg of a boat–train–boat–train service between New York City and Boston. After all, the Connecticut shore of Long Island Sound was

shot through with inlets, rivers, and harbors, making railroad construction there next to impossible. Why not be smart and build an inexpensive railroad out to the end of Long Island, let passengers change there to a cross-sound steamboat, and then continue on to Boston by train from, say, Provi-

The territory once dominated by the Union Ferry Company is quiet today; people cross the East River in automobiles and subway trains, not ferryboats. [Port Authority of NY & NJ]

dence, Rhode Island, or New London, Connecticut? The company was incorporated in 1834 and the line was finished to Greenport at the eastern end of Long Island in 1844, but, alas, by the end of 1848 the "next to impossible" all-rail line thorough Connecticut was in business as well. The Long Island R.R.'s *raison d'être* was gone, and furthermore in its haste to reach the steamer connection in Green-port the railroad was built through the relatively uninhabited center of Long Island; there was little local traffic it could easily or quickly generate to compensate for its lost Boston business.

The railroad's original western terminal – i.e., the one closest to New York City – was at the foot of Brooklyn's Atlantic Avenue, and it was from here that the very first L.I.R.R. passengers made their way across the mouth of the East River on ferryboats of an independent company. The route in question, Whitehall Street–Atlantic Avenue, began service in May 1836, four years before the railroad arrived, and it would later become part of the Union Ferry Company's network of East River lines. But the birth of this ferry-boat service was not easy.

When first proposed, the new

ferry was vigorously opposed by the company that had taken over the original Fulton–Cutting lease to operate the Fulton Street–Fulton Street line that *Nassau* had pioneered in 1814, a lease whose term was to run until 1839. The older company based its opposition on the legal construction it felt should be placed upon a phrase in its lease that gave it the exclusive right to operate a ferry in Brooklyn south of a specified point. But what exactly did "Brooklyn" mean? The boundaries of the incorporated village of Brooklyn had grown since 1814, and grew even more in 1834 when Brooklyn became a city. The holders of the older lease felt that all this political expansion and change of status merely served to extend their area of exclusivity; those proposing to initiate the new ferry from Atlantic Avenue felt that the 1814 lease granted franchise rights merely to a given and stable point – that is to say, the southern boundary of Brooklyn in the year 1814, a point which their proposed Atlantic Avenue landing was conveniently beyond.

The state legislature was finally petitioned for relief; when it ap-

peared that they were about to pass a law that would modify New York City's powerful control over ferryboat franchising and allow the new service, a lease was indeed granted by New York City to a group of Brooklynites to operate a ferry between Whitehall Street and Brooklyn's Atlantic Avenue, although it should be noted that the latter thoroughfare was known as Atlantic *Street* in the early 1800s. Thus a ferryboat route was in place and operating when railroad trains began to run eastward from the Brooklyn docks on the eighteenth of April in 'thirty-six – 61 years to the day after a more famous trip inland from an American waterfront.[5]

The corporate entity that was the Long Island R.R. actually took over and leased a previously-chartered railroad on its western end, the Brooklyn and Jamaica

5. The very first train on the L.I.R.R. was hauled by the company's very first locomotive, a machine that bore the name "Ariel" and had been turned out the previous November by Matthias W. Baldwin of Philadelphia. "Ariel" and her train, on April 18, 1836, ran from the foot of Atlantic Avenue to Jamaica.

R.R. The B. & J. received its own charter to 1832, the first issued to a railroad on "Nassau Island" and but the seventh in all of America. But it ran no trains of its own prior to its union with the L.I.R.R.

For one reason or another Brooklyn, village and city, never struck it off well with the Long Island R.R. Supposedly at the behest of street railway companies who saw the new railroad as a competitive threat, city fathers banned steam locomotives from the Atlantic Avenue line in 1859, just as the company was beginning to come to terms with its new and reduced status as a local island railroad and not part of a New York–Boston route. The railroad quickly became exasperated with the horse cars it was then forced to deploy on what it was attempting to develop into a major main-line operation, and so it set to work constructing a new route to the East River that would bypass Brooklyn entirely. Thus did the company wind up with its principal western terminus at Hunter's Point in Long Island City, and not in Brooklyn, and it was from Long Island City that the ferry service the railroad itself eventually took over and operated

The captain in the circular wheel-house on the Union Ferry Company's 1871-build sidewheeler Farragut *has just left Fulton St., Brooklyn, and is bringing his vessel around to head across the river and slightly downstream for a landfall in about five minutes at the foot of Fulton St., Manhattan. This route is one of two in the harbor that were instituted by Robert Fulton.* [Steamship Historical Society of America]

was inaugurated in the year 1859.

The original B. & J. main line was half abandoned and half downgraded with the shift to Hunter's Point. Trains continued to operate between Jamaica and East New York, the quarantine point for the company's steam locomotives, but the service was branch-line in status. Between East New York and the ferry slip at the foot of Atlantic Avenue the company abandoned its line, although a major

portion of it will be restored before the century is over.[6]

(This shifting of western termi-

nals of the L.I.R.R. in the late 1850s from Brooklyn to Hunter's Point is the fact that must be cited

---

6. A fascinating exercise in "what if" speculation is possible by positing that the Long Island R.R. retained its principal western passenger terminal at the foot of Atlantic Avenue in Brooklyn rather than shift to Hunter's Point. Would a single Long Island R.R. have evolved, or would the island be served, perhaps to this day, by separate rail entities? Would the railroad, or any portion of it, have been taken over by the Pennsylvania R.R. at the turn of the century? Would the Pennsylvania's own massive Manhattan terminal project (i.e., Penn Station and the river tunnels leading to it) ever have happened? How might the Atlantic Avenue corridor in Brooklyn have developed had the railroad remained in operation there?

It's around the year 1900 and visitors to New York anxious to send a postal card to the folks back home could find this interesting view in local shops; a Union Ferry Company sidewheeler out of Fulton St., Brooklyn is heading for Fulton St., Manhattan and a ferry slip directly "above" the vessel's smokestack. [author's collection]

Sky Scrapers from Brooklyn Bridge, New York.

to explain a most peculiar orientation of this unusual railroad, and it has an impact on operations to this very day – Jamaica, where the new line to Hunter's Point leaves the old line to Brooklyn, is a major junction where passengers must observe a venerable Long Island R.R. tradition: "Change at Jamaica for trains to Oyster Bay, Port Jefferson, Far Rockaway, Hempstead, and Long Beach." Daily commuters on the line understandably regard the "venerable tradition" as more of a deadly curse.)

There were two ferryboat routes out of Hunter's Point: a direct crossing to Manhattan's East 34 Street, plus a longer service that left Long Island City, headed down the East River, and deposited passengers closer to the commercial districts of Manhattan at James Slip. As was the case with many other early ferryboat routes throughout New York, the East 34 Street–Hunter's Point line was "longer" in 1859 when it was initiated than in subsequent years. Landfill would later reclaim considerable acreage from the river,

and the first ferryboats tied up in the vicinity of First Avenue in Manhattan, a full block inland from the river's edge today.

Prior to the Civil War four double-ended ferryboats can be identified as operating out of Hunter's Point: *Louise*, an 1853-built vessel, *Queens County* of 1859, *Suffolk County* and *Kings County*, both of 1860. The Long Island R.R.'s ferryboat operations on the East River much resembled those of the railroads terminating in New Jersey on the west bank of the Hudson River. But as with so

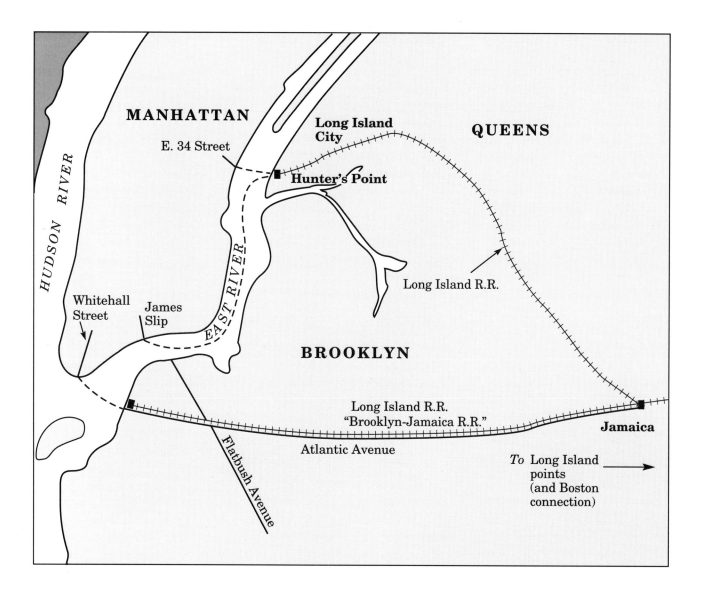

3. Access to Manhattan for the Long Island R.R.

many features of this unusual railroad they were also, as will be later seen, just a little bit different.

The Union Ferry Company was clearly the East River's major ferryboat operator, and even that claim may understate the facts. Of the company *The New York Times* would say, in 1870, that it was "the wealthiest and most important ferry company in the world." It grew to such status in several stages.

The nucleus of the Union Ferry Company was Robert Fulton's New York and Brooklyn Steam Ferry Boat Company of 1814. Indeed, the pilot of *Nassau* on her inaugural voyage in 1814, one Peter Coffee, remained an employee of the Union Ferry Company until after the Civil War. But in 1833 the company was not faring well. Fulton, of course, had died in 1815, and his partner, William Cutting, was never able to make the company a robust undertaking. In 1833 two men, David Leavitt and Silas Butler, secured control by purchasing a majority of the company's stock. Two new vessels were then purchased for the service, *Relief* and *Olive Branch*. They were bona-fide ferryboats of a conventional sort; Fulton's original twin-hull design was not replicated, in other words, and the pair were single-hull sidewheelers and much resembled the ferryboats that were evolving on the Hudson under the direction of the Stevens clan. As was the case on the Hudson, floating ice tended to be drawn into the area between the two hulls, clogging the paddlewheel, and one of the expectations both operators and passengers held out for powered ferryboats was an ability to make cross-river transport less dependent on winter weather than it had previously been. Prior to steam propulsion Brooklyn and Manhattan would often be isolated from each other for days and even weeks at a time during especially frigid periods when the periaugers dared not sail for fear of floating ice; fields of ice could even encompass and crush the frail hull of a small vessel, or even the not-so-frail hull of a medium-size vessel. Legends still abound of winters like 1816 when both the East River and the Hudson were so totally frozen that people were able to cross from shore to shore on foot! But this was an extraordinary happening; the more bothersome winter phenomenon were those days when the rivers were not dramatically frozen over, merely impassable.

Both the original Fulton Street–Fulton Street service and the new Whitehall Street–Atlantic Avenue route that had been inaugurated in 1836 had leases that expired in 1839. It was at this time that the first of many mergers took place, and both services were extended to 1844 under the terms of a single lease granted to a new firm, the New York and Brooklyn Union Ferry Company. Stockholders of the two older firms were able to exchange their securities for shares in the new firm. While the Union Ferry Company will go through several iterations of its formal name and additional routes will be added to the system, it is appropriate to say that the company had its beginnings with this 1839 merger.

The 1839–1844 lease was renewed through 1851 and the firm was re-organized as the Brooklyn Union Ferry Company. A third route was added to the company's service pattern in October 1846, linking the foot of Hamilton Avenue in Brooklyn with Whitehall

Street, roughly the route of to-day's Brooklyn–Battery Tunnel. With yet another lease extension from 1851 to 1861 it was stipulated that all surplus revenue at year's end, after paying operating expenses plus an eight-per-cent dividend to the company's investors, be given to the Brooklyn City Hospital and other Brooklyn charities.

This action served to cast Union as a genuine Brooklyn institution, and enabled its directors to say that their enterprise was hardly a profit-seeking corporation, but more a public service maintained for the benefit of the people of Brooklyn. Of course, some might argue that an eight-per-cent dividend is hardly philanthropy.

It's early 1909 and a sidewheeler of the Union Ferry Company is two-thirds of the way across the East River en route to Catharine St., Manhattan, from Main St., Brooklyn. Behind the ferryboat, steelwork is nearing completion on the two-deck Manhattan Bridge; it will open later in the year and further reduce the need for East River ferryboats. [Library of Congress]

While Union will eventually emerge as the principal Brooklyn–Manhattan ferryboat operator in the area downriver from where the Brooklyn Bridge now stands, it had to work hard to achieve that status. Competition soon developed in the Union's lower East River territory, and other independent ferries sprang up on a number of routes: Roosevelt Street, Manhattan, to Bridge Street, Brooklyn, in 1853; Wall Street, Manhattan, to Montague Street, Brooklyn, the previous year; also Catharine Street, Manhattan, to Main Street, Brooklyn, and Gouverneur Street, Manhattan, to Bridge Street, Brooklyn, both in this same general time-frame. And while its degree was surely modest in the land where Boss Tweed would soon roam and coin the nation's basic vocabulary for all subsequent discussion on the entire subject of municipal corruption, there is reason to believe that the awarding of leases for these several ferryboat lines was not free from graft. In 1851 the lease for the Catharine Street–Main Street ferry was supposedly awarded only after each alderman was secretly given a $500 bribe by the successful bidder,

and a similar situation is thought to have prevailed on the Wall Street–Montague Street line.[7]

But bribes to aldermen or not, none of Union's competitors were able to mount any kind of serious challenge to the older and larger company. They all fared poorly and pressure began to build throughout Brooklyn for Union to consolidate its own three services with the ailing newcomers; and that's exactly what happened.

December 6, 1853, saw all ferryboats on the lower East River flying flags and bunting from masts and railings. It was the first day of joint operation under Union auspices, a mind-boggling system that now included *seven* separate East River crossings: Fulton Street–Fulton Street, Whitehall Street–Atlantic Avenue, Whitehall Street–Hamilton Avenue, Wall Street–Montague Street, Catharine Street–Main Street, Roosevelt Street–Bridge Street,

and, finally, Gouverneur Street–Bridge street. (See map.) The consolidation had been effected and Union was now a company of virtually unimaginable proportions. It owned and operated *twenty-three ferryboats* – all of which are listed in Table III-1. Union was the world's largest ferryboat company, a status it would maintain for most of its years.

On the day the consolidation took place, Union's chronicler, Henry Pierrepont, tells an interesting story. He was sitting on a jury in Brooklyn and realized, all of a sudden, that proper attention had not been paid to assuring the validity of insurance policies on the now-enlarged fleet. He informed the judge of his problem and the understanding jurist excused Pierrepont so he could attend to the matter. And well that he did so, for that very night, *Montague*, one of the vessels whose insurance would have been in questionable status without Pierrepont's action, caught fire and burned. The insurance carrier made good $33,000 of her $38,000 purchase price.[8]

7. Bribes and corruption in the award of ferry leases during this period are discussed by Gustavus Myers, "History of Public Franchises in New York City," *Municipal Affairs*, 4 (March 1900), 71–206.

8. See Pierrepont, *Historical Sketch of the Fulton Ferry*, pp. 69–70.

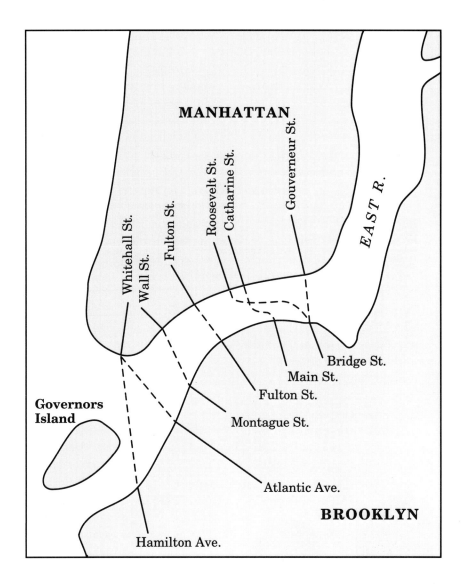

4. The Union Ferry Company of Brooklyn

Operation of seven ferryboat lines across so short a stretch of the East River proved to be just a little bit too much for the market, and in the late 1850s two poorly performing lines were dropped. The first to go was Gouverneur Street–Bridge Street; never a profitable or heavily used service, it was discontinued on January 10, 1857. Dropped in 1859 was the Roosevelt Street–Bridge Street service, thus reducing Union to five lines. But this remaining quintet were strong services that would form the heart of the Union Ferry Company for the next fifty years.[9]

The Union Ferry Company did not, of course, survive nearly as long as many lesser New York ferryboat services, and the reason relates to its success and importance. So vital was trans-river transportation in its territory that it was here that the area's first bridges and tunnels were constructed, starting with the Brooklyn Bridge in 1883. But in the years before the American Civil War, with loyal passengers like Brooklyn newspaperman Walt Whitman crossing the river regularly on its boats, the Union Ferry Company was in its years of ascendancy.

The third major East River operation linked Williamsburg with various points in Manhattan. A reference to contemporary geography and jurisdiction can help set the scene. Today Williamsburg is a section or neighborhood in the Borough of Brooklyn, but onward from 1827 it was an incorporated village of its own within the Town of Bushwick, and in 1851 Williamsburg achieved city status itself. It merged with the City of Brooklyn in 1854. Williamsburg, besides being a bustling place noted for its iron works and petroleum refining, was also a spot where inland residents from places like Bushwick reached the East River en route to Manhattan. The principal thoroughfare they traveled was called Broadway, but this was – and is – a different Broadway from the far better known Manhattan avenue of the same name.[10]

Compared to the Union Ferry Company, the Williamsburg ferries were a little slow in developing. When Union was consummating large corporate mergers and operating two dozen ferryboats, the Williamsburg lines were in their infancy. The general service pattern they developed involved routes to multiple Manhattan terminals from a single Williamsburg landing at the foot of Broadway. (The company had but one "non-Broadway" service; its Williamsburg terminal was at the foot of Grand Street, a little less than a half-mile to the north of Broadway.)

A rowboat ferry was established in the company's territory by one James Hazard in 1797. The first Williamsburg Ferry Company was established in 1824 and the first steam-powered service dates to 1826 – no challenge to the Fulton–Livingston monopoly here, obviously. The company's corporate title tended to change with some frequency over the years: Williams-

---

9. Brooklyn's Bridge Street deserves a brief mention. It is not named after or in relation to any existing East River span and the name predates the 1883 opening of the Brooklyn Bridge. The name derives from the fact that it was simply assumed that an East River Bridge, were one to be built, would vault upward from its alignment. None did.

10. Prior to the twentieth century, Williamsburg was spelled "Williamsburgh."

The Williamsburg ferries have been gone for decades, but, wonder of wonders, evidence of the old terminal at the foot of Broadway remains. When beam-engine sidewheelers regularly tied up to these ferry slips, the Manhattan skyline had a much different look to it. [author]

burg Ferry Company, New York Ferry Company, Brooklyn and New York Ferry Company, New York and Brooklyn Ferry Company. Just to increase the opportunity for confusion, the last title is one by which Union was formally known during a portion of its early history.

A lease renewal executed in 1849 provided for three routes out of Williamsburg to Manhattan: one to Roosevelt Street and one to Grand Street, these both from the company's Broadway terminal, and the service from the foot of Grand Street in Williamsburg whose Manhattan landfall was also at the foot of a street called Grand Street, the harbor's second "double name" ferryboat service. In the post–Civil War period the company will expand its operations with more routes out of the Broadway terminal and the fleet will grow to over a dozen sidewheel ferryboats.

The terminal at the foot of Broadway, understandably, became a focus for streetcar routes from many points, and for a short period after the Civil War there was even a railroad terminal here served by a company that was later absorbed by the Long Island R.R. – at which time the trains were rerouted to Hunter's Point.[11] In 1889 an elevated rapid transit line opened for business linking the Broadway ferry landing with inland communities.

11. The Broadway ferry terminal was located between Broadway and South 6 Street along the East River and can often be found referred to as the South 6 Street Terminal. As to the railroad: it was called the South Side R.R. and was built to compete with the Long Island between Jamaica, Babylon, and Patchogue – populated territory that the L.I.R.R.'s mid-

There were other East River ferryboat services with roots in the 1824–1860 era besides those of the three principal operators – the Union Ferry Company, the Williamsburg ferries, and the Long Island R.R. There was a Greenpoint Ferry Company established in 1853 that ran two routes from Greenpoint to Manhattan, one to East 10 Street and another to East 23 Street. (In 1889 the company's name was changed to the Tenth and Twenty-third Street Ferry Company.) The Nassau Ferry Company had a single route – Houston Street, Manhattan, to Grand Street on the opposite side – and it began service in 1842. A ferry was established in 1843 from upper Manhattan to Astoria, but it was discontinued early on. It will be resumed in later years and continue, under various auspices, until the opening of the Triborough Bridge in 1936.

There was also a ferry from the foot of Jackson Street, Manhattan, to the Navy Yard on Wallabout Bay in Brooklyn. Established in 1825, its first boat, the *General Jackson*, sank in 1836. Another early East River service was operated by the Roman Catholic Church; vessels used on the line were registered on official Federal documents as being owned by the trustees of Saint Patrick's Cathedral. (Not, of course, the current Saint Patrick's uptown on Fifth Avenue, but rather the 1809–1815-built downtown original at Mott and Prince Streets.) The line operated from the foot of East 23 Street in Manhattan to a point on Newtown Creek close to Calvary Cemetery, a burial ground that opened in 1848, and the ferry was established for the convenience of mourners heading for the cemetery. But while motivated by such a special purpose, the line was run under the auspices of a secular ferry lease issued by the City of New York and was, presumably, available to the general public as well. In 1853 the lease was transferred to the Greenpoint Ferry Company and service was rerouted from Newtown Creek/Calvary Cemetery to the foot of Greenpoint Avenue.

Table III-2 lists all the New York ferryboat routes in operation as the 1824–1860 era comes to a close.

Thus a general picture emerges over the past two chapters of the growth of harbor ferryboating in New York in the years after *Gibbons vs. Ogden* and before the Civil War. But what else can be

island route bypassed in its haste to reach the steamer connection at Greenport. To get to the East River and ferry connections with New York, South Side management first wanted to run their trains along Metropolitan Avenue east of Jamaica. That didn't pan out. Finally they were able to extend their line to Bushwick and Montrose avenues in Brooklyn, and passengers could proceed on to the ferry at the foot of Broadway aboard horse cars – first conventional streetcars to which they had to change, then horses hitched to the railroad cars themselves; no change at Bushwick and Montrose, in other words. This was in late 1869. The next year the South Side R.R. was able to substitute small steam engines, called "steam dummies," for the horses. The railroad's depot at the river's edge was located at South 8 Street and Kent Avenue. It was abandoned in February 1876 after the South Side R.R. had shifted all of its trains to Hunter's Point. The South Side was formally absorbed into the Long Island R.R. in October 1889.

said of New York during this interval when ferryboats grew from an experimental curiosity to a mainstay of local transportation? What stands out, not necessarily as a basic record of the history of the era, but to supply character, texture, and counterpoint to the ferryboat story?

New York has long been known for its skyline – and if it never gets to be said again let it be said here: there has never been a finer platform for viewing the city's skyline than the deck of a ferryboat! But what did the skyline look like in the 1840s and 1850s when wooden-hull sidewheelers were serving the various routes?

It was, to be sure, modest by contemporary standards. For the length of the 1824–1860 interval the "skyscrapers" of Manhattan were church spires, not office buildings. Saint Paul's Chapel on Broadway, between Vesey and Fulton streets, is today the oldest church in Manhattan – it was completed in 1766 – and for many years its steeple was the tallest structure in the city. The current Trinity Church at Broadway and Wall Street, in whose yard are buried the mortal remains of Robert

Fulton, was built in the 1840s. It and Saint Paul's, in a sense, could be called the "twin towers" one first saw approaching Manhattan by ferryboat. But other church steeples also gave form to the city's profile. There was the Old North Dutch Church, for instance, on William Street between Ann and Fulton, and many others.

In contrast to these saintly spires, the city's other architecture hugged the ground – three, four, and perhaps five or sometimes six stories were the limit during the period. Buildings wouldn't reach the dizzying heights of even ten stories until the 1890s. One result of such buildings is that as one drew away from Manhattan by ferryboat the natural elevations of the city were more obvious than they are today. One could better see the streets sloping down to the Hudson and East rivers and develop a sense for the natural contours that tall buildings would later disguise. There was also more greenery to be seen in Manhattan, on land or from the water.

Mention of the city's buildings calls to mind something that was a far more fearful peril in the early

nineteenth century than it is today – fire. Until techniques and equipment and building codes were deployed to fight and prevent urban conflagrations, it is hardly possible to imagine the catastrophe that necessarily resulted when a fire overwhelmed the city's firefighters and raged unchecked through block after block of vulnerable real estate. Everyone has heard of the Chicago Fire of 1871; less well known is the Great Fire of 1835 in New York that started in a store on Merchant Street (today's Beaver street) between Hanover and Pearl, burned for two days, destroyed as many as 700 stores, and resulted in damage of $40,000,000. Equivalent destruction today could only be caused by calculated and sustained military bombardment! Ten years later another epic fire erupted in New York and destroyed *three hundred buildings*; it began in a packing-box factory on New Street (today's Nassau Street).[12]

---

12. For an account of early New York architecture, particularly in the context of the peril posed by fire, see Kenneth Holcomb, *As You Pass By* (New York: Hastings House, 1952).

Pre–Civil War New York was not wanting for sources of enjoyment, though. In 1853 a marvelous World's Fair was held on the site of today's Bryant Park, West 42 Street and Sixth Avenue. A replica of London's Crystal Palace was erected and President Franklin Pierce journeyed to New York to inaugurate the festivities, traveling on the New Jersey R.R. and crossing the Hudson River on the Cortlandt Street–Paulus Hook ferry in all likelihood. But the premier entertainment event of the period was, surely, the visitation of a European singing star – a special appearance that would establish parameters for later conquests of America's aesthetic sensibilities by the likes of Enrico Caruso, Rudolph Valentino, John McCormack . . . the Beatles, the Rolling Stones, and Elton John.

The steamship *Atlantic* docked at Canal Street and the Hudson River on a late summer day in 1850, and down the gangplank walked

_____

Holcomb's work also includes a useful appendix that catalogues street names from Manhattan's past that are no longer in use.

Jenny Lind, the "Swedish Nightingale." Her American tour was arranged by Phineas T. Barnum and her concert at Castle Garden on the evening of September 11 was as total a conquest of New York as has been managed – before, since, or ever.

Castle Garden still stands in Battery Park. It served as an offshore fortification during the War of 1812, afterward it was a theater, a pre–Ellis Island immigration station, an aquarium, and now, fittingly, a place where one can buy tickets for the boat ride out to the Statue of Liberty and Ellis Island. There are lots of park benches around Castle Garden's walls – its surrounding land has been filled in, it's part of Battery Park, and no longer an "off shore" facility – and it's just a marvelous place to sit and relax and watch the ferryboats leaving and arriving from the nearby Whitehall Street terminal on the run to and from Staten Island. Chances are that many of the disappointed people who were unable to get into Castle Garden for Jenny Lind's concert on the evening of September 11, 1850, did the very same thing!

Thus, a critical thirty-five-year span from the issuance of the decision in *Gibbons vs. Ogden* to the onset of the American Civil War was accomplished. Ferryboats in New York Harbor grew from a just-mechanized infant industry serving a city of 200,000 people to a major transportation component in a city with a population over one million residents. Recall, though, that in discussing Robert Fulton's inauguration of Cortlandt Street–Paulus Hook service back in 1812 it was noted that the ferryboat *Jersey* was the area's only local transportation that was mechanized – that is to say, powered by machine, not by animals and not by the wind. But in 1860 virtually the same claim can be made of the city's 70-or-more vessel ferryboat fleet. It was the only form of local transport to be driven by the basic engine that was re-making the face of the world through the Industrial Revolution, the steam engine. True, by 1860 there were streetcars in New York; but they were hauled by horses. True, there were steam-powered railroad trains; but they were oriented more toward inter-city, and at best suburban, travel. And true, there were steamboats; but they, too, were primarily deployed to connect New York with distant points. It was the ferryboats alone that represented a large-scale use of mechanical power exclusively for local and short-haul transportation over and back across the two rivers and up and down the bay. New York – which is to say Manhattan – was thus able to evolve into an intense center of business and commerce and industry, and its workers were able to secure transport to more hospitable residential districts by ferryboat: to Brooklyn, to Hoboken, to Staten Island.

After the Civil War and onward toward the turn of the century ferryboats alone will be unequal to the task of providing Manhattan's growing workforce with access to healthy residential districts, and until other forms of mechanized urban transportation are in place awful tenement crowding in the city will become a national scandal. "What if" speculation is just that, speculation; but one cannot help but wonder how New York City might have coped with its 488% growth in population between 1824 and 1860 and its evolution into the nation's most important city without the one system of mechanized local transportation it had available, its fleet of steam-powered, double-ended ferryboats.

Edgewater, *Riverside & Fort Lee
Ferry Company, 1902–1948*

1. Henry Ward Beecher (1813–1887) became pastor of the Plymouth Church of the Pilgrims in 1847. He was, to use our contemporary term, an activist – an early supporter of the abolitionists, he worked as well on behalf of women's rights. Such concerns, understandably, earned the man quite a reputation, and he was frequently invited to give sermons and lectures away from his home parish. Plymouth Church, on Ann St. in Brooklyn between Hicks and Henry, was but a short walk from the ferry terminal at the foot of Fulton Street, and many of Beecher's trips began and ended with a passage across the East River on one of the Union Ferry Company's vessels – necessarily before the Brooklyn Bridge opened in 1883, by choice afterward. Beecher thoroughly enjoyed these voyages; he and Walt Whitman are often mentioned together as being the leading celebrity fans of the "Fulton Ferry."

The third era in the saga of the ferryboats of New York harbor is that four-year period in American history when eleven states formed themselves into the Confederacy, withdrew from the Federal Union, and took up arms against the government in Washington. The Civil War marks the end of an important period of growth for the harbor's various fleets and leads into the final years of the nineteenth century when New York ferryboats reached the zenith of their development. But the war years also saw some unique happenings of their own, the most improbable being the fact that two dozen or so double-ended New York ferryboats were "conscripted" for the duration and sailed off with Union forces to play a unique and interesting role in the Civil War itself, including participation in some of its more famous battles.

To discuss any aspect of New York City and the Civil War invites complex talk and, not infrequently, spirited debate – even today. There were, for instance, important roots of the Abolitionist Movement in both Brooklyn and New York. Henry Ward Beecher's fiery sermons from his pulpit in Brooklyn's Plymouth Church can hardly be overlooked.[1] But the area's overall reaction to civil war was far from simple and resists generalization most stoutly. Mayor Fernando Wood, for instance, proposed in early 1861 that New York City secede from the Union, establish itself as a "free city," and while not actually joining the Confederacy use its independent status to aid the southern cause. In 1863 when the Federal Government imposed upon the states the very first conscription in the nation's history, New York erupted in a July week of bloody rioting that saw a *thousand people killed* and was not put down until five regiments of the Army of the Potomac were ordered to the city to assist local police. The draft riots are linked to an absence of sympathy toward blacks on the part of city immigrants who saw in the freed slave an unwelcome competitor for the same unskilled jobs they themselves were seeking. Lynching of blacks within the boundaries of today's five boroughs was hardly unknown, and even among those who initially supported the Union cause with fervor and felt strongly about its nobility, a loss of ardor began to set in when casualties started to mount, casualties from battles whose decisiveness was less than obvious.

In New Jersey there was blatant support for the Confederate cause. State legislation there, alone among northern states, permitted fugitive-slave bounty hunters to frustrate the work of the underground railroad. Ferry slips especially, on both the Hudson and the Delaware, were likely locations for the slave hunters to lurk. Ferryboats steaming across the Hudson to Manhattan from Hoboken and Paulus Hook, in other words, often had to be avoided and bypassed by people fleeing a life of slavery.

Abraham Lincoln was elected president in November 1860 and was inaugurated on March 4, 1861, today's January inaugurations not becoming the rule until passage of the twentieth amendment in 1933. It was between Lincoln's election and his inauguration that secession began among the southern states; South Carolina, in December 1860, was the first to repeal its ratification of the United States Constitution, and on February 4, 1861, delegates from six secessionist states met in Montgomery, Alabama, adopted a provisional constitution for the Confederate States of America, and elected Jefferson Davis as provisional

president. Fort Sumter would be fired on two months later, on April 12.

The president-elect realized that he faced a mighty task in trying to preserve the Federal Union, and so, in journeying to the nation's capital from his Illinois homeland to assume his new constitutional responsibilities, Lincoln visited several important cities en route and met with key political people. After coming east in late February he left New York City for Washington, his inauguration, and the country's destiny.

Now, to reach Washington by rail from New York in the year 1861 was not today's three-hour dash on an electrified Amtrak Metroliner. Indeed, even the amalgamation of the New York–Washington rail service under the banner of a single company, the Pennsylvania R.R., was still years away. A routine journey went something like this: from the rail head in Jersey City to Philadelphia there was through service without change of trains, but it was over three contiguous, if related, railroads – the New Jersey Railroad and Transportation Company from the river to New Brunswick, the

Camden and Amboy R.R. beyond to Trenton, and the Philadelphia and Trenton R.R. from the New Jersey capital city on to Kensington Depot in Philadelphia, a service described in some detail in chapter 2.

In Philadelphia the Washington-bound traveler made the first change of trains and then rode the Philadelphia, Wilmington and Baltimore R.R. But this was neither a facile connection nor a straight and swift run. The P. W. & B.'s Philadelphia terminal was downtown on Broad Street, a fair haul from Kensington Depot in North Philadelphia. Furthermore, to cross the mouth of the broad Susquehanna River halfway to Baltimore, the entire train was put aboard a huge ferryboat, the 1150-ton *Maryland* (i); the first Susquehanna River bridge would not be completed until postwar 1866.[2] Once in Baltimore one made a final change, this time to

2. *Maryland* (i) was a bona-fide double-ended ferryboat built for the railroad in 1853. She had an iron hull, was 238 feet long – large by contemporary New York standards – and carried her passengers in main-deck cabins while the railroad cars were transported on

the Baltimore and Ohio R.R. The Philadelphia, Wilmington and Baltimore's depot at its southern extreme was the President Street Station. From there to the B. & O.'s Camden Station Washington-bound railroad cars were hauled, singly, along Pratt Street by horses – right past the site of today's bustling Harbor Place development – and then a new train was assembled for the final leg of the journey.

But even this relatively direct service wasn't Lincoln's planned route on his way to Washington from New York in 1861. He intended to head west from Philadelphia to the Pennsylvania state capital at Harrisburg for more meetings with state and local officials, and then south through York over the Northern Central Railway, connecting with the B. & O. at Baltimore. But while the president-elect's plans didn't call for him to cross the Susquehanna River aboard *Maryland* (i), he

would travel on another ferryboat en route to Washington from New York.

To reach their train in Jersey City on the morning of Thursday, February 21, 1861, members of the Lincoln traveling party first had to cross the Hudson River. Lincoln, man and president, likely crossed the Hudson by ferryboat many times. But his journey this day is one about which some details are known. The ferryboat, for one thing, was the 777-ton *John P. Jackson*, owned and operated by the New Jersey Railroad and Transportation Company.

The *John P. Jackson* was built in the Devine M. Burtis shipyard in Brooklyn in 1860, the same year Lincoln defeated Stephen Douglas, and two lesser candidates, and earned the right to be the nation's sixteenth president. Typical of ferryboats of her day, the *'Jackson* had a wooden hull and dimensions of 192 feet in length, 36 feet in hull width, and 12 feet in depth. She was powered by the usual vertical-beam engine; its single cylinder had a diameter of 45 inches and a stroke of eleven feet. *John P. Jackson* was named in honor of an official of the railroad and she was the newest vessel in

the fleet. As might be expected, the company laid on a bit of ceremony for the president-elect.

Lincoln had come down from Albany on Tuesday, February 19, and spent all day Wednesday meeting with officials in New York, including Mayor Wood, although his Honor let his secessionist feelings show and was noticeably cool to the president-elect. The party was staying at the Astor House, a fashionable downtown hotel on the west side of Broadway between Vesey and Barclay streets that had been built in 1836. Its six stories made it an imposing structure for its day.

Early Thursday morning Lincoln was picked up at his hotel for the short carriage ride to the foot of Cortlandt Street and his rendezvous with the *John P. Jackson*.[3] The ferryboat had left its Jersey City slip at eight in the morning

_____

a top deck. Laid up with the opening of a Susquehanna River bridge in 1866, *Maryland* (i) was brought to New York a decade later and again used to ferry entire railroad passenger trains. This phase of her career will be treated in chapter 5.

3. With language crafted, perhaps, less to inform his readers than to impress his editors, one reporter described the president-elect's leave-taking of his New York hotel thusly: "Bright and early yesterday morning Mr. Lincoln arose, and rapidly disposed of his early callers, his TIMES and his breakfast. . . ."

with the mayor and Common Council of Jersey City aboard and flags and bunting on all appropriate staffs and railings. Aboard the vessel martial music was provided by an aggregation called Dodworth's band, and as the '*Jackson* neared Paulus Hook on the return trip with Lincoln aboard a 34-gun salute was fired from the shore by the Hudson County Artillery Company, a tribute enthusiastically joined in by all manner of harbor craft. Whistles were sounded and cannons fired in honor of the president-elect. No American president before or since traveled to his initial inauguration with more imminent peril looming before the nation, and, arguably, no president's election ever engaged the emotional turmoil among the

The John P. Jackson *was built in Brooklyn in 1860 for trans-Hudson service between Cortlandt St. and Paulus Hook; in 1861 she carried president-elect Abraham Lincoln across the river en route to Washington and his inauguration. After that, though, the '*Jackson *became one of the almost two dozen New York ferryboats that were "conscripted" for Civil War service with the Union Navy. [Mariners Museum]*

electorate that did Lincoln's. Yet his passage to Paulus Hook was accorded due and proper tribute. Two visiting Cunard steamers fired salutes, alternately, at one-minute intervals while *John P. Jackson* steamed across the Hudson from Cortlandt Street to Paulus Hook, the very same route pioneered by Robert Fulton's *Jersey* fifty-nine years, three months, and eleven days earlier.

Lincoln gave a brief speech inside the huge railway depot before his train pulled out at nine o'clock behind the brand-new locomotive "William Pennington," itself decorated with flags and streamers. He spent that night in Philadelphia, the next in Harrisburg; then it was on to Washington and his inauguration on March 4. Soon afterward war was raging; it would continue for the full term of his presidency.[4]

John P. Jackson returned to her mundane assignments after her brush with immortality on February 21, 1861, and in the ordinary course of events it would likely have been said that she faithfully and quietly performed ferry service over and back across the Hudson River for many years. But the 1860s were far from ordinary times; later that same year *John P. Jackson* was sold by the New Jersey R.R. to the United States Navy and she remained in government service until October 1865. Once "mustered out" she resumed civilian merchant work, but not in New York. Instead she ran between New Orleans and Mobile – hauling cotton and helping the south rebuild its economy, an economy that had been ravaged in the months and years after she carried Abraham Lincoln across the Hudson River in February 1861. The

Lytle–Holdcamper List shows the *John P. Jackson* as having been abandoned in 1871.[5]

About *John P. Jackson*'s military service: in many later American wars New York ferryboats will be "conscripted" for use by the armed forces. During the Second World War, for example, several New York boats hauled shipyard workers to their jobs in South Portland, Maine, while others remained in New York but carried military personnel down the bay to Fort Hancock, or to troopships waiting to depart for the European Theater. During the Civil War, though, New York ferryboats were not used merely to transport men and equipment across rivers and bays. They were outfitted with armor plating, cannons were mounted in the same team gangways where fruit wagons were formerly hauled across

---

4. There was a frightful episode on Lincoln's trip after leaving New York that provides a grim presage of the man's presidency. Warned on the night of February 21 of a possible assassination attempt planned for the arrival of his Northern Central Railway train from Harrisburg at Baltimore, Lincoln secretly left the Pennsylvania capital well in advance of his widely-publicized departure time and traveled to Washington incognito wearing a Scotch plaid cap and a long military cloak. He doubled back to Philadelphia and there caught the Philadelphia, Wilmington and Baltimore R.R.'s southbound night train. His sleeping car passed quietly through Baltimore at three in the morning, with the president-elect under heavy guard inside. But note: this change of plans and routing meant that Lincoln did indeed cross the Susquehanna River aboard the ferryboat *Maryland* (i). This inci-

It takes a little doing to see the distinctive lines of a double-ended ferryboat in this photograph – where are the pilot houses, for example? But she's a ferryboat, all right, the Commodore Barney, *formerly the* Ethan Allen *of New York's Williamsburg ferries, here stripped down for action with the Union Navy during the Civil War. [Library of Congress]*

the East and Hudson rivers, and they became true fighting ships. Of twenty New York ferryboats purchased for service in the Union Navy, five were lost during the Civil War, four during actual combat. Table IV-1 lists the several vessels, and provides some details about their assignments, engagements, and post-war dispositions.

At the start of the Civil War the U.S. Navy was ill-prepared, and its lack of preparation was a double liability in that the foe's territory was not an ocean away. Strategically, interdiction of the Confederate cotton trade became the Navy's most important objective, and yet there were almost 12,000 miles of irregular coastline to blockade; it was here that shallow-draft inland and coastal steamers became especially desirable for the close-in patrolling needed to achieve this objective. Additionally, in the tidewater area of Virginia, up-river incursions into enemy territory became common, and the ability of a double-ended ferryboat to reverse direction quickly when Confederate resistance on shore stiffened proved a helpful asset: no awkward and vulnerable turning under hostile fire, in other words.

dent was reported in the press at the time and can be found in virtually every general work on Lincoln and the Civil War. For details of the railroad-related aspects of the episode, see Edward Hungerford, *The Story of the Baltimore & Ohio Railroad* (New York: Putnam, 1928), I, 351ff.

5. Per the Lytle–Holdcamper List, she was redocumented as the *J. P. Jackson* on October 3, 1865, a shorter version of her original name. The same source shows her as having been abandoned in 1871.

Maybe this Civil War woodcut from Frank Leslie's Illustrated Newspaper *explains why* Commodore Barney *has no pilot houses in the photo on page 95; in June 1863, while patrolling on the James River, she was rocked by a torpedo explosion. [Library of Congress]*

But the most important reason ferryboats went off to serve with the Navy had less to do with their design features or operational capabilities. It was simply this: at the start of the Civil War the entire complement of vessels in the Federal fleet was but 76 vessels, and of these a mere 42 were in active status. It would take months and years for northern shipyards to turn out sufficient numbers of new vessels for the Navy. Why not purchase existing bottoms right away and make do until proper vessels came on-line?

Initial efforts at purchasing ferryboats by the Navy hit a few shoals. First, mid-level naval officers were taken to the cleaners by vessel owners and paid excessively high prices for less than desirable craft. Recall, too, that the Civil War was not universally viewed as a patriotic crusade, and some owners undoubtedly felt no need to make sacrifices for the cause. To solve this problem, Secretary of the Navy Gideon Welles named his brother-in-law, George D. Morgan, to serve as a civilian purchasing agent in New York. Business-like procedures were quickly established to appraise and assess vessels properly and fairly, but the procedures turned out to be a little

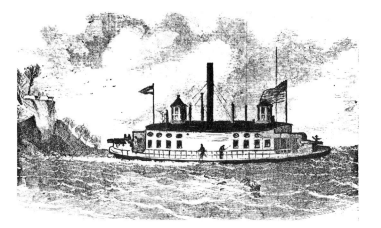

Another woodcut from Frank Leslie's Illustrated Newspaper *shows more Civil War action by a New York ferryboat.* Wyandank *was built for the Union Ferry Company in 1847, sold to the U.S. Government in 1861, and is here shown attacking Cockpit Point Battery on the Potomac River on March 11, 1862. [author's collection]*

too business-like. Unschooled in the ways of the public sector, Morgan followed normal commercial practice and tacked a modest commission for himself onto each sale he made or supervised. This caused a minor scandal when discovered, and in late 1861 Morgan was replaced by a naval flag officer, one Admiral Hiram Paulding. By this time, though, the Navy had already obtained eleven ferryboats – nine under Morgan and two prior to his appointment. Both Morgan and Paulding, of course, were under direction from the Navy to secure more than just ferryboats; their shopping lists included steamboats, schooners, sloops, work boats, and so forth.

New York ferryboats were assigned to the principal Civil War subdivisions of the Union Navy. Something called the Potomac Flotilla was an armada whose mission was to patrol waterways adjacent to the Potomac River and Chesapeake Bay, but down the rest of the Atlantic Coast and on around into the Gulf of Mexico there were a number of blockading squadrons, units whose orders were to stop Confederate cotton trade and cut off the flow of vital resources from Europe to the secessionist states.

The ferryboats served with all of these units, and while by war's end they were but a small fraction of the tonnage that the Union Navy comprised, they performed well and bravely and were on station well before Federal forces reached their peak wartime levels.[6]

A marvelous piece of scholarship was published at the time of the hundredth anniversary of the Civil War in the mid-1960s that describes this whole business in some detail, including accounts of many and various battles in which New York ferryboats participated.

6. From the 42 active vessels in the U.S. Navy when the Civil War began, the count eventually rose to 1,024. This was not the maximum number of vessels to serve at one time, but rather all the vessels that served from the war's beginning to its end.

Its author is Rachel Minick and her work consists of six articles that appeared in various issues of the *New-York Historical Society Quarterly* between 1962 and 1964 under the general title "New York Ferryboats in the Union Navy."[7] Reading Minick's work one can learn of the ferryboat *Whitehall*, late of the Union Ferry Company, which was sunk by enemy gunfire off Fort Monroe, Virginia, in the same engagement that saw the world's first clash of iron-hulled warships, the *Monitor* and the *Virginia*, a) *Merrimac*. Another story involves *Clifton* (i), an 892-ton vessel built for the Staten Island and New York Ferry Company in 1861 for service on the Whitehall Street–Staten Island line. She was purchased by the Navy in November 1861 for $90,000 and assigned to the West Gulf Blockading Squadron, along with her Staten Island sister ship *Westfield* (i) and fellow New Yorker *John P. Jackson*, the ferryboat that carried Lincoln on the first leg of his journey to Washington from New York on February 21, 1861.

Clifton (i), designated U.S.S. *Clifton* for the duration, participated in the capture of New Orleans in 1862, and the siege of Vicksburg in June 1862. Alternately, she could play three different roles: gunship – she had 9-inch mortars on her main decks; towboat – her shallow draft was useful in hauling larger vessels across sand bars; patrol craft – at night she would search for enemy troops trying to sneak up on Union vessels aboard rafts.

Clifton (i) suffered both damage and casualties at Vicksburg; eight of her crew were killed during the siege. Patched up, presumably at New Orleans, she saw action in Galveston Bay in January 1863, and in September of the same year in an engagement near Sabine Pass, Texas, she was disabled and fell into Confederate hands. Listen to how her final battle is described in David Porter's classic work, *Naval History of the Civil War*:

The attack, which was to have been a surprise at early dawn, was not made until 3 P.M. on the 8th of September, 1863, twenty-eight hours after the expedition had appeared off the Sabine. The "Clifton," "Sachem" and "Arizona" engaged a battery of seven guns. A shot struck the boiler of the "Sachem" and she was soon enveloped in steam. The "Clifton" ran directly under the fort and for twenty minutes fired rapidly grape, canister and shell, receiving a heavy fire in return. She soon afterwards got on shore, and not being able to back off, hauled down her colors – as did also the "Sachem."

Porter concludes: "This was rather a melancholy expedition and badly managed. It resulted in the loss of some twenty men killed and many wounded on board the 'Clifton' and 'Sachem' and was somewhat injurious to the prestige of the Navy. It did not, however, reflect any discredit upon the officers of the 'Clifton' or 'Sachem,' as both of these vessels were gallantly fought."[8]

---

7. See the Bibliography (Appendix A) for full citations to all six articles.

8. David W. Porter, *The Naval History of the Civil War* (New York, 1886; repr. Secaucus, N.J.: Castle, 1984), pp. 346–47. Further accounts of specific engagements can be found in *Civil War Naval Chronology, 1861–1865* (Washington: Navy Department, 1971), pp. II-6, II-66, IV-20, IV-44, 45, and V-64.

Now in Confederate hands, *Clifton* (i) was repaired, but her next service was not as a warship. She had excellent speed and so was put to work by the Confederacy as a blockade runner between southern ports and Cuba; there cotton was trans-loaded to neutral-flag vessels for shipment to European nations.

But this phase of the life of *Clifton* (i) was not to last long. In March 1864 she went aground trying to sneak out of Sabine Pass loaded down with southern cotton. To keep her from falling back into Union hands her captain ordered her set afire, and that was the end of her.

One New York ferryboat served with the Union Navy fresh from her builder's yard and never served under her civilian name, *Clinton*, until after the war; in the Navy she was the U.S.S. *Commodore Morris*. Following hostilities she was sold back to the Union Ferry Company, the firm that had had her designed and built before the war, and her distinctions would continue to accumulate for many years. Indeed, she remained in active service longer than any other of the ferryboats that went off to preserve the Union. The U.S. Army took title to *Clinton* during

the First World War, but for true ferry-like service in New York Harbor, not upriver expeditions behind enemy lines. In late 1920 she was mustered out of the military for the second time in her life, re-assumed the name *Clinton* – she had been the *General John Simpson* during her second tour of duty – and was sold to the Carteret Ferry Corporation for service between New Jersey and Staten Island across the Arthur Kill and, in all probability, between the foot of 69 Street in Brooklyn and Saint George, Staten Island, as well. It wasn't until the year 1931 that the old wooden-hull veteran was scrapped, a robust 70 years young. Her final enrollment certificate was surrendered at New York on February 24, 1931, and these words are written on the certificate in pen and ink: "Dismantled – sold for junk." When brand new, the ferryboat *Clinton*, official no. 4870, sailed off against the forces of Jefferson Davis. On the day she was retired, Adolf Hitler was forming his Third Reich and a new and different armed peril loomed ahead for the United States.

But the war itself wasn't the only ferryboat news between 1861 and

1865. While *Clinton* and *Clifton* (i) and *John P. Jackson* and the others were off with the Union Navy, there were important ferryboat developments back in New York Harbor. Several new services were introduced, for one thing.

A route across the Arthur Kill connecting Tottenville at the southern extreme of Staten Island with Perth Amboy, N.J., began service in June 1860, after the introduction of north–south railroad service across Staten Island's long dimension between Clifton and Tottenville in that same year. Initially this maritime operation used single-ended steamboats and not double-ended ferryboats, nor could the service be called a steady and permanent fixture onward from 1860. It wasn't until after the war's end that the 148-ton *Maid of Perth* became the line's first true ferryboat, in 1867. By then the ferry service had also become a corporate adjunct to the Staten Island R.R. passenger operation, not an independent service; it would remain so for 81 years.

On August 1, 1862, the New Jersey Railroad and Transportation Company supplemented its original Cortlandt Street–Paulus

Of all the New York ferryboats that sailed off to war with the Union Navy, Clinton remained in post-war service longer than any other and wasn't officially retired until February 24, 1931, when her final certificate of permanent enrollment, here illustrated, was surrendered at New York. "Dismantled – sold for junk" is the pen-and-ink notation at the bottom of the certificate's front page. [National Archives]

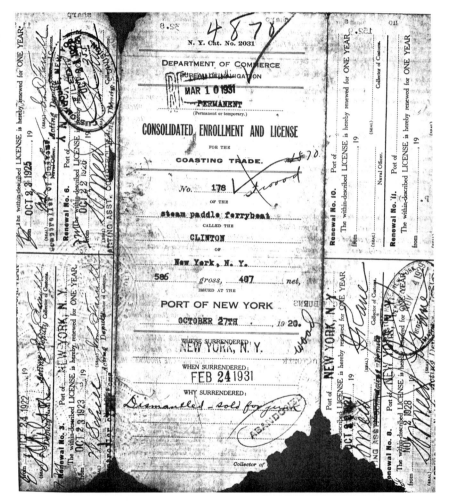

Hook route across the Hudson River with a second, Desbrosses Street–Paulus Hook. In 1861 steam-powered ferryboats began running between the southern tip of Manhattan and Governor's Island, a U.S. Army installation out in the bay, and two railroads extended their service to the west bank of the Hudson River opposite New York City and instituted ferryboat connections for their passengers during the Civil War, as well.

The Erie R.R. was opened in 1851, a full decade before the Civil War; its corporate mission was to link the Great Lakes above Niagara Falls – which is to say, a port on Lake Erie – with tidewater on the Atlantic Coast. Its original terminals were Dunkirk, N.Y., on the lake and to the west of Buffalo, and Piermont, N.Y., a landing on the Hudson 25 miles removed from the southern tip of Manhattan Island, thus forcing passengers to utilize a steamboat connection to get to their trains.[9] This arrangement was as short-lived as it was unsatisfactory, and in 1853 Erie

trains began to operate directly to Jersey City. Lacking its own terminal at the time, the Erie utilized the New Jersey R.R.'s Paulus Hook facility for eight years until, in 1861, the company opened its own depot in the Pavonia section of Jersey City just to the north of Paulus Hook.[10] A tunnel was cut

through the rock of Bergen Hill and the Erie created a subsidiary entity, the Long Dock Company, to construct the terminal itself and, in a complex way that American railroads seem to relish, lease the facility back to the Erie. Another firm was established in 1861, the Pavonia Ferry Company. It appears to have served purely technical and legal ends only – i.e., securing a proper ferry lease from the City of New York. The

---

9. The New York and Lake Erie R.R., to use the line's formal 1851 corporate

title, opened its line from Piermont to Dunkirk on May 14, 1851, and the inaugural celebration is worth hearing about. Up from Washington came President Millard Fillmore and four members of his cabinet, including Secretary of State Daniel Webster – one of the victorious attorneys in *Gibbons vs. Ogden*. Fillmore's party arrived on the banks of the Raritan River aboard a Camden and Amboy R.R. train on May 13th and were met there by the new railroad's equally new steamboat *Erie*, one of the vessels built for the New York–Piermont run. *Erie* then steamed up through the Narrows and docked at Castle Garden where a crowd of 50,000 people were waiting to see the Chief Executive. The party spent the night in New York and at six o'clock the next morning it was back aboard the *Erie*, this time from the railroad's own pier at Duane Street and the Hudson River, and off to Piermont.

10. For eight years, before moving into its own Jersey City terminal in 1861, Erie trains used another company's Hudson River depot and its passengers crossed the river on that railroad's ferryboats. The Erie R.R. came to an end in the year 1960 when it merged with the Delaware, Lackawanna and Western to form the Erie Lackawanna R.R. But here's an ironic parallel: in 1957, three-and-a-half years before the Erie R.R. surrendered its corporate identity, it moved its passenger trains into the Hoboken terminal of its eventual merger partner, and for these final days Erie passengers again crossed the Hudson on the ferryboats of another railroad. (The Erie sold two of its boats to the D. L. & W., but that's a story for a later chapter.)

The year is 1954 and the Erie R.R. is still running over and back service across the Hudson River between the foot of Chambers St. in Manhattan and the Pavonia section of Jersey City, where the line opened its New York passenger terminal in 1861. Arlington, shown here, was built in 1903 and is one of 18 ferryboats the Erie owned over the years. [Roger J. Cudahy]

railroad owned the boats and ran the service directly, a service that was initiated on April 15, 1861. At first the Erie fleet was a pair of East River veterans – *Onalaska* and *Niagara*. But before that first year was out, the company's brand-new *Pavonia* was down the ways, followed by *Susquehanna* (1864) and *Delaware* (1865).

The Erie's first Hudson River ferry route that began service on April 15, 1861, connected its new Jersey City depot with the foot of Chambers Street in Manhattan, and over the years this will remain the company's principal line. But it wouldn't be too long after the Civil War, in 1868, when the Erie

supplemented Chambers Street–Pavonia with a second crossing, West 23 Street–Pavonia. On toward the turn of the century West 23 Street will become a virtual "Union Station" in Manhattan, with ferryboats of many railroads operating there. But to repeat: the Erie's first trans-Hudson ferryboats began operating on April 15, 1861. Two days earlier the Federal garrison at Fort Sumter had surrendered.[11]

Another railroad, the Central of New Jersey, also began its rail operations out of a waterside terminal removed from New York Harbor proper, not unlike the Erie at Piermont; its early passengers bound to and from New York thus had to begin and end their trips not with a cross-river ferryboat ride, but on a steamboat plying a more lengthy course. The C.N.J.'s original depot (and train-to-steamer transfer point) was

---

11. General information on the Erie R.R. is available in Edward Hungerford, *Men of Erie* (New York: Random House, 1946). More detailed material on the railroad's many subsidiary companies and their relationship to the larger entity can be found in *The Erie System*, 2d ed., comp. and rev. George H. Minor (New York: Erie Railroad, 1936).

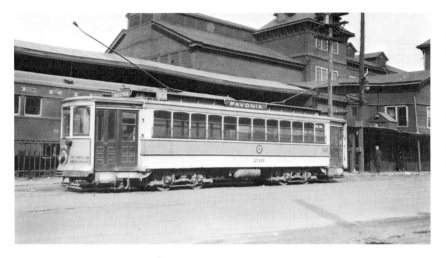

The Erie R.R.'s Jersey City passenger terminal was a place where many modes of transport came together: trans-Hudson ferryboats; local and long-distance trains to various points along the Erie's main line; subway trains of the Hudson & Manhattan R.R.; and, shown here ca. 1939, trolley cars of the Public Service company. [author's collection]

Elizabethport, N.J., a spot on the Arthur Kill across from the northwesternmost point on Staten Island. The first "train" to reach Elizabethport did so in 1835; it was a mere horsecar plying a line between Elizabethport and what's today called Elizabeth – but this used to be called Elizabethtown, so the company was the Elizabethtown and Somerville R.R. Steam locomotives arrived in 1839; the line pressed westward, and by the 1860s it had become the Central Railroad of New Jersey, a major force in the new industry. It, too, felt the inadequacy of a lengthy steamboat connection to New York City for its passengers –

lengthy, in this case, being 12 miles or so.

For its rails to reach the Hudson River in the New York City area the C.N.J. had two choices: it could push northward on the west side of Newark Bay and then turn east and assault Bergen Hill; or it could bridge the bay, run north up the Bayonne penninsula, and get to the site of its proposed terminal, the Communipaw section of Jersey City, that way. The railroad selected the latter course. Thus in the middle of the Civil War, on July 29, 1864, the first ceremonial train was operated to the new terminal from Flemington, N.J., some 40-odd miles inland. Many

invited guests from New York took the New Jersey R.R.'s noon ferry from the foot of Cortlandt Street and a connecting train at Paulus Hook and caught the C.N.J. special at Elizabeth, where the two lines crossed – and after a fashion still do.

Now, those familiar with the Jersey Central's Hudson River depot in later years – i.e., during the twentieth century – tend to think of a rather conventional depot built rather conventionally on the bank of the Hudson River. But this wasn't the arrangement in 1864. Then, to reach what is today the river's edge required a mile-and-a-half wooden pile trestle built

A hundred-and-three years after it opened in 1864, the Jersey Central R.R.'s passenger terminal in the Communipaw section of Jersey City is about to close down. Henceforth, New York-bound passengers will transfer to PATH rapid transit trains in Newark and the old waterside depot – as well as the connecting ferry service – will be abandoned. Passenger equipment has been cleared out of the coach yards to the left, and a five-car local train heads into suburbia with homeward-bound commuters. [Howard W. Serig, Jr.]

Plainfield *was one of the Jersey Central's latter-day propeller ferryboats, and she is shown here approaching the Liberty St. ferry slip in Manhattan on an August day in 1953. Originally her boilers burned coal, and the* Plainfield *then had a tall smokestack to help support the coal's combustion. Shorter stacks were retrofitted to the fleet when coal gave way to oil as the fleet's fuel. C.N.J. was also the only one of the trans-Hudson railroad ferries to equip its vessels with radar.* [author]

across swampy tidelands and a terminal that resembled, to use an anachronistic parallel, an off-shore oil-drilling rig. That first ceremonial train, which puffed and whistled itself into the new terminal shortly after one o'clock in the afternoon, was met by the railroad's first cross-river ferryboat, the 1023-ton single-deck *Central*, turned out the previous year by the Devine Burtis yard in Brooklyn and skippered this day by Captain George W. Howe.[12] Rather

than a direct crossing to lower Manhattan as would thereafter be the custom, *Central* took her ceremonial passengers on a leisurely luncheon cruise around the harbor, and the railroad's president, John T. Johnston, averred as how

the new rail link that day opened brought Chicago "60 miles closer" to New York – over, obviously, the Central of New Jersey and connecting lines through Pennsylvania and beyond. Johnston saw his C.N.J. as a railroad with a long-

---

12. From at least 1860 onward the Central Railroad of New Jersey itself owned the vessels that connected with

its trains at Elizabethport. In 1860 three vessels are shown enrolled at the port of New York for the service: *Wyoming*, a 382-ton steamboat built in New York in 1853; *Red Jacket*, 424 tons and built in 1858 at New York; and *Kill Van Kull*, a massive 1191-tonner with registered dimensions of 252 × 35 × 14 feet. *Kill Van Kull* was built in New York in 1858 and was a bona-fide double-ended ferryboat. As

far as I can tell she never ran on the C.N.J.'s Liberty St.–Communipaw service, but I mention her to qualify the assertion that *Central* was the railroad's first ferryboat. *Kill Van Kull* ended her days running between Manhattan and Sandy Hook, yet another maritime venture of the Central Railroad of New Jersey. *Kill Van Kull* was destroyed by fire at Elizabethport in 1889.

distance potential and dreamed dreams of formal corporate links with lines to the west, nor was he the only person in American railroading who so regarded the C.N.J. The Pennsylvania R.R.'s decision to press beyond Philadelphia to New York Harbor in 1871 by leasing the Joint Companies was significantly motivated by fear that the Jersey Central, with its own line to the Hudson River firmly established, might press westward and become the major railroad power the P.R.R. itself desired to become – and in fact became.

The New York Times lavished uncommon praise on the new *Central*: ". . . largest and most elegant ferryboat afloat . . ." and called her in addition a ". . . model of its kind, moving gracefully upon the water, and its appointments would be no discredit to the more pretentious vessels that ply between New York and Albany." The luncheon cruise ended in Manhattan at 4:30 P.M.[13]

13. For a treatment of the Jersey Central's trans-Hudson ferryboat operations, see Harry Cotterell, Jr., "Jersey Central Ferries," *Steamboat Bill of Facts*, No. 13 (April 1944), 225–28.

This story, incidentally, shared space in the *Times* of Saturday, July 30, with news that General Sherman was closing on Atlanta, and also that Confederate guerrillas such as Mosby's Raiders were staging hit-and-run attacks in northern-Virginia counties that are today bedroom communities of Washington, D.C. A letter-to-the-editor in the same edition called upon patriotic Americans who were seeking ways of aiding the Union cause to send blackberries to their nearest Army hospital – they were useful in the treatment of various intestinal problems. And to get still another perspective on life in New York in the year 1864: elsewhere in the same 'paper was to be found an account of a game of baseball played that Thursday on the Olympic Ballground in Philadelphia between the Resolute club of New York and the Athletic club of Philadelphia. The latter team is still doing business today, but under slightly different circumstances: they've added an "s" to their name and they now wear their home uniforms when they play in Oakland, California. But as they would do to the New York Mets in the 1973 World Series, so did the Athletic club do to the New York Resolute in 1864 – they beat 'em. The score was 29 to 12, and it was ". . . a creditable display of the attractive features of the game, and a well-earned victory for the Philadelphia party."

There were other developments during the Civil War involving local ferryboat service in New York Harbor. In early 1864 the Staten Island and New York Ferry Company, a firm that had been founded in 1853 to operate vessels between Manhattan and points along the Eastern Shore of Staten Island, was sold to the Staten Island R.R. The ferry operation then became a subsidiary of the rail line and was called the Staten Island Railway Ferry Company. (The "R" in the parent company stood for "railroad"; in the subsidiary it meant "railway.") This new marine entity continued the operating scheme of service from Whitehall Street to three Staten Island landings, Tompkinsville, Stapleton, and Clifton, the last also being the point where the S.I.R.R. trains from Tottenville terminated. In addition, prior to the take-over of the service by the railroad in 1864, a major fleet replacement program was begun to compensate for the five company vessels sold to the U.S. Navy for Civil War service, none of which returned. *Westfield* (ii) of 1862, *Northfield* of 1863, and *Middletown* of 1864 were all built by Jeremiah Simonson's Brooklyn yard to virtually identical specifications; they were double-deck side-wheelers with beam engines and wooden hulls, and they will form the backbone – but not the entirety – of the Manhattan–Staten Island fleet until the arrival of the five Borough-class boats under municipal auspices in 1905.

Thus did the ferryboats of New York Harbor complete the third era of their history, the years of the Civil War. But there is one more incident to relate, a counterpoint to the story of *John P. Jackson* carrying president-elect Lincoln across the Hudson on February 21, 1861. It happened on the New Jersey Railroad and Transportation Company's new Desbrosses Street–Paulus Hook line on the morning of April 24, 1865. That was the day the funeral train of Abraham Lincoln reached the west bank of the Hudson River opposite New York City.

Lincoln was shot in Washington on the evening of April 14, and died early the next morning. The train that bore his remains to their final resting place became the focus of an emotional outpouring of national grief as it solemnly made its way out of Washington on April 21, 1865, for a two-and-a-half-week journey to Springfield, Illinois, Lincoln's home and final resting place. America has never seen anything at all like the Lincoln funeral train; it never will. Later national tragedies were turned into common national experiences in different ways – through radio, with newsreels, and on television. But in 1865 railroads were the link between slain president and grieving people – railroads and a ferryboat named *Jersey City*.[14]

The Lincoln funeral had been in Philadelphia, one of fourteen cities where the president would lie in state, and it was early on the morning of April 24, 1865, that a nine-car train left the Philadelphia and Trenton R.R.'s Kensington Depot there. Departure was at 4:02 A.M. – ". . . just as the eastern horizon began to purple with the first rays of dawn," in the words of a reporter for *The Newark Daily Advertiser* – and, as was, and still is, standard practice when railroads dispatch especially important trains, an engine running alone left ten minutes ahead of the funeral train to ensure that the right-of-way was in order, and to absorb any trauma, accidental or otherwise, should it not be. This pilot engine, so called, would stop

---

14. There is some uncertainty about the identity of the ferryboat that bore Lincoln's remains across the Hudson River on April 24, 1865. *The New York Tribune* says the boat was the *New York*, while *The Newark Daily Advertiser*, which presents an otherwise very detailed technical account of the journey of the Lincoln funeral train from North Philadelphia to Jersey City, identifies the ferryboat as the "*New Jersey*."

The railroad owned a *New York* in 1865, and it would have been a plausible vessel for the assignment. But I find no evidence of any ferryboat named *New Jersey* on the roster at this time.

The New York Herald identifies the vessel as *Jersey City*, as does David Valentine, the prodigious compiler of official information of and for the City of New York (see David T. Valentine, *Obsequies of Abraham Lincoln in the*

at each station along the way and not move on until word was received by telegraph that the funeral train had reached the station one back. Camden and Amboy R.R. locomotive No. 24 was assigned the pilot duty; the train was hauled by locomotive No. 72 and it consisted of a restaurant car, six passenger coaches, the funeral car in which were both Lincoln's casket and that of his little son Willie, who had died in 1862 and was to be buried with his father in Springfield, and finally a special car for the chief dignitaries.[15]

All through Pennsylvania the tracks were lined with people; likewise in New Jersey, when the special crossed the Delaware River at 5:30 A.M. and a trackside ceremony was held in Trenton. Then

_____

City of New York [New York: Edmund Jones and Company, 1866], p. 116). Carl Sandburg, Lincoln's definitive biographer, does likewise (see Carl Sandburg, *Abraham Lincoln: The War Years*, Vol. 4 [New York: Harcourt, Brace and World, 1939], p. 395).

With this evidence I have concluded that the vessel was more than likely the *Jersey City*; but some uncertainty remains.

onward along the Joint Companies' right-of-way – today's high-speed Northeast Corridor. New Brunswick was reached at 7:30. Here the Camden and Amboy locomotives were cut off and engines of the New Jersey R.R. substituted. Pilot duties fell to a locomotive named "H. R. Remsen," while No. 40 handled the funeral train itself. Through Rahway at 8:25 and Elizabeth at 8:45; a stop at Newark, and then off on the final segment to Jersey City at 9:07. Arrival at Paulus Hook was scheduled for 10:00 A.M.

_____

15. Historians such as Bruce Catton have decried the ". . . most elaborately contrived funeral procession in American history . . ." as an effort on the part of radicals within the administration, led by Secretary of War Edwin Stanton, to make of Reconstruction an instrument for revenge on the Confederacy. "Lincoln had been murdered by Jefferson Davis' agents," Stanton purported to the nation, a nation that then ". . . felt an anger so black that Lincoln's own vision [of peaceful reconstruction] was blotted out." And the lengthy train journey drove the point home to millions, Catton argues (see Bruce Catton, *The Civil War* [New York: American Heritage, 1985], pp. 270–71).

Long before the Lincoln funeral train reached Jersey City people began to gather. About 9:00 o'clock, an hour before arrival time, finely dressed men and women appeared on the iron balcony inside the vast 1858-built trainshed. These were people of means and station holding special invitations; at trackside on the northernmost platform where the train was to arrive there was assembled a procession of military units and important public officials who would help form the cortège. On the wall at the station's western end the big railroad clock was stopped and its hands had been set at 7:22 – the hour of Lincoln's death. "A Nation's Heart Is Struck," said a banner encircling the clock. A similar banner on the eastern wall read "Be Still and Know That I Am God." But beyond the immediate confines of the terminal itself people of all walks of life and people with no public distinction had gathered. They, too, wished to pay their respects to Lincoln. People had climbed atop railroad cars and buildings and poles and were waiting, in near total silence, for the train to arrive.

Finally, "Almost unheard, the nine cars of the funeral train, all draped with black, glide steadily in through the western gates of the station." The train stops. Eight soldiers remove the president's coffin from the train; salutes are rendered. Then a procession forms for the march to the ferryboat. And while this is happening, a choir composed of four Hoboken singing clubs renders, ". . . in a great volume of strong and manly voices, and with much feeling and good execution, an impressive *Graberuhe*, or Requiem."

The procession moves east down the platform to the head of the track, then turns and proceeds back along another parallel platform and out into the street, Exchange Place, beyond the west end of the building. Here the honor guard places Lincoln's casket in a hearse drawn by six gray horses, each covered with a heavy black pall. The procession then heads east again toward the ferry slip.

Jersey City had been built in Brooklyn in 1862; as she moved out of the Exchange Place slip on her assignment ". . . the requiem singers continued their solemn chorus . . ." and ". . . from down the bay came the echo of the distant cannons." *Jersey City* performed her task well: ". . . the

powerful steamer moved across the river with hardly any perceptible vibration, as if it were a thing of life and conscious of the precious nature of its charge." [16]

If the trackside gatherings in Pennsylvania and New Jersey were large, they were as nothing compared to the vast throngs gathered on the Manhattan side at Desbrosses Street. It was one huge sea of people, with merely a narrow but respectful corridor through its midst left for the funeral procession, a procession that moved up Desbrosses Street to Canal, Canal to Broadway, and down Broadway to City Hall where Lincoln's body would lie in state.

The ferryboat *Jersey City* enjoyed a fine and long career. She was, typical of her day, a wooden-hull sidewheeler with statutory dimensions of 192 × 34 × 13 feet. She helped the eventual operator of the Desbrosses Street–Paulus Hook ferryboat service, the Pennsylvania R.R., become one of the most important operators in New

York Harbor, and she remained on the rolls until April 28, 1917. By that time there were tunnels under the Hudson River for P.R.R. trains, the Paulus Hook railroad depot had been downgraded for commuter service only, and the United States had just entered the Great War against the Central Powers. The wooden sidewheeler thus served for 55 years. In her third year, though, on April 24, 1865, *Jersey City* performed the most solemn service ever asked of any New York ferryboat.

---

16. Quoted descriptions of the train's arrival and the passage across the river are taken from editions of *The New York Times* and *The New York Tribune* of April 25, 1865.

Sometime between the end of the Civil War and the beginning of the twentieth century is in all likelihood to be found the apogee of harbor ferryboating in New York. Fleets expanded, new routes and services were introduced, and vessel design saw the advent of such improvements as steel hulls, screw propellers, and high-pressure engines. But the period also saw the arrival of something else: competition! By the turn of the century the Brooklyn Bridge will be seventeen years old, work will be underway on the Williamsburg Bridge, and plans will be firming up for rapid transit tunnels under both the Hudson and East rivers. The exclusivity ferryboats enjoyed in 1865 for transporting people and vehicles will be gone forever by 1900. Indeed, it was a mere two years into this era, in 1867, when John A. Roebling completed his design for the Brooklyn Bridge; it opened in 1883.[1]

But it was the Civil War itself that gave this postwar era a most important characteristic from its outset. For the Civil War accelerated the growth of industrialization in northern cities like New York to such a degree that, in the words of Bruce Catton, ". . . [b]y 1865 the northeastern portion of America had become an industrialized nation, with half a century of development compressed into four feverish years." Catton continues: "Altogether, it is probable that the Civil War pushed the North into the Industrialized Age a full generation sooner than would otherwise have been the case."[2]

Apart, then, from the oddity of New York ferryboats' sailing off with the Union Navy and the tragic irony of Lincoln's term in office involving a ferryboat passage across the Hudson River at both its beginning and its end, the major impact of the Civil War on ferryboat transportation in New York Harbor may well be that it signaled, and even caused, the start of an expansive era of new maturity, a coming of age of New York City as an industrialized urban center.

A good deal more regular information about ferryboats also begins to emerge from official source materials after the Civil War, and onward from this point the story of New York ferryboats can begin to shape itself with more confidence at what might be called a statistical level. In 1868, for example, shortly after war's end, the Federal Government began to

Borough Class, City of New York, *1905–1947*

1. For the full story of the design and construction of the Brooklyn Bridge, see David McCullough, *The Great Bridge* (New York: Simon and Schuster, 1972).
2. Catton, *The Civil War,* pp. 162–64.

Here's a gloomy-day look at the first major New York bridge to offer an alternative to ferryboat travel – Roebling's Brooklyn Bridge, completed in 1883. There's even symbolism in the trailer truck; it's turning at the foot of Brooklyn's Main St. If it weren't for the bridge, the truck wouldn't have to turn – it could continue straight ahead onto the Union Ferry Company's Catharine St.–Main St. ferryboat line. [author]

publish its annual register *Merchant Vessels of the United States*, providing a steady report on all commercial vessels enrolled in the country. As another instance, the Steamboat Inspection Service, a Federal agency mandated to assure the riding public that minimum safety standards were met on powered vessels, will begin issuing annual reports on what vessels the agency inspected each year, the names of persons licensed to operate such vessels, and details about safety violations and accidents within the agency's jurisdiction.[3]

New York itself, of course, will continue to grow by leaps and bounds. Despite losing over 15,000 of her sons in the Civil War, and realizing that births tend to be low when young males are off in the army, immigrants came to New York during the Civil War in sufficient numbers to give the city a

small net population increase from 1861 to 1865. But this was nothing compared to the virtually unrestrained growth that began – or, more properly, resumed – after the war. The city's population reached three-and-a-half-million persons in the Federal census of 1900, compared to just over one million in 1860. And even population figures fail to tell the full story. This was also the period when New York emerged as the nation's premier city in so many ways – the leader in trade, manufacturing, commerce, business, and the arts. To understand how this 1865–1900 era put its own distinctive mark on the development of New York ferryboating, it is useful to begin with a review of the harbor's very first line, Cortlandt Street–Paulus Hook.

(One minor change is terminological: with the development of Jersey City in the later years of the nineteenth century and the reclamation of additional acreage from the river, the terminal is more properly identified by a major thoroughfare to which it is adjacent, Exchange Place – and will be henceforth so called in the narrative.)

The principal development affecting this ferryboat service was neither minor nor terminological, though: it was the takeover of the New Jersey Railroad and Transportation Company by the Pennsylvania R.R. in December 1871, an evolution touched upon in chapter 2. Negotiations between the parties were protracted, but once completed the Pennsy made extensive investments in its facilities on the bank of the Hudson. A new rail–ferry terminal in Jersey City was quickly constructed to replace the 1858 edifice, the station where the Lincoln funeral train once paused. The P.R.R. also expanded its harborside facilities northward from Exchange Place into the Harsimus Cove area, land recently reclaimed from the river. While this was primarily for freight and cargo, the Pennsylvania did operate a short-lived ferryboat service to the site between 1891 and 1901, the railroad's sole service that did not land on the Jersey side at the Exchange Place depot. It terminated in Manhattan at the foot of West 13 Street. But if this route was less than successful, the railroad began other new services in the final years of the nineteenth

---

3. The Steamboat Inspection Service dates to an act of Congress initially approved in 1838. For additional details on the agency, see Lloyd M. Short, *Steamboat-Inspection Service: Its History, Activities and Organization* (New York & London: Appleton, 1922).

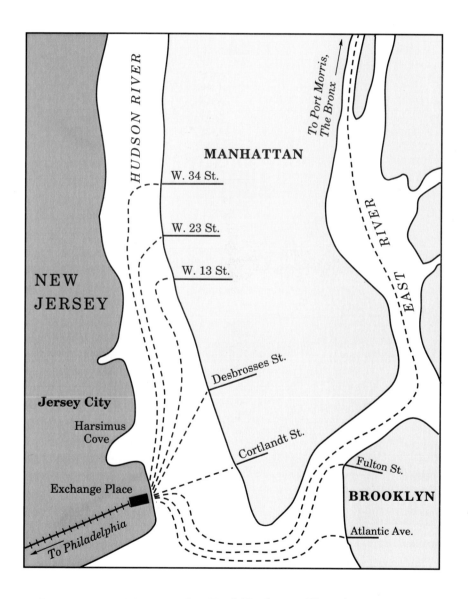

5. Services to and from Paulus Hook/Exchange Place Area

In addition to trans-Hudson ferry-boats, passengers getting off Pennsylvania R.R. trains had an option of taking a boat that proceeded directly to Brooklyn, bypassing Manhattan entirely. For many years this service was operated for the Pennsy by a separate company; eventually it was absorbed by the railroad. The service always required a separate fleet of ferryboats, though; regular P.R.R. vessels were too large for the Union Ferry Company's Fulton St. slip in Brooklyn, where this "annex service" terminated. Annex 2, shown here, was typical of the Jersey City–Brooklyn boats. [Mariners Museum]

century for its expanding ferry-boat fleet that were quite the opposite. In 1897 the Pennsylvania R.R. initiated a service between Exchange Place and the foot of West 23 Street in Manhattan. Yet another new route out of Exchange Place was begun in 1877, not by the railroad itself, but by a separate company. It was unusual in that it bypassed Manhattan island entirely and operated to the Union Ferry Company's terminal at the foot of Fulton Street in Brooklyn. In 1897 the railroad took over this route itself, but it always enjoyed an identity separate from the basic Pennsylvania R.R. operation. It was called the "Brooklyn annex," or the "Pennsylvania annex," during the days of both independent and P.R.R. operation.

The vessels assigned to this service bore the imaginative names *Annex, Annex No. 2, Annex No. 3*, and so forth.[4] Even after the takeover of the operation

The foot of Fulton St. in Brooklyn in 1901, but the ferryboat heading away from the slip is not one of the Union Ferry Company's vessels. She's Annex (ii) *and she'll head around the southern tip of Manhattan to the Pennsylvania R.R.'s passenger depot in Jersey City, thereby permitting passengers from Brooklyn bound for, say, Philadelphia to bypass the congestion of Manhattan. [Library of Congress]*

4. The Erie R.R. operated a similar "annex" service from its depot in Jersey City to Brooklyn, bypassing Manhattan. Rather little is known of this operation, and it is thought to have run from 1885 until about 1900.

by the railroad itself in 1897, a separate fleet was required for Annex service, since the railroad's conventional Hudson River vessels were too large and cumbersome to berth at Union's Fulton Street slip in Brooklyn. Potential Pennsy passengers in major on-line cities found this service described in the railroad's newspaper advertisements as follows: "For Brooklyn, N.Y., all through trains connect at Jersey City with boats of the Brooklyn annex, affording direct transfer to Fulton street, avoiding double ferriage across New York City."

What may well have been the most unusual ferryboat service of all time in New York Harbor also operated out of the Pennsylvania R.R.'s Jersey City complex. It conveyed not pedestrians and ordinary street vehicles but entire railroad passenger trains – passengers and all – thus permitting through inter-city service between Boston to the north and Philadelphia, Baltimore, and Washington to the south. While not operated by the Pennsylvania R.R., it deserves a brief description at this point.

Recall that in chapter 4 mention was made of a ferryboat named *Maryland* (i) that transplanted trains of the Philadelphia, Wilmington and Baltimore R.R. across the mouth of the Susquehanna River half-way, roughly, between Philadelphia and Baltimore. With the construction of a bridge across the river in 1866 the ferryboat was no longer needed and she was placed in lay-up by the railroad, there not being any market on the east coast for such a vessel at the time. Almost a decade later *Maryland* (i) was purchased by the New York and New England R.R., a predecessor of the later-day New York, New Haven and Hartford, extensively re-built, and brought to New York.[5] There, her assignment was to carry trains out of Boston away from the New York and New England's railhead at 130 Street and the Harlem River and convey them to the Pennsylvania at Jersey City for dispatch to Philadelphia and beyond – *trains and their passengers*. The upcoming 1876 Centennial Exposition in Philadelphia prompted this service, but it proved popular and survived the close of the exposition to become a regular option for passengers traveling through New York City and not wanting to stop off there, until 1912 when it was annulled.

Maryland (i) was a large ferryboat when she came to New York in 1876; her 238-foot length and 1150 gross tons compared to 210 feet and 758 tons for *Southland* (ii), the newest vessel then on the Whitehall Street–Staten Island run and as large a ferryboat as was operating in the harbor.

Maryland (i) came to an unfortunate end in late 1888. She left Jersey City at 10:30 in the evening on December 8 with two sleeping cars, a coach, and a baggage car aboard that had earlier arrived from Washington as "The Federal Express." As she was nearing the 130 Street slip fire broke out in one of the passenger cars; all 30 passengers aboard, 19 in the coach and eleven in the two sleepers, escaped uninjured, but the 35-year-old vessel burned to the waterline and was a total loss. In February

---

5. In her original configuration for Susquehanna River service, *Maryland* (i) carried railroad cars on her upper deck, with a passenger cabin on the lower deck, a most unusual arrangement. When re-built for the New York phase of her career this was reversed: railroad cars on the main deck, passengers above.

One of the more unusual ferryboat services ever to operate in New York was that provided by Maryland *(i) and* Maryland *(ii), the latter shown here from the Manhattan shore heading down the East River under the Brooklyn Bridge.* Maryland *(ii), and* Maryland *(i) before her, transported not foot traffic and ordinary vehicles, but entire railroad trains. [Library of Congress]*

1889 the railroad's directors voted to have another built. Thus was *Maryland* (ii) launched at Wilmington, Delaware, on October 23, 1889, and placed in service four months later on February 20, 1890. She, too, was big – 859 gross tons and 238 feet long.

Maryland (ii) was the mainstay vessel of the service from then until 1912, although various single-ended steamboats worked the route along with her from time to time. A story from June 1892 helps illustrate the style and tone of this unusual service; it was rather different, say, from Union Ferry Company's penny-a-ride trips across the East River for working people heading for the factory and a day on the job.

Incumbent Republican president Benjamin Harrison was about to be renominated by his party to seek re-election in 1892 when, on June 4, his irrepressible Secretary of State, James G. Blaine, resigned from the cabinet and announced that he, Blaine, would challenge Harrison for the nomination. It was a major political development and dominated the newspapers for several days.

On June 7, with the G.O.P. convention just getting underway in Minneapolis, Blaine departed from Washington for his family home in Maine, there to await the outcome of his late-starting candidacy. He left his house at Lafayette Square across from the White House at 2:30 in the afternoon and rode

with his wife in a carriage to the Pennsylvania R.R.'s station in Washington, a depot then located directly on the Mall, roughly at the alignment of 4 Street to the west of the Capitol. (The current Washington Union Station did not open until 1908.) The Blaines, senator and spouse, needed seven large trunks to carry belongings required for the trip.

Blaine was, in 1892, but a year from death and many years removed from earlier and vigorous exploits in American politics – United States Senator, Secretary of State on two different occasions, Republican presidential candidate against Grover Cleveland in 1884. But as the 1892 election loomed, many Republican stal-

The New York skyline is of more modest proportion than it is today as the ferryboat Maryland *(ii) turns to enter her slip in Jersey City and deliver passenger cars from Boston to the Pennsylvania R.R. for continuing service on to Philadelphia, Baltimore, and Washington. The train is "The Colonial," and the era is the turn of the century. Today one can still travel Boston-to-Washington on a train called "The Colonial." It's a fully land-bound service, though: no more waterborne transfer across New York Harbor. [Library of Congress]*

warts were convinced – correctly, as it turned out – that their incumbent, Harrison, was no match for Cleveland, the Democrat, who was seeking his second, albeit non-consecutive, term as president. They actively sought Blaine's candidacy for many months, but when it was finally announced it proved to be too little and too late, although quite dramatic, to be sure.

Blaine boarded an afternoon train in Washington and secreted himself in a private railroad car provided him by P.R.R. vice-president Frank Thomson. (Today such a gesture would likely result

in Thomson's being cited for making an illegal campaign contribution!) "Had he been the Czar of Russia in imminent peril from a bombshell full of dynamite, he could have been no more closely guarded," noted one reporter of the arrangements at the railway station in Washington. As to Blaine himself, he was described as being ". . . pallid as a marble slab."

Keeping the ever-inquisitive press at bay was important to the ever-secretive Blaine, and the P.R.R. did its best to help. Conductor W. Kennedy was successful as the train left Washington for the north at 3:15 P.M.; Blaine relaxed in the car Thomson had provided, and reporters were easily kept from entering it by railroad personnel as the train sped through the countryside. At various stations along the way Blaine appeared on the train's observation platform and spoke briefly to crowds that had gathered to see the man some felt might yet dislodge the incumbent president. Blaine received several telegrams from his political operatives in Minneapolis when the train paused in Philadelphia.

When they reached Exchange Place, Jersey City, on time at 9:10 P.M. Blaine's car was quickly removed from the tail end of the train on which it had arrived by a switch engine and was coupled to another train, "The Federal Express," which had reached Exchange Place earlier but was being held for Blaine's private car. Then the train was moved aboard *Maryland* (ii) for the 90-minute cruise down the Hudson, around the Battery, and up the East River to the Harlem River at the foot of 133 Street, and the rails of the New York, New Haven and Hartford R.R.

But here was where the privacy and security that had prevailed back along the railroad broke down. Reporters wandered around the big ferryboat and managed to catch Blaine – perhaps through an open window of his car – and queried him on the kinds of things reporters perennially like to ask presidential candidates. One resourceful scribe even managed to sneak aboard Blaine's car during the switching maneuver at Jersey City. But Blaine was Blaine and the only quote the enterprising reporters were able to elicit from the elusive candidate was this: "I am not going to be interviewed. I refuse absolutely to say anything whatever about anything."

This car-ferry service of the New Haven R.R. was the only instance in New York Harbor that saw passenger-carrying trains regularly moved across the water with people aboard.[6] Transit of

freight cars, on the other hand, has always been popular in New York and continues to this day, although at substantially reduced levels from earlier times. And while even *Maryland* (i) and *Maryland* (ii) and their single-ended running mates hauled freight cars from time to time, the conventional equipment for this service in New York was, and is, unpowered barges pushed along by tugboats.

Returning, now, to Exchange Place and the Pennsylvania R.R.'s trans-Hudson operation: the ferryboat fleet continued to expand throughout the later years of the nineteenth century, but the Pennsy was also perennially unsatisfied with its Jersey City terminal facilities. A major upgrading of both the depot and its contiguous ferry slips was undertaken in 1891, the principal improvement involving the complete elevation of the railroad's main line through Jersey

6. The New York, New Haven and Hartford R.R. carried railroad trains across the Hudson River on another ferryboat line 50 miles or so upstream from New York City. The *William T. Hart* was 295.5 feet in length, constructed in Philadelphia in 1881, and beginning in that year worked a route between Fishkill Landing, N.Y., on the east bank of the Hudson River, and a point near Newburgh on the west bank. Construction of a Hudson River bridge by the railroad at Poughkeepsie in later years eliminated the need for the service. *Maryland* (ii) is known to have filled-in on this route

Before the Pennsylvania R.R. ordered propeller-driven ferryboats, beam-engine sidewheelers like Chicago *were the backbone of the company's trans-Hudson fleet.* [*Steamship Historical Society of America*]

City. This same grade was retained all the way to the bumper posts at Exchange Place, and it meant that passengers getting off their trains there were at the same level as the upper decks of the railroad's ferryboats – and so upper-deck boarding of the boats was arranged for rail passengers; vehicles, of course, stayed at "ground level." Other ferryboat lines will later feature *supplementary* upper-deck passenger loading, and on the Whitehall Street–Saint George line it became standard at both terminals. But among the railroads only the Pennsylvania had a Jersey terminal where, thanks to the elevated railroad alignment, this was the ordinary passenger flow. A fire in 1898 destroyed the seven-year-old terminal, but it was quickly rebuilt to an even improved design.

There were five separate ferryboat slips adjacent to the Exchange Place depot, and this reflected common practice with the Hudson River operators. This is to say that there were always many more ferry slips on the New Jersey side than there were at the individual Manhattan terminals. It was on the New Jersey side that vessels were usually laid-up during off-hours, fueled, and given routine servicing; demand for dock space

---

from time to time; it seems perfectly reasonable to suspect that the '*Hart* may have run in New York now and again to spell *Maryland* (i) or *Maryland* (ii), but I have come across no evidence to that effect. There were also passenger car–carrying steamboat services on Long Island Sound over the years, but none appear to have utilized double-ended ferryboats.

in Manhattan precluded building extra ferry slips there for such activities. In addition, all the railroads operated to multiple Manhattan terminals from their New Jersey rail depots at one time or another. The Pennsy's five-slip facility in Jersey City, for instance, while used to lay-up out-of-service boats in off-hours, would be kept quite busy during peak traffic periods with ferryboats heading for Cortlandt Street, Desbrosses Street, West 23 Street, and Fulton Street, Brooklyn.

Another New York ferryboat service that saw important developments during the post–Civil War years of the nineteenth century was that which linked Staten Island with the foot of Whitehall Street, in Manhattan. Since this is the operation that will see, in 1905, the very first publicly owned and publicly operated ferryboats, it is useful to review the 1865–1900 interval in some detail to understand better how and why such a development came to pass.

As was discussed earlier, in chapter 4, even before the end of the Civil War the Staten Island and New York Ferry Company was purchased by the Staten Island R.R., a small "island-only" line that had been organized in the 1850s and completed a right-of-way from the ferry landing at Clifton in the north to Tottenville in the south in 1860. S.I.R.R.'s first locomotive was built by the New Jersey Locomotive Works and bore the name "Albert Journeay," honoring the railroad's president. The company was not prospering, though, in part – or so its backers claimed – because of an inability to coordinate train arrivals at Clifton with ferryboat departures. The company felt ferryboat captains were pulling out for Manhattan just as the trains came into view! Since both the railroad and the ferry company were, in essence, Vanderbilt interests, the merger was not difficult to accomplish. (Why the Vanderbilt people could not have coordinated the service without a formal merger either remains a mystery or suggests that there were other reasons for its consummation.) In any event, railroad and ferry operations were united from 1864 through 1884 under a single management; then yet another realignment took place.

It, too, was a merger of previously separate operations. Under the impetus of two Staten Island businessmen, William Pendleton and Erastus Wiman, the Eastern Shore ferryboats – i.e., the double-ended vessels of the Staten Island Railway Ferry Company – were corporately united with the single-ended steamboat operations serving the North Shore, and a new and single Staten Island ferry landing was established at the point on the island closest to Manhattan as the crow flies but which

up until this time had no ferryboat or steamboat service at all.

To make this largely undeveloped locale a useful place for a ferry landing, the S.I.R.R. was extended northward to the site of the new facility from its former terminus at Clifton, and then, to tap the area where the single-ended steamboats previously operated, the railroad was also extended westward along Staten Island's North Shore. The idea was a single ferry landing with the railway carrying passengers to other points on the island. The newly combined rail–water entity was this time called the Staten Island Rapid Transit Railroad Company, and it dates to 1884. Use of the term "rapid transit" did not mean that the service was any

kind of electric railway, a concept then in its infancy, at best. It featured ordinary steam-powered trains, although electrification of the S.I.R.T. would come to pass 40 years later.

In 1886 the new terminal was ready; it was called Saint George.[7] The "George" in question, though, can boast of no ecclesiastically-recognized sanctity. One George Law, active in railroad and ferryboat financial circles around New York and regarded by many as something of a minor scoundrel, owned the hitherto unused land Erastus Wiman needed for his new ferry terminal. Wiman held an option to buy the land, but his option was expiring and he lacked cash to complete the deal. To get his option extended Wiman is said

---

7. The merger of North Shore steamboats and Eastern Shore ferryboats into a single S.I.R.T. service to and from St. George caused this bureaucratic problem; S.I.R.T. was actually taking over two pre-existing ferry leases issued by the City of New York, but each stipulated a different fee that the lease holder was obliged to pay the city for the right to run its boats. The Eastern Shore lease called for the payment of 5% of total revenue, while

the North Shore lease was a much higher 14%. Understandably, S.I.R.T. chose to regard the great bulk of its newly-established St. George service as being operated under the old Eastern Shore lease, at a lease payment of 5%. But two trips per day between Whitehall St. and St. George were designated by the company as "North Shore" service – there were special connecting trains to North Shore points, the passengers were kept septo have promised Law that he not only would name the new ferry terminal in Law's honor, but would do so with a title Law could hardly expect to earn either on his own or in his lifetime. Law thought it was all a fine idea, gave Wiman what he wanted, and to this day the place where the ferryboats land on Staten Island may be thought to honor a venerable third-century martyr who is the patron saint of England, but if it does, it's only because another guy named George once gave Erastus Wiman something he needed.[8]

This 1884 merger and unification involved more than Staten Island businessmen and Staten Island transport companies, though. One

of Wiman's key financial backers in the deal was a wealthy gentleman from Maryland by the name of Robert Garrett whose entry into the world of Staten Island ferryboating will have extraordinary consequences. Garrett was the president of the Baltimore and Ohio R.R., the country's oldest, and he invested with Wiman in the Staten Island venture to help se-

cure for his railroad a major toehold in New York Harbor, something it then lacked. The financial package Wiman and Garrett put together called for the B. & O. to lease the island railroad for 99 years. (In 1899, after a network of competitive trolley lines was built on Staten Island and the S.I.R.T. itself went bankrupt, the B. & O. used this occasion to buy the line outright.)

Five years after the 1884 merger the B. & O. built a railroad bridge over the Arthur Kill – the first structure of any kind to link Staten Island with the American mainland. As matters developed, this rail connection served freight traffic exclusively, and a rather modest amount of it at that. But in the late 1880s the Baltimore and Ohio saw Staten Island as an opportune spot for the construction of a major long-distance passenger depot, as well as extensive waterfront freight facilities. The B. & O.'s own rails extended no farther north than Philadelphia; here their trains from Baltimore took first to the tracks of the Reading Company and finally to those of the Jersey Central, and passenger trains terminated at the latter's terminal on

arate from the rest of the company's customers, and the fares they paid were kept separate as well. And then from this sum of money, but this sum only, S.I.R.T. paid the city 14%. In 1892 politicians claimed that the city was being cheated by S.I.R.T.'s tactics, but an investigation quickly determined that the company's tactics were perfectly legal under the leases.

8. In 1873 *The New York Times* excoriated Law for purchasing the Grand Street–Grand Street ferry across the East River but not bothering to pay the city any of the rentals it was due under the lease. ". . . George Law has no right to the exclusive use of this ferry, and . . . the subject is one deserving the attention of the Common Council," concluded the *Times*. George Law also had dealings with the Staten Island Ry. Fy. Co. in 1872–73, over a decade before the "St. George" business. From September 21, 1872 through April 8, 1873 Law's name appears on official Federal enrollment certificates of the company's *Northfield*, *Westfield* (ii), and *Middletown*. He owned the three boats, in other words, even though they continued to run in S. I. Ry. Fy. Co. service and continued to carry that company's name on their flanks.

the banks of the Hudson. Passengers could then continue on to Manhattan aboard C.N.J. ferryboats. But with the developing plans for Staten Island, a new alternative seemed to be in the offing. Onward from the 1884 merger, then, all discussion of ferryboat service between Staten Island and Manhattan had to be conducted around various possibilities relating to the B. & O.'s moving in, making major investments, and playing a bigger role.

As matters turned out, Baltimore and Ohio passenger trains never reached Staten Island: they continued to terminate at the C.N.J. depot in Jersey City, save for the extraordinary days of the First World War when, with the Federal Government in control of all American railroads, arrangements were made for them to operate into Pennsylvania Station in Manhattan.

When B. & O. trains returned to the Jersey Central depot after the war, something different was added to its service to compensate for the fact that passengers no longer stepped off their trains on Manhattan island. A fleet of motor coaches connected with the com-

pany's trains at trackside and provided passengers with connecting service to such New York City locations as Columbus Circle, the Grand Central area, and even downtown Brooklyn. These railroad buses were given priority treatment on the ferryboats – no waiting in line, for instance – and motor coach passengers were permitted to get out and stroll the deck during the short trip across the Hudson River. The buses continued to run right up until the B. & O. eliminated passenger service into the New York area in 1958.

Exactly why the Baltimore and Ohio's passenger trains never managed to terminate on Staten Island will be seen shortly, and it involves a personal tragedy to each of the two movers and shakers behind the 1884 merger, Wiman and Garrett. Before the onset of tragedy, though, each man achieved a brief moment of glory. Each had a fine new ferryboat named in his honor.

Under B. & O. control in 1888, the S.I.R.T. built two most unusual ferryboats to supplement the line's largely Civil War–era fleet. Steel-hulled and 225 feet long, the double-deck sister ships

were built in Baltimore – the railroad's influence, no doubt – and featured an advanced form of paddlewheel design that represented the epitome of that propulsion system. They were named *Erastus Wiman* and *Robert Garrett*.

Each of the two vessels was equipped with something called an inclined compound steam engine, and the engine was connected to paddlewheels that featured "feathering buckets." First the engines.

The inclined compound differed from the vertical-beam engine, the ferryboat industry's standard up until that time, in that it had multiple cylinders set in a line perpendicular to the paddlewheel shaft in such a way that the paddlewheel shaft served as the crankshaft for the engine. The ungainly transfer of energy from piston to paddlewheel through an overhead walking beam was thus eliminated. The cylinders were also set at a slight downward angle from the paddlewheel shaft into the ferryboat's hull, whence the name "inclined."

Inclined engines, per se, on New York ferryboats had been tried earlier. The Union Ferry Company, as an instance, dabbled with such designs back in the Civil

War era, as did other East River operators. But these were single-cylinder low-pressure power plants that were not so successful as to dislodge the vertical-beam engine from its position of prominence in the ferryboat industry. The *'Wiman* and the *'Garrett* had much advanced forms of inclined engines.

The multi-cylinder design meant that the laborious task of urging a beam engine into motion with a manual starting bar was eliminated. One cylinder was always at a different phase of its stroke from the other(s), and so the chance of a compound engine's stalling was greatly lessened. If starting a beam engine can be likened to hand-cranking an automobile engine, the inclined compound is analogous to the introduction of the electric starter.

Another feature of a compound steam engine – inclined or other-

Thanks to its corporate links with the Baltimore & Ohio R.R., the Staten Island Rapid Transit was able to design and build a pair of distinctive sidewheel ferryboats in 1888 – the Robert Garrett *(left) and the* Erastus Wiman *(right). Both were powered by 2-cylinder inclined compound steam engines and driven by an improved kind of paddlewheel. [Staten Island Historical Society]*

The Whitehall St. ferry terminal, ca. 1899, and a look at a lower Manhattan skyline rather different from today's. (See photograph on page 71 for a more contemporary view from exactly the same angle.) The Staten Island Rapid Transit's 1888-built sidewheeler Erastus Wiman, *on the right, has been renamed* Castleton *to avoid association with the luckless Wiman. The small white ferryboat with the tall smokestack is the 1898-built* General Hancock, *then working the Whitehall St.–Governors Island run.* [*Library of Congress*]

wise; maritime, railroad, or stationary – explains its name: it uses its steam twice. (Power plants that use their steam thrice are called triple-expansion engines, and they will be discussed later.) Both the *'Wiman* and the *'Garrett* had two-cylinder engines, and each engine featured cylinders of different diameter. Steam directly from the boiler courses first through the smaller of the two, the high-pressure cylinder so called, and while the steam loses some of its muscle in so doing, there is still sufficient energy in the exhaust from the first cylinder to perform more work. This "second-hand" steam will, however, have to be brought to bear against a much larger surface to compensate for its lost energy. Thus it is then fed into the larger, or low-pressure, cylinder to complete the circuit before being exhausted away into the atmosphere. Both cylinders, while of different diameter, have the same stroke and are connected to the same crankshaft.

The inclined compound engines on the *Erastus Wiman* and the *Robert Garrett* had cylinders that were much smaller than those on the S.I.R.T.'s older beam-engine ferryboats, but they called for steam at considerably higher pressure, adequate boiler designs to permit such pressure with safety having by then been developed. The S.I.R.T.'s *Northfield* of 1863, for example, had a 600-h.p. beam engine whose single cylinder had a diameter of 50 inches, a stroke of ten feet, and an allowable boiler pressure of less than 30 p.s.i. On the new 1888 S.I.R.T. boats the compound engines had cylinders of 39 inches and 70 inches in diameter, and a stroke of only five feet; they generated 1200 h.p., but operated with a boiler pressure of 110 p.s.i.

Of course, one reason the ungainly beam engine retained a degree of popularity into the last third of the nineteenth century, and beyond, was precisely that its cavernous cylinder could be worked with low-pressure steam, lower than was needed for more compact and efficient steam engines such as the inclined compounds on the S.I.R.T.'s 1888 vessels. Smaller and less stable ferryboat companies that lacked the backup of engineering support from the likes of a Baltimore and Ohio R.R. were quite comfortable in letting others pioneer new designs while they themselves stayed with proved concepts.

But the inclined compound engine wasn't the only new feature of the '*Wiman* and the '*Garrett*; there was also the matter of what were called feathering-bucket paddlewheels.

In the older or radical-bucket design, flat paddles ("paddles" and "buckets" are synonymous; they refer to the broad portion of the paddlewheel that does the pulling) were rigidly fixed to the arms of the paddlewheel. While the paddlewheel turned on its shaft, it had no additional moving parts. With a feathering-bucket wheel, however, the paddles are not rig-

idly fixed and are always maintained perpendicular to the water's surface, not unlike cars on a ferris wheel. Thus they cut sharply into the water and yet always bring the full surface of the paddle to bear in affecting a "pulling" action, much as swimming coaches instruct their young Olympic hopefuls. The paddles pivot, in other words, and accomplish this by virtue of rod-like connections attached to the hub of the wheel. (Here the "ferris wheel" analogy falters; its "cars" remain perpendicular by the force of gravity alone.) Feathering-bucket wheels are considerably more efficient than the slapping action of fixed-bucket, radical paddlewheels – and the B. & O./S.I.R.T. adopted this feature for the two new steel-hull double-deckers.[9]

It should also be noted that the

'*Wiman* and the '*Garret* were the first vessels built for Whitehall Street–Saint George service to feature steel hulls. The very first New York ferryboats ever to be so constructed were Union's *Brooklyn* and *Atlantic*, beam-engine vessels built a mere three years earlier in 1885. Iron hulls for ferryboats, on the other hand, had been introduced some years previous; interestingly, the use of iron for a ferryboat hull was one of the few innovations *not* pioneered in New York. The ferryboat *Delaware*, built in 1846 for service in Boston Harbor, was the very first American double-ender whose hull could rust, but not rot.

The *Erastus Wiman* and the *Robert Garrett* entered service in August 1888 and represented a great advance over the company's earlier vessels, particularly from

9. Later-day paddlewheel vessels in New York Harbor that were the only experience many people ever had with this propulsion system were the Hudson River Day Line steamers *Hendrick Hudson* (1906–1948) and *Alexander Hamilton* (1924–1971), both powered by inclined engines and driven by feathering-bucket paddle-

wheels. The Day Line's *Robert Fulton* (1909–1954) had feathering-bucket paddlewheels, but a vertical-beam engine – the last operating instance of the famous old power plant on the East Coast. For further information on the Day Line and its vessels, see Donald C. Ringwald, *Hudson River Day Line* (Berkeley: Howell-North, 1965.)

the perspective of ferry passengers. Engineering innovations down below deck are interesting, but passengers were more concerned with comfort, and here the new vessels earned high marks. But the relationship between S.I.R.T. and its captive customers on the Whitehall Street–Saint George line, never terribly good to begin with, worsened in January 1889 when the company pulled the two new boats out of service and put them in winter lay-up at Tompkinsville. By this move S.I.R.T. was saying that they would use their new vessels during warm-weather months when they were seeking to lure discretionary customers to ride the ferry to visit sites such as Wiman-owned amusement parks. But when it came to hauling native Staten Island residents to and from work in Manhattan each day, winter as well as summer – well, listen to what an S.I.R.T. official told *The New York Times*: "What do Staten Islanders want for 10 cents – 10 miles of ferriage and palatial steamboats. The old boats are good enough."

(Less than a week later, on Sunday, January 6, a fierce winter gale was pounding New York,

but S.I.R.T. had only a single vessel working the Whitehall Street–Saint George line, *Westfield* (ii) – "the decrepit old Westfield," in the words of the *Times*. In calm weather a single boat was sufficient to maintain the one-boat-an-hour Sunday service the line operated in the winter months, but on this day *Westfield* (ii) had all sorts of problems holding to her schedule in the teeth of the storm. Staten Islanders in Manhattan for the day, of course, still had to get home. It was early evening and ". . . a crowd gathered in the stuffy little ferry house that threatened to bulge out its wall . . ."; large numbers of people actually had to wait for the late-running *Westfield* (ii) outdoors in the driving rain. "Why the Southfield was not put in service to help out her sistership is a conundrum that can be answered only by the managers of the Staten Island Ferry Company," concluded the account in the next morning's *Times*.)

The *Erastus Wiman* and the *Robert Garrett* did not, as things turned out, represent the future of harbor ferryboat design in New York; inclined compound engines and feathering-bucket paddle-

wheels would never become popular and indeed were never repeated by any New York operator. In the same year in which S.I.R.T. took delivery of its twin side-wheelers a descendant of Colonel John Stevens had a new vessel designed and built for the Hoboken Ferry Company, a double-ender that bore the unassuming name *Bergen*. *Bergen*, though, marked the first successful use of screw propellers on a harbor ferryboat, and so successful was Stevens' design that it was soon emulated throughout the harbor and became, by the end of this 1865–1900 era, the conventional power and propulsion system for New York Harbor ferryboats. The *Erastus Wiman* and the *Robert Garrett*, while different, turned out to be the last of the old, not the first of the new.

Before going on to discuss *Bergen* and the design she introduced, a word or two, please, about the men after whom the S.I.R.T.'s final ferryboats were named; their stories are sad.

Erastus Wiman was born in Toronto in 1834 and early on became associated with a mercantile agency there founded by one R. G.

Dun. Soon it became Dun, Wiman and Company, and while it would later evolve into Dun and Bradstreet, that would happen only after Wiman and Dun had parted company. Wiman moved to New York in 1866 and established an affiliated agency; soon enough he had become a very prosperous man. His manor house on Staten Island overlooking Upper New York Bay was one of the finer residences in the area.

Wiman was tireless, and after learning of Garrett's desire to establish major terminal facilities for his Baltimore and Ohio R.R. in New York he not only became a supporter of the idea, but saw the railroad's arrival in Staten Island as an opportunity for both community development in his adopted homeland and personal return from private real-estate investments.

Wiman begged and borrowed every dollar he could and bought acre upon acre of Staten Island waterfront property, all of it mortgaged to the hilt. (Recall that Erastus Wiman, a very wealthy man, was unable to come up with the cash to exercise an option he held to buy land from George Law ca. 1884.) Then, as so often happened in the days of fast fortunes and free-wheeling speculation, it all came unglued.

The B. & O. eventually arrived on Staten Island, but not on the scale Wiman expected – or, more importantly, *required* – to justify his investing. A downturn in financial markets in 1893 caught Wiman short: ". . . the greater part of his money was tied up, so that it was hard to realize quickly when urgent necessity came," noted the *Times* many years later. His empire collapsed and his future evaporated, and, to make matters worse, R. G. Dun brought a charge of forgery against him in 1894 on which he was convicted, although the conviction was later reversed on appeal. Erastus Wiman died on Staten Island in 1904, a broken man. While he retained his fine home until the end, the week before he died his furniture was sold at auction to help pay off creditors, and even the S.I.R.T. felt compelled to abandon its one-time friend. The ferryboat *Erastus Wiman* was re-named *Stapleton* in 1894 to avoid identification with the luckless financeer.

Why the astute Erastus Wiman guessed so wrongly about the B. & O. involves the other tragic figure, Robert Garrett. Garrett took over the presidency of the Baltimore and Ohio R.R. in 1884 upon the death of his father, John Work Garrett, and he immediately began to expand the railroad into new markets and subsidiary activities that had long been discussed but which Garrett-the-elder with his conservative business instincts had continued to approach more cautiously. Among these was a greatly enlarged New York terminal for the line, and it was here that Garrett and Wiman stood poised to make common cause. A lavish reception and party hosted by Wiman for Garrett at the Pavilion Hotel in New Brighton to signal the start of their joint venture just after the latter became president of the B. & O. was spoken of for years as a social event *par excellence.*

Garrett, though, was unable to sustain the level of effort on his railroad's part that was necessary to realize his and Wiman's plans. His tenure as president of the railway was brief, and the line's directors were very uncomfortable with his expenditures and expansion. Perhaps had Garrett survived and pressed forward with his ideas the whole story might have unfolded differently, but he didn't. He was visiting William H. Vanderbilt, the Commodore's son, on December 8, 1885, at the latter's Fifth Avenue home to work out certain agreements between the Baltimore and Ohio and Vanderbilt's New York Central and Hudson River R.R., when Vanderbilt collapsed while the two men were alone and died. Garrett later insisted that he and Vanderbilt had reached accord on a number of matters, absent which the B. & O. could not sensibly proceed with its New York terminal plan. But the Central's management remained unconvinced or unwilling, and in the face of continued misgivings from his own board and his own people, poor Robert Garrett was no longer equal to the demands of leading a major industrial corporation. His health, physical and mental, failed. He retired from the railroad in 1887, only three years after becoming president, and he died in July 1896, a man of but 49 years. And the Baltimore and Ohio R.R. never became that major a factor in the port of New York.[10]

These are the basic facts, but they certainly invite speculation. Did Vanderbilt's death so disturb Garrett as to render him unstable? One of Garrett's obituaries suggested as much. Had Garrett retained his health, might the whole Garret–Wiman dream have been realized? And if so, would a major B. & O. presence on Staten Island have given that line such a share of the intercity passenger market that the Pennsylvania R.R. would not have been in a position to built its Hudson River tunnels in 1910? Indeed, if the Baltimore and Ohio had gotten to Staten Island in the 1880s, might *it*, and not the Pennsy, have been the company that was later in a position to build a bridge or tunnel to Manhattan? Might both railroads have reached Manhattan? Would major B. & O. investment in Staten Island ferry-boat operations have precluded the City of New York from taking over the Whitehall Street–Saint George service in 1905?

The Baltimore and Ohio R.R. continued a lesser affiliation with the S.I.R.T. until the 1980s, but it was never of the sort envisioned by two men in 1884. As matters developed, the men who dreamed that dream are remembered only as the namesakes for a pair of inclined compound paddlewheel ferryboats built in 1888 – vessels, ironically, which while of a new design did not presage the future of ferryboat evolution.

As to the vessel that did, *Bergen*, it is totally appropriate that she was designed under the direction of a direct descendant of Colonel John Stevens.[11] The Stevens people had long been interested in the notion of a screw-propeller ferryboat, and as that became the conventional form of marine propulsion elsewhere, its application to the ferryboat industry continued

10. For a discussion of the Baltimore and Ohio R.R.'s efforts to expand into the New York area, see Edward Hungerford, *Story of the Baltimore & Ohio*, II 145–62. Hungerford virtually dismisses the short presidential tenure of Robert Garrett, but provides valuable perspective in his treatment of John Work Garrett, Robert's father and predecessor as president of the railroad.

11. See Smith, pp. 69–80, for a discussion of the development of *Bergen* and the role played by various third-generation members of the Stevens family.

to excite naval architects and ship designers. But as discussion proceeded, a natural conservatism started to develop among ferryboat operators. Would not a screw propeller at each end of a boat be especially vulnerable to damage? How about shifting passenger loads and maintaining vessel stability while entering ferry slips, something at which paddlewheel boats excelled? Was the claimed efficiency of the high-pressure engines and high-pressure boilers worth the increased precautions – and expense – it would require?

The issues were genuine, sidewheel propulsion was a relatively proved and stable commodity, and thus the first successful deployment of a screw propeller didn't happen until 1888 when *Bergen* slid down the ways of the Delamater Iron Works in Newburgh, N.Y.

It could have happened a little earlier, though. The Hoboken Ferry Company had desperately needed two new boats in 1885, and while the company's thinking was rapidly coming around to the notion of screw propellers, the need for these two boats was too severe to permit the necessary design

work, not to mention run the risks inherent in such experimentation. Thus the sidewheelers *Montclair* and *Orange* were turned out by the T. J. Marvel yard in Newburgh, *Orange* going down the ways on October 6, 1886, and *Montclair* on November 27. They proved to be the last sidewheelers the company would ever build, though. (*Orange* and *Montclair* did pioneer something for the Hoboken Ferry Company: they were the firm's first vessels built with steel hulls.)

And so with the Hoboken Ferry Company's basic fleet-replacement needs addressed by the addition of the two sidewheelers, proper attention could be turned to the vessel that became *Bergen*.

Bergen's hull and boilers were designed by the Hoboken Ferry Company, but the all-important engine that would make or break her major design innovation was designed by J. Shields Wilson, an operator of day boats on the Delaware River and the man whose Wilson Line will continue to run excursion boats on the East Coast until well after the Second World War. While new to the world of ferryboating, the engine was the epitome of steamboat conven-

tionality for the day – a three-cylinder engine mounted along the center line of the boat, with cylinder heads at the top and crankshaft at the bottom. In today's automotive parlance *Bergen*'s 800-h.p. engine would be called "in-line," while in the maritime world a popular phrase was that she had an "up-and-down" engine.

More precisely, *Bergen* had a triple-expansion engine: which is to say that, if a compound engine uses its steam twice, in a triple-expansion steam is fed, in turn, into three different cylinders, each of a larger diameter. (It's also possible to have a *four*-cylinder *triple*-expansion engine; in such cases two equal-size cylinders are paired and use steam at one of its three phases.)

And now for the interesting part. Two identical 4-blade propellers were affixed to *Bergen*, one at each end. But they were attached to the same length-of-the-boat propeller shaft, a shaft that was also connected to the engine. Thus, in either direction, *Bergen*'s forward propeller "pulled," and her aft propeller "pushed."

Scientific American magazine took proper note of *Bergen*'s nov-

The first successful double-ended ferryboat to be powered by a screw propeller was Bergen *of the Hoboken Ferry Company, built in 1888 and here shown in later years wearing the livery of the Delaware, Lackawanna & Western R.R. [Mariners Museum]*

elty, commenting especially on the increased deck room – ". . . twenty percent for trucks and carriages and thirty-five percent for passengers . . ." – that was freed by elimination of the paddle boxes on both sides of the boat wherein the paddlewheels rotated in earlier designs, as well as mid-vessel space-saving from being able to mount the smaller triple-expansion engine totally below deck.

Following her introduction into trans-Hudson service and a proper period of "breaking in," *Bergen* was put through an exhaustive series of technical tests to determine how her performance compared with a beam-engine sidewheeler. For these tests the company selected the 1886-built *Orange* as the vessel against which they would measure the newcomer. (It's a pity they didn't use the slightly newer *Montclair*; then it could have been said that Hoboken's very last beam-engine side-wheeler was pitted against the first screw-propeller ferryboat, but *Orange* was only 57 days "older" than *Montclair*, so the point has no technical import at all.)

There were three aspects to the evaluation: one, both vessels would be carefully measured on fuel consumption and work output during a 14-hour period in regular ferry service; then, each vessel would be similarly measured during the course of a non-stop 120-mile cruise up the Hudson River to Newburgh, N.Y., and back; and finally, *Bergen* would have one of her screw propellers removed and her performance would be carefully documented during several runs over a 2-mile course. The last test was especially critical because, for complicated reasons that could be explained only by marine architects talking to each other in lengthy algebraic equations, identical screws on both the fore and aft of a vessel turning at the exact same speed were theoretically expected to produce some degree of inefficiency as certain forces counteract and cancel out other forces. It was important to measure exactly what this "inefficiency" was in real terms: were it too great, of course, the concept *Bergen* pioneered might not be the expected step forward in the evolution of ferryboat design.

On August 15, 1889, *Orange* made her Newburgh round trip, *Bergen* made hers a month later, and on September 28, *Bergen* was put through a number of tests with one of her screws physically removed from the propeller shaft.

A large quantity of engineering data was generated during these tests, and it provided considerable grist for technical papers that were read at meetings of various professional organizations in the maritime field over the next months and years. But in simple terms it boiled down to this: *Bergen* won, and as Stevens put it, "Practically, the *Bergen* is preferred by passengers and pilots alike. While the boat is by no means perfect, she is the best we have, has proved a successful experiment, and will furnish a type for our future boats."

Furnish it she did, and not just for Stevens' company. In 1891 the Erie R.R. brought out their *John G. McCullough*, the second steam ferryboat to operate in New York *sans* paddlewheels. She was built at the famous Neafie and Levy shipyard in Philadelphia, and again *Scientific American* hauled out the superlatives: "She is lighted all over by the incandescent light, and is in all respects the 'most modern' ferryboat in the fullest sense of the word, and she will be the model ferryboat of New York harbor." Later that same year, 1891, and early the next, 1892, four more propeller-driven ferryboats entered service, *Hamburg* and *Bremen* on the Hoboken line, and *Cincinnati* and *Washington* wearing the colors of the Pennsylvania R.R. The Central Railroad of New Jersey built its first propeller boats in 1892, and with but a single exception there would be no further sidewheelers built for the railroads.

One minor-but-important modification to the original *Bergen* design included in many, if not most, subsequent steam-powered propeller ferryboats was abandonment of the triple-expansion engine and substitution in its place of a pair of 2-cylinder compound engines. The twin compounds were permanently fixed to a single propeller shaft, just as was *Bergen*'s triple-expansion engine – it was *not* a case of one engine driving the forward screw and the other the aft, as has sometimes been suggested. In fact, for all intents and purposes a ferryboat outfitted with a pair of two-cylinder compound engines could be said to have a single four-cylinder engine – with two equal-size high-pressure cylinders and two equal-size low-pressure ones.

But while screw propellers quickly became standard on Hudson River railroad ferryboats, they still were new technology, and this proved troublesome to some operators. As was the case when the B. & O. built the S.I.R.T.'s two 1888 ferryboats, the Hudson River railroads, in the 1890s, were prosperous organizations with large engineering departments, and they were both comfortable with the notion of pressing forward with technical innovation in steam-engine design and adequately financed to pay for it all. But over on the East River, and elsewhere,

Following the success of Bergen *in 1888, the Hoboken Ferry Company took delivery of a pair of similarly-powered vessels in 1891,* Bremen *(shown here) and* Hamburg. *The Hoboken line gave many of its trans-Hudson ferryboats Germanic names because German-flag passenger liners docked adjacent to its ferry slips on the Jersey wide of the Hudson. At the time of the First World War, however, with a rash of anti-German feeling in the country, what ferryboats remained with such designations were quickly rechristened with the names of nearby cities and towns as part of the patriotic fervor. [author's collection]*

such was hardly the case – all the more so with shadows beginning to be cast across ferry routes from the towers of new suspension bridges. Neither the Union nor the Williamsburg ferry company, for example, was buttressed with such resources; hence what new ferryboats they purchased in the post-*Bergen* era were, essentially, built to pre-*Bergen* specifications – i.e., while steel-hulled, they continued to be beam-engine side-wheelers, sometimes even utilizing second-hand engines salvaged

from older vessels as a further economy move.[12] Indeed, even a steel hull was not always a requisite. The final beam-engine ferry-

---

12. The generalizations I am making here about railroad ferry operations *vs.* smaller independent companies retains its validity, I believe, even though the Hoboken Ferry Company was not, in the year 1888 when *Bergen* was built, formally affiliated with the Delaware, Lackawanna and Western R.R. The Hoboken operation was, simply, more like a railroad-run ferry than it was like the East River companies.

boat to be built for New York service dates to the year 1922, and she had a wooden hull!

(For the record: she was the *Charles W. Galloway*, 587 tons and 140.8 feet long and powered by a vertical-beam engine built by the W. and A. Fletcher Company, arguably the most renowned manufacturer of these power plants. She was built by the Pusey and Jones Company in Wilmington, Delaware, and operated for the Staten Island Rapid Transit – not, obviously, in Whitehall Street–

Saint George service, since that was taken over by the City of New York in 1905; rather the *'Galloway* spent her years linking the S.I.R.T.'s Tottenville terminal at the southern tip of Staten Island with Perth Amboy. She remained thus employed until 1948 when S.I.R.T. gave up this service and a new operator took over with modern, though small, diesel boats. On October 16, 1948, when *Charles W. Galloway* made her last trip across the Arthur Kill, she was the sole ferryboat operating in New York Harbor still driven by the style of engine that once powered the entire industry.)

Thus the story of *Bergen*, and the introduction of the screw propeller to over and back ferryboat operations. One of the trans-Hudson services that would eventually replicate *Bergen*'s pioneering design nine times can likely be called the most important new ferryboat line to be inaugurated in New York in the 1865–1900 period. It served the fifth – and the final – rail depot to be built on the west bank of the Hudson River. Its advent was nothing if not complicated, although eventually the service settled down to become a

conventional trans-Hudson connection for a conventional railroad, the New York Central, the terminal of whose West Shore line was in Weehawken, N.J., across the Hudson from Manhattan.

To keep things clear: the New York Central R.R.'s principal line into New York City from upstate and the west crosses the Hudson River at Albany, N.Y., 150 miles north of Manhattan, hugs the east bank of the river, and terminates in New York City at Grand Central Terminal. The about-to-be-discussed West Shore operation, which provides a parallel main line along the Hudson's opposite bank, was a secondary line for the New York Central. On the other hand it wasn't *always* part of the New York Central System, and that's where the story picks up in the years after the Civil War.

Two related rail ventures were begun to link New York City with the port of Oswego, N.Y., on Lake Ontario – the New York and Oswego Midland R.R. from Oswego to Middletown, N.Y., and the New Jersey Midland R.R. from there to New York Harbor. The ventures, while doomed to failure, made their mark.

For one, in seeking a site for a Jersey-side passenger depot, the "Midland enterprise" selected Slough's Meadow. This was a rather northerly location with reference to the business and commercial districts of New York City, but all the more preferable sites in the Hoboken–Jersey City area were spoken for by other railroads. Here, as was discussed in chapter 2, a ferryboat service already existed; it would be absorbed, eventually, by the new company.

But the two Midland ventures weren't soundly financed and they bellied-up in the late 1870s. Afterward, much of the partly completed right-of-way in New York State west of Middletown became the New York, Ontario and Western R.R., itself never an epitome of sound transport financing. But this is also where the story begins to get *very* confusing.

In addition to the O. & W. spinoff, a group of investors headed by George Pullman, he of sleeping-car fame, as well as other interests associated with the Pennsylvania R.R., made an effort to rescue from the Midland breakup the nucleus of a railroad that

Although its early corporate evolution was a little on the complex side, the railroad and ferry depot in Weehawken, New Jersey eventually became the New York terminal of the New York Central R.R.'s West Shore line, a supplementary service to that company's principal operation out of Manhattan's Grand Central Terminal. The 'Central long used the slogan "the water level route you can sleep" in advertisements for its long-distance passenger trains. Somehow, though, using the expression on a ferry terminal seems to be over-stressing the obvious. [author]

might parallel, and compete with, Cornelius Vanderbilt's New York Central. It was called the New York, West Shore and Buffalo R.R. Its route was to be north out of Weehawken along the west bank of the Hudson to Albany, and then west to Buffalo.

The new line retained Slough's Meadow/Weehawken as its New York terminal, and also entered a long-term agreement whereby the N.Y., O. & W. would connect with its road at Cornwall, N.Y., 50 miles up the Hudson from New York City, and operate trains down the West Shore to Weehawken.

Construction proceeded and in 1884 trains of both new railroads – the New York, Ontario and Western and the New York, West Shore and Buffalo – began running into and out of the Weehawken terminal, and passengers were then ferried to Manhattan aboard a fleet of four fine new ferryboats that were *built* by the O. & W. but transferred immediately to the N.Y., W. S. & B. for operation.

And what of the New York Central R.R.? How did the older line react to this new competitive threat to its main-line operation? Well, it retaliated, that's what it did. The

Vanderbilt interests began to build a new railroad to compete with the Pennsylvania on *its* home turf. Construction began across Pennsylvania on what was to be called the South Pennsylvania R.R.; right-of-way was graded and tunnels even built, but in mid-1885 J. P. Morgan stepped in and mediated the whole dispute. Pullman et al. agreed to sell the New York, West Shore and Buffalo R.R. to the New York Central, and Vanderbilt walked away from his half-finished South Pennsylvania project. (Years later the Pennsylvania Turnpike was built along much of its right-of-way and even made use of tunnels the Vanderbilt people had drilled through the mountains of central Pennsylvania.)[13]

And so the line out of Weehawken that has always been popularly called the West Shore R.R. came under formal control of Vanderbilt's New York Central. The Ontario and Western's contractual arrangements with the N.Y., W.S. & B. were honored by the Central after it took over the West Shore and, until the O. & W. abandoned its passenger service entirely in 1953, its trains continued to operate into and out of the Weehawken terminal – and its passengers traveled to and from Manhattan on New York Central ferryboats. Of course the railroad didn't go to any great pains to emphasize this point in its advertisements and timetables, a reading of which would lead one to presume that O. & W. trains connected with O. & W. ferryboats.

The railroad depot eventually built in Weehawken wasn't exactly in the Slough's Meadow area

where the older ferryboat line operated. It was a mile or so to the south, and from here two principal ferryboat services were established. One crossed the Hudson more or less directly to the foot of West 42 Street, also the Manhattan landing for the earlier Slough's Meadow service. But the second route out of Weehawken will always remain one of New York's more interesting ferryboat routes. Trans-Hudson lines often avoided a direct crossing, and their route took them a mile or so up or down the river before landing on the opposite side. Barclay Street–Hoboken was a good example of such a style of service, the foot of Barclay Street being a little over a mile to the south of Hoboken. But a line out of Weehawken to the foot of Cortlandt Street in downtown Manhattan involved a 4½-mile voyage up and down the Hudson River that gave the traveler a priceless view of Manhattan and the constantly changing maritime traffic on the river. Toward the middle of the twentieth century when the city's deep-water piers for major trans-Atlantic ocean liners were located just north of the West 42 Street ferry slips and

directly opposite Weehawken, morning commuters off their trains from places like Nyack on the West Shore line would routinely be heading downriver to Cortlandt Street on a New York Central ferryboat just as the likes of the *Île de France* or the *Mauretania* was heading up the Hudson. Blasé ferry passengers *sometimes* never looked up from their crossword puzzles and box scores in the face of such drama, but more often than not everyone headed for the railing of the ferryboat for a better view, and the captain had to compensate for a slight list to the boat.

"What's that, the *Queen Elizabeth*?
"Naw, I think it's the *Queen Mary*. She's got the three stacks."
"Sure is big, isn't she?"
"Sure is."

Back to the nineteenth century: the four original "O. & W. boats" that inaugurated the service out of Weehawken for the railroad in 1884 remained in service for the New York Central R.R. until, roughly, the time of the First World War. All were removed

13. For discussion of these complicated corporate developments, see Condit, pp. 70–75.

from service as more modern ferryboats joined the fleet; all found second careers with other companies after they were sold off by the railroad. For one reason or other this new York Central/Weehawken ferryboat operation waited longer than any of the others to design and build its first propeller-driven ferryboat – the *West Point* of 1900; it was also the only railroad-related service to build a new sidewheeler after *Bergen* came out in 1888 – that being *Buffalo* of 1897. One more oddity of the railroad ferry service from Weehawken was that it was the only one of the five serving a passenger depot on the west bank of the Hudson that never instituted a supplementary service to the foot of Manhattan's West 23 Street, a landing that at one time or another the other four all served.[14]

And thus did the 1865–1900 era continue. The Brooklyn Bridge story has been recounted many times and need not be explored here; what can't be overlooked, of course, is that the Brooklyn Bridge *was built*, and it opened for traffic in 1883. And with the reality of the Brooklyn Bridge dominating the East River, talk of other bridges – tunnels, too, for that matter – could not be dismissed out of hand by the various ferry operators. On the Hudson there was even talk of a massive "Union Bridge" that might carry the trains of all the New Jersey–bound railroads to a direct landfall on Manhattan. Such a project, of course, would have been undertaken by the railroads themselves and would have represented investment decisions on their part about how best to get their passengers to their final destination. The railroad ferryboats would have been rendered obsolete by such a structure, but that would have been an obsolescence born of decisions made by the railroads themselves. With the independent ferry companies on the East River, on the other hand, bridges (and tunnels) were quite something else again. There it would become a case of the public sector building whatever river crossings were warranted – for general traffic, for streetcars, for rapid transit trains, and for pedestrians. The impact such investments might have on the economic well-being of the ferryboat companies was of little consequence in the overall scheme of things, and a decision to build a particular bridge or rapid transit tunnel was totally out of the hands of the ferry companies.

Another matter that always caused concern for ferryboat owners, workers, and passengers – and still does and always will – is the question of safety. The water is an alien place for humankind, and all the legends of infamous tragedies at sea do not lose their poignancy when the "sea" in question becomes the Hudson River or Upper New York Bay. Fire, shipwreck, collision, a boiler explosion: all are potential hazards.

On the evening of Monday, November 26, 1866, the *Idaho*, a 496-ton ferryboat that had been built in Brooklyn the year before and was owned by the Williamsburg company (then formally known as the New York and Brooklyn Ferry Company), left the big terminal at the foot of Broadway for a short and routine passage across the East River to the foot of Roosevelt Street in Manhattan – across

---

14. For a treatment of the ferryboat operations out of Weehawken, see Harry Cotterell, Jr., "The Weehawken and West Shore Ferries," *Steamboat Bill of Facts*, No. 70 (Summer 1959), 38–42.

and down the river actually, Roosevelt Street being in the area where the Brooklyn Bridge stands today. Aboard were about 30 passengers and two teams of horses, fortunately a light load. Because no sooner was *Idaho* clear of her Williamsburg slip than fire erupted on the boat; the action of her pilot, one Richard Stillwell, in not immediately putting back to the Broadway terminal was later faulted. The fire spread quickly through the all-wood vessel and soon *Idaho* was out of control – hopelessly ablaze and helplessly drifting. Here is how it was described in the next morning's *Times*:

"About 7:10 last evening an immense blaze was seen to rise behind the sugar refinery of HAVEMEYER & ELDER, on First-street, Williamsburgh. At first it was thought that the refinery was on fire, and the fire companies crowded to the place as rapidly as possible. On arriving there, however, they soon discovered that the flames rose from a burning ferry-boat that was fast drifting down the stream, and seriously imperiling the vessels lying in her track. The flames rose high and burned with extraordinary brilliancy, lighting up the East River everywhere within range of vision. The docks all along the river on the New York and Williamsburgh sides were soon crowded with spectators. Of course the fire companies, on reaching the docks, were powerless to render assistance, the burning boat being about two hundred yards from shore. As the boat still had on a considerable amount of steam, the spectators every moment expected to see and hear the explosion of the boilers."

Well, it didn't turn into an out-and-out tragedy. One of *Idaho*'s fleetmates, the 338-ton *Canada*, managed to get a line aboard the stricken vessel before she was fully engaged in flames and passengers and animals were safely gotten off – although several of the former, including a woman with an infant in her arms, had to jump overboard into the cold November-night water and be rescued from there.

Official hearings followed. Company witnesses were asked to speculate what might have happened had *Idaho* been carrying several hundred passengers. They, naturally, said everything would have gone just as smoothly during the rescue. ("I don't think there would have been any great loss if they had only kept cool.") The ability of passengers aboard a crowded ferryboat to keep cool, though, was quite another matter. The hearing also brought out the alarming fact that on the evening of the fire, passengers aboard another Williamsburg ferry, the *Minnesota*, were of a mind to lynch that vessel's captain and crew for putting them, the *Minnesota*'s passengers, at peril by venturing near the burning *Idaho*. And always there was the balancing of the company's economic well-being with the physical well-being of its passengers. "**Q.** Would it not have been better, don't you think, had there been another man having charge of those two deck hands to direct their efforts in the emergency? **A.** No, Sir."[15]

It was during this same post–Civil War period that the worst

---

15. Citations taken from a hearing held by the New York City Board of Health on December 7, 1866, and quoted in *The New York Times*, December 8, 1866.

tragedy ever to befall a New York ferryboat took place. On a sunny Sunday afternoon in July 1871, the Staten Island R.R. *Westfield* (ii) exploded at the Whitehall Street ferry slip. Sixty-six people were killed, making it not only the worst tragedy in New York ferryboating, but one of the more serious losses of life from any disaster in

---

16. Measured solely by loss of human life, the *Westfield* (ii) explosion would appear to rank as the New York area's eleventh worst disaster. Herewith the awful list:

June 16, 1904	– fire aboard passenger steamer *General Slocum*	1030
June 30, 1900	– Hoboken dock fire	326
Dec. 5, 1876	– Brooklyn theater fire	295
Mar. 25, 1911	– Triangle Shirtwaist fire	145
Dec. 16, 1960	– crash of 2 airliners following mid-air collision	134
June 24, 1975	– plane crash at JFK Airport	113
Mar. 1, 1962	– plane crash in Jamaica Bay	95
Nov. 1, 1918	– rapid transit crash in Brooklyn	93
Feb. 6, 1951	– train wreck in Woodbridge, N.J.	84
Nov. 22, 1950	– train wreck in Richmond Hill, N.Y.	79
July 30, 1871	– boiler explosion aboard *Westfield* (ii)	66

and around New York.[16] It happened like this.

On Sundays in the summer of 1871 the S.I.R.R. maintained hourly ferry service out of Whitehall Street, but supplemented this schedule with extra boats on the half-hour as traffic warranted. Sunday, July 30, was a hot day, and the nine-year-old *Westfield* (ii) was assigned to make such a run at half-past one. She was a 609-ton wooden-hull sidewheeler; her vertical-beam engine had a cylinder diameter of 50 inches and a stroke of ten feet, and was rated at 700 h.p. She was the railroad's second vessel to bear her name. *Westfield* (i) was an 1861-built ferryboat that had perished in U.S. Navy service during the Civil War. Both were built in Brooklyn at the Jeremiah Simonson yard.

Captain John Vreeland was in the after pilot house supervising the loading of passengers below. *Westfield* (ii) had arrived from Staten Island at 1:10 P.M., and while the railroad regarded the 1:30 departure time as a schedule they expected Vreeland to meet, there was more flexibility than with the regular "on the hour" departures. In addition, for the passengers this was merely an un-

scheduled extra sailing so there was not the usual rushing to get aboard.

One thing that proved devastating was a decision Vreeland made to hold his departure from Whitehall Street until the 1:00 P.M. boat out of Staten Island had come into view around Governor's Island. Had the ferryboat gotten under way before the explosion the call on the boiler for steam would likely have reduced pressure and precluded the accident – at least for awhile, but maybe forever.

Another circumstance that was hardly fortunate was that passengers coming aboard *Westfield* (ii) inevitably made for the Staten Island end of the boat, a behavioral phenomenon that prevails at Whitehall Street to this day. In the wistful prose of the next day's *Times*: "All of those who were on the boat crowded naturally but unconsciously to the one fatal spot on board. The day was sultry, and for the sake of the breeze from the Bay everybody sought the end of the vessel furthest from the dock."

Now, New York Harbor ferryboats like *Westfield* (ii) are normally asymmetrical, which is to say that down in the hold the boil-

This is the way Frank Leslie's Illustrated Newspaper *depicted the tragic* explosion *aboard the Staten Island Rapid Transit's ferryboat* Westfield *(ii).* [*author's collection*]

ers and coal bins are placed to one end of the vessel and the engine to the other. Looking at such a vessel broadside one sees that the smokestack is off-center, marking where the boilers are positioned; the walking beam is to the opposite side of midship, and this is where the engine is. The S.I.R.T. specified the boiler end of their ferryboats as the "Staten Island end," and it was this that made "the end of the vessel furthest from the dock" "the one fatal spot on board." Departure time was approaching; there were about 250 people aboard.

Down below fireman Robert Carresan heard an irregular sound, a different kind of hissing of steam. An unschooled ear would hear nothing but undifferentiated white noise in a ferryboat boiler room, but an experienced man like Carresan detected something irregular. The boilers were rated for a top pressure of 25 p.s.i., and they were apparently at that, or perhaps a little above, as the safety valves were blowing off steam, a normal enough circumstance just before a vessel gets under way. Again *The New York Times*:

He listened for a moment; it was an ominous sound, full of peril. No such noise could be heard coming from the boilers consistent with safety. He started forward to investigate the matter, and had taken but a few steps when he encountered a dense volume of steam. At that instant something struck him in the face and he became insensible. The history in the hold was closed. It was 1:27 P.M. The boilers exploded. The force from the explosion was upward and outward toward that "one fatal spot on board" where passengers were relaxing and anticipating the pleasure of a breezy Sunday afternoon sail down the bay. Carresan, for example, survived, and he was *down in the boiler room* where the explosion happened, although to landward of the rupture. A woman on the second deck of *Westfield* (ii) was hurled into the air higher than the top of the steeple on the ferry house.

The Eastern Hotel, standing at the corner of Whitehall and South streets, became a receiving station for the dead and injured pending their transfer to Park Hospital, on Centre Street. Through the after-noon and evening rescue work continued, and it was a grisly task. The very presence of *Westfield* (ii) in the ferry slip made it difficult to search for victims who might be alive but, perhaps, clinging to a piece of floating timber under the vessel's paddlewheel guards. So at half-past four the railroad's *Northfield* began to tow the still-floating *Westfield* (ii) to the foot of East 8 Street and the East River, a spot about two-and-a-half miles away. At 4:35 P.M., *Middletown* landed at the very slip where the accident happened, its load of 1000 passengers homeward bound from a day of relaxation on Staten Island mutely watching the still-continuing rescue operations and search for victims.

Sixty-six people were killed and over two hundred injured, many of whom were disfigured for life. The year 1871 was but 62 summers since Robert Fulton powered his *Claremont* up the Hudson to Albany, and while exploding steam boilers were not the frequent tragedy they were in the early days of steam navigation, the accident aboard *Westfield* (ii) demonstrated that the technology still had its dangers. *Westfield*'s boilers had been inspected as recently as June 15, 1871, by Federal officials to a hydrostatic pressure of 34 p.s.i., and this fact was registered in the U.S. Customs House in New York on July 15, a mere 15 days before the disaster. One final quotation from the *Times* on the morning after the accident: ". . . a copy of this [inspection] certificate furnished to the boat hung in horrid mockery to a portion of the timbers of the vessel left intact. . . ."

Westfield (ii) herself survived, although damage was estimated to be $30,000 – perhaps half the cost of a similar new vessel in 1871. She was re-built by the railroad and continued to serve through municipal take-over of the Whitehall Street–Saint George service in 1905.

As to official findings: the Steamboat Inspection Service laid responsibility for the mishap on two individuals. First to be cited was Henry Robinson, the chief engineer on *Westfield* (ii), ". . . who was acting without a license, not duly appreciating his responsibility, and being ignorant of many of his duties, became reckless in their discharge, and was in constant habit of carrying steam

greatly in excess of the pressure allowed by the certificate." Also held to be at fault was Superintendent Braisted of the ferry company who ". . . employed an ignorant and careless person to fill the position of engineer on his ferryboat, and permitted him to openly violate the requirements of the steamboat laws."[17]

THE POST–CIVIL WAR ERA, for purposes of this narrative, comes to an end at the turn of the century and will lead, presently, to a time that will witness the emergence of a new concept not merely in the world of ferryboating but of urban mobility itself:

public ownership and operation of a transport service. The final piece to the 1865–1900 chapter, though, sets the stage for this development. It is the consolidation of previously separate jurisdictions into today's five-borough City of New York.

Following earlier legislative efforts, the question of amalgamation made its way onto the ballot for a popular referendum in 1894 across all the territory proposed for inclusion in what was commonly called, at the time, Greater New York. It was, to be sure, a serious and even an emotional issue, but it was neither the dominant nor the only judgment

---

17. *Proceedings of the Twentieth Annual Meeting of the Board of Supervising Inspectors of Steam-Vessels* (Washington: Government Printing Office, 1872), p. 53. The same report also said this: ". . . the primary cause of the explosion was a defective sheet located on the lower side of the boiler, near forward end, but in such a position as not to be seen by any internal examination or developed by the usual hydrostatic test. Constant use during nine years increased this defect and consequently materially weakened the boiler, rendering it unable to sustain

the excessive pressure to which it was frequently exposed. The amount of pressure allowed for this boiler was twenty-five pounds, but it was an ordinary practice for the engineer to carry an excess of from two to five pounds, and his gauge, only a few moments before the explosion, indicated a pressure of twenty-seven pounds, and it is probable, from the appearance of the boiler after the accident, that at the time of the explosion the steam may have been raised to thirty-five pounds" (pp. 52–53).

voters were being called upon to make on Tuesday, November 6, 1894. New York City residents were electing a mayor, and statewide the governor's race was being decided. Amalgamation carried, but by a very close margin. In the wards of New York City the tally in favor of forming a new metropolis was 63,641 to 62,240 – a mere 1401 votes! In Brooklyn it was just as close, but the drama was higher because it took longer to count the votes. Results were in from all the other jurisdictions and amalgamation had passed in all of them; but as late as Thursday, November 8, newspapers were reporting that the outcome was very much in doubt. Unanimity was required among all the jurisdictions, but negative ballots were still outnumbering affirmative ones in Brooklyn. When all the votes were finally counted, however, Brooklyn had joined the others in saying "yes," and Greater New York began its final (albeit four-year-long) journey to reality. Good-bye City of Brooklyn and good-bye bucolic Staten Island down the bay; hello Borough of Brooklyn and Borough of Richmond, soon to be compo-

nents of a five-borough City of New York.[18]

Next, a charter had to be prepared for the new municipality, and the task fell to a wonderfully large commission with lots and lots of committees and subcommittees. Hearings were held, options explored, drafts prepared, revisions made. At one point it was suggested that the new muncipal entity be divided into *nine* boroughs! Eventually a product was ready for submission to the state legislature for final ratification. It passed the General Assembly (New York State's lower house) on March 23, 1897, by a vote of 118 to 28; it cleared the Senate 39 to 9, two days later; and at 9 o'clock in the morning on Wednesday, May 5, 1897, Governor Frank S. Black signed the measure into law. "It is

---

18. Some population figures at the time of amalgamation: Manhattan, 1,825,000; The Bronx, 135,000; Brooklyn, 1,133,000; Queens, 150,000; Richmond, 70,000; total, 3,313,000. Greater New York thus became the world's second largest city, behind London and its population of 5,600,000 and ahead of Paris and its 2,444,000 residents.

probable that no question ever received so much legislative and executive consideration before its culmination as the creation of this city," editorialized *The New York Times*.

On November 2, 1897, voters within the boundaries of the soon-to-be-created new city elected their first mayor. He was Robert Van Wyck, a Tammany Hall Democrat. He defeated Seth Low, who ran under the banner, not of a national political party, but of something called Citizens Union. Low, a major force behind amalgamation, a former mayor of the City of Brooklyn, and later the president of Columbia University, was a Republican by choice and conviction. But as would often prove necessary in the new New York with an overwhelmingly Democratic electorate, he ran on a "fusion ticket," an ad hoc coalition put together across party lines to challenge the Democrats.[19] (Low

---

19. Low's fusion candidacy failed to stop the Republicans from nominating their own candidate whose 125,000 votes clearly did Low little good in his 233,450 to 146,142 loss to Van Wyck.

persevered, though, and in 1901, four years later, a subsequent fusion candidacy of his was successful.)

So, with a charter approved as the new city's instrument of governance, and a mayor elected to serve as its chief executive, it was time to launch the ship – and to celebrate a little, too. Conveniently, the new municipal entity was to begin its formal existence with the start of the new year, 1898. One celebration could mark both milestones.

Some New York newspapers paid scant attention to the merriment, though, since it was sponsored by one of their rivals, *The New York Journal*. In addition to

---

Low's inability to keep the G.O.P. from running a candidate against his fusion ticket can be traced to his strongly-held view that national partisan issues are out of place in municipal government. As mayor of Brooklyn – "all the people of Brooklyn," as he put it – he refused to work in support of James G. Blaine's presidential campaign against Democrat Grover Cleveland in 1884. Elephants, it would seem, do indeed have long memories.

the expected fireworks, music, and torchlight parades, at precisely the first stroke of midnight in New York, three thousand miles away the mayor of San Francisco pushed a button and sent a telegraph signal eastward, which flipped a relay and started an electric motor that hoisted the new flag of the new city to the top of a mast in City Hall Plaza. Artillery pieces manned by the New York National Guard let out a 100-gun salute from the grounds of the Post Office at Park Row and Broadway, and a choir of "3000 trained voices" added a gallant touch to the midnight extravaganza. Searchlights swept the grounds from the tops of buildings – ". . . the tall buildings, ten, twelve, fifteen and eighteen stories," in the words of one awe-struck reporter. The U.S. Army was unwilling to fire its cannons in the middle of the night for some reason of long-standing policy having to do with not wanting to alarm a sleeping citizenry to non-existent perils; but with the first light of dawn came another 100-gun salute from the battery on Governors Island, and at noon on New Year's Day, Mayor Van Wyck

was sworn in as the first chief executive of the newly amalgamated city.

Thus was contemporary New York City pieced together. At an indeterminate time years later, some guileless fool decided that the entity whose political advent was so enthusiastically welcomed that cold and rainy New Year's Eve can somehow be appropriately symbolized by, of all things, an apple: a big one, though; not a small one.

What impacts will be seen on the ferryboat story as a result of this landmark action? One point is that equity will prevail with respect to matters such as New York City claiming Brooklyn real estate below the limit of high tide; the borough boundaries were established at mid-river. While this may be more symbolic than anything else, it draws attention to the fact that the lease-granting instrumentality will now be a government representing citizens on both ends of a ferry service, something not previously the case.

The political re-alignment that amalgamation sought, and after a fashion brought about, will have another important effect on ferry-boating. One of the major goals that Republicans were after in pressing for the creation of Greater New York in the first place was breaking the hold of the established Democratic Party in New York City – that is to say, Tammany Hall. While it is doubtful that the goal was achieved to the G.O.P.'s satisfaction, it will be during two important non-Tammany mayoral administrations, Seth Low's fusion government between 1902 and 1904 and the 1918–1926 term of Brooklyn Democrat John Hylan, that City Hall will sponsor several important ferryboat initiatives, the first of which being the direct take-over of the Whitehall Street–Saint George service in 1905. Absent amalgamation – or even given amalgamation but absent alternatives to Tammany rule of City Hall – it is difficult to imagine how these initiatives would have come to pass.

Before moving ahead to a discussion of the first decade of the twentieth century in chapter 6, hear the words of New York state senator Thomas C. Platt in summary description of the amalgamation of 1898:

"We are about to enter upon the greatest experiment in municipal government that has been undertaken in this country. We have performed a consolidation of interests quite comparable with the union of the thirteen Colonies. It insures to the people brought within its operation better and cheaper transportation, more comfortable homes, lower rents, vastly improved facilities for the transaction of their business, and the innumerable benefits that proceed from a simpler administration and a larger control of their affairs."

Senator Platt was *not* the man after whom the notorious Platt Amendment would be named in 1903; he was a local Republican politican who had worked hard for the passage of the five-borough amalgamation – through all the pulling and hauling needed to secure passage of so monumental a legislative triumph – and his characterization and prediction, while perhaps overly enthusiastic and certainly subject to some qualification, is probably more right than wrong.

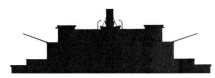

6. The Road to Municipal Operation

1900–1910

Perhaps this chapter should be entitled "the road to municipal operation *and* the demise of the first major New York ferryboat network." Both are significant developments from the first decade of the twentieth century. In 1905 the city government will take over one of the harbor's major routes and turn it into a municipally-run public service. (And in 1906 will take over a second!) But in 1908 the Williamsburg ferry system will collapse in the face of competition from bridges and rapid transit tunnels and will abandon outright its important five-route system across the East River.

About the onset of municipal operation in 1905 there is this ironic curiosity: the service that first left the private sector of risk and profit and became part of the public sector of subsidy and service was the one major operation in town that was least affected by competitive inroads from bridges, tunnels, and rapid transit – the Whitehall Street–Saint George service. Other ferryboat lines will later be "municipalized" when their corporate viability becomes threatened by virtue of a diversion of traffic to, say, the Manhattan Bridge or the Interborough subway. But Whitehall Street–Saint George was not of such a sort; its traffic was reasonably assured by the slow but steady growth of Staten Island's population and the new borough's apparently unbridgeable remove from the rest of the city to which it now belonged. One has to probe further to generate possible reasons for the extraordinary advent that *Manhattan*'s voyage down the bay represented on the overcast Thursday morning of October 25, 1905.

One matter that must not be overlooked is that Staten Islanders, dependent as they were on their ferryboats, were also rather convinced that the service they were being provided in the years leading up to 1905 by the Staten Island Rapid Transit Company was in many ways decidedly substandard, and more likely outright dangerous. Those who were inclined to be of such a mind had their opinions dramatically confirmed on the afternoon of June 14, 1901. Clearly it does not stand as the most serious mishap ever to befall a New York ferryboat – the explosion aboard *Westfield* (ii) in July 1871 was far worse. But what happened to S.I.R.T.'s ferryboat *Northfield* on that day may well have led to more significant

Reliance, *New York & Engelwood Ferry Company, 1921–1979*

The ill-fated Northfield *of the Staten Island Rapid Transit Company.* [*Staten Island Historical Society*]

long-term changes in New York ferryboat history than any other tragedy. Ironically, both *Westfield* (ii) and *Northfield* were sister ships, having been turned out by Jeremiah Simonson's yard in Brooklyn in 1862 and 1863, respectively. Each was a double-deck 202-foot wooden-hull sidewheeler powered by a 700-h.p. vertical-beam engine. Each had a tall, thin, black smokestack and a fully-exposed walking beam atop the hurricane deck.

By late afternoon on Friday, June 14, 1901, the temperature in New York was holding in the mid-seventies, there were fresh variable winds from the south-west – that would prove to be important! – and, while the skies were cloudy and showers were forecast for later in the evening, there was no problem with visi-bility off the southern tip of Man-hattan where *Northfield* was se-cured to one of the company's two Whitehall Street slips – the slip closer to the Battery, slip Number One, and that would also prove to be important. She was loading passengers for a scheduled 6 o'clock sailing for Saint George, a trip that routinely carried more pas-sengers than any other daily de-parture. This day was no exception; an estimated 800 or more Staten Islanders were heading home after a day's work in Manhattan. Twelve horse-and-wagon teams were also aboard, secured in the gangways in the center of the vessel's main deck.

Captain Abraham Johnson was in the forward wheelhouse of the 38-year-old *Northfield*, and when departure time came and he was assured that loading was finished at the other end of the vessel, he signaled the lines be let loose and sounded several loud gongs in the vessel's engine room for power ahead. As a matter of fact, it wasn't until 6:02 P.M. that *Northfield* began to pull out of her slip for the scheduled six o'clock trip, but this was neither an intolerable nor even a significant delay. It would, however, prove to be fatally costly, for what was about to happen wouldn't have happened had she left her slip a minute earlier. Or a minute later!

Slowly the ferry's single-cylinder walking-beam engine began to transmit energy to the two paddlewheels; Saint George was a halfhour or so away, a trip the aging *Northfield* had made thousands of times before. But this day something tragic would keep the vessel from ever reaching Staten Island.

Unaware of what was about to happen, passengers began to settle in for the 30-minute ride. Most were on the upper deck. While *Northfield* had conventional passenger cabins on her main deck, they were enclosed and mid-June made the upper deck and the option of an outdoor seat along the promenade a more appealing alternative. It also got one farther removed from the horses, and that was always desirable. Many passengers unfolded evening newspapers to catch up on world, national, and local developments. A major scandal in Philadelphia filled the front pages; it involved questionable tactics by that city's mayor in the award of certain franchise rights for the operation of city streetcars. The nation of Cuba was also a topic of concern on June 14, 1901, with strong doubts being expressed by some members of the McKinley Administration that the island's native people, in the wake of the Spanish-American War and the demise of colonial government, were capable of self-governance. The impact of yet another war was also in the news;

Great Britain was considering placing a ten-per-cent tax on the profits generated by mines in South Africa to help finance its fight there against the Boers. And for those who were able to get the very latest editions of their favorite afternoon papers with wire dispatches from the middle west there was this baseball news: the New York Giants moved back into first place in the National League on June 14 when they beat Chicago 4 to 1, despite a triple play turned in by the men from the Windy City. (It was not an omen of eventual success, though. The team finished the 1901 season in seventh place, 37 games behind the pennant-winning Pittsburghs.) Some Staten Islanders followed the fortunes of New York's other baseball team, the crazy one from Brooklyn: they hadn't fared too well on June 14. They were soundly beaten in Saint Louis by a score of 10 to 2. (But they finished the season in third place.) And what of New York's American League entrant, the team later to be called the Yankees? Well, they didn't exist yet. The summer of 1901 was only the first season for the brand-new American League, and the "junior

Front page of Northfield's *final certificate of permanent enrollment.* [*National Archives*]

circuit" wouldn't field a team in New York until 1903.

Flood tide (i.e., high tide) at Governor's Island was at exactly six o'clock that evening, and pilot tables to this day describe the complex way currents swirl around the Whitehall Street ferry slip where the Upper Bay, Buttermilk Channel, and the East River join and react to the tide's rise and fall. On this trip, Captain Johnson had determined that he would bring his vessel straight out from the slip toward the Brooklyn waterfront for several hundred feet before turning to starboard and the bay. His reason was that strong close-in tidal currents could easily endanger *Northfield* by driving her back toward the Manhattan shore were he to bring his vessel around too quickly. He wanted plenty of open water to starboard before turning, in other words – a normal practice under the given tide conditions coupled with the fact that there were fresh breezes coming across the bay from the southwest.

As paddlewheel *Northfield* was making her way out of the White-hall Street slip, another ferryboat appeared on the scene. She was

the Central Railroad of New Jersey's steel-hull *Mauch Chunk*, one of two propeller boats the railroad had purchased in 1892 as it began to re-orient its ferryboat fleet around the design pioneered by Hoboken Ferry's *Bergen* in 1888. Jersey Central's principal route – then and for as long as the railroad operated ferryboats – was the Liberty Street–Communipaw service connecting the railroad's passenger terminal in Jersey City with lower Manhattan's Hudson River waterfront. But since 1897, because of corporate links between the Staten Island Rapid Transit and the Baltimore and Ohio R.R., on the one hand, and the B. & O. and the Jersey Central, on the other, a number of daily ferry trips were also run between S.I.R.T.'s Whitehall Street terminal and Communipaw, thus making the busy South Ferry complex accessible to rail passengers on both the Jersey Central and the Baltimore and Ohio, whose New York–bound passenger trains terminated in the Jersey Central depot (a relationship touched upon in chapter 5). South Ferry was an advantageous Manhattan landfall for railroad passengers, as the place was an intense focus of street-car and elevated-train activity. In addition, the Whitehall Street ferry slips provided opportunities for still further connecting services for the railroad patrons – to Staten Island and to several places in Brooklyn.[1]

Staten Islanders, for their part, resented what they felt was an intrusion by the Jersey Central Railroad into "their" terminal. Indeed, they felt their opposition had a legal basis to it and continually argued that C.N.J. was operating into Whitehall Street without having received a proper lease from the city government for doing so.

But proper ferry lease or no, *Mauch Chunk* was nearing Whitehall Street from Jersey City at 6 o'clock in the evening of June 14, 1901, just as *Northfield* was leaving for Staten Island. Unlike the crowded conditions on the Saint George–bound vessel, *Mauch Chunk* was virtually empty. Captain Sylvester C. Griffin was in the wheelhouse of the C.N.J. boat.

Griffin was obviously taken by surprise at Johnson's decision to swing *Northfield* wide, and even after he saw the vessel getting under way he must have felt he could pass the Staten Island boat to his port, assuming a sharper turn by *Northfield*. But *Northfield* didn't come about as Griffin had expected she would, *Mauch Chunk* was moving along at a good speed, and before either vessel could do anything to avoid its happening, they collided, the steel-hulled *Mauch Chunk* driving its bow into the wooden hull of *Northfield* forward of the starboard paddlewheel and under the guard. When *Northfield* was later hauled out and examined, *Mauch Chunk*'s print was a T-shaped hole ten feet high and 20 feet across at the top.[2]

Fortunately, there were two full deck crews aboard *Northfield*, and death and injury were held low by their swift actions. But the Staten Island–bound vessel was instantly disabled and the sharp pre-collision whistle exchanges between the two ferryboats now reached crescendo proportions as nearby vessels attempted to signal shoreside authorities, in pre-radio days, that rescue forces were needed.

Northfield quickly started down by her Staten Island end as water poured into her hull, a hull lacking any real subdivision into water-tight compartments. Water was over the main deck in a matter of minutes, and the same tidal currents that prompted Captain Johnson to leave the slip as he did now caught the disabled ferryboat and began to carry her up the East River. The ocean tug *Unity*, owned by the Chapman Derrick and Wrecking Company, was the first to reach *Northfield* and

---

1. Jersey Central ferry schedules put into effect on July 19, 1897, when the Whitehall St.–Communipaw service began, called for 36 round trips on weekdays, 33 on Sunday, and no service between midnight and dawn. This was only about 25% of the service the railroad operated on its principal route, Liberty St.–Communipaw.

2. This account of the accident incorporates some conclusions and assumptions on my part. Testimony at two subsequent hearings will find Griffin saying that the accident happened

with *Northfield* barely, and perhaps not even totally, out of her Whitehall Street slip. Both captains, however, spoke of extensive whistle exchanges that took place between the time

quickly began to nudge her toward the Manhattan shore. Nine other tugs, plus the *Atlantic* of the Union Ferry Company, maneu-vered to help, but in a very few minutes *Unity* – and the tide – had managed to get *Northfield* into the space between piers 9 and 10 on the Manhattan side of the East River and there, a half-mile and ten minutes removed from the collision, *Northfield* sank.[3] The site

---

Northfield began to move and the moment of impact. I am assuming, therefore, that Griffin was wrong and that the point of collision was several boat lengths out from the slip, and on the basis of this I am speculating about Griffin's intentions. Excerpts from statements prepared by each captain and transmitted to the U.S. Steamboat Inspection Service follow; these statements were likely prepared in consultation with legal counsel from the respective railroads.

GRIFFIN: New York, June 14, 1901. "Making for the Whitehall street ferry slip with the ferry-boat Mauch Chunk, within one and a half lengths off Whitehall street ferry slip, at 6:03 P.M., I noticed the ferry-boat Northfield, of the Staten Island Rapid Transit Company, had started to come out of her New York slip, foot of Whitehall Street, with the wheelsman at the wheel in the head end pilot-house.

"The wheelsman blew me two whistles and continued on coming out, headed directly for my slip. I then rang two bells to stop my engine, two bells to back, and single bell to back full speed astern, then blew an alarm whistle five different times to Northfield as a danger signal.

"The Northfield continued coming out of her slip. The tide was running strong flood. When she was three-quarters of her own length out in the stream and headed across the mouth of my slip it was just a half minute from the time she started. We came in collision."

JOHNSON: New York, June 15, 1901. "Concerning the sinking of the ferry-boat Northfield, I beg to report as follows:

"We left New York for St. George, Staten Island, at 6 P.M., June 14, 1901. The tide was flood and there was a light breeze blowing from the southwest.

"Started my boat at one bell and blew the alarm whistle as the lines were cast off. [*Not a signal of impending danger; merely a normal practice when leaving the slip.*] I saw the Mauch Chunk coming around the Battery.

"The quartermaster blew two whistles to the Mauch Chunk, and the Mauch Chunk responded with two whistles. The quartermaster then hooked up the boat and rang the jingle bell.

"As the Mauch Chunk was still coming ahead, I blew two more whistles and then the alarm whistle. She still continued her course and struck our boat forward of the starboard wheelhouse."

Johnson's talk of "hooking up the boat" refers to the peculiar way in which vertical-beam engines had to be started. See chapter 2 for more details, but "hooking up" – or "dropping the hooks" – meant shifting the engine from what might be called manual feeding of steam into the cylinder by the engineer to automatic feed. After his boat had gotten under way, Johnson still felt his course was proper, and he gave a signal to the engine room to "drop the hooks" and continue *Northfield*'s passage to Staten Island. This is clearly not consistent with Griffin's testimony that the accident happened at the very mouth of the ferry slip. However I readily admit I am making assumptions and drawing conclusions in this matter.

of her foundering is just below today's South Street Seaport. (See map, page 155.)

Passengers, all 800 or so of them, scrambled off the fatally-stricken ferryboat and onto Pier 10, the *Unity*, and several other tugs. The city's big fireboat *The New Yorker* was quickly on the scene from her berth at the Battery, and if every tragedy produces its hero, the mantle this day was to fall on Manuel Fernandez, a watchman on Pier 10. (The quay was largely empty, having been used by the Spanish Line until the start of the recent war.) Fernandez hauled a woman out of the water and gave her to people aboard *Unity*, took a small child from a woman on *Northfield*'s hurricane deck and jumped himself to the *Unity* with his precious cargo, and later dived into the East

River to save a slightly older child.

Captain Johnson supervised the evacuation of his stricken charge; he didn't leave *Northfield* until water was lapping into the ferry's forward wheelhouse. At this point his vessel was resting on the muddy river bottom. She had sunk, in other words.

As late as one o'clock the next morning, the New York City Police Department was insisting there were no fatalities in the *Northfield* accident. But they were wrong. Five people died in the tragedy, some only discovered when the 38-year-old vessel was inspected the next day by divers. Others drowned and were carried away from the site by the area's swift currents; one man's body drifted ashore a week later across New York Bay at Greenville, N.J., for instance. But if the human death toll was relatively low, the same cannot be said for the twelve teams of horses harnessed to heavy wagons in the twin gangways of the ferryboat: they all perished.

Salvage, of course, became the S.I.R.T.'s next problem. The same Chapman Derrick and Wrecking Company whose tug *Unity* was

the first to come to the *Northfield*'s aid was retained. The next day their divers were inspecting the sunken ferryboat and they assigned two floating derricks to the job of raising *Northfield*. One was the new *Monarch*, claimed to be the largest such in the world; the second was a veteran of the unsuccessful effort to raise the U.S.S. *Maine* from the bottom of Havana Harbor two years earlier. But a 600-gross-ton wooden ferryboat hardly posed the same challenge as a battleship with a displacement of 6682 tons, and a week later *Northfield* was sitting in a Brooklyn dry dock. Not only was her hull cut open from keel to deck level by the force of *Mauch Chunk*'s blow, but her all-wood upper works were also badly collapsed from tidal action while she was partly submerged in the East River. Rehabilitation was out of the question.

Johnson, in a state of shock, was arrested Friday night. The New York police couldn't locate Griffin, but the Jersey Central produced him the next day as officialdom began its search for the causes of the episode.

"The whole fleet of so-called fer-

---

3. According to the next day's *New York Times* these were the ten tugboats: *J. Jewett, Shohola, Unity, Baltimore, Pusey, Arrow, President, Emperor, Lehigh Valley Tug No. 14,* and *Catasaqua. The New York World* also mentioned the tug *Mutual* as playing an important role.

Eighty-two years after municipal ferryboat service was inaugurated between Manhattan and Staten Island, the operation is alive and well as one of the large vessels of the Barberi *class waits to begin a trip down the bay. The waters off Whitehall St. no longer see as much commercial traffic as they once did, and pleasure craft will now often venture into the area. It's very doubtful, though, if the folks aboard the sailboat realize they are in the precise spot where* Mauch Chunk *collided with* Northfield *on a day in June 1901!* [author]

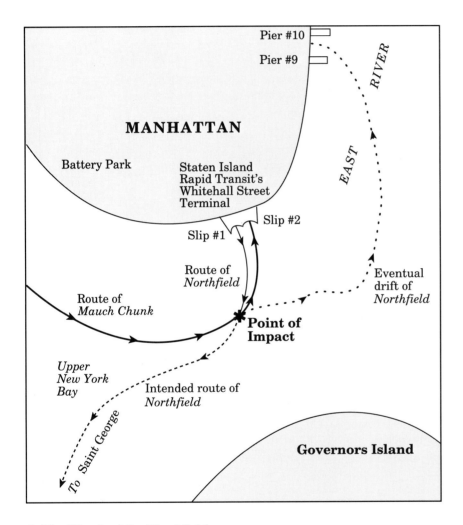

Pier #10

Pier #9

EAST RIVER

MANHATTAN

Battery Park

Staten Island
Rapid Transit's
Whitehall Street
Terminal

Slip #2

Slip #1

Route of
Northfield

Route of
Mauch Chunk

Eventual
drift of
Northfield

**Point of
Impact**

*Upper
New York
Bay*

Intended route of
Northfield

To Saint George

Governors Island

6. The Wreck of the *Northfield*

ryboats is not fit to haul garbage in," complained one veteran Staten Island commuter on the day after the crash. He was attending the arraignment of both ferryboat captains in the Tombs Police Court before Magistrate Crane. While the legal proceedings were attempting to deal with technical matters such as "rules of the road" and vessel right-of-way, the reaction of ordinary citizens spoke to the general condition of S.I.R.T.'s ferryboat fleet. "The company refuses to give us decent boats," another man claimed, nor was there any sense in which such opinions could be said to have begun with the *Northfield–Mauch Chunk* accident. In 1899 a committee of the Staten Island Chamber of Commerce declared that "Middletown, Westfield and Northfield are in no manner, and by no means adequate for the service for which they are intended, being too small, poorly ventilated and at times ill-smelling. The sanitary arrangements on these boats are abominable."

An interesting reaction to the accident was to be found in the Letters-to-the-Editor column of *The New York Times* on Sunday, June 16, two days after it happened. A man suggested that the crash might very well have been avoided had Jersey Central boats been assigned by the S.I.R.T. only to the slip closer to the Battery, slip Number One, thus precluding the Staten Island boats from having to cross their path, as they would be the exclusive users of slip Number Two, and users of slip Number One only in the absence of C.N.J. traffic.

Both ferryboat captains were declared free of criminal blame at a later coroner's inquest, Johnson totally so while Griffin was "censured" for navigating his vessel too fast. Griffin was also faulted for heading his ferryboat directly into its Whitehall Street slip after the accident and not attempting to assist the stricken *Northfield*. (After landing his few passengers he took *Mauch Chunk* immediately back to Jersey City, thus putting himself beyond the immediate reach of the New York police.) Professionally, the two men were not quite so fortunate as they were before the bar of justice; on July 24, 1901, the U.S. Government's Steamboat Inspection Service imposed a 30-day suspension of each man's operating license.

Interestingly, though, the Steamboat Inspection Service was far more forgiving of *Northfield*'s age, per se, as a contributing factor in the whole episode than were most New York commentators. In the agency's annual report for the year 1901 it was suggested that the ferryboat sank because her hull was not subdivided into watertight compartments, and that a similar vessel of any age would likely have suffered a similar fate. (Of course a newer vessel, just because it *was* newer, would have been far more likely to have had watertight compartments, and so the technical point made by the Federal agency, while correct, failed to lessen the outrage that was growing over the fact that the S.I.R.T. should have replaced its Civil War–era ferryboats a long time before.)

Another reaction to the crash was concern over the quantity as well as the accessibility of life jackets – there had been some criticism that passengers couldn't easily reach *Northfield*'s, and she was equipped with only 318 of them in any event, although such a complement was in and of itself quite lawful. (*Northfield*'s previous Federal inspection on July 3, 1900, cited this number of life jackets as being aboard quite matter-of-factly.) The New York City Police Department undertook a rapid inspection of other ferryboats, but they were unsure what standards they were seeking to enforce; the campaign quickly died down. The S.I.R.T., for that matter, even questioned the police department's right to conduct such inspections.

But the overall point is this: the Whitehall Street–Saint George ferry, and its 1901 lessee the Staten Island Rapid Transit Company, had suffered a major tragedy, and the antiquated condition of the 38-year-old *Northfield* furthered a frame of mind in New York that major changes were needed. The trade journal *Marine Engineering* reported on the accident in its August 1901 issue with this observation: "The *Northfield* is a very old boat and should have been condemned long ago," and a month later when *Northfield*'s sister ship *Westfield* had a minor and otherwise inconsequential brush with the Starin Line's steamer *Howard Carroll* off the Whitehall Street slip under much the same conditions as the *Northfield–Mauch Chunk* accident, *The New York Times* called the railway's wooden ferryboat the "... most anti-

quated boat in the harbor."

Northfield never returned to service. She was removed from the official rolls on October 29, 1902, and in the space on her final Certificate of Enrollment where the cause for her removal is cited are to be found these words, written in pen and ink and with a firm hand: "Broken up." The S.I.R.T. fleet was thus reduced to five boats.[4]

On June 22, 1901, eight days after the accident, the S.I.R.T. leased the Williamsburg ferry company's new steel-hull paddlewheeler *John Englis* to fill in for *Northfield*. How long *John Englis* stayed on the Whitehall Street–Saint George run is not clear.[5] But what *is* perfectly clear is that the company had little reason to consider serious investment in any new vessels of its own. Its lease was scheduled to expire in early

1904, and, with so brief a period of potential return from a major investment, the S.I.R.T.'s inaction is quite understandable.

So *Northfield* never sailed again. *Mauch Chunk* went on to a rather unusual career. When built by the Jersey Central in 1893 she was one of the railroad's first two steel-hull and propeller-driven boats, but her 145-foot length soon proved too small for the demanding Liberty Street–Communipaw service. Thus when newer 200-foot ferryboats began to join the Jersey Central fleet she and her 1893 sister ship *Easton* were sold. *Easton* became *Leonia* and worked the West 125 Street–Edgewater service across the Hudson River until after the Second World War when she again migrated north along the Hudson River and finished her days working the Yonkers–Alpine, N.J., ferry. *Mauch Chunk*'s sec-

---

4. The five being *Westfield* (ii); *Middletown*; *Southfield* (ii); *Robert Garrett*; *Castleton*, (a) *Erastus Wiman*.
5. This much is known: *John Englis*, together with her sister ship *Harry B. Hollins*, inaugurated a new service for the Williamsburg company on December 2, 1901, between the foot of Broadway, in Brooklyn, and East 42

Street, in Manhattan. Thus her lease to the S.I.R.T. did not exceed six months. At some point prior to municipal take-over in 1905, two vessels of the Hoboken Ferry Company, *Moonachie* and *Netherlands*, were leased to S.I.R.T. for Whitehall St.–St. George service.

ond owner was the Philadelphia and Reading R.R., and, bearing the name *Margate*, she ran between Camden, N.J., and Philadelphia. Around 1930 she returned to New York and worked briefly on a short-lived ferryboat service that linked Long Island City with the foot of Manhattan's East 34 Street.[6] For this final phase of her career she was *Mount Hood*; the 1936 edition of *Merchant Vessels of the United States* lists her as abandoned. But despite all her ramblings, *Mauch Chunk, b) Margate, c) Mount Hood* played her most critical role in the New York ferryboat story at a few minutes after six o'clock in the evening of Friday, June 14, 1901.

And so, triggered to one degree or another by the accident, an important sequence of events began to unfold in New York that would culminate with *Manhattan*'s inau-

gural trip under municipal auspices on October 25, 1905.

The S.I.R.T.'s seven-year lease to operate the ferry service was due to expire on May 1, 1904, and attention quickly began to focus on what kind of changes should be incorporated in any renewal. Staten Islanders, now part of the municipal entity that would award the new contract, were determined to have a say in the whole process. The old style of business – with a New York City of which Staten Island was not a part making all the calls and paying little apparent regard to the needs of the outlanders across the water whose citizenship was in alien municipalities – why, this approach was out. Staten Islanders were now just as much "New Yorkers" as residents of Manhattan.

On February 21, 1902, a delegation of 200 people from the island led by the borough's Chamber of Commerce journeyed to Manhattan and met with the city's commissioner of the Department of Docks and Ferries, MacDougal Hawkes, in the latter's office on Pier A. The subject of the meeting was the Whitehall Street–Saint George ferry service, Hawkes' de-

partment having jurisdiction over the award of ferry leases and the enforcement of their terms.

The group demanded newer, safer, and faster boats; they felt that a long-term lease of twenty-five years or so would be better than the shorter leases then the practice and encourage investment in new vessels; they wanted only Staten Island boats to use the S.I.R.T.'s Whitehall Street slips – no more C.N.J. service, in other words – and they even felt that it would be a better idea if the city itself, and not the ferry company, owned the various shoreside terminals. But above all, they voiced their general dissatisfaction with the B. & O.–owned S.I.R.T.

"The rapid transit company has Richmond by the throat," claimed one of the delegation's leaders, a real estate man who was then serving as secretary to the Chamber of Commerce and whose Dutch-origin surname was a trifle difficult to pronounce. Forty-nine years and one month after the meeting, on March 21, 1951, later generations of Staten Islanders were afforded ample opportunity to stumble again over the man's name. That's the day the City of New

---

6. Known as the East 34 Street Vehicular Ferry, the service operated from 1927 until 1936 and used shore facilities, at least on the Manhattan side, that were abandoned when the Long Island R.R. discontinued its East River ferryboats in 1925. See chapter 8 for further details.

York put a new 2285-ton ferryboat in service that was named in his honor – the *Cornelius G. Kolff*.

But before '*Kolff* the ferryboat would carry the municipal flag over and back across New York Bay, Kolff the civic activist would see, and participate in, considerable discussions and negotiations between the New York City government, the Staten Island Rapid Transit, other potential ferry lease-holders, and Staten Island representatives.[7] Some of it was serious and substantive, most of it had considerable political overtone, but every now and again there was the puffy stuff that in later years would be called, simply, a photo opportunity.

One such took place in the summer of 1902 as the debate was raging. A man by the name of H. H. Rogers invited a group of New York reporters and city officials to take a ride on his steam-powered yacht, the *Kanawha*. But it was to be no ordinary pleasure cruise around the bay. Rogers felt he had a point to make.

The guests boarded *Kanawha* at Pier A in mid-morning on July 6 and Rogers ordered *Kanawha* to sail around the Battery and maneuver, stern first, into one of the Whitehall Street ferry slips. Then, as a stop watch was started, *Kanawha* was off – off for Saint George where, 13 minutes later, she was brought to a halt inside one of the ferry slips, suggesting to anyone willing to draw such a conclusion that Mr. Rogers appeared to have the wherewithal to reduce ferryboat running times.

From a technical perspective the stunt proved nothing, of course, since a racing yacht *vs.* a ferryboat is hardly a fair fight.[8] But it

did call attention to H. H. Rogers and his apparent concern over improving the lot of Staten Island–bound ferryboat passengers. For Rogers was associated with a group who owned and operated a streetcar network on Staten Island, a company affiliated with Standard Oil of New Jersey, and a company that soon began to challenge the S.I.R.T. for the next contract to operate the ferry service to Manhattan.

Through the rest of 1902 and early 1903 rival proposals began to firm up, one from the S.I.R.T. and one from the Rogers group. An important meeting was held in Hawkes' Pier A office on November 11, 1902, and the outlines of the rival proposals were presented. "It is my purpose to give the people of Staten Island the best transit facilities possible, regardless of the people interested in furnishing them," said Hawkes.[9]

The Standard Oil plan called for sailings every 15 minutes during most of the day, a 20-minute run-

7. When the ferryboat *Cornelius G. Kolff* entered service – and when Mr. Kolff passed away in early 1950 – there was considerable mention in the newspapers of his work in real estate, and his general civic activism. But there was no mention of the fact that the man had played a key role in the displacement of the S.I.R.T. by the city government as the operator of the Whitehall St.–St. George ferry service back in the century's first decade.

8. A case can be made that while mere humans quickly forgot about *Kana-wha*'s demonstration trip of July 6, 1902, New York ferryboats remembered the stunt, and held a grudge against Rogers' yacht for some time. On August 20, 1902, *Kanawha* was heading up the East River toward the

ning time, service all night long, and, for passengers willing to pay in advance for a multi-ride ticket, the equivalent of a three-cent fare. Perhaps the most interesting aspect of the ferry plan advanced by the trolley-car people involved the proposed Staten Island terminals. Saint George, Erastus Wiman's creation back in 1886, was the sole landing spot on the island for S.I.R.T. ferryboats. The trolley group had little interest in Saint George, though, largely because the geography of the place made it a difficult spot for trolley-car passengers to transfer to the ferryboats. S.I.R.T. trains, on the other hand, were quite handy for ferry passengers at Saint George.

Capitalizing on Staten Islanders' known desires to have island ferry landings at places besides Saint George, Rogers proposed no Saint George service at all, but rather dual terminals at Tompkinsville and West Brighton. Not surprisingly, at these spots Staten Island-bound passengers would find it more convenient to continue their travels inland aboard the trolley cars than aboard S.I.R.T. trains.

The S.I.R.T. plan, as presented during the November 11, 1902, meeting, called for retaining Saint George as the principal terminal, but held out some possibility of supplementary service to other landings if traffic warranted. Specifically with respect to using Tompkinsville for a terminal, the S.I.R.T. people pointed out that the waters off Tompkinsville were a "man of war anchorage" and it certainly wouldn't be wise for the ferryboats to have to pick their way through the Atlantic Fleet when it was in port. On the matter of passenger fares, the S.I.R.T. failed to match the trolley proposal of a 3-cent fare and suggested retaining the existing straight nickel tariff, but said that it would certainly be willing to invest in some new vessels, given a sufficiently long contract. The S.I.R.T. representatives were at a decided disadvantage at the meeting in Commissioner Hawkes' office that day. They found themselves largely defending their own past performance, while Rogers' people were saddled with no such disadvantage and were able to talk only about the glowing future they planned to bring to Staten Island.

"This beautiful spot, the prettiest within a hundred miles of New York, is paralyzed because the B. & O. is not progressive and does not consider the interests of the people," said Edward Lauterbach, an attorney representing Rogers. *The New York Times* said that Lauterbach ". . . aroused the crowd to a high pitch of enthusiasm."

In the months after the November 1902 meeting the two pro-

---

foot of East 23 Street, carrying Rogers to work from his Staten Island home. Just north of the then a-building Williamsburg Bridge the Long Island R.R.'s *Rockaway* engaged her in a minor collision – no injuries, no significant property damage, but a point made. Four years later on July 11, 1906, *Kanawha* was steaming on the Hudson River near the New York Central's West 42 Street ferry slip when that line's *Newburgh* gave her another shove.

9. Pier A still stands. Listed on the National Register of Historic Places, it is the headquarters of the New York Fire Department's Marine Division and is the berth of Marine Company No. 1, currently the *John D. McKean*.

posals were debated – and, for that matter, each was altered to respond to the competition. Borough President George Cromwell of Staten Island had important conditions to lay down, among them being that Saint George must be retained as the principal ferry terminal, although this was not an endorsement of the S.I.R.T. proposal as such. A borough hall and a Carnegie-endowed library were planned for the site, but Cromwell did press for *additional* service to alternate locations.

In February 1903 Hawkes felt that his department had reached a decision, and he recommended to Mayor Seth Low "that the unanimous approval of the Commissioners of the Sinking Fund be given to the proposition made by the Staten Island Rapid Transit Railway Company, which is also guaranteed by the Baltimore & Ohio Railroad, and which is embodied in the terms of a proposed lease."

Staten Islanders erupted in anger. Hawkes made his recommendation to Low on February 21, and the matter came up for discussion at a meeting of the Sinking Fund Commission on February 25.

Kolff sounded off against the proposal before the commissioners, and a property owner from Staten Island by the name of Andrew Power said this of the S.I.R.T.: "Their boats are rotten and their train service is worse."

Hawkes' recommendation wasn't accepted, and again the two proposals were subjects for debate and discussion. But then something a little different happened.

The 126th session of the New York State Legislature convened in early 1903, and when the session adjourned, among its legacies was Chapter 624 of the Laws of 1903, "An Act to amend the Greater New York Charter, relative to the operation of ferries and the acquirement of property therefor." The act became law over the signature of Governor Benjamin B. Odell, Jr., on May 15, 1903, and what it provided was quite new. The city was now empowered to enter 25-year ferry leases, for one thing (it previously lacked this authority). But the city was also empowered by the new legislation to own and, if necessary, itself operate a ferry from Manhattan to Staten Island, as well as a route from Manhattan to the foot of 39

Street in Brooklyn. The latter was a lesser service out of Whitehall Street that had been initiated by the S.I.R.T. back in the early 1880s, but which by the turn of the century was being operated by the New York and South Brooklyn Ferry and Steam Transportation Company.[10] In any event, Mayor Low quickly announced that he would sign the appropriate affidavits and accept, as it were, the authority to take over the two services – a necessary condition of the enabling legislation.

With the passage of the new legislation, the possibility of an old-style ferry lease to a private operator – the S.I.R.T. or anyone else – quickly faded, and it was clear that *some* added municipal presence would eventuate when the whole business was finally settled, although full-scale municipal ferry operation was not necessarily a foregone conclusion. Mu-

10. The president of this South Brooklyn line was W. Bayard Cutting, a descendant of William Cutting, Robert Fulton's partner in the venture that saw *Nassau* inaugurate ferryboat service between Manhattan and Brooklyn in 1814.

nicipal ownership of terminals and boats, with private operation under contract, remained an option, and this was essentially the style of management being implemented on the city's then a-building new subway system.[11]

With such a possibility in mind, in early July 1903 the Sinking Fund Commission adopted Mayor Low's preliminary proposal to begin design work on a fleet of ferryboats for the Staten Island service; "only the minor question of operation of the service by the city itself, instead of leasing the property under definite terms, and rates, was left unsettled," as the *Times* noted.

Of course, full municipal operation was a near crusade with some people. Thundered Alderman John McCall of Manhattan: "You have the opportunity, Mr. Mayor, to make your administration memorable long after you and I are

gone. I am opposed to the part of the resolution you propose, which makes it possible to lease the ferry after it has been built and equipped by the city. The time is ripe for a municipal ownership of such a ferry." McCall was addressing the same meeting of the Sinking Fund Committee in July 1903.

But Low himself was hardly a William Randolph Hearst pressing for public operation at any cost, although as 1903 became 1904 the prospects for private operation began to dim. By the time 1905 dawned it was clear that the city would implement all aspects of the 1903 state legislation and operate the ferries as well as own them.[12]

Early 1904 saw final technical decisions reached on the matter of vessels for the Whitehall Street–Saint George service. To begin with, Staten Islanders had high expectations. They wanted big boats – 3000-or-more passenger capacity; and they wanted fast boats – 19 m.p.h. to ensure a 20-minute running time. But such vessels would be expensive, in the range of $375,000 each according to preliminary engineering specifications that the city had drawn up. Somewhat smaller and slower boats – 25-minute running time and a passenger capacity in the low 2000s – would cost but $275,000, and budget-conscious members of

---

11. The subway situation was a parallel to this extent: the city built and owned the tunnels and leased them to the Interborough Rapid Transit Company for operation. The Interborough, however, was required to provide its own rolling stock.

12. I have cast this chapter so the *Northfield–Mauch Chunk* accident serves as an introduction to the period when the public policy decision was made in New York to municipalize the Whitehall St.–St. George service. It's also worth noting that during the five-year period from 1900 through 1904 Jersey Central ferryboats were involved in *nine separate collisions* adjacent to the Whitehall Street ferry slips. To be sure, they were, for the most part, minor incidents that never

even rated mention in the newspapers. But nine incidents over five critical years may well have helped to create a frustration in City Hall that contributed to the eventual decision.

The nine were:

Feb. 5, 1900: 10:05 A.M. – *Mauch Chunk* collides off Whitehall Street with towing steamer *R. J. Moran*; slight damage; no injuries.

June 14, 1901 – *Mauch Chunk–Northfield.*

May 19, 1902: 9:58 A.M. – *Mauch*

the Board of Aldermen pushed for such an alternative. Staten Islanders would have none of it, of course, and expressed themselves with the kind of vigor they had been showing throughout the whole business. At a meeting of the Sinking Fund Commission held on Thursday, February 11, 1904, President Forbes of the Board of Aldermen argued on behalf of the slower boats, drawing angry roars from the largely Staten Island crowd in attendance. Four days later the Sinking Fund Commission authorized Dock Commissioner Maurice Featherson to go ahead with the larger vessels. Featherson had succeeded Hawkes

following the 1903 election, when the municipal administration of Mayor George McClellan replaced that of Seth Low.

The next month a curious thing happened. The Erie R.R. had just taken delivery of a new ferryboat, the *Arlington*. She was an example of the smaller, slower, and cheaper boat the city had decided *not* to buy for service to Staten Island, but she was also a perfect example of post-*Bergen* state-of-the-art in Hudson River railroad ferries. On Tuesday, March 15, *Arlington* was brought around to the Whitehall Street terminal and put through a series of tests – namely, trips from Whitehall Street

to both Saint George and the foot of 39 Street in South Brooklyn. It's possible – but unlikely – that this demonstration was staged to change some minds on the matter of what style of vessel to order for the Saint George service; bids had already been requested from shipyards for the larger boats. But when the city later opted to take over the Whitehall Street–39 Street/Brooklyn service as well, *Arlington*, with one major design alteration, became the kind of ferryboat ordered for the city's second route.

For its new fleet of ferryboats for the Whitehall Street–Saint George service, the city retained A. Cary Smith, a noted naval architect, to prepare plans and specifications. Based on Smith's design, bids were sought and on March 28, the sealed envelopes were opened in Commissioner Featherson's office. But the quotations that came in were all too high, and no contract was awarded. Instead, the Department of Docks re-advertised the vessel procurement and sought fresh bids. This time a different design was used, one that had been prepared by the New York firm of Millard and

---

Chunk collides off the Battery with towing steamer *Eli B. Conine* with car float in tow; no injuries.

Oct. 21, 1902 – *Mauch Chunk* hits towing steamer *R. S. Carter* off barge office; no injuries; tug seriously damaged.

June 10, 1902 – *Easton* and car float in tow of tug *Nannie Lamberton* in collision off Whitehall Street; slight damage; no injuries.

July 24, 1903: 6:30 P.M. – *Easton* and Union Ferry Company's *Pierre-*

pont collide off Whitehall Street; no injuries; slight damage.

Nov. 16, 1903: approx. 5:00 P.M. – *Mauch Chunk* and steamboat *Shinnecock* collide off Whitehall Street; slight damage; no injuries.

Jan. 28, 1904 – *Wilkes-Barre* collides off the Battery with the S.I.R.T.'s *Middletown*; slight damage; no injuries.

May 9, 1904 – *Easton* collides off the Battery with excursion steamer *Angler*; slight damage; no injuries.

When the City of New York took over the Whitehall St.–Saint George ferryboat line in 1905 and turned it into a municipally operated service, a fleet of five twin-stack ferryboats was designed and built, each named after one of the city's boroughs. Here is Brooklyn *with a large crowd of finely dressed people aboard, indicating, perhaps, some kind of special or charter trip. [Library of Congress]*

Maclean. On June 10, this second round of bids was opened; these proved more reasonable. After carefully reviewing the prices that were submitted by eight different shipyards, Featherson selected the Maryland Steel Company, and on June 20 the city entered a contract with that firm for five 250-foot double-deck ferryboats. Maryland didn't wind up building all five boats, though; they sub-contracted with the Burlee Dry Dock Company of Staten Island for one of them and built the other four at their facility in Sparrows Point, Maryland, just outside Baltimore.[13]

Bidders had been asked to submit two classes of quotes for other-wise similar ferryboats; "Class X" called for the installation of either Babcock and Wilcox or Niclausse boilers, while "Class Y" called for Mosher, Hoehstein, or Seabury boilers – all common equipment at the time. The contract signed with Maryland was for "Class X" at a total price of $1,709,000 – which worked out to an average of $341,800 per boat, although bids were submitted in a way that specified a price for a first boat, and then additional vessels beyond that. This was somewhat below earlier engineering estimates; and it was a good deal below the bids that had earlier been received on the design which A. Cary Smith had developed. The contract with the Maryland Steel Company was the largest single order for ferryboat construction up until that time.

(An interesting aside on the contract is this: today, with capital money for all kinds of mass transit facilities and equipment being supplied by government at all levels from Federal to local, it is common for such public funds to entail various kinds of "labor protection" as a condition of their acceptance. Equipment must be built in America, organized labor must agree that a project proposed for funding does not harm existing workers, and so forth. The City of New York's contract with Maryland Steel in 1904 included an early version of these now-common provisions: the ". . . boats are to be built in compliance with the labor laws of New York state, which provide for an eight-hour working day . . ." for shipyard employees, reported the September 1904 issue of *Marine Engineering*.)

Before the ink was dry on the contract for the construction of what became the Borough-class ferryboats, though, considerable fear was voiced over the vessels' safety. This was not because of any flaw that had been detected in the specifications drawn up by Millard and Maclean; rather it was because the day the contract was signed, June 20, 1904, was but four days after the excursion steamer *General Slocum* caught fire in the East River with a loss of *over a thousand lives*. The fears were understandable, but the Borough-class ferryboats represented the best and finest design of the time, and they served their owners well and safely for many, many years.

---

13. I have no direct evidence to advance in support of such a suggestion, but it is quite likely that Maryland Steel's subcontracting for the construction of one vessel with Burlee Dry Dock was brought about far more as a result of jaw-boning by the city government with its contractor than by purely business decisions reached in Baltimore. Over the years there will always be considerable political pressure to spend local tax dollars at local shipyards so local businesses – and local workers – may benefit from municipal expenditures.

Few vistas are as captivating as the Manhattan skyline receding behind a Staten Island–bound ferryboat out of Whitehall St. Long after the festive inaugural of municipal operation in 1905, and with the twin towers of the World Trade Center now dominating the downtown skyline, another boat load of people enjoy the experience. [author]

Even after the principal details of the municipal take-over had been worked out, there were problems. The S.I.R.T., for example, felt that it had some leverage all of a sudden and started talking about not continuing to operate the service at all after its lease expired in early 1904. The city was clearly in no position to take over the service before the Borough-class boats were ready, and the railway agreed to a short-term extension, June 1, 1904 through June 1, 1906, but subject to cancellation on 30-days' notice by the city – only, though, in exchange for a firm agreement by the city to purchase the S.I.R.T.'s interest in the two terminals, plus its five ferryboats, for a specified price.[14]

14. Ownership of the terminals was complicated, reflecting certain elements of municipal investment and other elements of investment by the private lease-holder, with even more complex terms for the buy-out of private assets in the event a lease is not extended. The short-term lease ex-

In early 1905 it was announced that the city also planned to "municipalize" its second ferry line, that linking Whitehall Street and the foot of 39 Street in Brooklyn, the authority to do so having been part of the same legislation that enabled the Whitehall Street–Saint George take-over. And then on April 8, 1905, it was time to celebrate a little and launch the four Maryland-built Borough-class ferryboats. What a mess that turned out to be!

A special train headed south that day with festive New York officials aboard, a delegation headed by Featherson and President Fornes of the Board of Aldermen. Their Maryland colleagues – which is to say, Democratic politicians from Baltimore and its environs – were on hand to meet their northern brethren, and at the shipyard the first vessel to be launched, *Man-hattan*, slid smoothly down the ways. She was sponsored by Anna Ahearn, the 16-year-old daughter of the Manhattan borough president, and the plan was to launch the other three vessels in turn. As it developed, though, only *Man-hattan* took to the water that day.

Frances Tierney, the daughter of Justice John M. Tierney of the Bronx, mounted a platform to christen a vessel named for her home borough. But try as shipyard workers would, even using battering rams, the *Bronx* wouldn't budge on her ways. She was stuck tight. That's when everybody moved over to *Brooklyn* on an adjacent way; Marion Brackenridge was her sponsor. But *Brooklyn* wouldn't budge, either. Except while everyone was paying attention to *Brooklyn*, *Bronx* started to slide down toward the water on her own and Miss Tierney, who had dutifully stayed at her post just in case, gave the vessel a ceremonial smash with the traditional bottle of champagne. But *Bronx* wasn't really cooperating! When she reached the water's edge she stalled again. *Queens*, which was to have been christened by Marie Lahondra, couldn't even have her launching attempted because she was built behind *Brooklyn* and required the latter to be launched and out of the way before she could take to the water. Or try to . . .

Nobody was terribly upset over it all; a banquet was served aboard *Manhattan*. "We have been having a spell of very warm weather here. The grease and tallow spread on the ways was put on with the idea that this weather would continue, or at least with no thought that cold weather would congeal it. It apparently did congeal," explained a slightly-but-not-terribly embar-

---

tension between the city and the S.I.R.T., which wasn't actually executed until January 1905 after the earlier lease had expired, specified these dollar values for the assets the city would take over: for the company's investments in the Whitehall Street facility the city would pay $125,000; for investments in the Saint George terminal, $75,000; for the *Garrett* and the *Castleton*, the two 1888 inclined-compound sidewheelers, $245,000; for *Southfield* (ii), $30,000; for *Westfield* (ii), $23,000; and for *Middletown*, $22,000. With respect to the ferryboats these figures were their appraised values as of May 1, 1903, and they were subject to any changes "as may be found to have taken place in the boats at the time when the city takes possession." *Proceedings of the Sinking Fund Commissioners* (January 31, 1905), pp. 62ff.

This is the route of the Whitehall St.–Saint George line. The towers of lower Manhattan loom in the background, Brooklyn is off at the far right, and Governors Island guards the mouth of the East River to the top right-center of the picture; Saint George is out of view at the lower left. Ocean liners heading out to sea use the very same route for a portion of their trip, and often a municipal ferryboat out of Whitehall St. would overtake and pass *a famous Atlantic greyhound during the five-mile trip down the bay. It won't be the case on this day in the early 1930s, though; Cunard Line's R.M.S.* Mauretania, *a sister ship of the ill-fated* Lusitania, *is being chased by a municipal ferryboat, but the Cunarder is beyond being caught. White steamer on the liner's port is a Jersey Central R.R. vessel heading for Atlantic Highlands and connecting trains to points farther down the Jersey coast. [Library of Congress]*

rassed President Frank E. Wood of the Maryland Steel Company, who served as master of ceremonies for the affair. But the bad luck wasn't over yet. When the New York delegation boarded their special train for home one of the cars derailed at slow speed. No injury or even damage; just an hour's delay.

The New York Times probably added a little to the confusion at Sparrows Point that day, too.

"The contretemps was a great disappointment," noted the reporter covering the launching, and that's surely a fair assessment. But the newspaper also reported the following; "At the yard the New York visitors had . . . taken positions of vantage on a new battleship under construction. . . ." This raises some questions. No U.S. battleships have ever been constructed at Sparrows Point, and through the time of the First World

War the only U.S.N. fighting ships built at the yard there were three destroyers that were a subclass of the larger *Bainbridge*-class vessels – U.S.S. *Truxton*, U.S.S. *Whipple*, and U.S.S. *Worden*. The trio should have been finished and delivered to the fleet before the day of the New York ferryboat ceremony, but if one of them was the "battleship" the *Times'* reporter was talking about, the poor chap had misidentified a vessel that was only *four feet longer* than the Borough-class ferryboats. (A review of *Jane's Fighting Ships* for the year 1907 fails to show any other warships in the world that were built at Sparrows Point!)

The *Bronx* was finally launched three high tides later, the others soon afterward, and on May 20 the fifth vessel in the order, *Richmond*, was successfully launched at the Burlee Dry Dock Company in Port Richmond, Staten Island.

The mayor himself, George McClellan, traveled to Port Richmond for the ceremony; he rode in the city's small steam launch *Manhattan*, and all of Staten Island was in a festive mood. McClellan toured the new vessel before she was sent down the ways and actu-ally stayed aboard during the launch. *Richmond* was sponsored by Mae Frances Davidson, the 17-year-old daughter of a vice-president of the Burlee company, and the vessel easily slid into the waters of the Kill Van Kull on the high tide at 9:30 A.M.

As to the ferryboats themselves (their technical specifications, that is): they were steel-hull vessels driven by two four-bladed eleven-foot propellers, one at each end; power came from a pair of 2-cylinder compound steam engines located amidships and affixed to a single center shaft that ran the length of the vessel. An interesting difference between the Millard and Maclean design (the Borough-class boats as built) and the earlier design executed by A. Cary Smith (the design that *wasn't* built because the bids came in too high) is that the latter called for each vessel to be powered by a single 4-cylinder triple-expansion engine.

A unique feature of the Borough class was that each vessel had two boiler rooms, one on either side of the engine room and each fitted out with two Babcock and Wilcox boilers. The engine was thus at dead center of the boat and, viewed broadside, *Manhattan* and her four sisters had a perfectly symmetrical profile – that is to say, smoke stacks equidistant from the center, one over each boiler room, with the engine located in the area between and defined by the twin stacks.

The trade press was more than passingly interested in the Borough-class boats; *Marine Engineering* devoted lengthy technical articles to their design features during the winter of 1904–1905, and provided steady news about their progress toward completion through the months of 1905.[15] And then at a few minutes after eleven-thirty in the morning on Wednesday, October 25, 1905, *Manhattan* steamed down the bay to Saint George and the new order was underway.

A year later, on November 1, 1906, Mayor McClellan's administration inaugurated municipal ferryboat service on a second once-privately-operated line, that

---

15. See *Marine Engineering*, 9 (July 1904), 333; 9 (September 1904), 407–10; 9 (October 1904), 472–74; 10 (January 1905), 35–37; 10 (September 1905), 374–75.

linking Whitehall Street in Manhattan with the foot of 39 Street in South Brooklyn. It was a somewhat lengthy run of three miles through Buttermilk Channel and around Red Hook – not as long as Whitehall Street–Saint George, but longer than the average river crossing. The foot of 39 Street was once a spot where steam-powered suburban railroad trains of the Brooklyn, Bath and West End R.R. allowed passengers from such inland communities as Bath Beach, New Utrecht, and even the seaside resort areas of Coney Island to transfer from train to ferryboat on their journey to Manhattan. By the turn of the century the steam-powered railroad had been upgraded into an electrified rapid transit service, the West End line, of the Brooklyn Rapid Transit Company, and trains were able to eschew the ferryboat connection and make their own way to Manhattan over the company's elevated system and the Brooklyn Bridge. As a result of an agreement reached in 1913, the West End line was tied into New York's growing subway network, and it continues to function in such a fashion to this day. (See map, page 176.)

Thus in 1906 the Whitehall Street–39 Street/Brooklyn ferry service was seen not as an important connection for Brooklyn, Bath and West End trains, but rather as something to serve the growing industrial and shipping interests adjacent to the 39 Street ferry slips.

"While other portions of Brooklyn will be served by the three bridges over the East River and the tunnel beneath it, it is claimed that this portion of the borough is the only section which will not be directly benefited, and thus the improvement of this ferry appears to those making this claim to be at present the only feasible way by which it can be helped," stated Seth Low's Commissioner of Docks and Ferries, MacDougal Hawkes, back in 1903 when the issue was under discussion. And indeed a major factor influencing the city's decision to take over this service was precisely the question of equity – which is to say that South Brooklyn wouldn't benefit directly from the new subway or the new river bridges, or from the new ferry to Staten Island for that matter – so here was a tailor-made opportunity for balancing the scales.

But if Hawkes and his boss, Low, were interested in pressing forward with taking over the Whitehall Street–39 Street ferry, Featherson and McClellan were a good deal less enthusiastic. The Commissioners of the Sinking Fund had passed a resolution empowering the mayor to proceed in December 1903, but by April 1905 no action had been taken and Featherson was asked to explain why.

Holy smokes, said Featherson in effect. We're up to our necks trying to take over Whitehall Street–Saint George. We're thinking as well about supplementary service from Whitehall Street to Stapleton or Port Richmond in Staten Island and maybe both, and the Union Ferry Company's talking about going out of business within a year and we may have to step in there, too. Let's hold off on this one for now, Featherson urged. It'll run at a big deficit, and it's largely for the benefit of business, not ordinary passengers. Why, business in South Brooklyn ought to throw in some money for the terminals, Featherson suggested, and they haven't.

Featherson's arguments may have had merit, but they didn't carry, and in May 1905, a month

Kennedy *class close-up. American
Legion (ii) is tied up at the Saint*   *George terminal between runs to
Whitehall St., providing an*   *opportunity to appreciate the fine
lines of this three-boat class. [author]*

later, the Sinking Fund Commission authorized the acquisition of the line for a sum of $750,000. New city ferryboats probably wouldn't be ready in time for the take-over, planned for November 1, 1906, so, as reported to the Sinking Fund Commissioners on June 26, 1906, ". . . the ferry company agrees to let and furnish for the use of the city their two ferryboats, the West Brooklyn and the South Brooklyn."

These two leased boats would be sufficient, under ideal conditions, to maintain the company's schedule of service from each terminal every thirty minutes. But a spare boat was also needed; *West Brooklyn* and *South Brooklyn* were iron-hull sidewheelers built in 1887, and the city got hold of a third vessel the same way the older company had. It agreed to charter the Union Ferry Company's *Mineola*, just as the South Brooklyn company had been doing. *Mineola* was a true old-timer. Built in Brooklyn in 1868, she was a beam-engine paddlewheeler with a wooden hull, and the city agreed to pay $42 a day for her use. The $42, incidentally, included more than just the boat; it also included

a flesh-and-blood Union engineer who knew the old *Mineola* like the proverbial back of his hand.

As to the new vessels that were designed from the keel up for the Whitehall Street–39 Street service: this second municipal line was seen as providing ferryboat service primarily for vehicles, and commercial vehicles at that, and so the trio of vessels the city purchased had their main decks laid out to accommodate four lanes of vehicles, and had no passenger cabins at all, passengers being accommodated on the upper deck. As New York moves further into the automotive-oriented twentieth century, ferryboats with, essentially, a "vehicles only" sign on the main deck will become more common, understandably enough.

The Whitehall Street–39 Street boats were smaller than the Borough-class boats, and generally were modeled after contemporary Hudson River railroad ferries. (A result of that trial trip made by Erie R.R.'s *Arlington* in 1904, perhaps.) The builder was the firm of Harlan and Hollingsworth of Wilmington, Delaware, and the three 182-foot vessels were called *Gowanus*, *Bay Ridge*, and *Nassau*,

the last recalling an earlier ferryboat that linked Manhattan and Brooklyn. Each was powered by a pair of 2-cylinder compound steam engines, the same arrangement used on the Borough class.

As expected, though, these new city boats were not delivered in time for the inauguration of municipal service on the Whitehall Street–39 Street line (they arrived in 1907), and so on November 1, 1906, it was the old *Mineola*, all decked out in red, white, and blue bunting, that handled the first trip over the line under municipal auspices. As was the case when Whitehall Street–Saint George was taken over by the city, William Randolph Hearst was in the midst of a bloody electoral campaign. In this, his campaign for the New York State governor's office, he ran as a formal nominee of the Democratic Party, but he was beaten by Republican Charles Evans Hughes. "Except that the deck hands and officers of the ferryboats now wear the municipal uniform the change would not be noticed," commented *The New York Herald* of this second venture in municipal ferryboat operation.

And thus did the City of New

York become an owner and operator of harbor ferryboats in the first decade of the twentieth century. While the city will go on to be the owner and operator of the largest single ferryboat fleet ever to sail New York waters, the same first decade of the twentieth century also witnessed the initial instance of an old and venerable ferryboat company abandoning its network of routes entirely.

Critical to the demise of the Williamsburg ferries in late 1908 was that, in the years and months previous, a massive public investment had been made by the City of New York in alternate facilities for crossing the East River. Two massive and even dramatic suspension bridges had been built, the Brooklyn in 1883 and the Williamsburg in 1903. But perhaps even more important than the bridges per se was the fact that they were both eventually transited by electric-powered streetcars, as well as multi-car electric rapid transit trains. Furthermore, in addition to the two bridges – plus a third and a fourth that would open in 1909, the Manhattan and the Queensboro – there was a publicly-constructed underwater

tunnel through which high-speed subway trains of the Interborough Rapid Transit Company began to operate in 1908. The first leg of the subway, between City Hall and Harlem, all on Manhattan island, opened on October 27, 1904, a year before the ferryboat *Manhattan*'s inaugural voyage. By 1908 this same subway had been extended down Broadway from City Hall to South Ferry, and then under the East River to the Borough Hall section of Brooklyn. From there the new subway was quickly extended inland to Flatbush and Atlantic avenues in Brooklyn, and this too is critical to the ferryboat story, because here was a Brooklyn passenger terminal of the Long Island R.R. (Recall from chapter 3 that in 1859 the L.I.R.R. truncated its original Brooklyn–Jamaica line after disputes with Brooklyn city fathers over the operation of steam locomotives. Service was later restored as far west as Flatbush and Atlantic avenues.) Travelers from points on Long Island were able to take advantage of the subway connection at Flatbush and Atlantic and were thus afforded an alternative to the L.I.R.R.'s Hunter's Point ferry-

boats for reaching destinations in Manhattan.

Despite making possible new options for Long Islanders, the new Interborough subway tunnel chiefly affected patronage on various lines of the Union Ferry Company, since it crossed the East River in that company's territory. As early as December 1903, Union's president Julian Fairchild was commenting on the traffic already diverted from his ferryboats by the Brooklyn Bridge and its elevated trains, and looking to the future: "We will not be able to afford to run our boats at the present rate of fare when the new bridges and tunnels are finished." In January 1908, immediately after the Interborough subway's Joralemon Street tunnel under the East River was opened, Union reported the Wall Street–Montague Street ferry as being "practically deserted," 3000 fewer rush-hour passengers on the Whitehall Street–Atlantic Avenue line, and, in general, a much heavier impact from the new subway tunnel than had been expected.

But Union would survive the first decade of the new century with its routes pretty much intact,

The Manhattan Bridge opened for traffic on December 31, 1909; here it is earlier that year, and workmen rush to complete the span. Photographer's vantage point is along Main St. in Brooklyn; ferry slip is that of the Union Ferry Company's line to Catharine St., a service the new bridge will eventually doom. [Library of Congress]

although with diminished traffic. Fate dealt the Williamsburg ferries a more sudden blow.

The Williamsburg ferries primarily operated from a single Brooklyn terminal to multiple landings on the Manhattan side, and this terminal was at the foot of Broadway – Brooklyn's Broadway, not Manhattan's.

By 1908 there were four different routes operating out of this terminal: Grand Street–Broadway, a direct river crossing that was the company's busiest single route; Roosevelt Street–Broadway, a route that took passengers farther downtown on the Manhattan side to a point adjacent to the Brooklyn Bridge; East 23 Street–Broadway and East 42 Street–Broadway, services to landings farther uptown on the Manhattan side. The company's fifth service, and the one that did not use the busy Broadway terminal, linked Manhattan's Grand Street with the Brooklyn street of the same name.

The two "uptown" routes – i.e., East 23 Street–Broadway and East 42 Street–Broadway – were the company's newest ventures. The line to East 23 Street was begun in 1885, and the company's

final effort at ferryboat service expansion involved the line to the foot of East 42 Street. It was initiated on December 2, 1901, a game effort to retain viability for the corporation as the shadow of the Williamsburg Bridge was then starting to be cast, literally as well as figuratively, over the Broadway terminal. Indeed, for this final expansion the company even had two new vessels built – their first, last, and only steel hulls. *John Englis* and *Harry B. Hollins*, named after two directors of the company, were also the only double-deck ferryboats ever to be owned by the Williamsburg company. The pair were built in Newburgh, N.Y., but while modern in some respects were throwbacks to an older era in matters of propulsion: they were both equipped with vertical-beam engines and sidewheels.

But neither the company's venturesome new uptown services nor its traditional older ones would be able to stand up to the bridge, a bridge that was soon outfitted with four tracks for electric-powered trolley cars and two more for elevated and subway trains.

The elevated rapid transit trains that eventually ran across the

Williamsburg Bridge – and helped thereby to destroy the Williamsburg ferries – did provide those same ferries with a steady source of Manhattan-bound passengers in the years before the bridge was built. The el that reached the ferry terminal in 1889 was part of the Brooklyn Rapid Transit Company's system and operated service inland to such places as Bushwick, East New York, Ridgewood, Ozone Park, and Canarsie. Streetcars also converged on the ferry terminal; they served even more neighborhoods than the el trains.

But the Williamsburg Bridge changed all the familiar patterns. The bridge itself opened for traffic on December 19, 1903. A year later, in November 1904, many of the trolley cars that had been terminating at the ferry terminal were rerouted over the bridge to the Delancey Street terminal at the Manhattan end of the span, and still other streetcars were rerouted so as to terminate at the Brooklyn end of the bridge, rather than to the foot of Broadway. (Generations of Brooklynites would become familiar with the reading "WMSBG. BRIDGE PLAZA" on the destination signs of their local

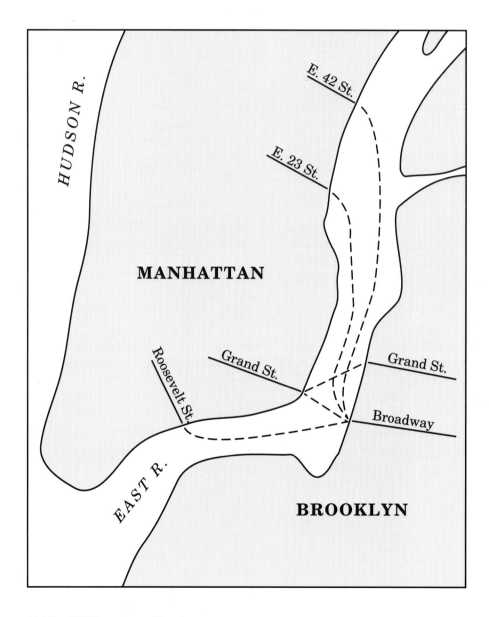

7. The Williamsburg Ferries

trolley cars.) And there was this technical feature of the several East River bridges as well: since they were all fixed-span structures that yet had to provide mid-stream clearance for heavy water-borne traffic navigating the East River, they began their assents well back inland from the river's edge. "Wmsbg. Bridge Plaza" is actually several blocks – and half-a-mile – away from the Broadway ferry terminal and its environs.

Yet consider the general notion of the "environs" of a ferry termi-nal for a moment. It wouldn't hap-pen all at once, but for the next three-quarters of a century New York will struggle with the conse-quences of the fact that the sev-eral East River bridges managed to create economic disaster areas in their very shadows – areas that were prime city real estate before the construction of the bridges, with much of their activity based on the traffic generated by the fer-ryboat lines. The number of Holly-wood movies, over the years, that have managed to create a mood of poverty and urban decay merely by shooting a few scenes in the neighborhoods under the on-land portions of the East River bridges

is quite lengthy. *The New York Times* recognized this early on; in an editorial in June 1909 it put the matter in a proper Hamlet-like context thusly: "If the city aban-dons its ferries entire neighbor-hoods will fall into decadence. If the city sustains its ferries upon its present scale of expenditure and deficit the taxes thus saved will be dearly earned. It is a di-lemma from which there seems no escape."

Getting back to the Williams-burg ferries and 1908: rerouting of trolley cars was bad enough, but on September 16, 1908, the Brook-lyn Rapid Transit completed an extension to its Broadway ele-vated line permitting its trains the options of terminating at the old Broadway Ferry station as had long been the custom or of cross-ing the new bridge into Manhat-tan. And that did it.

At five o'clock in the morning on December 14, 1908, company workers posted notices in the vari-ous ferry houses saying that serv-ice was being abandoned on all the company's lines, effective imme-diately.[16] There was no public-sector regulatory body needed to authorize this cessation, and

the principal sanction for non-performance built into the leases under which the company ran its boats was the threat of no renewal at term. (As this matter was sub-sequently discussed in New York it was determined that the state's newly-created Public Service Com-mission did indeed possess power to enforce performance by ferry-boats that were operated in con-junction with railroad service. But independent ferry lines, like Williamsburg, fell outside that body's jurisdiction.)[17]

16. The text of the posted notice is as follows:
"To the Public:
"Notice is hereby given that all the ferry service from the foot of Broad-way, Brooklyn, to New York, and also from the foot of Grand Street, Brook-lyn, will be permanently discontinued at 5 A.M., Dec. 14, 1908."
17. Although the New York State Public Service Commission lacked for-mal regulatory control over the Wil-liamsburg ferries, the commission's staff helped to assemble information for the city about the operation. In early November 1908, the P.S.C. col-lected patronage data on the five Williamsburg routes that clearly sub-stantiate that the company was ailing:

The sudden stoppage created a maelstrom of traffic snarls in Brooklyn that required calling out reserve police officers to unsnarl. The company's action also brought forth plaintive calls from many quarters that the city government should just step in and take over the old operation, the theoretical matter of the appropriateness of municipal operation presumably having been settled on October 25, 1905. But Mayor McClellan was not especially interested in expanding the city's ferryboat fleet and responsibilities, and his administration proved unreceptive to the calls for such action, although McClellan's people were active in attempting to broker private-sector replacement service, and thus can't be said to have been indifferent to the whole matter. The Nassau Ferry Company, operators of the Houston Street–Grand Street line across the East River, were asked to consider taking over some or all of the Williamsburg routes, but they replied that they were interested more in getting out of the ferryboat business entirely than in assuming new responsibilities.

The state legislature gave the city the power to acquire the Williamsburg network in 1909, the year after the service was abandoned, specifying in very detailed language the right of the municipal government to equip, maintain, and operate any privately-operated ferries – unless they should happen to be owned by a railroad and so long as they ran from the Brooklyn side of the East River between the northerly side of South 6 Street and the southerly side of South 9 Street (which is to say, the Broadway terminal). The city was also empowered to retain all of the company's employees who were on the rolls on January 1, 1908, without the bother of civil service competition.

But the McClellan Administration wasn't interested:

> For my part, I am not, as a general proposition, in favor of committing the city to the operation of ferries at a loss. I look upon municipal operation as a last desperate resort and something that should not be resorted to until all other resources have failed. For that reason, while we

Route	No. of Daily Trips	Total Daily Patronage	Average Patronage per Trip
E. 42 St. – B'way	40	800	20
E. 23 St. – B'way	65	1279	19
Grand St. – B'way	72	1704	24
Roosevelt St. – B'way	51	1678	33
Grand St. – Grand St.	25	361	14
TOTALS	253	5822	23

I'm not certain of its relevance, but the entire passenger traffic the Williamsburg ferries were carrying on 253 trips over a 24-hour period in November 1908 could be carried today on but one trip aboard the city's *Andrew J. Barberi* or *Samuel I. Newhouse.*

were obliged to take over the Staten Island and Thirty-ninth Street Ferries, I am not inclined to look favorably upon taking over other ferry properties,

said his Honor.

Eventually service was restored on two of the old Williamsburg routes. A new entity, this one called the Brooklyn and Manhattan Ferry Company, formed and, armed with an agreement that called for the city to subsidize its service, purchased five of the old Williamsburg boats. On March 16, 1911 – two years, three months, and two days after the service had been curtailed – the old iron-hull sidewheelers *Oregon* and *Maine* of the former company began running between Williamsburg and the foot of Roosevelt Street in Manhattan. The previous day, service had been restored on the East 23 Street–Broadway route. This replacement service would last only a few years, but it helped to ease the transition for many of the old line's customers from dependence on cross-river ferryboats to travel across the bridge on trolleys and el trains.[18] The larger fact remains, though, that the old Williamsburg ferry company, that

entity with so many different corporate names over the years, threw in the towel completely in December 1908. Earlier, there had been various corporate realignments among ferry providers and even out-and-out service abandonments from time to time. But December 14, 1908, was the first time a major ferryboat operator simply called it quits. It should come as no surprise to learn that it wouldn't be the last.

Before leaving the first decade of the twentieth century, a quick

word on one of the harbor's more unconventional ferry services, that which linked the immigrant station on Ellis Island with Whitehall Street.

Ellis Island survives today as a monument to the masses who came to American shores during the great periods of European immigration, and indeed a brand-new ferry – although single-ended and thus beyond the scope of this narrative – again links it with the mainland. But the Ellis Island of current celebration is not the Ellis

18. The Commissioners of the Sinking Fund approved a plan for these two routes on July 22, 1909 and authorized the Dept. of Docks & Ferries to advertise for bids from prospective private operators. None were received, but eventually the city accepted a proposal from the newly-formed Brooklyn & Manhattan Fy. Co. that called for the company to operate the West 23 St.–Broadway/Brooklyn line for the payment of a mere $1.00 per annum lease. For the Roosevelt St.–Broadway service the *city* would pay the *company* an annual subsidy of $132,000.00, but, should profits be realized on the service, the city was to receive an equal share with the company. The agreement was for a period

of ten years, but shortly after the first year the parties were in court, the city claiming that it had been denied profits justly due under the contract, and the city prevailed. The relationship between the city and the Brooklyn & Manhattan Fy. Co. was never good, and when the company abandoned the operation in 1918, three years before the contract expired, the city's comptroller, Charles Craig, estimated that the city's out-of-pocket cost for the seven years of service was $1.7-million, this a combination of direct subsidies and capital investment in slips, terminals, and so forth. See *Proceedings of the Sinking Fund Commissioners* (August 1, 1918), pp. 620–23.

As will be seen in subsequent chapters, the initial excursion into public-sector operation of harbor ferryboats in New York in 1905 did not prove to be an isolated incident; over the next two decades many more routes will come under City Hall's management, including three of the Union Ferry Company's routes. Here, in a stereoscopic view from the 1923–1925 era, a pair of second-hand sidewheelers repainted in the colors of the city's Department of Plant and Structures head out from the big ferry terminal at the foot of Whitehall St., one likely heading to the foot of Brooklyn's Atlantic Ave., the other to Hamilton Ave. There must be traffic heading into Buttermilk Channel, though, as the two ferryboats seem to be swinging pretty far into the East River en route to Brooklyn. [author's collection]

Island where 20 million people were processed en masse between 1891 and 1954. *That* Ellis Island was a harsh place where many dreams of a new life in a new country were dashed on the hard realities of then-current immigration policy – or sometimes just its implementation by fallible people.

There was ferryboat service between Whitehall Street and Ellis Island from 1891 when the immigration station moved there, and for the first 13 years there were a number of different vessels operated by different companies under contract to the Federal Government. In 1904, though, the Immigration Service decided to take over the ferry operation itself, and from then until Ellis Island closed on November 29, 1954, the route was worked by a single vessel – called, fittingly, *Ellis Island*.[19] (Various substitutes were leased, of course, when *Ellis Island* was due for dry docking or was otherwise laid up.)

Keep in mind, of course, that *Ellis Island* provided only the regular over and back service. As needed, steamboats and even

---

19. *Ellis Island*'s immediate predecessor wasn't a ferryboat at all; it was *John G. Carlisle*, a wooden-hull steamboat with dimensions of 135.6 × 29.8 × 11.7 feet. *MVUS* gives her the des-

Ellis Island, *the U.S. Government's double-ender that long connected*

Manhattan with the immigrant station out in the harbor, is tied up at

Slip 7 in the big municipal terminal at Whitehall St. [author]

ignation "I.p.," which stands for "inland; passenger." Listen to the kind of "passengers" *The New York Times* claims she was to haul after being bumped off the Ellis Island run: ". . . now destined for use as a transport for horses between the Aqueduct, Morris Park, and the Gravesend race tracks." barges of various sorts would transport immigrants from arriving ocean liners directly to Ellis Island, and in some cases there

Assuming this 1904 rendition of Ellis Island *represents the way she was actually built, a number of subtle changes were made to the vessel over her lifetime: pilot houses were raised, doubtless to provide better visibility; more lifeboats were installed; engine-room ventilators were added to the top deck. [author's collection]*

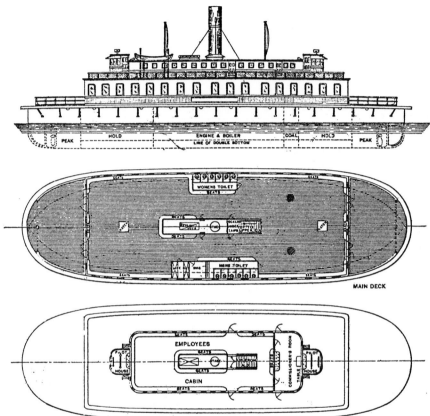

was such service *from* Ellis Island to various railroad terminals along the New Jersey side of the Hudson River. (Most of the major railroads had ticket offices on Ellis Island to solicit business from immigrants whose final destinations were points inland from New York Harbor.) But in more routine instances when processing was complete, or when immigration officials were going to work and returning, the trip would be aboard the 160-foot, double-deck ferryboat. Of the 20 million immigrants who passed through Ellis Island, it is estimated that 12 millon completed their journey to the New World with a short voyage across New York Bay aboard *Ellis Island.*

Ellis Island was built by Harlan and Hollingsworth in Wilmington in 1904. She had a 2-cylinder "up and down" compound engine – not a common arrangement – and screw propellers on the usual end-to-end shaft. While she clearly looked like a typical harbor ferryboat from broadside, head-on there was a perceptible difference: her entire main deck was devoted to passenger accommodation, and was enclosed. She carried no teams or vehicles at all, her namesake island being little more than a collection of buildings out in the bay with no roads, much less a need for vehicles. And she was something different still, a two-class ferryboat, perhaps the only one ever to sail New York waters. On her larger main deck there were accommodations for 1000 people – immigrants, usually. The upper deck was reserved for immigration officials, visitors, and so forth.

Ellis Island was equipped with a hospital room that had twelve beds – not, obviously, for persons who might become sick en route, but to transfer patients to and from the immigration station – plus another specialized facility for the unwell that *The New York Times* mentioned in these words: ". . . there is also a padded cell for the reception of any violently insane immigrants."

Some waterfront observers in 1904 felt that *Ellis Island* looked a little like the Jersey Central R.R.'s two early propeller boats, *Mauch Chunk* and *Easton*, and she was close to them in length – 160 feet for *Ellis Island*, 145 feet for the C.N.J. boats. But surely the most remarkable thing about *Ellis Island* turned out to be her longevity, 1904 through 1954. She deteriorated badly at her Ellis Island slip in the years after 1954, but wonder of wonders, funds have materialized for her restoration, and, with luck, people who visit Ellis Island in future years will be able to see *Ellis Island*, the ferryboat, as well.[20]

So, the major themes of the ferryboat story in the twentieth century have been sounded: corporate interest in ferryboat investment and operation is on the wane, save for the Hudson River railroads; bridges and tunnels have become a fact of life, and rapid transit trains are running over or through them; the city government is on its way to becoming the largest single owner and operator of ferryboats in the harbor; and if anyone has any ideas for retaining the viability and the value of real estate down by the old ferry slips under the bridges, he or she is managing to keep it a closely guarded secret.

The next era in the narrative will be the period from 1910 through 1925, and it will be explored in chapter 8; the next chapter, chapter 7, will see a pause in the narrative story of New York ferryboats so that some statistical information may be examined.

---

20. A marvelous report – a book, actually – was published in 1969 which I believe I can safely call the most detailed and lengthy treatment of a single New York ferryboat yet written. See Edwin C. Bearss, *The Ferryboat* ELLIS ISLAND*: Transport of Hope* (Washington: U.S. Department of the Interior, National Park Service, 1969).

U p to this point the story of the ferryboats of New York Harbor has been told as an historical narrative, moving more or less serially from one development to another. For this chapter, and this chapter only, that style will be interrupted and a different approach employed. Certain statistics covering broad spans of time will be introduced and examined, statistics that help to put the narrative story in a more complete context and perspective. The first portion of this chapter will explore a variety of ferryboat information over an interval that begins in 1866 and ends in 1975. This, surely, is not a case of "giving away the ending" of the ferryboat story by exploring events beyond the point reached thus far in the narrative: the general pattern of reduced ferryboat service in the twentieth century is hardly a secret! The second portion of the chapter will take a detailed look at ferryboat safety performance during a twelve-year interval, a period when ferryboat operations in New York Harbor were at a rather intense level, 1899 through 1910.

General Trends (1866–1975)

Seven benchmark years have been selected from 1866 to 1975 and a variety of information items presented to see how they fluctuated over a period from, essentially, the Civil War to the present. The initial year is 1866, the first year following the Civil War; 1904 is the second point of reference, the last year before municipal operation of harbor ferryboats began; the third of the seven years is 1919, like 1866 the first after a major war; how harbor ferryboats were faring in the depths of the Great Depression can be seen by looking at data from 1936; 1945 shows the various fleets toward the end of the Second World War; a decade of post-war change will be reflected in statistics from 1955; and 1975, the last of the seven benchmark years, will show how harbor ferryboats were performing twenty years later. While there have been considerable ferryboat developments between 1975 and the present day, these have little long-term statistical import, for all intents and purposes, and it is reasonable to consider the information presented for 1975 as an approximate description of

Elmer W. Jones, *Electric Ferries, Inc., 1926–1953*

The wheelhouses of the two classes of larger vessels currently working the Whitehall St.–Saint George service represent an interesting contrast: the classic lines of the 1965-built John F. Kennedy; *the more contemporary look of the* Barberi-*class boats.* [*author*]

the way things stand today. (The few cases in which 1975 statistics differ markedly from the late 1980s will be noted.) Ferryboat data presented in this 109-year overview are taken largely from *Merchant Vessels of the United States.*[1]

Number of Vessels in Operation

An important ferryboat statistic is the one that tells how much service was being provided by the various operators, and Table VII-1 displays this in three different ways. The first column lists the number of vessels documented in each of the seven years.[2] Mere numbers of vessels can be mislead-

ing, of course, if the vessels are not of the same size and carrying capacity. The middle column, therefore, calculates the average gross

tonnage of the ferryboats in service in each of the years examined. The final column is a calculation of the total ferryboat gross tonnage operating in New York Harbor at the same seven intervals.[3]

One interesting variation is the relatively low figures shown for

---

1. I have used *MVUS* for all years save 1866 where my source was *Proceedings of the Sixteenth Annual Meeting of the Board of Supervising Inspectors of Steam Vessels* (Washington, D.C., 1867), pp. 92–101. See below, note 6, for further details about this agency and its operations. Patronage statistics displayed in Table VII-6 are derived from "Marine Transit Operations in the Tri-Sate Region," an unpublished staff report of the Tri-State Regional Planning Commission (New York, 1975).

2. The number represents all ferryboats enrolled with New York as a home port for a given year. Other than in 1975 when any such vessels have been excluded, the figures include a small percentage of ferryboats that operated in geographical areas adjacent to New York but outside the scope of this book, such as trans-Hudson routes north of New York City whose vessels were normally enrolled in Gotham.

3. Gross tonnage is a measurement of the amount of permanently enclosed space in a vessel according to carefully established procedures and is widely regarded as the best single-number expression of a merchant vessel's overall size. It is a surrogate for a vessel's carrying capacity, with one gross

An old photograph of the Hoboken terminal from the days when the Delaware, Lackawanna & Western R.R. still painted its ferryboats white. Vessel on the left is the propeller-driven Elmira, a vessel that survived to be the last steam-powered ferryboat on the lower Hudson River; to the right is Montclair, the last sidewheeler built for Hoboken service. [author's collection]

the year 1919 in all categories; inability of operators to secure new vessels during the First World War, plus the loss of vessels to the military for war-related services, are undoubtedly factors at work here. Another factor, however, is

ton arbitrarily equaling 100 cubic feet of capacity. Warships eschew measurement in gross tons, on the other hand, since carrying capacity is not an important measurement for such vessels. Their common yardstick is displacement tonnage, which is an index of how much a given vessel weighs.

that 1919 was a year in which many smaller ferryboat operators, especially on the East River, had begun to reel under the competitive impact of new bridges and tunnels. Many ferryboat routes had been abandoned by then, and other operators had reduced the size of their fleets. The City of New York would later build new ferryboats and restore a fair number of these services under municipal auspices; hence by 1936 a quite different profile has emerged.

Table VII-2 is a graph that attempts to display the number of

vessels owned in contrast to total gross tonnage. Of interest is that, while 1904 was the maximum for number of vessels, 1936 saw more tonnage than any other year. Table VII-3 charts the increase in the average tonnage of a New York ferryboat over the 109-year time span being examined. It is worth noting that while the 1955–1975 interval saw the heaviest decline in numbers of boats and total tonnage, this same time-frame witnessed a very substantial increase in average tonnage per vessel. This can be explained by the

The hurricane deck was generally off-limits to passengers. These two views show the difference between the tall stack on the Erie Lackawanna R.R.'s steam-powered (and coal-fired) Elmira *and the squat stack-housing the Erie Lackawanna's predecessor, the Delaware, Lackawanna & Western R.R., installed on* Lackawanna *(iii) when that vessel became the only* Hudson River railroad ferryboat to be converted from steam to diesel propulsion. [Howard W. Serig, Jr.]*

fact that the principal route in operation in 1975, Whitehall Street–Saint George, has always operated the harbor's largest ferryboats.

Ferryboats and
Population Changes

To understand the role ferryboats were playing in the evolving social and economic life of New York, it is useful to examine more than simply the number of vessels the various operators were running. Table VII-4 charts the growth of the residential population of the territory that is today the City of New York. Table VII-5 is an effort to relate the city's population and its growth over the 109-year period to the amount of ferryboat service provided. The table is oriented *backward* from the year 1975, which is established as the base year and is assigned a value of 1.0. This 1.0 represents an index derived from and standing for the gross tonnage of ferryboats operating in the harbor divided by the city's total population in the year 1975. The process is then performed on the other benchmark years, and the difference between 1975's 1.0 and, say, 1904's 7.9 is that in 1904 there was 7.9

times more operating ferryboat tonnage in New York per capita than there was in 1975. This table is a crude measure of how much more important ferryboats were to New York in past years than they are today (1975 being roughly equivalent to "today" for comparison purposes).

Of course, ferryboats alone – mere vessels or total gross tonnage – are not the best measure of the role the industry was playing in New York's economic and social life at any given time. Ferryboat utilization – patronage – is a far more important statistic. Unfortunately this information is not available for all seven benchmark years that have been examined thus far, nor is the consistency of what information is available quite as steady as the vessel registration data in *MVUS*. Table VII-6 endeavors to show a patronage profile onward from 1908, in terms both of raw number of passengers carried and of the percentage reduction each interval represents. This downward trend must be seen in contrast to some other statistic, of course, to understand what a loss, in 1975, of 90% of the ferryboat patronage of 1908 represents. Again using city population

figures, Table VII-6 also shows the number of annual ferryboat trips per capita taken in the various years examined. In 1908 each person who resided in the City of New York took the equivalent of 54.4 ferryboat rides a year. Today (i.e., 1975) that number is 2.5.

Ferryboat Operators

In the narrative portion of the ferryboat story three separate kinds of ferryboat operators have been identified, although the distinctions are not always razor sharp between them: private companies, railroads, and after the year 1905 the municipal government of the City of New York. (Operations of the Federal Government to Ellis and Governor's islands, while interesting and worthy of narrative consideration, are not statistically important, nor are services once provided by the State of New York to various health and welfare institutions on islands in the East River.) Table VII-7 shows changes in the percentage relationships of these classes of operators over the seven interval years, the percentages being of the total number of ferryboats operated in each of the years. For purposes of this analy-

Interior views of a typical Hudson River ferryboat. The stairway is at mid-vessel and provides access to the upper deck; main-deck cabins were traditionally designated one for smokers one for non-smokers, but the distinctions were largely ignored. [Howard W. Serig, Jr.]

sis such ferryboat operators as the Hoboken Ferry Company that began independently and were later purchased by railroad companies are regarded as "railroad or railroad-related" at all seven intervals. Ferryboats operated by the Staten Island Rapid Transit Company, or various trolley car companies, are not considered railroad ferries, but are classed with the independent operators. Had Erastus Wiman's ventures with the Baltimore and Ohio R.R. developed differently in the mid-1880s, perhaps the S.I.R.T. would have to be regarded differently. But they didn't; so it doesn't.

Ferryboat Builders

A much larger phenomenon in American life than the construction of New York Harbor ferryboats can be seen in Table VII-8, where shifts are displayed in where the vessels were built. Over time the banks of the East River and the Hudson River closed their shipyards, and vessel construction, as an industry, moved to other locations – elsewhere in the general New York area, then southward to the Delaware River Val-

ley, and finally outside the northeastern portion of the United States entirely and to shipyards in Texas and Louisiana. New York's limited waterfront-land supply grew too valuable for use as shipyards when such work could as well be performed on less expensive real estate. New York was the nation's shipbuilding leader in the early days of wooden ships, but as the Industrial Revolution altered the shape of America's commercial and industrial activities, Manhattan's waterfront became a priority location for ships to load and unload cargo, and the shipyards went elsewhere.[4]

Ferryboat Construction and Equipment

Table VII-9 shows how ferryboats themselves changed between the end of the Civil War and 1975. Hull composition went from wood, through iron, to steel. Steam-

powered paddlewheelers eventually gave way to diesel-powered vessels with screw propellers – and in a development beyond the scope of this data table to depict, even conventional propellers have recently been superseded on some recently-constructed municipal ferryboats.[5] Data table VII-9 may also contain the only information in this chapter where the 1975 entry presents a totally incorrect picture of the current state of affairs in New York ferryboating. While 1975 shows a reasonable

---

4. For further discussion on the evolution of ship building in New York City, see John H. Morrison, *History of New York Shipyards* (New York: Sametz, 1909). Morrison identifies the Union Ferry Company's 1869-built *Winona*

as "among the last" wooden-hull vessels to be built by one of the old-line New York shipbuilders, Webb and Bell, the same company that built the massive wooden caissons for the Brooklyn Bridge.

5. When the City of New York took delivery in the early 1980s of the massive ferryboats *Andrew J. Barberi* and *Samuel I. Newhouse*, it became the first maritime agency in the United States to own vessels propelled by a new German-developed system which some refer to as an "egg-beater drive." In lieu of conventional screw propellers, the new city boats are driven by a system of rotating, variable-pitch, paddle-like devices designed

Night is starting to fall over Upper New York Bay on a winter evening in 1954 and a Merrell-class ferryboat stands in outline against the western sky. A steam-powered tugboat moves toward the East River, and the beacon on Governors Island is flashing its warning to navigators. [author]

percentage of steam-powered vessels, today New York ferryboats are 100% diesel-powered. The very fact that one could ride a steam-powered anything in New York as late as 1975 came about as a result of a marvelous bit of happenstance from the 1950–1951 era that will be savored, to the full, in chapter 9. The three unusual ferryboats that are part of all this were removed from service in the early 1980s, and the chance that any of them will ever return to active ferryboat service is quite unlikely.

Safety Performance (1899–1910)

The early years of the twentieth century saw, arguably, more in-

by the West German firm of Voith Schneider. For further general discussion, see Theodore W. Scull, *The Staten Island Ferry* (New York: Quadrant Press, 1982), pp. 88–91; for a detailed technical treatment, see Ulrich Sturmhoefel, "The Cycloidal Propeller and Its Significance for the Propulsion of Special-Purpose Vessels," *Proceedings of the Second International Waterborne Transportation Conference* (New York, 1978), pp. 323–57.

tense ferryboat service in New York than any other period. Steel-hull propeller boats were becoming common; the City of New York inaugurated municipally-operated service; and while bridges and tunnels were being built across the Hudson and East rivers, they had not yet caused any great reduction in the amount of ferryboat service provided, even if patronage was starting to reflect the advent of the new options.

Table VII-10 provides a wealth of information on ferryboat safety performance during the twelve-year interval 1899–1910. These statistics have been gathered from annual reports of the U.S. Steamboat Inspection Service; however, this raises a procedural problem.[6] In Table VII-10 the data element "number of ferryboats" indicates the vessels that the service reports as having been inspected at the port of New York in the year indicated. In discussing numbers of vessels, though, previous tables in this chapter used information from *MVUS*, and in those tables "number of ferryboats" means vessels enrolled and showing New York as home port. These are, simply enough, two different numbers. In some kind of ideal order they might be expected to be the same, but there are many reasons why they often were not. A vessel could be inspected elsewhere than in its home port, for instance, and as bureaucracy is often wont, the two Federal agencies with important jurisdiction over steamboating defined a "year" differently.

MVUS operated on a fiscal year that ended each June 30, while the Steamboat Inspection Service reported information on the basis of calendar years. An owner could also keep the enrollment active on a vessel that was in a lay-up status and thus not subject to annual inspection.[7] In 1904, for example, the only year common to both the preceding tables and this safety review, the Steamboat Inspection Service places the number of ferryboats in New York at 132, while *MVUS* says it was 147.

Another issue that requires raising, although it will resist being solved, takes the form of a question: how reliable, and hence how accurate, are these safety-related numbers from the Steam-

boat Inspection Service? Well, they are *official*, for whatever that's worth. But they involve a period of time when the agency itself was seriously faulted in the steamboat community for what were claimed to be poor inspection practices, and this shortcoming – alleged or otherwise – relates to the awful tragedy aboard the excursion steamboat *General Slocum* in New York on June 15, 1904. In what remains the worst disaster in New York history, 1030 people died when that wooden vessel caught fire in the East River en route to Locust Grove, Long Island, from the foot of Manhattan's East 3 Street, and the Steamboat Inspection Service was cited for failure to enforce proper safety standards.[8] Better *reporting* of safety-related incidents may well have followed the 1904 disaster, though. Note, for example, that out of 17 fires and groundings over the twelve-year period reviewed, 14 of them appear in Table VII-10 in the years after the *General Slocum* disaster. Likewise the collision rate for ferryboats also rose

6. For further information about the Steamboat Inspection Service, see Lloyd M. Short, *Steamboat Inspection Service: Its History, Activities and Organization* (New York & London: Appleton, 1922).

7. In December 1940, the ferryboat *John Englis* was removed from documentation and scrapped. Because her inspection had been revoked on January 12, 1939, but her enrollment had not then been canceled, her owner had to submit a sworn deposition that she had indeed remained out of operation from January 12, 1939. This affidavit is included with the *John Englis'* final enrollment certificate in the National Archives.

8. See Short, pp. 18–19.

Tuxedo *was an Erie R.R. boat,*
typical of the propeller-driven vessels
built for Hudson River Railroad
service in the twentieth century. The
staff extending outward from under
the wheelhouse is not for flags or
decorations; it's a navigational aid
that by visual alignment with a
distant reference point can give the
wheelhouse crew early warning that
the vessel is starting to come about.
[*author*]

after the 1904 tragedy, or so it
would seem. Before 1904 there
was an average of 0.28 collision
per ferryboat per year in New
York, while after 1904 that number rose to slightly over 0.37. Was
this a deterioration of ferryboat
performance? Did the true collision rate rise by 42% after the
General Slocum disaster? Or was
it simply a case of more conscien-
tious reporting of whatever inci-

dents were happening all along?
The question defies answering,
but the issue it raises is of more
than passing interest. Table VII-10
requires little explanation beyond
itself. A collision? Anytime two
vessels made contact and the incident was reported to the Steamboat Inspection Service. Many
were of virtually insignificant
consequence, with both vessels
continuing in service after the

maritime equivalent of exchanging
drivers' licenses. A ferryboat–
ferryboat collision is one episode
involving two (or more) ferryboats. (On the foggy morning of
February 28, 1903, the Pennsylvania R.R.'s *New Jersey*, on a 7:45
trip out of Jersey City, collided
with both her fleetmate *Saint
Louis* and the Erie R.R.'s *Passaic*, and since it all happened at
about the same time, it is listed

The last ferryboat built for service on the New York Central R.R.'s Hudson River routes was Albany *of 1925, shown here at the line's Weehawken terminal in 1959. [author]*

Waiting room in the ferry terminal at Saint George, Staten Island. Sliding doors along the back wall are rolled open to give passengers access to the ferryboats. [author]

as but one ferryboat–ferryboat collision. Two other ferryboat–ferryboat collisions happened on that same foggy morning, making three out of the year's total of five. None was serious. In fact, *New Jersey* recovered from her earlier three-way episode and was involved in one of the later accidents.)

Despite all these numbers, and despite the treatments presented earlier of the tragedies that befell S.I.R.T.'s *Westfield* (ii) and *Northfield*, ferryboat transportation in New York has generally been, and

been perceived to be, a safe enterprise. Occasionally, though, perils at sea can arise from the behavior of passengers. On November 10, 1907, for example, a man was seriously injured aboard the Long Island R.R.'s *Garden City*, and the wonder is that more weren't. A thousand men – *a thousand men* – squared off as the ferryboat headed back to Manhattan that Sunday evening, half of them a group of Irishmen who had spent the day at a football match in Celtic Park, the rest a group of Germans homeward bound from a day's picnic in

Astoria. Let a *New York Times* reporter describe the incident: the groups "started to poke fun at each other," and soon enough "a German and an Irishman became engaged in a fight." Quickly "the friends of the two got into arguments," and then "fighting started all over the boat." "While the men were fighting in and out of the cabins women fainted, and many were knocked down" by the combatants.

The ferryboat captain frantically blew *Garden City*'s whistle, "bringing out the reserves of the East Thirty-fifth Street Station," who

Contemporary action off Whitehall Street! Inbound from Staten Island, The Gov. Herbert H. Lehman *is about to call for reverse power as the captain eases his boat into one of the slips in the terminal; outbound on a short trip to Governors Island is the U.S. Coast Guard's* Governor, *the only New York ferryboat to be built in a West Coast shipyard.* [author]

rushed to the slip to restore order once the ferryboat docked. Fortunately, *Garden City*'s run was but a half-mile across the East River. Had it been longer, the outcome might have been far more tragic. Since this episode was a matter solely for the local police to handle, it is not even listed in the Steamboat Inspection Service's report for 1907.

Two collisions that were reported to Federal authorities in 1906 bear a brief examination. One took place on May 16, and in the middle of the evening rush hour, but the involved ferryboat was running against the dominant flow of traffic and carried few passengers. She was the Pennsylvania R.R.'s iron-hull paddlewheeler *Baltimore* and was nearing the company's Desbrosses Street slip on a run from Exchange Place, Jersey City, when the steam lighter *Greenwich*, riding low in the water, struck her below the guard and ruptured her hull. *Baltimore* was able to continue to her Manhattan slip and discharge safely both pedestrian and vehicular traffic. But two-and-a-half hours later, despite valiant efforts with emergency pumps and *Baltimore*'s moving herself out from the south slip, pivoting, and moving back into the north slip to allow emergency crews better access to the damaged area of the hull, she settled onto the mud bottom of the slip. She sank, in other words, although most of her superstructure remained above water.

The second episode took place early on the morning of December 29. It was clear and the ferryboat captain later reported that he could see lights from both shores at mid-river. The Erie R.R.'s 23-year-old iron-hull sidewheeler *Paterson* was en route to West 23 Street from Pavonia Avenue, Jersey City. Proceeding up the Hudson and off Christopher Street, it was 5:15 and she was attempting to pass a tug and barge. The tug was the *Joshua Lovett* out of Boston and the barge she was towing was the *Flora*, and it was with *Flora* that *Paterson* collided. The ferry's hull was pierced and, lacking water-tight bulkheads, she sank in ten minutes. Once she came to rest on the river bottom sixty feet below mean high water only the top of her stack was visible – her "smokepipe," in the words of a contemporary press account. The small handful of early-morning passengers were rescued by several passing tugs, including the *'Lovett* and the *John S. Smith*. The city's fireboat *George B. McClellan*, built in 1904 and then serving as Engine 78 at the foot of Gansevoort Street, was also on the scene.

The Steamboat Inspection Service reported that all aboard, passengers and crew, were rescued – "as far as known." But press accounts the day after the accident claimed that one crew member drowned. In addition, as so often happened in ferryboat disasters in pre-automotive days, all the horses aboard perished, despite efforts by teamsters to set the frantic

animals free from their fatal harnesses and let them fend for themselves in the river.

Pennsy's *Baltimore* was quickly patched up and returned to service. (Her place in the schedule was temporarily taken by the railroad's "emergency boat," the 27-year-old wooden-hull sidewheeler *Princeton*.[9]) Erie's *Paterson*, though, fared much less well. Once dragged along the bottom to the New Jersey shoreline from mid-river by Merritt–Chapman and raised, she was judged unworthy of further investment and does not appear again on the active rolls. The new *Jamestown* went into service the following year.

But the point is that two sinkings – or at least *these* two sinkings – were not major disasters. New York was, surely, acutely conscious of maritime safety in

---

9. *Baltimore* remained in the Pennsy's fleet through June 24, 1916, when she was sold. Her new owners cut away her superstructure, removed her engines, and converted her to a barge. As such she worked in both Boston and Savannah. The 1879-built *Princeton* was removed from documentation on June 29, 1909, and dismantled.

1906, a year but two removed from the *General Slocum* disaster and five from the *Northfield–Mauch Chunk* collision. Yet press coverage of *Baltimore* and *Paterson* was restrained. The former rated a small story on the front page of the next day's *Times*, but the latter did not; her demise was not thought worthy of such coverage, and readers had to turn to an inside page to find out what happened off Christopher Street on the morning of December 29, 1906.

One last statistical phenomenon from the 1899–1910 time period must be mentioned, even though it is both morbid and depressing. It involves passengers' taking their lives by jumping from moving ferryboats – but the statistics reveal some patterns that are difficult to understand.

Over the twelve-year period, 39 unfortunate souls jumped or fell from New York ferryboats, and 36 of them perished. But 25 out of the 39 instances, sixty-four per cent, happened aboard Pennsylvania R.R. ferryboats, a fleet that constituted less than 10% of the harbor's total of enrolled ferryboats, and carried approximately

A quiet moment on the main deck of the ferryboat The Gov. Herbert H. Lehman *as the vessel passes Robin's Reef Light en route from Manhattan to Staten Island.* [author]

35% of all the harbor's ferry passengers. But even stranger is the fact that nine of the 25 cases happened on a single vessel, *Cincinnati,* an 1891-built steel-hull propeller boat.[10]

No possible reason can be advanced to explain this state of affairs – it's simply an irrational phenomenon that emerges from the otherwise orderly world of data and statistics.

In any event, the narrative portion of the New York ferryboat story now can resume. As it investigates, in chapter 8, developments from the 1910–1925 era, a sense of statistics and numbers is now available to help place individual events and episodes in their proper context.

---

10. *Cincinnati* was built in 1891 at the Samuel Morse & Sons yard in Elizabethport, N.J. She was a steel-hull propeller boat with an original gross tonnage of 1255. Great pains were taken with the woodwork of her passenger cabins, and this double-deck vessel was widely reported at the time to be the finest ever built for ferryboat service in New York. In later years her passenger cabins were removed and she was converted into a very spartan single-deck, vehicles-only ferryboat. In 1929 the railroad sold *Cincinnati* to the Delaware–New Jersey Fy. Co. of Wilmington, and she remained on that company's roster until she was withdrawn from documentation on May 29, 1952, and subsequently scrapped.

In years gone by, waterborne traffic on the Hudson River was intense. It is about 1930, and ten separate ferryboats are in motion on the river. River traffic had fallen by 1967 when the Erie Lackawanna R.R.'s Barclay St.–Hoboken ferryboat service was the final over and back route operating on the Hudson. [Port Authority of NY and NJ] [Howard W. Serig, Jr.]

8. Here Comes Red Mike

1910–1925

With the establishment of municipal operation on two major services in 1905 and 1906, the next interval in the story of New York ferryboats runs through the years of the First World War and ends in 1925. It was a curious time: curious for a nation whose importance as a world power was growing, and curious for a New York ferryboat industry whose overall importance in the local scheme of things was definitely on the wane and yet whose future would still see some altogether remarkable developments.

Most of the railroad-related ferryboat operations across the Hudson River remained more stable than not during this era, replacing older paddlewheelers with the newer propeller boats that would see the various services through their eventual abandonment in the 1950s and 1960s. But at the end of this interval in 1925, whatever equilibrium the railroad ferries earlier enjoyed was on the verge of being lost. For by then construction workers with the peculiar nickname of "sandhogs" were toiling on a project under the Hudson River that would become, in 1927, the region's first tunnel under a body of navigable water designed for the passage of vehicular traffic – the Holland Tunnel. In addition, the Holland Tunnel represented a new form of public-sector participation in local transport matters. It was built by a bistate agency, the Bridge and Tunnel Commision, an organization that was later absorbed by the larger Port of New York Authority, now called in proper deference to both of its contiguous entities The Port Authority of New York and New Jersey. The Port Authority itself had been created in 1921.

But the Holland Tunnel was not the first subaqueous crossing of the Hudson. The initial year of this era, 1910, was also the year that saw the long-cherished dream of all the Jersey-bound railroads – direct all-rail entry onto Manhattan Island – achieved by one of their lot, the Pennsylvania, and the Long Island R.R. managed a similar feat from the other side of Manhattan at the same time and as part of the same project. (Save the New Haven R.R.'s access to Penn Station from New England in 1917 via the Hell Gate Bridge, save the use of the Pennsy's tunnels by other railroads during the Great War and afterward, and save the various corporate successors to the L.I.R.R. and P.R.R., no other railroads would ever

General Charles F. Humphrey, *U.S. Army, 1928–n/a*

fulfill the dream. Commodore Vanderbilt's New York Central, of course, as well as the New Haven's principal line down from New England long reached Manhattan from the north, sans bridge, tunnel, or ferryboat, and terminated at Grand Central.)

The Pennsylvania R.R. aside, though, the other four Hudson River railroad operations posted rather steady ferryboat patronage figures between 1910 and 1925, as the information displayed in Table VIII-1 shows. In response to this steady traffic during the 1910–1925 era, eleven new screw-propeller ferryboats were put into service by the railroads. The railroads continued to replace their older paddlewheel boats, had funds available for such capital investment, and felt that the expenditures were justified.

East River ferryboat services, on the other hand, remained vulnerable to competition from bridges and tunnels between 1910 and 1925. Although some of the old routes were given temporary protection from market forces by virtue of municipal take-over and operation, none of these city ventures achieved the kind of permanence

Whitehall Street–Saint George managed, and even some close observers of the New York ferryboat scene are unaware of the fact that the city actually operated this route or that one during its final years. This was the era during which the venerable old Union Ferry Company of Brooklyn lowered its house flag for the last time, a public–private "loss sharing" arrangement collapsed that permitted some of the Williamsburg routes to be reopened after that company ceased operations in 1908, the Long Island R.R. got out of the ferryboat business entirely, and several smaller companies threw in the sponge as well. In 1900 there was but one fixed crossing of the East River, the Brooklyn Bridge; by the end of 1910 there were three more bridges, one subway tunnel, and one railroad tunnel in operation; by 1925 these would be supplemented by five more subway tunnels, and both trolley cars and rapid transit trains would be running across all four bridges.[1]

But if competition was taking its toll among the East River private operators, the municipal presence began to assert itself during the

1910–1925 era, on the East River and elsewhere. Whitehall Street–Saint George carried 11.3 million passengers in 1910; by 1925 the count had risen to 24.8 million, an increase of 118%. And if the city's second municipal venture, Whitehall Street–39 Street/Brooklyn, was a good deal less successful – it carried 1.5 million passengers in 1910, a mere 485,000 in 1925 – public operation would expand vigorously to new routes during the era. In 1910, 12.8 million passengers rode municipally-operated ferryboats on two lines; in 1925 the total was 33.5 million on a greatly expanded network of ten routes. Stated differently, these numbers say that, in 1925, 8.3 million annual ferryboat passengers rode on municipally-operated routes that weren't even part of the municipal network in 1910.

Overall (public and private combined) ferryboat patronage

---

1. For an excellent study of the various bridges (but not the tunnels) that replaced ferryboat service across the East River and throughout the rest of New York City, see Sharon Reier, *The Bridges of New York* (New York: Quadrant, 1977).

throughout the harbor exhibits a decline between 1910 and 1925. As the era begins, 158 million passengers are using ferryboats annually; in 1925 the count will be 137 million, a drop of 13%. Is this a little or a lot? Well, municipal population, a useful statistic to view in contrast with ferryboat patronage, was not following a similar trend. It was on the increase – 4.8 million according to the 1910 U.S. Census and something in the range of 6.2 million in 1925, an increase of almost 30%. In 1910, therefore, each municipal resident took the equivalent of 32.9 ferryboat rides; by 1925 that figure had dropped to 22.2 and the percentage loss is 34%, almost three times the decline in sheer patronage.

In general, then, the railroads were stable, municipal operation was expanding, and the other private operators were feeling the pinch. In this chapter, developments from the era will be seen through a series of vignettes touching upon a number of interesting episodes. Some of these will carry a bit beyond the 1925 cut-off date for the chapter to allow integral units to be examined to their conclusion.

The Pennsylvania R.R.'s River Tunnels

On November 27, 1910, something happened in New York that had never happened before; since that day it has been a commonplace. Set the scene: William Howard Taft was in the White House, Jack Johnson was the heavyweight champion of the world, Cunard Line's sister ships R.M.S. *Mauretania* and R.M.S. *Lusitania* were the pride of the North Atlantic ("The fastest steamers in the world," boasted the company's advertising). And at 12:02 A.M. on that decisive Sunday the Pennsylvania R.R. dispatched the first passenger-carrying train out of its new Manhattan terminal at West 33 Street and 7 Avenue. Onward from that time the railroad's fleet of Hudson River ferryboats would play a much less important role in the P.R.R.'s scheme of things as the bulk of the company's long-distance trains were diverted away from the older Exchange Place terminal in Jersey City and its new successor became one of the best-known places in town – Penn Station. There were, would be, and still are many "Penn Stations" throughout the territory served by the Pennsylvania R.R. But this is the *real* one! When later generations would jitterbug to a tune about a fictional train for Tennessee leaving Penn Station each day at 3:45 P.M., they weren't dancing to a tune about the railroad's depot in Newark, or Trenton, or Baltimore.[2]

(Another song from the same era popularized the telephone number of a major hotel that was built on the opposite side of Seventh Avenue from Penn Station and to which incoming passengers often repaired to await 'phone calls and messages. "PEnnsylvania 6-5000" was not only a Glen Miller favorite but the actual telephone number of the Hotel Pennsylvania, an establishment still in business in 1989 as the New York Penta

2. Volumes have been written about Penn Station, the river tunnels, etc., including even a small one by me (see *Rails Under the Mighty Hudson* [Brattleboro, Vt.: Stephen Green Press, 1975]). I will refrain here from retelling stories about DD-1 electric locomotives, the architectural grandeur of Penn Station itself, or alternate schemes the railroad explored before embarking on the course of action it took.

Hotel, a contemporary establishment that can be reached by dialing this number: 212 736-5000. Remove the area code and convert the numbers back to an exchange and one finds some refreshing stability in the deregulated world of contemporary communications. *It's the same number!*)

In any event the project that built Penn Station and the Hudson River tunnels in 1910 also included a pair of twin-tube tunnels under the East River, and these eventually served three purposes: they provided the Pennsy's own trains from the south and west access to huge storage and inspection yards in Long Island City; they gave the Long Island R.R., since the year 1900 owned outright by the Pennsylvania but operated as an independent company, its own direct route into Manhattan; and with the completion of the Hell Gate Bridge in 1917, they allowed through rail service to be instituted, via New York, between Boston and Washington – joint service over the Pennsylvania R.R. and the New York, New Haven and Hartford similar to that which previously required the waterborne efforts of a *Maryland* (i) or a *Maryland* (ii) to effect.

The New York Tunnel Extension, as the whole project came to be called, was an undertaking of monumental proportions, and, given the architectural grandeur of the original Penn Station, the pun can even be acknowledged. Its cost was staggering for the day – $116-million. The original New York subway of 1904 cost but $38-million and that was a public-sector expenditure. Penn Station with its river tunnels was a corporate investment – and risk – made to enhance a private company's earning power. One would have to turn to a project like the Panama Canal, opened in 1914 at a cost to the United States of $352-million, to find an effort of greater cost in the 1910–1925 period, and again this was a public-sector investment. But whatever Penn Station's price tag, the project had a direct, major, and to some extent immediate impact on three harbor ferryboat networks, services that were operating seven separate over and back routes before Penn Station opened for business.

As mentioned earlier, in chapter 6, the New York, New Haven and Hartford R.R.'s ferryboat operation between Exchange Place and the Bronx folded in 1912. This was, of course, the service that transported entire railroad passenger trains and effected, thereby, through service without changing trains between, on the extremes, Boston and Washington. Hell Gate Bridge, when it opened in 1917, allowed this through service to resume in an all-rail fashion, but with routine New York–Washington railroad service operating into and out of Penn Station after 1910, which was just a short taxi ride across town from Grand Central where the New Haven R.R. had long terminated its principal Boston–New York service, the complexity of the *Maryland* (ii) operation was not felt to be necessary in the interim. But the cessation of *Maryland* (ii) service was still a little on the strange side.

On Friday, October 18, 1912 – nearly two years after Penn Station opened and five years before the then a-building Hell Gate Bridge would be ready – the railroad issued a sudden and unexpected announcement from its headquarters in New Haven saying that, effective immediately, *Maryland* (ii) would sail no more. Period. Her last trip was made that very night. "The abandonment of the car floats for handling the heavy passenger trains between the Harlem River and the Jersey shore is due to many hazards beyond the control of the railroad transfer steamers," read the cryptic formal release, with no explanation at all as to what the "many hazards" actually were. There has been some speculation that the railroad was just plain nervous in the year of the loss of R.M.S. *Titanic* about the very notion of operating passenger-carrying vessels. Better to stay on dry land where the company's experience was its long suit than run the risk of a disaster off-shore in an alien environment, the thinking might have gone. In any event the ferryboat service, unusual as it was, terminated, and through passenger-train operations between Boston and Washington via New York City were annulled for a period of five years.

But Hell Gate Bridge, when completed, would serve only a dozen or so passenger trains. (The ferryboat *Maryland* [ii] operation provided connections for but *two* daily trains in each direction.[3]) The Hudson and East River tunnels, on the other hand, quickly established traffic flows of *hundreds* of passenger trains each day,

and the ferryboat operations of both the L.I.R.R. and the P.R.R. were greatly affected.

The Pennsy made a major ferryboat service adjustment coincident with the opening of the Hudson River tunnels on November 27, 1910. It completely eliminated two of the four services that had been operating out of Jersey City, West 23 Street–Exchange Place and Exchange Place–Fulton Street/Brooklyn. The railroad's operating plan for the New York area did not call for the outright elimination of the Exchange Place terminal, however. It was to be retained, although its traffic would be mostly suburban and commuter trains; longer-distance operations would use the new Manhattan sta-

tion uptown at West 33 Street and 7 Avenue. And so the Cortlandt Street–Exchange Place and the Desbrosses Street–Exchange Place ferryboat services were retained as they were oriented largely for passengers heading toward the downtown business districts of Manhattan, proper commuter-like destinations.

Over the years, though, even these two ferry routes saw their patronage slowly diminish, and eventually they both were abandoned, Desbrosses Street in 1930 and Cortlandt Street in 1949, making the mighty Pennsylvania the first railroad operating trans-Hudson ferry service in New York to abandon its vessels entirely. The Exchange Place railroad de-

---

3. "The Colonial" was a Boston–Washington day train that utilized the *Maryland* (ii) connection, and the other train was "The Federal Express," an overnight schedule. After 1912 the latter remained a through train, but it bypassed New York City completely and crossed the Hudson River on the New Haven R.R.'s bridge at Poughkeepsie, some 75 miles upriver. This added 100 miles, and three hours, to the train's journey, but since it traveled an overnight schedule, the additional time was tolerable.

"The Colonial" continued to appear in the timetables between 1912 and 1917 as a Boston–Washington train through New York City, but it was actually two separate trains in each direction and passengers had to utilize a motor-coach connection between Penn Station and Grand Central. Both trains were rerouted over the Hell Gate Bridge when it opened in 1917 and, wonder of wonders, they continue to run for Amtrak to this day. "The Colonial" is still a Boston–Washington day train, although it continues south

pot itself managed to hang on for a few years after the boats were discontinued, serving a diminishing schedule of commuter trains. It was abandoned outright in 1961 and Penn Station, 51 years after it was built, then became the railroad's sole New York passenger terminal. A major impetus for shutting down Exchange Place came from Jersey City civic leaders who wanted to tear down the railroad's elevated approach to the Exchange Place terminal that had been built by the P.R.R. back in 1891, and which gave the railroad's passengers level access to the upper decks of the company's ferryboats. But this advantage for ferry passengers in the nineteenth century had become a blight on Jersey City in the twentieth; the terminal was closed and the elevated approach dismantled.

There was another important development that had an impact on passenger traffic on the Pennsylvania R.R.'s trans-Hudson ferryboats in the early years of the twentieth century, and it was this: when that railroad opened its own trans-Hudson tunnels in 1910 they were not the first rail tunnels under that river. A rapid transit enterprise called the Hudson and Manhattan R.R. had earlier in the decade built a network of lines connecting Hoboken, Jersey City, and Newark with Manhattan, and the company constructed two pairs of twin-tube Hudson River tunnels for its electric-powered trains. One of these ran directly under the Pennsy's Cortlandt Street–Exchange Place ferry line, and it was as easy for a passenger stepping off a P.R.R. train at Exchange Place to take an elevator

down to the H.& M. rapid transit line as it was to walk ahead to a Pennsy ferryboat, level access to the second deck and all. The new rapid transit service could deposit passengers inland in Manhattan at Cortlandt and Church streets before a P.R.R. ferryboat even reached mid-river.

(The H. & M. also had subway stations adjacent to the D. L. & W.'s Hoboken terminal and the Erie's Jersey City depot. When the company opened its first trans-Hudson line in 1908, its irrepressible president, William Gibbs McAdoo, suggested that, were all passengers then using the railroad-operated ferryboats to switch to his trains, over the course of twelve months' time they would collectively save the equivalent of nine hundred years! And more on the company that would become

---

of Washington and terminates at Newport News, Virginia. Amtrak's overnight train between Boston and Washington performs the same service as did "The Federal Express," but it does so under a different name, "The Night Owl." Schedule comparisons between 1904 and 1989 are as shown in the chart.

	"COLONIAL"		"FEDERAL EXPRESS" "NIGHT OWL"	
	1904	1989	1904	1989
LV Boston	8:45 A.M.	7:30 A.M.	7:45 P.M.	10:10 P.M.
AR Washington	9:44 P.M.	3:45 P.M.	9:45 A.M.	7:55 A.M.
LV Washington	7:40 A.M.	12:30 P.M.	5:35 P.M.	10:20 P.M.
AR Boston	8:30 P.M.	9:10 P.M.	7:18 A.M.	8:34 A.M.

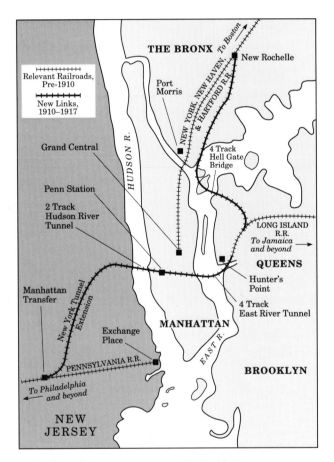

Relevant Railroads, Pre-1910

New Links, 1910–1917

THE BRONX

To Boston

New Rochelle

Port Morris

Grand Central

NEW YORK, NEW HAVEN, & HARTFORD R.R.

HUDSON R.

Penn Station

2 Track Hudson River Tunnel

4 Track Hell Gate Bridge

LONG ISLAND R.R. *To Jamaica and beyond*

QUEENS

Hunter's Point

4 Track East River Tunnel

Manhattan Transfer

New York Tunnel Extension

Exchange Place

MANHATTAN

E.A.S.T. R.

PENNSYLVANIA R.R.

BROOKLYN

To Philadelphia and beyond

NEW JERSEY

8. Railroad improvements, 1910–1917

best known as the Hudson Tubes: thanks to an agreement worked out in 1903 between McAdoo and Alexander J. Cassatt, the president of the Pennsylvania R.R., the new rapid transit company shared trackage with the P.R.R.

out across the Jersey Meadows en route to Newark. The H. & M. and the P.R.R. also both served what was surely America's most unusual railway station, Manhattan Transfer. Built along the banks of the Passaic River near the junc-

tion where the P.R.R.'s new line to Penn Station and the Hudson River tunnels connected with its old route to and from Exchange Place, Manhattan Transfer was a station that could be reached only by train—not by trolley car, not by taxi, not even on foot, and certainly not by ferryboat. It was here that passengers made transfers to and from McAdoo's H. & M., as well as to and from P.R.R. trains bound for both Penn Station and Exchange Place.[4])

The Pennsylvania R.R. bought no new ferryboats after *Newark* (ii) was built in Newburgh, N.Y., in 1902. The company's first venture in screw-propeller vessels was in 1891, three years after

4. Manhattan Transfer was also the place where inbound P.R.R. trains swapped their steam engines for sootless electric locos before heading under the Hudson River. Two developments later rendered Manhattan Transfer obsolete. One was the expansion of electrified service on the Pennsy beyond the New York terminal area; the other, the construction of a new railroad station in Newark in 1937 where the H. & M. and the P.R.R. could better, or at least as well, do their transferring activities.

When she was new in 1891, the Pennsylvania R.R.'s Cincinnati *was a double-deck ferryboat with an expansive passenger cabin on the second deck. Before she was sold to Delaware River interests in 1929, she had been converted into a simple single-deck boat for vehicular traffic only. [Steamship Historical Society of America]*

Bergen, when iron-hull *Washington* and steel-hull *Cincinnati* joined the roster, the former built in Chester, Pennsylvania, the latter in Elizabeth, N.J. Railroad equipment observers at trackside along the P.R.R. system will readily attest that railroad's penchant, over the years, for unique "company designs" on its steam locomotives and rolling stock, and a little bit of that "our way is best" mentality is apparent in its ferryboat fleet as well. Four of the propeller boats were equipped with two three-cylinder compound engines, an unusual arrangement, and the two engines turned separate propeller shafts, thus providing two screws at each end, or "twin screws" in the sense in which that term is usually understood today. (Conventional post-*Bergen* single-shaft ferryboats have *two* screws, but it's not correct to call them *twin* screws: only one is at each end of the boat.)

Before continuing the tale of the demise of the Pennsylvania R.R.'s ferryboat operations in New York in the post-1910 era, one little story from the bygone days of 1902 when the company's *Philadelphia,* a "twin-screw" ferryboat, stepped out of her mundane role for a day, hobnobbed with the rich and powerful, and gave global destiny an ever-so-slight brush. On February 25, 1902, a 161-foot schooner named *Meteor* was launched at the Townsend and Downey shipyard on Shooter's Island, a piece of geography off Staten Island in the Arthur Kill and territorially part of Staten Island. *Meteor* was owned by a rich German nobleman of royal blood who was known to the world as Kaiser Wilhelm II, and *Philadelphia* was chartered to carry the official party from Manhattan to the launching. The Kaiser himself remained in Europe, but President Theodore Roosevelt was aboard *Philadelphia* that day, as was his daughter Alice who christened the new yacht, as well as

Prince Henry of Prussia who was representing the Kaiser, and well he should have, because he was the man's brother.

Twelve years later, on June 28, 1914, Kaiser Wilhelm was entertaining the British ambassador aboard his yacht *Meteor* when he received a most foreboding piece of news. Archduke Franz Ferdinand of Austria had been assassinated in Sarajevo, and the German monarch's battleships, which the men were reviewing, would soon be engaged in mortal combat with the fleet of the ambassador's country. But this yacht was *Meteor IV*; the Staten Island–built vessel was *Meteor III*, and the P.R.R.'s *Philadelphia* had more of a near-miss with history than anything else.

As the Pennsy's Hudson River traffic diminished after 1910 – 33.3 million passengers in 1909, down to 5.1 million in 1919, and but 1.7 million in 1929 – the company was able to sell off many of its still serviceable vessels. Something of a steady customer for ex-P.R.R. boats was a line on the Delaware River that connected Deepwater, N.J., and New Castle, Delaware, just south of Wilmington, and there's something of an irony here.[5]

The P.R.R. boats were rendered surplus, as has been seen, when the passengers they once carried across the river were provided with direct service to Manhattan through subaqueous tunnels. The ferryboats were done in by the railroad trains, in other words.

But when the boats went to work for their second owner, the Delaware–New Jersey Ferry Company, they helped, after a fashion, to drive the Pennsylvania R.R. itself out of business. For their new service was far less a local connection between two river landings than a link in an evolving intercity highway corridor up and down the East Coast, where the P.R.R. had long prevailed. The line was always oriented more to autos and trucks than foot passengers; it began operating only

in the mid-1920s, for example, and hardly dated to the Fulton–Stevens–Vanderbilt era. Many of the ex-P.R.R. boats had their main-deck passenger cabins torn out to accommodate more vehicles. When the Deepwater–New Castle ferryboat service was finally abandoned in the summer of 1951 it was carrying almost four million vehicles a year, and the service was annulled only when the Delaware Memorial Bridge had been completed and was set to open.[6] Today, of course, the Delaware Memorial Bridge with its connecting turnpikes is the primary traffic artery between New York and Washington, and the ex-Pennsylvania R.R., now Amtrak's Northeast Corridor, plays a decidedly secondary role; the corporation that was the P.R.R. is long

---

5. The following Pennsylvania R.R. ferryboats were sold to the New Jersey–Delaware Ferry Company, a subsidiary of the Wilson Line of Wilmington, whose founder J. Shields Wilson designed the engine for Hoboken Ferry's *Bergen* back in 1888: *Cincinnati* in 1929, *Washington* in 1937, *Pittsburgh* in 1939, *Philadelphia* in 1948, and finally *Chicago* in 1949.

6. To place a four million annual vehicle rate in a recent New York context, when the 69 St./Brooklyn–Saint George line was phased out in New York with the opening of the Verrazano–Narrows Bridge in 1964, its annual vehicle count was in the range of 2½ million. One of the two ferryboats that made the final Delaware River crossing for the New Jersey–

When the Pennsylvania R.R. began to reduce its ferryboat fleet after its trans-Hudson tunnels were opened in 1910, the company found a willing buyer for many of its vessels in the Delaware & New Jersey Ferry Company, whose line across the Delaware River has since been replaced by the Delaware Memorial Bridge. The double-stacker in the foreground is Pittsburgh, *an ex-Pennsy boat now shorn of both upper- and lower-deck passenger cabins to afford maximum room for vehicular traffic. The far vessel is unidentified, but the middle boat is* Philadelphia, *another ex-P.R.R. ferryboat. [Delaware River & Bay Authority]*

gone. Thus, in a manner of speaking, it is perfectly correct to suggest that the old ferryboats helped to do in the railroad trains.[7]

The Long Island R.R.

The Long Island R.R.'s East River ferryboats suffered a fate not un-

like parent P.R.R.'s once the company's trains were able to reach dry land on Manhattan Island on their own. The L.I.R.R. actually

---

Delaware Ferry Company, incidentally, on the evening of August 15, 1951, was the ex-P.R.R. vessel *Washington*, then a robust 60 years old. (The other was the diesel-powered *Jersey Shore*, a vessel that has no bearing on our story.) *Washington*'s final enrollment certificate was surrendered on May 29, 1952, and she was scrapped.

7. The public agency that operates the Delaware Memorial Bridge, the Delaware River and Bay Authority, deserves a further citation in a book dealing with ferryboats. In addition to the twin suspension bridges at the southern extremity of the New Jersey Turnpike, this agency also owns and operates a fleet of sleek single-ended ferries that link Cape May, N.J., with

Lewes, Delaware. For further information see two books that have been written by the authority's executive director, William J. Miller, Jr.: *Crossing the Delaware: The Story of the Delaware Memorial Bridge* (Wilmington: Delapeake, 1983); *A Ferry Tale: Crossing the Delaware on the Cape May–Lewes Ferry* (Wilmington: Delapeake, 1984).

began serving Penn Station from the east two-and-a-half months before the inauguration of Pennsy service from the west, and thus it was on September 8, 1910, that the first tuscan-red, electric, multiple-unit trains carried passengers through the new tunnels.

The railroad's ferryboat service was immediately affected. In a manner not unlike what P.R.R. would do ten weeks later, the L.I.R.R.'s plan was to retain the old waterside terminal at Hunter's Point, continue to serve it with some daily trains, retain, as well, some ferryboat operations, but route the bulk of its service under the river into Penn Station. Which it did, except that the L.I.R.R. boats failed to survive nearly so long as the P.R.R.'s. Indeed, L.I.R.R. ferryboat patronage had begun to fall off even before it began to use the Pennsy's new East River tunnels in 1910, as subway and bridge alternatives to its boats had begun to have their impact. The "downtown" ferryboat route from Hunter's Point to James Slip was abandoned on October 1, 1907, and another L.I.R.R. waterborne service—a route between Hunter's Point and the foot of Wall Street

that utilized single-ended steamboats, not ferryboats, and was called the "annex service"—gave up the ghost on September 30, 1908.[8] Thus when Penn Station opened in 1910, the Long Island R.R. was operating only the East 34 Street–Hunter's Point route.

But it was the new tunnels that finally did in the L.I.R.R. ferryboats. (The tunnels even assaulted the ferry operation while they were under construction. In early 1908 the railroad had to dredge out its Hunter's Point facility because the construction of the subaqueous bores near by but below the river bottom was forcing silt into the ferry slips.) As would

8. The Montauk Steamboat Company was an L.I.R.R. subsidiary that operated passenger vessels between Manhattan, Long Island City, and points on Long Island, including overnight service to places like Greenport and Sag Harbor on the far eastern end of the island. It was Montauk's steamboats that handled the annex service between Hunter's Point and the foot of Wall Street, and while this operation was terminated in 1908, other Montauk Steamboat Company services continued, under L.I.R.R. auspices, until 1927. For further details, see Seyfried, part 7, pp. 210–22.

be the case with the P.R.R., the Long Island R.R. imposed an extra fare for passengers traveling through the new tunnels, 14 cents on many tickets. This caused some consternation among its riders – one man is reported to have indignantly written out a check for that amount when the trainman told him his older ticket required supplementing. But while the Long Island's ferryboats were eventually abandoned, and sooner rather than later, they were not all that immediately affected by the new tunnels. Despite the routing of many new electric-powered trains into Penn Station, on the day after the tunnels opened ferryboat traffic on the East 34 Street–Hunter's Point line was a robust 77% of normal. And there was also this to consider: unlike the Hudson River ferry slips and terminals in Manhattan where the only connecting city transit was that provided by streetcars, the L.I.R.R.'s East 34 Street facility was adjacent to a spur line of the Manhattan elevated lines that connected with the Second and Third Avenue els, and certain locations in downtown Manhattan's business district could thus be reached easier, faster, and cheaper than via Penn Station.

The year is 1948 and this ferryboat is working far from New York. She's called Islander *and she's operating in Cape Cod waters between Martha's Vineyard and Woods Hole, where she's seen arriving. Previously she worked in New York for the Riverside & Fort Lee Ferry Company as* Hackensack, *but her original owner was the Long Island R.R., in whose service she bore the name* Hempstead. *[Steamship Historical Society of America]*

Penn Station, in 1910, lacked any subway stations in its neighborhood, and the Sixth and Ninth Avenue els were each a long block away.

But too many factors were working against a long-term future for L.I.R.R. ferryboats. As was mentioned earlier, in chapter 6, the Interborough subway was extended to the Long Island R.R.'s Brooklyn terminal at Flatbush and Atlantic avenues in 1908. Suddenly this was an alternate and all-rail way to reach downtown Manhattan; with two subsequent subway tunnels under the East River between Manhattan and Queens in the general neigh-

borhood of Hunter's Point – plus the extension of Manhattan elevated train service across the Queensboro Bridge in 1917 – the Long Island R.R.'s ferryboat business began to erode. Almost 30 million annual passengers and a profit to the railroad from ferryboat operations alone of $250,000 in 1906 became a net loss of $30,000 in 1923 and a traffic volume of but 850,000 passengers.

The ceremonial last trip was run by the iron-hull sidewheeler *Southampton*, an 1869 product of Harlan and Hollingsworth – "shabby old Southampton," in the words of the *Times* – and while at 59 years she

surely was old, she had also pioneered an important innovation not too many years earlier. She and her fleetmate *Manhattan Beach* became, in the post-tunnel year of 1915, the very first New York ferryboats to be converted to oil fuel, and, indeed, the first to burn oil fuel.

In any event, Captain Thomas Hinchley was in command of the 59-year-old vessel on her final trip, which left Hunter's Point at half-past six that evening. Aboard were her crew, two policemen, a newspaper reporter, and "ten phlegmatic passengers" – again language from the *Times*.

Rockaway is another ex-Long Island R.R. ferryboat that finished up her career working for another operator. Rockaway once crossed the East River between E. 34 St. and Hunter's Point for the railroad; here she's shown in her later days in Norfolk, Virginia. [Steamship Historical Society of America]

The occasion of the line's demise brought forth much reflection on the "good old days" when the ferry to Hunter's Point was the principal gateway to the beaches and race tracks of Long Island. There were interesting stories, as well, of earlier times when automobiles first made their way to the railroad's ferry slips and sought passage aboard the boats along with the more common teams and wagons. Recalled Captain William Hamilton, then with the municipal fleet, but a 26-year veteran of L.I.R.R. service: "When I was a deckhand automobiles arrived. These funny looking vehicles were so undependable that people were afraid of them. Hence there was a rule that no machine should enter or leave a ferryboat under its own power. The cars had to be pushed aboard and hauled off by the deck hands."

This was a nominally free service provided by the ferryboat company, but deckhands expected something for the effort from the obviously well-heeled owners of the new-fangled horseless carriages. Hamilton then went on to describe an impasse that developed one day when a millionaire actress – diplomatically, the old ferry captain did not divulge her name – refused to tip the deckhands who, in turn, refused to move her car off the boat. Police were called; friendly persuasion brought no resolution. Finally the railroad secured a truck and towed the woman's car ashore, thus permitting neither party to the dispute to lose face, but allowing the ferryboat to get back to work.

Now a word or two about the Long Island R.R.'s less-than-modern ferryboat fleet. After the railroad was taken over by the Pennsylvania in 1900, plans were developed under Pennsy auspices for a pair of state-of-the-art steel-hull propeller boats, and these were built by Harlan and Hollingsworth in 1906. *Babylon* and *Hempstead* were appropriately distinctive, though more so above deck than in the engine room. While not all that long – 188 feet – they sported tall twin stacks, a P.R.R. characteristic, and, though their compartment was on the main deck only, passengers had access to a fully open upper deck where there was an around-the-boat promenade. Power came from a pair of compound engines linked to the usual single shaft – the conventional ferryboat arrangement, if anything can be called that.

Babylon and *Hempstead* were requisitioned for military service

during the First World War – in New York Harbor; no hostile operations behind enemy lines this time – but as patronage steadily fell off after the war, the line's only propeller boats were sold to a subsidiary of New Jersey's Public Service Gas and Electric Company for use on a Hudson River route between the foot of West 125 Street in Manhattan and Edgewater, N.J. (Public Service was, as its name suggests, a gas and electric utility. But it was also the largest operator of streetcars in the Garden State, and the ferry line fed passengers to the trolleys.) The West 125 Street–Edgewater route had begun service under a previous operator in 1888, with Public Service formally entering the picture in 1911.[9]

The Pennsy also sent a few of its own older ferryboats to the Long

Island R.R. after its acquisition of the line; *Hudson City*, a wooden sidewheeler originally built for the New Jersey Railroad and Transportation Company in 1867, became L.I.R.R. property in 1903, and *Pennsylvania*, built in 1874 for the P.R.R.'s Delaware River operations, joined the fleet at Hunter's Point in 1923 after the propeller boats were sold. She and *Southampton*, in fact, were the final two vessels to work for L.I.R.R., on May 3, 1925.

But if the fleet struggled along with less-than-modern ferryboats as the service was coming to an end, and had but two steel-hull vessels ever, in earlier days this was a premier operation: ritzy, classy, and smart. *Southampton*, for instance, in 1869 was the harbor's very first iron-hull ferryboat, and her accommodations were

---

9. Public Service called its ferryboat subsidiary the Riverside and Fort Lee Ferry Company. The West 125 Street–Edgewater route began as an independent ferry operation in 1888, and it was absorbed by a newly-organized electric railway company in 1900, the New Jersey and Hudson River Railway and Ferry Company, more popularly known as the Hudson River Line. The entire operation, electric railway and ferryboats, was, in turn, absorbed by Public Service in 1911.

The Hudson River Line achieved a degree of acclaim in the trade press of the maritime industry in 1902 for their new ferryboat *Edgewater*. Colonel Edwin A. Stevens was a member of

thought to be quite comfortable, if not downright luxurious. She and her fleetmates carried generations of famous people en route to various ocean-front resorts in the days when palace hotels in places like Manhattan Beach were the epitome of luxury and the Long Island R.R. and its predecessors was the proper way to get there – after, of course, crossing the East River on one of the company's double-ended sidewheelers.

Hempstead and *Babylon* will surface later in the ferryboat story with different names and different

---

the vessel's design team; she was a steel-hull propeller boat, 180 feet long, driven by a single 3-cylinder compound engine. *Edgewater* had a somewhat different-looking profile from other harbor ferryboats in that her lower-deck passenger cabins extended almost to the very ends of the vessel (more commonly, the cabins were set back to allow some open deck area beyond the cabins). *Edgewater* also revealed the trolley-car orientation of her owners in this feature: the seats in her main-deck cabin were made out of rattan, a woven cane material quite common in the streetcar business, but hardly so among ferryboat operators.

owners, and, for that matter, the L.I.R.R. ferryboat service itself was resurrected two years after its demise under somewhat different circumstances. In 1927 a new company instituted a line over and back across the East River between the L.I.R.R.'s old slip at the foot of East 34 Street and a different Long Island City landing, one at the foot of Borden Avenue, slightly downstream from the Hunter's Point site. As was the case with the Deepwater, N.J.–New Castle, Delaware, service to which many ex-P.R.R. boats migrated, this operation saw itself principally as a carrier of motor vehicles, not railroad passengers, and the new corporation's name made it all rather clear: it was called the East 34 Street Vehicular Ferry Company.

Service was instituted on the afternoon of Friday, September 16, 1927, when the reconditioned ferryboat *Mount Hope* left Manhattan at 4:35. Acting Mayor McKee took a turn at the helm en route to Borden Avenue, and for the return trip to Manhattan, Queens Borough President Maurice Connolly drove his own automobile aboard the boat. (No pushing by deck-

hands; no arguments over tips.) The second vehicle was a large truck owned by the National Sugar Refining Company, whose plant was near the Long Island City ferry slip. But if the truck's cargo, a load of sugar, was urgently needed by a Manhattan customer, there was likely some disappointment, because *Mount Hope* took a leisurely steam down the East River past the Manhattan Bridge before returning to East 34 Street. There a buffet supper was served in the ferry house and one and all predicted a prosperous future for the new venture.

But the East 34 Street Vehicular Ferry Company was short-lived and it came to an end on July 15, 1936, almost nine years (and one Great Depression) later. Under the best of circumstances the route could never have survived much beyond the opening of the Queens Midtown Tunnel in 1940 – a facility built to relieve crowding on the older Queensboro Bridge and following the route of the ferry line almost perfectly. Given the business conditions that prevailed in the 1930s, the service didn't last even that long.

Mount Holly *was one of three second-hand ferryboats owned by the East River ferryboat service between Manhattan and Long Island City after the Long Island R.R. abandoned its East River crossing. Mount Holly certainly has the look of an old vessel in this view from the early 1930s, with circular pilot houses that just reek of nineteenth-century design. But guess what?* Mount Holly *was still running in ferryboat service in 1989! See "The Oldest New York Ferryboats" for further details, plus a later-day photograph of* Mount Holly. [*Mariners Museum*]

A word about the company's reconditioned ferryboats – *Mount Hope*, the inaugural vessel, and her two running mates, *Mount Holly* and *Mount Hood*. All were second-hand vessels, all were steel-hull propeller boats, all had been reconditioned to permit maximum vehicle carriage. But the 1893-built *Mount Hood* had a secret past! While her previous assignment was in the port of Philadelphia as *Margate*, back before that she had toiled in New York for the Central Railroad of New Jersey. She was, in fact, the infamous *Mauch Chunk* that on June 14, 1901, sent the S.I.R.T.'s *Northfield* to the bottom of the East River after colliding with her off Whitehall Street.[10]

Red Mike and Municipal Expansion

Seth Low and George McClellan were both cautious mayors who hardly rushed head-long into municipal take-over of the Whitehall Street–Saint George and the Whitehall Street–39 Street/Brooklyn ferries. William J. Gaynor, who succeeded McClellan in 1910,

was no different. Indeed, Gaynor harshly attacked the city's buy-out of the Whitehall Street–39 Street line during his campaign in 1909, charged the McClellan Administration with paying an excessive price to the private owners for the property, and felt that the city's management of its two ferries was undisciplined and in need of major improvement. Shortly after assuming office in 1910 Gaynor sent a letter to his Commissioner of Docks and Ferries, Calvin Tompkins, saying that he, Tompkins, should develop plans to reduce ferryboat operating costs by at least $300,000 a year. Gaynor felt that the boats were not being economically managed and the crews were too large; the mayor was especially incensed at the practice of paying crews while their boats sat idle. Tompkins, like Gaynor new to his job, reacted by firing the su-

perintendent of ferries and bringing in an ex-Navy commander to take over. But it wasn't until the subsequent administration of John Purroy Mitchel that the municipal ferry operation started to use black ink in its annual reports. The year 1915 was the first since municipal take-over, in other words, that the ferry operation broke even, although both Low and McClellan had continually given assurances that such a state of affairs would come to pass much sooner. But on this critical question of municipal operating expenses and the very notion of "breaking even" it is quite important to keep in mind that terms and points of reference are quite different as between public and private agencies. For the former, a break-even situation can be said to have been achieved if operating revenues (i.e., passenger fares)

---

10. *Mount Holly*, built in Jacksonville in 1913 as *South Jacksonville*, has this distinction: still in service in 1989 on Lake Champlain as *Adirondack*, she may yet become the longest-lived ferryboat of any that ever worked in New York; see The Oldest New York Ferryboats, pp. 325–32. For details on

the celebration of this extraordinary vessel's 75th anniversary in 1988, see my article "Long Live *Adirondack*," *Yankee* (August 1988), 18; see also "Ferry Boat South Jacksonville," *International Marine Engineering* (December 1913), 512–14.

match day-to-day operating expenses (i.e., fuel, crew salaries, maintenance, etc.). The one-time cost of basic capital equipment needed to run the service (i.e., ferryboats and terminals) *isn't* regarded as an operating expense at all, nor is the servicing of any notes or bonds that were used for their purchase. Such costs are handled separately in a typical municipal finance set-up, and while there is no overt effort to deny that they exist and must be paid, it can lead to a certain imprecision in understanding. A private ferryboat operator lacks such bookkeeping flexibility, and necessarily must carry on the books as a cost of doing business a "line item" to retire the debt from past capital expenditures and/or to establish a reserve for the future. Municipal operation was able to split "capital" and "operating" costs, and public mass transit in America today continues this style of double bookkeeping. There's nothing particularly evil about the practice, but it has to be mentioned lest incorrect conclusions be drawn.

Thus in 1915 the two municipal ferries were said to "break even" with combined expenses of about $1 million and revenues (i.e., fares) of the same. But if the annualized cost of equipment replacement were added to the ledger the way a private company would normally do, then the ferry operation would have to be said to have "lost" a half-million dollars.

The city's operating losses before 1915 were, of course, quite understandable – which is to say that they can be traced to clear causes. For one thing, the municipal government was obliged to observe an eight-hour workday for its employees; the S.I.R.T. had not done so. Furthermore, there was widespread agreement that the city simply took on far too many employees in 1905. Indeed, when McClellan acceded to Richmond's long-standing requests and established a secondary Staten Island ferry landing at Stapleton in 1909, the city was able to afford the additional expense largely by utilizing its existing workforce – and fleet – more efficiently.

Over the years, municipal operation of harbor ferryboats will continually be cited as an instance of bloated workforces, excessive capital resources, and operating practices that would never be tolerated in the profit-conscious private sector.[11] Proposals for reintroducing corporate operators on various city-run routes became a perennial part of the municipal scene almost as soon as the ferryboat *Manhattan* completed her ceremonial voyage down the bay in 1905. But of all the ferryboat services the city ever took over, none was ever returned to private auspices for operation. Campaigning office-seekers, "watchdog" citizen groups, editorial writers, and, of course, potential private ferryboat operators kept the notion alive – and, to one extent or another, keep it alive to this day.

---

11. Although I do not have information from a private company with which to compare it, and thus cannot make judgments about whether it is a large complement or a small one, in 1905 the following numbers of people were on the city's payroll to operate its ferryboats: 9 executives and their immediate support staff; 5 junior clerks; 2 financial clerks; 34 attendants – presumably on-board cabin attendants; 76 deckhands; 34 oilers; 16 captains; 14 quartermasters; 6 carpenters; 30 marine engineers; 99 stokers; 32 water tenders; and 8 others for a total of 385 employees. See *Thirty-*

In any event, in the fall of 1917 the city was operating but its original two routes; a "loss-sharing" arrangement had been put into effect in 1911, under Gaynor, to assure the return of certain routes that had been abandoned by the Williamsburg ferries in 1908, as was discussed in chapter 6. And this was the totality of the city's ferryboat responsibilities – operating responsibilities, that is, since the awarding of leases and franchises continued, of course, as a municipal function, as it had since pre-Colonial days.

Mitchel, the incumbent, was defeated in the mayoral election of 1917. A Republican by conviction, he was elected in 1913 as a fusion candidate, but he was solidly trounced when he sought reelection under a similar rubric four years later. The victor? A 49-year-old Brooklyn Democrat by the name of John Francis Hylan, who had been a judge and a magistrate since 1896 and who was solidly

endorsed by William Randolph Hearst, still a force in New York politics. Hearst had earlier let it be known that he would not support the mayoral candidate whom Manhattan Democrats (i.e., Tammany Hall) were expected to nominate, Alfred E. Smith. As a result of Hylan's impressive ability to gather votes in his most recent judicial re-election in Brooklyn, a Democratic ticket was put together, with Hylan from the Brooklyn Democrat organization at its head and Smith, from Tammany Hall, the candidate for president of the Board of Aldermen. Hylan received 313,956 votes, Mitchel 155,490, two other candidates split 201,766, and John Francis came close to gaining a clear majority in a 4-man field; he bested Mitchel head-to-head 67% to 33%. (Al Smith was also elected president of the Board of Aldermen, whence he would later advance to governor and, in 1928, the Democratic Party's unsuccessful candidate for president.)

Hylan would serve two marvelously frantic terms as mayor before being himself ousted by Tammany Hall's Jimmy Walker in the 1925 primary. And if Stevens,

in the early 1800s, was said to be the surname that put the single most significant mark on New York ferryboating, the one that's clearly in second place is Hylan. For that matter, an altogether believable case can be made that John Francis, all by himself, outdid the Colonel and his whole clan.

In Hylan's time the city ferry operation that Mitchel had recently managed to bring into a lean and break-even posture chalked up these accomplishments: 18 new ferryboats were ordered, five for Staten Island service, the rest for other routes Hylan took over or established; a new, small ferryboat design was developed primarily for East River operation that will ultimately see sixteen members of the class—twelve ordered by Hylan, four by Walker—making it the largest single class of ferryboats ever in New York history; and while the city was operating but two ferryboat services on the day Hylan took the oath of office in 1918, during his term in City Hall *eight more routes* will come under municipal auspices.

"Red Mike" Hylan—the man had a full head of red hair and a big, bushy mustache—was a staunch

fifth Annual Report of the Department of Docks and Ferries for the Year ending December 31, 1905 (New York, 1906), pp. 31–41.

believer in the concept of public control and public operation of local transport services, and while his efforts and passions during his eight years in City Hall were largely directed against the two private operators of the city-owned subway system and culminated in the construction of the city-owned and city-operated Independent Subway System, Hylan's activities in the waterborne area were substantial. And, oh, was he colorful!

Before They Built the Verrazano–Narrows Bridge

When the United States Congress enacted an appropriations bill for the Federal Department of Transportation's money needs in what bureaucrats like to call "fiscal year 1986" – which in plain English means the 12-month period that began on October 1, 1985 – the measure included an unusual proviso. Proposed by a congressman who represented Staten Island, it sought to use the leverage of the Federal budget to solve a traffic problem back home. Certain of the congressman's Staten Island constituents were becoming annoyed over the noxious automobile and truck exhausts that tended to waft through their neighborhoods from day-long traffic jams that continually backed up from the toll plaza of the Verrazano–Narrows Bridge, a revenue-collection facility that did its coin gathering on the Staten Island end of the bridge from traffic in both directions – "one-way fares," so to speak. The congressman's amendment said that, unless the Triborough Bridge and Tunnel Authority revised its procedures and collected, in essence, "round-trip fares" from Staten Island–bound traffic only, all sorts of routine Federal transportation assistance would be denied the region. The congressman sought to isolate the traffic congestion and place its unwelcome emissions back out across the bridge. Brooklyn-bound motorists would sail right through the toll plaza and, presto, no more smelly fumes in Staten Island neighborhoods from cars waiting to pay their tolls.

The frustration is understandable. Each year over 60 million vehicles use the Verrazano–Narrows Bridge!

It wasn't always like this, of course. Time was when there weren't any exhaust fumes drifting into Staten Island neighborhoods from the toll plaza of the bridge and people who wanted to take their cars from Staten Island to Brooklyn had to use a ferryboat. In fact, for several years they had their choice of two different lines. Both operations are interesting and have this in common: they each inaugurated and abandoned service wholly within the twentieth century.

The longer-lived of the pair began first and ended last. It linked Bay Ridge and Saint George and began amid what may be a touch or two of apocrypha in 1912. In the June 1952 issue of *Steamboat Bill of Facts*, a veteran ferryman by the name of Clifford Hawkins weaves a tale of how he and a group of associates leased the good ship *Garden City* from the Long Island R.R. and in the early morning hours of July 3, 1912, quietly ran the old sidewheeler over the proposed route and thereby laid claim to the service under some arcane section of municipal law, and thus did the Brooklyn and Richmond Ferry Company arrive on the scene.

Newspapers tell a slightly different, although not necessarily inconsistent, story. They identify opening day as July 4, 1912, the following day, and say that *Garden City* was joined by another ferryboat leased from the Long Island R.R., the *Flushing*. And just a bit of undocumented legend to make things a little more interesting. When the successor line was eventually abandoned 55 years later with the opening of the Verrazano–Narrows Bridge, a 74-year-old passenger aboard the final trip told a reporter that she clearly remembered the inaugural trip many years ago, because she was aboard. It was her birthday, July 29, 1912, she claimed. And more: she even remembered the name of the ferryboat and said it was the *John Englis*, a vessel that she also said was retired from service in 1939. Add all these reports together and this seems certain – the service began in mid-1912.

The Brooklyn and Richmond Ferry Company appears to have owned no boats of its own over the years and maintained operations with vessels leased from other companies, just as it did on opening day. In the 1930s, for example, the company was using the ferryboat fleet owned by the Carteret Ferry Company, a related firm whose own service across the Arthur Kill linking Carteret, N.J., and Staten Island was eliminated in 1929. Carteret continues to appear each year in *Merchant Vessels of the United States* through the early 1940s with four, or five, or six paddlewheel ferryboats on its roster each year. *John Englis*, the vessel the woman recalled as being on the Bay Ridge–Saint George line in 1912, was owned by the Carteret company from 1917 through 1939, for instance – when, as the passenger quite correctly recalled, she was retired and scrapped. Indeed, it was also in 1939 that the Brooklyn and Richmond Ferry Company gave way to another operator, but that will be a story for chapter 9.

As to the second Brooklyn–Staten Island ferry route: it was a municipal service begun under Mayor Hylan on June 14, 1924, and it lasted until June 1946. The inaugural trip between 39 Street/Brooklyn and Saint George was run with *Nassau*, one of the three 1907 vessels the city bought for the Whitehall Street–39 Street service. Calvin Coolidge had just been nominated at the Republican Convention in Cleveland (and would, of course, destroy John Davis, the Democratic candidate, in November). But a contender for the nomination to run against Coolidge in 1924 is of more than passing interest, as he played an earlier role in the New York ferryboat saga. On the day *Nassau* was making her way from 39 Street to Saint George, William Gibbs McAdoo, now a Californian, was leaving Los Angeles by train en route to the Democratic Convention in New York, where he very confidently predicted that he would be nominated on the fifteenth ballot. McAdoo was the man who built the Hudson Tubes in 1908, the first rail tunnels under the Hudson and the first alternative to ferryboat travel on the North River. His platform in 1924 called for outlawing demon rum and championing what he called "progressive democracy."

The 39 Street–Saint George service quickly established a steady market of about a million or so passengers a year, but drew continual protests from the Brooklyn and Richmond Ferry Company

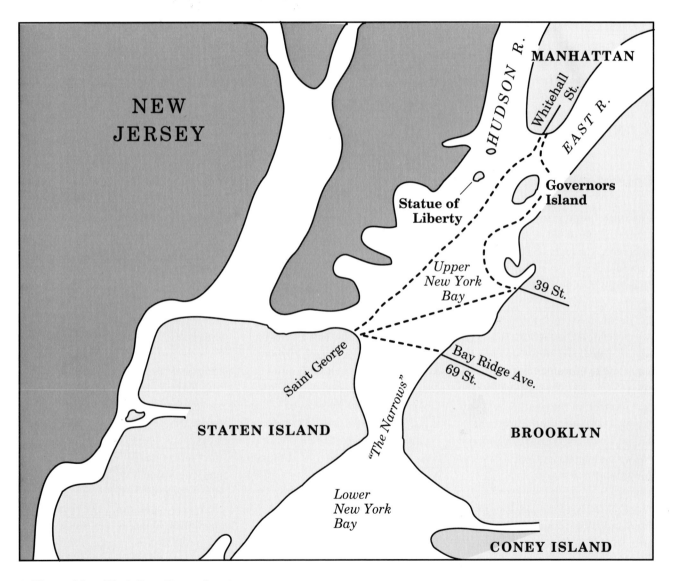

9. Upper New York Bay Ferry Services

who saw the whole business as deadly competition – deadly competition they themselves had to help pay for with their city taxes. The service came to a strange halt in 1946, an episode that will also be described in the next chapter.

Union Lowers the Flag

The once-mighty Union Ferry Company went out with a whimper, hardly a bang. Sure, there was plenty of talk about the civic importance of retaining the value and the desirability of real estate in the shadows of the new East River bridges, and those who predicted that the complete abandonment of the various ferryboats, and the consequent total diversion of ferry traffic to the bridges and subways, would bring on decay and blight along the waterfront proved to be dead right. But it's difficult to build four major bridges and ten two-track rapid transit crossings of the East River between Long Island and Manhattan and *then* ask how the areas around the ferry terminals can be kept viable.

Three of the Union Ferry Company's routes – recall that its network principally involved five East River crossings onward from 1857 – were taken over by the city during the Hylan Administration and operated for some years as part of the municipal system. But two routes were abandoned outright by the company in 1912, Catharine Street–Main Street and Wall Street–Montague Street. The other three, Fulton Street–Fulton Street, Whitehall Street–Atlantic Avenue, and Whitehall Street–Hamilton Avenue, in poor health for most of the early twentieth century, were taken over by the city in December 1922. New state legislation had by this time been passed giving the city broad authority to take over ferryboat services, and the shift to municipal auspices went smoothly enough. Oh, there was a little bit of seeming acrimony at the end and the technical form for the city take-over was a revocation of Union's operating rights signed by Grover Whalen, Mayor Hylan's Commissioner of Plant and Structures. (Chapter 646 of the New York State Laws of 1918 amended the Greater New York Charter by shifting ferry responsibilities from the city's Department of Docks to the Department of Plant and Structures.) But whatever the legal technicalities of it all, municipal take-over of Union's lines had been a matter of protracted debate in New York, and when it finally happened it was hardly an earth-shaking development. The old company operated for the last time on Saturday, December 16, 1922. Whitehall Street–Hamilton Avenue, which ran service all night long, saw its first municipally-operated ferryboat shortly after midnight, on Sunday morning, December 17. Whitehall Street–Atlantic Avenue operated its first municipal service at 7:00 o'clock that same morning, but Fulton Street–Fulton Street wasn't running Sunday service at all in 1922, and its inaugural trip under the new order didn't happen until early Monday morning. Nine Union ferryboats were sold to the city as part of the deal – for $350,000 – and one immediate and quite visible result of the take-over was that passenger fares were immediately lowered to a nickel from the seven-cent rate to which Union's tariff had escalated in the company's unsuccessful effort to survive.

131.   FERRY BOAT, N.Y.   COPYRIGHT 1898, BY J.S. JOHNSTON, N.Y.

Brooklyn (iii) of the Union Ferry Company was built in 1885, and she proved to be the next-to-the-last ferryboat built for that venerable company. [Library of Congress]

Whitehall *(iii) was built in 1890 for the Union Ferry Company. She was the fifty-seventh and last ferryboat to join up with the famous Brooklyn company and its predecessors.* [*Mariners Museum*]

While Hylan had little theoretical difficulty with the Union take-over, and indeed had earlier engineered the municipal take-over of three other East River services whose private operators had no interest in continuing running the routes, the mayor still had to fight for his program. He was not without political enemies, either, who sought his embarrassment with regularity. In early 1923, just after the formal municipal take-over of the three ex-Union routes, the mayor was enjoying a winter vacation in Florida. In his absence the Board of Estimate was scheduled to debate – and approve – a special appropriation to pay cer-

tain operating costs of the new ferry lines, presumably a totally routine piece of business. But City Controller Charles Craig, a Hylan foe, capitalized on the mayor's absence and blocked the action.

Grover Whalen, who had been with Hylan in Palm Beach, hurried home to attend to the crisis. Whalen joked with the press: Hylan, still in Florida, played the Palm Beach Country Club in 108, he recounted, and the mayor was "the Gene Sarazen of City Hall" in the opinion of the man who ran the municipal ferryboat fleet. The money Craig managed to block in February Hylan didn't get until June, and then the Board of Esti-

mate only approved less than half the mayor's requested amount. Hylan may have been colorful, but the man had to work hard to pursue his agenda.

For one of the three former Union Ferry Company lines that the City of New York took over in 1922, even municipal operation failed to ensure any long-term continuity of service. The two Brooklyn routes out of Whitehall Street, one to Atlantic Avenue, the other to Hamilton Avenue, remained in operation for a number of years, but the East River's first steam-powered ferry line, Fulton Street/ Manhattan, to and from Fulton Street/Brooklyn, proved to be too great a drain on the growing municipal ferry network and it was eliminated early in 1924 after but thirteen months in the public sector.

At 7:01 on Saturday night, January 19, 1924, which was a minute behind schedule for a reason to be explained presently, Captain John O. Androvette headed the wooden paddlewheeler *Union* out of her Manhattan slip on the "Fulton Ferry's" final trip. *Union* had been built for the Union Ferry Company in the Civil War year 1862 and was purchased by the city as part of the municipal takeover in 1922. Androvette, who at age 63 was a year older than the ferryboat he was commanding, was a 38-year ferryboat veteran and he delayed the final sailing in hopes that a cash-paying passenger might come along. "Steamboat" Sloan, the ticket agent on the Manhattan side, walked out into South Street from the two-slip ferry terminal in search of such a patron, but he had no luck. The only person he saw was a policeman quietly walking his beat along the deserted street, and the final passage was made with not a single customer aboard, symbolic of the very reason for the finale.

Strangely, on a Saturday evening today the area would be bustling with New Yorkers and visitors enjoying themselves at the shops and restaurants adjacent to the South Street Seaport as the city creates new values for its waterfront in a new age. But in 1924 only that lone policeman was to be seen. High overhead in the darkened winter sky, pale yellow lights from the windows of trolley cars and elevated trains could be seen making their way across the Brooklyn Bridge, and on the streets of Manhattan inland from the ferry slips pedestrians could feel the rumble of subway trains under the sidewalks of New York heading for Brooklyn through the East River tunnels. It was the golden age of that new form of urban mobility, but ferryboats would steam over and back across the East River from the foot of Fulton Street no more. *Union* had sailed not only across the East River, but ". . . down the toboggan of disuse to absolute obscurity," in the somewhat unusual metaphor coined by a reporter for *The New York Times*.

Of course, some people can take just about anything in stride, and one of *Union*'s deckhands, James Baulsir, was quite impatient over all the delay associated with finale. To Baulsir it was just another day at work, and yet the man's father and grandfather were once pilots on the very same ferry route, his grandfather back in the days of the horse boats!

Whitehall Street–Atlantic Avenue remained in service until 1933 when it was phased out after eleven years of public operation. Whitehall Street–Hamilton Avenue, virtually the route of the Brooklyn–Battery Tunnel today, lasted longer and wasn't abandoned until mid-1942. With its quiet demise the last remnant of the Union Ferry Company's network of lines passed from the scene. Passenger traffic on the line dwindled under municipal operation from almost a million-and-a-half in 1930 to 405,000 in 1941.

The ex-Union Atlantic Avenue ferry terminal in Brooklyn saw the inauguration of an interesting new service in January 1929, "new service" and "1929" not being otherwise terribly compatible notions in the ferryboat story. It survived until 1935, two years after the Whitehall Street–Atlantic Avenue route was phased out in 1933. What happened? Well, shades of the old Pennsylvania Annex ferry operation, the Pennsylvania R.R., no less, negotiated the establishment of a service that bypassed Manhattan island and connected Brooklyn and Exchange Place, Jersey City. Intended for automotive traffic only, on Saturday, January 19, 1929, an old-fashioned ferryboat inaugural was staged. The P.R.R.'s *New Brunswick*, an 1897-built double-deck propeller ferry, handled the first trip. The city had spent $300,000 sprucing up the Atlantic Avenue terminal and put on a first-class show for the inaugural. *New Brunswick* was led across the harbor by the city's 135-foot ceremonial launch *Macom*, technically registered as a police boat but regularly used for any and all gala events. (The vessel's name was a foreshortening of *Ma*yor's *Com*mittee, the semi-official group of citizens City Hall called on to help out with matters of high protocol.) The flagship of the city's fireboat fleet, the *John Purroy Mitchel*, moved out from her berth as Engine 57 at the Battery and threw streams of water skyward in proper celebratory fashion. (The *'Mitchell* was the last steam-powered fireboat in the city fleet: last to be built in 1922 and last on the roster in 1966.) But it was *New Brunswick* that was the star of the show as she did something no Hudson River railroad ferryboat had done since the Jersey Central's *Red Bank* steamed into the West 23 Street terminal from Communipaw on June 5, 1905, and none has done since—she inaugurated a new service. Two political bigwigs who were expected to attend the inaugural failed to appear, Mayor Walker of New York and Mayor Frank Hauge of Jersey City.

The operation was abandoned in 1933 with these touches of irony: the Pennsylvania R.R. was the last agency to operate a ferryboat out of Union's Atlantic Avenue ferry slip, and the final ferryboat to depart from the place where the Long Island R.R. once had its in-town terminal was owned by the line that, since 1900, was its parent company.

New City Boats!

John Hylan's policy of expanding municipal ferryboat service created a need for more municipal ferryboats. In many cases the first day of municipal operation on an old route saw the city's standard flying from the mast of an old vessel purchased or leased from the erstwhile private operator. But access to municipal funds allowed new double-enders to be designed and built for these services, and in New York shipyards if at all possible; he wasn't always able to prevail on this score, but Mayor Hylan had little use for laws and regulations that allowed New York City tax dollars to be spent in such far-away places as Elizabethport, N.J.

In addition to boats for the new municipal routes, increasing traffic on the heavy Whitehall Street–Saint George line created an almost constant demand for more tonnage there, and the Hylan ferryboat-building program addressed such needs as well.

The Borough-class boats of 1905 proved to be the backbone of the Whitehall Street–Saint George route for a quarter-century or more. They also proved to be a generally well-designed boat, although by no means free from all flaws. Perhaps their principal drawback was in their twin boiler-room design, the problem being one of excess operating expense: two sets of fuel bunkers, boilers, and so forth, and not just one, meant that *Manhattan* and her sisters required two sets of coal passers and other boiler-room workers, and labor expense was an especial vulnerability for a municipal operator, since from the day it took over from the Staten Island Rapid Transit in 1905 the city was required to restrict its employees to an eight-hour day.

(Until general labor legislation enshrined the notion of an eight-hour workday throughout the economy, it was common among the old-line ferryboat operators for a given vessel to have but a single crew, who slept and took their meals aboard the vessel. For such men, a "day off" was more akin to "shore leave.")

The five Borough-class ferryboats were not the only vessels the city owned from 1905 that could work the Whitehall Street–Saint George service. Purchased from the Staten Island Rapid Transit at the time of the municipal take-over was its entire fleet of five double-enders: *Westfield* (ii), built in 1862; *Southfield* (ii), built in 1882; *Middletown*, an 1864-built

vessel, all three of these being wooden-hull sidewheelers that saw little and possibly no municipal service; also, *Castleton, a) Erastus Wiman*, as well as *Stapleton, a) Robert Garrett*. These last two were the inclined compound sidewheelers of 1888. The *'Garrett* was renamed in late 1906 and it would seem safe to speculate that her second name indicated that she saw a good deal of service on the supplementary route between Whitehall Street and Stapleton that the city established in 1909.[12] On November 5, 1910, as an instance, she developed a minor problem in her propulsion system that merited inclusion in that year's annual report of the Steamboat Inspection Service: "While

ferry steamer *Stapleton* was on regular trip from Stapleton, N.Y. . . ."

The 1888 sidewheelers had originally been designed with rather unusual pilot houses. For one thing they were big; not that many years before, and on many vintage craft still plying New York waters in the early 1900s, ferryboat pilot houses tended to resemble telephone booths in size and proportion. But the *'Wiman* and the *'Garrett* not only had pilot houses that were large, the pilot houses had a different shape to them. The front was flat. The Department of Docks and Ferries rebuilt the pilot houses sometime after the vessels were acquired to a curved-front design similar to the Borough

---

12. This service was intended primarily for vehicles, as Stapleton was a growing industrial and shipping district. There was also concern that the grade up from the slips at Saint George was too hard for horse-drawn wagons; it was more benign at Stapleton. The first trip was made on Thursday, May 27, 1909; Mayor Mc-Clellan was aboard the *Richmond*, which handled the inaugural, and she arrived at Stapleton at 3:45 P.M. Service was scheduled to operate every

90 minutes from each terminal, indicating that a single vessel was all that was needed for this supplementary operation. Service began at 4:00 A.M. and ended at 8:00 P.M., unlike Whitehall St.–St. George which ran 24 hours a day. The Whitehall St.–Stapleton service was eliminated on December 31, 1913. For further details, see Herbert B. Reed, "The Stapleton Ferry," *The Staten Island Historian*, 21 (April–June 1960), 19–20.

class. As a result, *Stapleton* and *Castleton*, although sidewheelers, blended visually into the city fleet, at least to some degree.

Stapleton and *Castleton* also found a good deal of work on the second municipal ferryboat line, Whitehall Street–39 Street/Brooklyn, until they were disposed of just before 1920. The trio of vessels purchased nominally for *that* service in 1907 – *Bay Ridge*, *Nassau*, and *Gowanus*, steel-hull propeller boats with no passenger accommodations on the main deck – took turns on the Whitehall Street–Saint George run from time to time as well. In November 1910, for instance, *Nassau* had a bit of a time one evening en route from Saint George to Manhattan. Attempting to pass a tug and barge, she ran aground up against the Governors Island seawall. Most of her passengers were able to jump ashore and then make their way to Manhattan aboard the U.S. Army's *General Hancock*, the regular vessel then working the Whitehall Street–Governors Island run, which made two extra trips for the benefit of the "survivors" of the "wreck of the *Nassau*." Some people, though,

preferred to remain aboard the grounded ferryboat until she was later pulled free of her predicament by fleetmate *Bronx*, assisted by a pair of tug boats.

(*Nassau* was damaged but little – a twisted propeller repaired at a cost of $7000 – but the name of her captain that evening is of note. He was Sylvester Griffin, the very same man who was in the wheelhouse of the Jersey Central R.R.'s *Mauch Chunk* the day she collided with the S.I.R.T.'s *Northfield*. We may seem to be picking on Captain Griffin, but he got his name in the 'papers on yet another occasion. Before joining the municipal service, while skippering Jersey Central's *Bound Brook*, on July 14, 1904, he collided with the excursion boat *Cetus* of the Iron Steamboat Company while the latter was returning to Manhattan from Coney Island. It was, fortunately, a minor mishap.)

Still, there was a need for more vessels to supplement the Borough-class boats. The first such was *Mayor Gaynor*, built in Camden, N.J. in 1914 during the Mitchel Administration, but hardly the most successful design ever. She was named after former mayor

William J. Gaynor, Mitchel's predecessor, but a year after he left office. The poor man was shot on board a trans-Atlantic ocean liner and died soon afterward. While ex-mayors were routinely honored by becoming the namesake of a city fireboat in those days, sympathy for Gaynor caused him to be doubly honored: *William J. Gaynor* was a fireboat built in 1914; *Mayor Gaynor*, the 1914 ferryboat.

Mayor Gaynor avoided the inefficiency of dual boiler rooms and pioneered what would later become the standard profile for Whitehall Street–Saint George boats: twin stacks toward one end of center indicating a single boiler room there, engine room toward the opposite end. But she was seriously under-powered with a single 4-cylinder triple-expansion engine. *Mayor Gaynor* never really fit into the regular Whitehall Street–Saint George service pattern because she couldn't maintain schedules, and downgrading schedules from the performance levels easily met by the Borough class to hers was out of the question. She served primarily as a supplementary boat, and in later

President Roosevelt *of the municipal
ferryboat fleet has the same general
profile as the Borough class of 1905.
Her widely separated stacks indicate
separate boiler rooms, one on either
side of the engine room. Vessel to the
left is* Miss New York. [*Roger J.
Cudahy*]

years her main deck was converted to handle vehicular traffic only, something that will become an increasingly common configuration in New York, and elsewhere, as the nation turns more and more to automotive transport as its basic means of getting around. (For all her faults, *Mayor Gaynor* enjoyed a long life in municipal service. She wasn't withdrawn from active service until 1951, 37 years after she joined the fleet.)

The next new addition to the city's ferryboat fleet was virtually a complete return to the Borough-class design, separate boiler rooms and all. She was *President Roosevelt* of 1921, built at Staten Island Shipbuilding in Mariner's Harbor. In later years when "that man" was in the White House, many took umbrage at having to ride aboard a ferryboat that was obviously named after "T.R.," but absent a first name or initial did so with a title that could be confusing. *American Legion* of 1926 was the first of what would be a standard design through the Second World War, a design that would be repeated seven more times – a single boiler room toward one end of center, engine room with twin

compounds toward the other. *Mayor Gaynor*'s profile and the proven engine of the Borough class, in other words. *American Legion* had an usual hull design, however, which managed to douse her main deck with sea water in all but dead-calm conditions; it was a feature not repeated on subsequent vessels.

American Legion triggered a controversy over her name, though – of more than passing interest since the name survives today in the municipal fleet on the 1965-built *American Legion* (ii). When it was announced that a vessel would be named to honor people who had served their nation under arms, who could fault the idea? But the American Legion was only one veterans' organization; others, while strongly applauding the general notion, disagreed just as strongly with the way it was going to be done. Letters, petitions, discussions, and even a grand compromise proposal to call the 1926 ferryboat "*Abraham Lincoln*" proved of no avail; *American Legion* (i) she became.

Between *President Roosevelt* and *American Legion* (i), three vessels were ordered and built that

may well rank as New York Harbor's most unusual ferryboats. Recall that in discussing the advent of screw propellers on double-ended ferryboats in 1888 it was pointed out that fore-and-aft screws turning at the same rate of speed generate some mechanical inefficiency. Perhaps "hydrodynamic inefficiency" is a more precise term, but whatever it might be called it was clearly offset by other advantages when compared to earlier side-wheelers, and this was the whole point of the tests the Hoboken Ferry Company ran in 1889, pitting *Bergen* and her screw propeller against *Orange* and her sidewheels.

Still, the inefficiencies remained, to be brooded over by naval architects. With conventional "up and down" steam engines, the complex gearing needed to disengage one screw and apply power solely to the other was felt to be too cumbersome, and the inefficiencies of the single shaft continued to be tolerated. But the break-through that caused designers to give a serious look at an alternative – a "split-shaft" design, so called – was the possibility of turning a ferryboat's screws by electric

American Legion *(i) joined the municipal fleet in 1926 and was scrapped in 1963. Vessels used on the Whitehall St.–Saint George service stayed rather constant in size from 1905 until the delivery of vessels like the* Pvt. Joseph F. Merrell, *shown on the right, in 1951.* Merrell-*class vessels featured three passenger decks, while older boats like* American Legion *had but two. Scene is the city's ferryboat maintenance base in Staten Island.* [Roger J. Cudahy]

motors: one motor attached to each screw, and relatively simple electric switches and controls to determine how much power would be applied to each screw at any given time. The ideal arrangement, according to the thinkers and designers, was not to disengage the front screw anyway – that might be even worse – but to let it turn over at a slightly slower rate than the aft screw, something that seemed eminently "do-able" with a split-shaft design and electric motors powering the screws.

And as long as the screws were to be turned electrically, why not see if a better power plant than the reciprocating steam engine might be available to generate the electricity? Thus was born the turbo-electric ferryboat! (*Turbo* – power was generated by a single 2200-h.p. Curtis 8-stage condensing marine steam turbine engine that could run up to 3000 r.p.m.; *electric* – the steam turbine drove a 3-phase a.c. electric generator, and each propeller was turned by its own electric motor.)

Running at top speed, the stern propeller would turn over at 176 r.p.m. and contribute 2100 h.p. to the voyage, while the forward screw would "idle," so to speak, at 132 r.p.m. and produce a nominal 100 h.p. Either or both screws could be used, at the captain's discretion, while maneuvering and berthing, and the whole process would be reversed on the return trip.

When the trio was built in the early 1920s it was, of course, a time when steam turbine engines

What looks like a "normal" ferryboat of the municipal fleet is in fact a highly experimental vessel. Whitehall (ii) was one of three double-enders built in 1923 and powered by a unique steam/turbo-electric propulsion system. Alas, the experiment failed to elicit orders for additional vessels. [Mariners Museum]

were in their ascendancy. Direct-drive turbines had become the standard power plant for the likes of battleships and express ocean liners. H.M.S. *Dreadnought* of 1906 is generally regarded as the initial deployment of steam turbines on a major ship of the line. Cunard's R.M.S. *Mauretania* of 1907 was also turbine-powered, as was her sister ship, the *Lusitania*. But ocean-going ships were one kind of turbine application; ferryboats, quite another. On the former the engine-room telegraph would often remain on "full ahead" for days at a time, and the turbine drove the propellers directly – which is to say, through mechanical reduction gears. But in over and back ferry service, constant engine reversing is required, and this is simply not possible with direct-drive steam turbines. But if a fast-running steam turbine can be matched up with an electric drive to turn the screws, well, maybe this might be the ideal combination!

But it wasn't. The experiment, while noble, failed to produce orders for any more steam turbo-electric ferryboats in New York, and the three vessels were stricken from the rolls in the years just after the Second World War. The steam turbine engine, while not requiring to be reversed in the way it was deployed on these three ferryboats, did have to have its speed constantly adjusted – full power, idle, half-power, more full power, idle again – and the cycles were just too short to tap the engine's inherent advantages, which

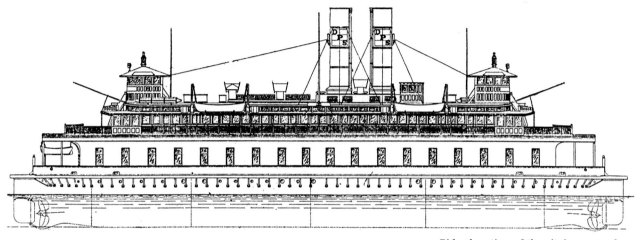

Side elevation of the city's unusual turbo-electric ferryboats, a three-boat fleet built in 1923. [author's collection]

were, in simple terms, to run at very high speeds for very long periods of time.[13]

There is also some reason to believe that the trio was intended to work a municipal ferryboat route for trucks and other commercial vehicles, which never materialized:

---

13. For further information and discussion on the city's turbo-electric ferryboats, see "New Turbo Electric Ferryboats for New York City," *Marine Engineering*, 27 (May 1922), 297–301. The three had registered dimensions of 218 × 64 × 18 feet.

Cortlandt Street–Staten Island. Instead, they filled in on all of the city's Upper New York Bay services – Whitehall Street–Saint George, Whitehall Street–39 Street, and 39 Street–Saint George. In profile they resembled *Mayor Gaynor* and *American Legion* (i) – twin stacks off center; in configuration they were similar to *Bay Ridge, Nassau,* and *Gowanus* – vehicles-only main deck.

Now, as to their names: here was vintage Hylan.

All three were launched in the spring of 1923 just a few weeks apart, and each vessel's name was kept a City Hall secret until the last possible moment, like nominees for Academy Awards or winners of the Nobel Peace Prize. First to go down the ways of the Staten Island Shipbuilding Company at Mariner's Harbor on March 17 was (the envelope, please) the *William Randolph Hearst*, lest anyone fail to appreciate the genesis of Hylan's political philosophy. There was some suspicion in New

York that Hylan's plan for the next two turbo-electrics was to name one of them after himself and the other after Grover Whalen, his commissioner of the Department of Plant and Structures. (It was even said that Hylan wanted to name the ferryboat that became *President Roosevelt* in 1921 the *John F. Hylan*, but somehow or other he was talked out of it.) The Municipal Art League, a self-appointed custodian of good taste in such matters, registered strong disapproval of any incumbent's plastering his own surname on so public an entity as a ferryboat, and when the second of the three vessels was christened on the morning high tide of April 7 by Mrs. Hylan – with the "foam of what was said to be champagne trickling over the starboard bow" – the vessel bore the name *Rodman Wanamaker*, the chairman of the mayor's reception committee and a member of a famous family of retailers. Mrs. Hylan's role in sponsoring the *'Wanamaker*, though, gives some support to the suspicion John Francis did indeed want to – and had planned to – name the vessel after his favorite mayor. The last of the trio hit the water in early May and was called *George Loft* after a New York political eminence whose name is better associated with a chain of shops that sold chocolates in and around New York.

The three new vessels were put into service simultaneously over the Memorial Day weekend in 1924, and Sunday, June 1, proved to be the heaviest traffic day the Whitehall Street–Saint George ferry had ever experienced up until that time. Six regular boats were in operation plus the three new turbo-electrics, and over 5000 automobiles were transported across the bay. In the late-evening peak travel hours – i.e., 9 o'clock until midnight – thousands of people and their vehicles were lined up at Saint George awaiting passage back to Manhattan, en route home from the beaches of Staten Island and New Jersey. There were, of course, no bridges and no tunnels in 1924, and there were no parkways, either. New Yorkers heading back to the city from the beaches of New Jersey who came through Staten Island thus had to use two different ferryboat services, Tottenville–Perth Amboy and Whitehall Street–Saint George. Selecting one's route home involved these trade-offs: the uncertainty of two ferryboat crossings on the Staten Island route, or the congestion of Newark and Jersey City streets if one cast one's lot with a single ferry trip across the Hudson on one of the railroad-operated lines.

So much, then, for the larger municipal boats – 200 feet and more in length – that handled the various Upper Bay assignments. The Hylan Administration also put its hand to designing a smaller ferryboat for the various East River services Red Mike was rapidly bringing under municipal responsibility. The effort produced one of the more remarkable vessels in the entire story of New York ferryboating. What Hylan began eventually became a fleet of sixteen – *sixteen*! – vessels. They were delivered between 1925 and 1931, and the 16 represent the largest class of ferryboats built to a single design by any New York operator, at least so far.

While the vessels appear on their official documents as having a registered waterline dimension of 143.6 feet in length, the fleet has been commonly called the

Rockaway, *built in 1925 as the*
Murray Hulbert, *was the first of the*
16-boat class of 151-foot ferryboats to
be launched. This single-deck vessel
was built for municipal service on
various East River lines recently
taken over from failed private
companies. [Steamship Historical
Society of America]

Outline drawing of the City of New York's 151-foot-class ferryboats. [*author's collection*]

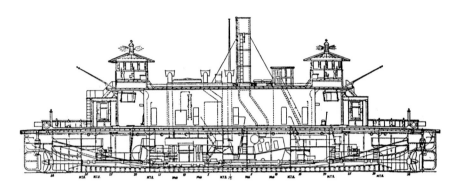

"151-footers" – this their end-to-end deck measurement. First reasonably developed indication of what would become the 16-vessel fleet (there had always been vague talk that "we need new boats for the East River") came in early 1923 when Commissioner Whalen requested approval from the city's Board of Estimate to buy eight new all-steel ferryboats that would be assigned to the various ex-Union lines, plus Grand Street–Broadway, East 23 Street–Greenpoint, East 92 Street–Astoria, and Clason's Point–College Point, all by then municipally operated. But action was not forthcoming in early 1923, and just as well. The design Whalen submitted with his spending proposal was for a totally unexceptional-looking 130-foot boat with a tall single stack dead amidships. Nice, small, even cute;

but a much better boat was to evolve.

The early design spoke in terms of either steam or diesel power – had the latter been selected the tall stack would undoubtedly have been shortened. When Whalen and his engineers and consultants finally got the go-ahead in 1924, however, here is what they bought: an all-steel single-deck ferryboat 151 feet in overall length and powered by conventional twin-compound steam engines. And because the vessels were primarily justified for carrying vehicles, and not passengers, their main deck included three parallel gangways with passenger cabins outboard of this vehicle space. This left precious little room for passengers. The big Borough-class boats with two main-deck vehicle gangways were 66 feet over guards at their

beam, while the 151-footers, with three gangways, measured only 53 feet from side to side. To repeat: the passenger cabins were small, a mere six feet in width – narrower than a trolley car, in fact. They featured bench-type wooden seating for a mere 62 passengers along the inside bulkheads away from the cabin windows, and precious little else by way of accommodation. Passengers had no access to the upper deck, for example, although, oddly enough, the sole member of the species to survive and be preserved (at South Street Seaport) is one of but two of the sixteen to have an upper-deck cabin added in later years.[14]

---

14. This is the *Maj. Gen. Wm. H. Hart, a) John A. Lynch, b) Harlem.* Her final assignment was service be-

The 151-footers were nifty little craft. Because they had twin boilers with little room to design efficient duct work for a single stack, they were built with two side-by-side stacks, each astride the space that separates the center gangway from the outside ones. Thus they had a delightful inland riverboat look to them at a time when most marine architects were thinking and talking about diesel engines and totally different kinds of exhaust systems. The 151-footers were also the city's first – but hardly its last – oil-burning ferryboats.[15]

The first of the sixteen to be launched hit the water just a few minutes ahead of the second. And their names? Why, here Hylan put on another show. After all, the

man was coming up for re-election in 1925, it looked as if he was in for a serious primary fight, and so, long before politicians had to hire expensive consultants to get themselves elected, John Francis Hylan came up with a better idea. Maybe he'd never get to name a boat after himself, but at least he could name some after political cronies, or somebody else whose support he might require in his forthcoming campaign. And he could stage a big ceremony and have the man's daughter or spouse crack the champagne across the vessel's prow. (Or whatever other liquid the rigors of Prohibition dictated.) And the shipbuilder could host a nice party after the launching and give the vessel's sponsor a little memento of the occasion – some diamond earrings, or a gold wrist watch, but nothing cheap, because, after all, this is the City of New York.

Hylan, as it developed, wasn't renominated in 1925. He was beaten for the Democratic nomination by Jimmy Walker, and the final four 151-footers that were ordered during Walker's term came from the shipyard with more prosaic names of various New York neighborhoods on their letterboards. For

that matter, Hylan's largesse was quickly painted over by Walker, and the twelve floating testimonials to the good character of people Mayor Hylan wanted to help him become a three-term mayor were renamed *Sea Gate*, *Flatbush*, *Astoria*, and so forth. Indeed, Hylan's naming the three big turbo-electrics after Messrs. Wanamaker, Loft, and Hearst was partially undone under Walker, as well. The *'Loft* became b) *West Brighton*, and *'Hearst* became b) *Whitehall* (ii). Only *Rodman Wanamaker* retained her original name all of her days, and that was because Wanamaker himself had passed away and such a gesture might have seemed cruel.

But this is to get ahead of the story. The location of the first launching – a dual launching – was the Tebo Yacht Basin Company in South Brooklyn, a subsidiary of Todd Shipyards. Ready to go on Saturday, December 27, 1924, were *Murray Hulbert* and *Herbert Riegelmann*, named, respectively, after the president of the city's Board of Aldermen and the borough president of Brooklyn, the latter then being a justice-elect of the New York State Supreme Court, as well.

---

tween Whitehall Street and Governors Island for the Federal Government, and she was the last of the 16-vessel fleet to be retired from active service, an event that happened in 1968.
15. For additional material on the 151-footers, see "New York's New Oil-Burning Ferryboats," *Marine Engineering*, 31 (1926), 70–71; "New York's New Ferryboats," *Marine Engineering*, 34 (1929), 243–50.

*Fifteen of the sixteen 151-foot-class
ferryboats were scrapped – or allowed
to rot away, as was the case with
Astoria, originally the* William T.
Collins, *shown here at a Staten Island
ships' graveyard in the late 1970s.
[Howard W. Serig, Jr.]*

One reason why the Major General William H. Hart *has managed to survive and join the marvelous maritime collection of the South Street Seaport is that she ran in New York service for the U.S. Army after her days with the municipal fleet were over. Shown here in 1954 on the Whitehall St.–Governors Island run, her original lines were dramatically altered when the Army installed a second-deck cabin to accommodate additional pedestrian traffic. [author]*

The two ferryboats stood poised on parallel ways. Shipyard workers had carefully removed virtually all of the cribbing holding back the two vessels, all but one key timber under each boat. And then after Hulbert's wife and Riegelmann's niece had dutifully christened the twin vessels, the men after whom they were named were each handed a large saw and set to the task of cutting through that final timber. It was a good old-fashioned take-off-your-coat-and-roll-up-your-sleeves country-fair competition (although the metaphor must respect the fact it was late December), a competition that the larger and stronger Hulbert won by several minutes. Both vessels were scheduled to be assigned to the old Union line between Whitehall Street and the foot of Brooklyn's Atlantic Avenue. (Appendix C provides additional information on the whole 16-vessel fleet of 151-footers.)

The Rockaways

One of John Francis Hylan's last ceremonial functions as mayor of the City of New York took place on Saturday, October 17, 1925, several weeks after he had been beaten in the Democratic mayoral primary by State Senator James J. Walker. He opened a brand-new ferry line that day. It was his last, and a highly unusual one, as well.

The Rockaway peninsula in New York is a sandy spit of land that

Only one of the 16-boat class of 151-foot ferryboats survives. Originally the John A. Lynch, *later the* Harlem, *and finally the* Major General William H. Hart, *she is shown here in retirement at the South Street Seaport. [author]*

fronts the Atlantic Ocean many miles away from the city's business and commercial districts. While it is connected to Nassau County at its eastern end, the peninsula is not contiguous with any part of New York City. Rockaway is, though, very definitely a part of New York City, within Queens County, even while separated from both Brooklyn and mainland Queens by the waters of Jamaica Bay.

There had long been various steamboat services operating to points on the Rockaway peninsula from places like Canarsie and Sheepshead Bay, often under the formality of official ferry leases issued by the municipal government, but these were not over and back ferryboat operations.

One of Hylan's many road-building projects had been to extend Brooklyn's principal thoroughfare, Flatbush Avenue, out across some rather barren swampland – called, appropriately, Great Barren Island – to the shores of Jamaica Bay opposite Rockaway. How else to get across than by ferry?

In typical Hylan fashion a motorcade with a thousand people participating made its noisy way out Flatbush Avenue to the new ferry slip. A band struck up a lively rendition of "Down Went McGinty to the Bottom of the Sea," whether in acknowledgment of Hylan's recent electoral reversal or in anticipation of maritime perils is uncertain. The mayor and other officials then boarded the 151-footer *John H. McCooey* for the inaugural ride across the narrow neck of the bay to Rockaway, Queens County, U.S.A. Other less important participants followed on the '*McCooey*'s sister ship, the *Maurice E. Connolly*. But then things came a little unraveled, even if no "McGintys" so much as got their feet wet.

The '*Connolly* went aground on the soft mud bottom of Jamaica Bay thanks to a swiftly running tide and strong winds, and stayed there for a half-hour until a city-owned tug pulled her free. Meanwhile the mayor went on with the second half of the ceremony over on the Queens side, saying that this was one last thing he wanted to do before leaving office, and wasn't it too bad that Governor Smith had thwarted his plan to build a tunnel under the Narrows between Brooklyn and Staten Island.

Then it was everybody aboard the *Edward Riegelmann*, a third 151-footer assigned to the ceremony, for the return to Brooklyn. Two-and-a-half months later, Hylan left City Hall and, actually, it wasn't all that long until the new Rockaway ferry line was itself rendered superfluous by the construction of a smart-looking vertical-lift span, the Marine Parkway Bridge. (Today it's called the Gil Hodges Marine Parkway Bridge in honor of the late first baseman of the Brooklyn Dodgers.) The bridge is now owned and operated by the Triborough Bridge and Tunnel Authority, but its construction bears noting. It was built by the Marine Park Bridge Authority, a special-purpose agency with but a single individual on its governing board, and that man was Robert Moses, the impresario of New York's adapting to the automotive age in the 1930s and later. Incredibly, the Marine Parkway Bridge was built in but one year. With its opening on July 3, 1937, the Flatbush Avenue–Rockaway ferry was no longer needed and was abandoned. But much of the rhetoric that flowed at the opening of this bridge is quite germane to the ferryboat story. For no longer was New York building East River crossings to link the outer boroughs with the city's epicenter. Now the emphasis is on circumferential thorough-fares, and the travel mode these new facilities are designed around is the private automobile – not the streetcar, not the subway train. And that's exactly what Moses said in his speech on the day the bridge opened.

The Flatbush Avenue–Rock-away ferry was a different kind of service in New York, right from its inception. The rapidity with which all kinds of new mobility patterns and needs would soon change the shape and style of New York to its core can be seen fore-shadowed in the fact that this serv-ice didn't even exist before October 17, 1925 – and yet it was replaced by a bridge on July 3, 1937.

Summary

At the end of the 1910–1925 era several things can be said about the ferryboat scene in New York. The railroad services across the Hudson River seemed to be in stable condition – but it was a false stability. Their years of growth were over and only *one more new ferryboat* would be built for the five networks after 1925. Furthermore, their steady patron-age figures will begin to erode in the next era, 1925–1955. For on November 12, 1927, after seven years of work, the area's first sub-aqueous vehicular tunnel, the Hol-land Tunnel, will open for business linking the northern end of Jersey City with Canal Street in Manhat-tan. And in that same fall of 1927, yet another trans-Hudson vehic-ular venture was begun. On Sep-tember 21, 1927, ground was broken for the George Washington Bridge. While this Hudson River crossing was up near 180 Street in Manhattan and arguably not all that "competitive" with the more downtown-oriented railroad fer-ries, the larger fact is that the new uptown bridge was part of a whole new set of automotive op-tions soon to be available for a new generation of New Jersey sub-urbanites who work each day in Manhattan. The George Washing-ton Bridge will not just have an impact on the railroad ferryboats; it will knock off a few railroad lines themselves, and help to drive the others into the public sector.

Even the municipal ferryboat system that grew so rapidly under Mayor Hylan will see many of its routes abandoned after he leaves office in 1925. The public service they provided was judged to be too expensive for the municipal budget to bear, especially dur-ing the lean years of the Great Depression.

And the independents? Well, the older style of such operators – the Union Ferry Company and the Williamsburg ferries – will be gone before the era even begins. Here and there a small operator will stay in business up through and even after the years of the Second World War – some "up-river" lines across the Hudson somewhat beyond the scope of this narrative come to mind, as do services linking Staten Island with the New Jersey mainland. But, wonder of wonders, the 1925–1955 era will also see some new kinds of gutsy entrepreneurship develop in the private sector, cleverly blend-ing new technology and new capi-tal to make an era of overall retrenchment see some interesting initiatives, as well.

But finally, before seeing more of the 1925–1955 period in chapter 9, what, in closing, can be said of Mayor Hylan?

With the benefit of hindsight it is easy to dismiss Hylan as a free-spending profligate whose legacy in the harbor was merely temporary protection from market forces for a half-dozen or so doomed ferryboat lines. But the man was not without vision and his purposes were far from venal. It is purely speculative to inquire if there were better strategies and policies that might, if pursued, have avoided massive deterioration in the unbelievably valuable urban real estate located under the East River bridges. But the cold fact is that John Francis Hylan took steps in that direction: he *did something*! It's easy to laugh at Hylan's boat-naming foibles, but none have ever found in his boat-building program any hint of scandal or abuse. Hylan may just have been something America has seen little enough of, complains all the time that it needs, but has difficulty recognizing when one comes along – an effective urban manager.[16]

---

16. John Hylan returned to the bench after his two terms in City Hall and served as a justice in Children's Court. He was appointed by Mayor Walker, the man who defeated him in the 1925 Democratic primary. Although long associated with Brooklyn, in his later years Hylan made his home in Forest Hills, Queens, and it was here that he died of a heart attack in his 68th year early on the morning of January 12, 1936. For an unusual look at this unusual man, see John F. Hylan, *Autobiography of John Francis Hylan* (New York: The Rotary Press, 1922).

Here, finally, the era when the ferryboat story begins to assume the shape of its current condition.

Between 1925 and 1955 the Hudson River railroad ferries found themselves faced with competition from three separate vehicular crossings, the Holland Tunnel of 1927, the George Washington Bridge of 1931, and the Lincoln Tunnel of 1941. During its early months of operation, the Holland Tunnel cut into vehicular traffic on the Erie R.R.'s ferries by 50%, prompting the railroad to slash its own fares. The 45¢ charge for a typical "roadster" was cut to 20¢, for instance, shortly after the tunnel opened. The D. L. & W. was equally affected; vehicular traffic dropped by thirty to forty per cent on its routes. Here, though, the ferry operator's reaction was not one of aggressive competition with the newcomer: in January 1928, the railroad shut down the Christopher Street–Hoboken service at night and on Sundays.

The overall result of all the new construction was further changes in travel behavior, and further deterioration in ferryboat patronage. The five railroad ferryboat operators carried over 91 million passengers in 1925 and operated twelve separate routes over and back across the Hudson. By 1955 this had dropped to 21 million passengers on six routes, and the first of the railroad ferryboat services to cease operations entirely did so on New Year's Eve in 1949 when the Pennsylvania R.R. shut down the Cortlandt Street–Exchange Place service. This cessation was supposedly of a temporary nature, but in fact it turned out to be quite permanent. Table IX-1 displays these 1952 *vs.* 1955 contrasts on a route-by-route and railroad-by-railroad basis.

Oddly enough, when the P.R.R. shut down its New York ferryboat operation there was no mention of the event in the major New York newspapers, so insignificant had the service become in its final years—two old boats, *Chicago* and *Newark* (ii), on a half-hour schedule, with the deckhands collecting fares at the Manhattan end of the line. This was, of course, the very same Cortlandt Street–Paulus Hook service that had initiated steam-powered ferryboat service under Robert Fulton's leadership 137 years, 5 months, and 28 days earlier, when *Jersey* first made her way across the mighty Hudson to the cheers of throngs lining both shores.

Fulton *(ii)*, *Union Ferry Company,*
1852–1867

But there were no throngs in 1949, not even a one-paragraph story in the next morning's newspaper. And what *was* in the press? What happened in New York on December 31, 1949, that was more important than the ferryboat finale down in the old Third Ward where Cortlandt Street meets the Hudson River and where for so many years the old Northern Hotel gave nineteenth-century travelers a place to rest from their journey when they first reached New York City? Well, maybe the shape of the future was best captured in a small item on an inside page of *The New York Times* on January 1, 1950. It told how on the day the ferry to Paulus Hook sailed for the last time, out in Queens at the new Idlewild Airport on the shore of Jamaica Bay, a KLM Royal Dutch airliner revved up its four piston engines and took off into the wind, bound eastward for Gander, Amsterdam, and Rome. Aboard was the young monarch of a middle-eastern nation whose then-strange-sounding name, Mohammad Reza Pahlavi, would become more familiar in the decades to follow and whose title, the Shah of Iran, would become

even more so. Representing New York's Mayor William O'Dwyer on the tarmac at Idlewild that day to bid the Shah and his party the city's official farewell was none other than Grover Whalen, then the city's official greeter and meeter and the man who, a quarter-century earlier, had been Red Mike Hylan's "shah" of the growing municipal ferryboat fleet.

Whalen had stepped down from his post with the city's Department of Plant and Structures in 1924, and in his place Mayor Hylan appointed William Wirt Mills, Whalen's deputy, to manage the agency that ran the city's ferryboats. Mills implemented Hylan's policies for the rest of Red Mike's term. Then, with the return to power of a Tammany Democrat in 1926, Jimmy Walker, a new crew of political appointees took over the city agencies; Plant and Structures went to one Albert Goldman.

In the early years of the Walker administration there was no discontinuity in ferry management from the days of John Francis. New vessels continued to be ordered and none of the services begun by Walker's predecessors was abandoned, or even felt to be

under threat. On the other hand, there was no effort to inaugurate any new municipal services, either. One might speculate whether Hylan, had he been re-elected in 1925, might have moved in and established a city-run service to replace the Long Island R.R.'s operation across the East River between the foot of East 34 Street and Hunter's Point, which was phased out in March 1925. Walker didn't, although his people were active in negotiating the arrangements that saw a privately-operated East 34 Street Vehicular Ferry Company begin operations in 1927 as a substitute, of sorts, for the L.I.R.R. service.

So the point is this: Walker–Goldman didn't rock any of the boats that Hylan–Whalen–Mills had set on their various courses. They didn't until October 1929, that is, when the onset of the Great Depression gave an enormous jolt to the whole municipal fiscal apparatus. City expenses had to be trimmed, as a downturn in general economic activity translated into reduced tax yields. What better piece of the budget was there to cut than ferryboat services across the East River, which were vainly attempting to realize some wholly indirect objective like retaining the viability of neighborhoods under the East River bridges and whose patronage was not only marginal, but marginal and falling? (In 1925, Hylan's last year in office, the East River municipal ferry lines carried 7.6 million passengers; in 1930, the first year after the crash of the Stock Exchange, this total was down to 6.7 million. Two years later it was 5.2 million.)

On May 27, 1931, the last two vessels in the fleet of sixteen 151-foot ferryboats were launched— the *Murray Hill* and the *Washington Square*.[1] Less than eight months later, on January 14, 1932, Goldman was asking the Sinking Fund Commission for authority to abandon outright the East 23

Street–Greenpoint and Whitehall Street–Hamilton Avenue routes, services that the new vessels were, in essence, purchased to work. This, then, became the new policy direction. Indeed the first of the Depression-induced cutbacks happened even *before* the last of the 151-footers were launched; on May 1, 1931, the Grand Street–Broadway/Brooklyn service was discontinued and additional abandonments followed, the details of which can all be seen in Appendix B. By the end of the 1925–1955 era the only municipally-operated ferryboat service still in business in New York was the one that began it all back in 1905, Whitehall Street–Saint George. There was a small number of municipally-run institutional services, so called, still in business in 1955 – ferry routes serving various health, welfare, and penal institutions located on islands in the East River and the approach to Long Island Sound. Many of these had previously been operated by the state government, using single-ended steamboats. Whalen was successful in bringing them under the umbrella of his then-rapidly-growing empire in the early days of the

Hylan Administration, arguing, among other things, that emergency vehicles like fire engines could better and faster reach these islands aboard true ferryboats. Indeed it was for these institutional routes that the city designed and built its first diesel-powered ferryboats, the 1927 sister ships *Mott Haven* and *Greenwich Village*, each 245 gross tons and 99.4 feet long. These were both direct-drive diesels; a third sister, *Chelsea*, built in 1930, was diesel-electric. The institutional services also explain the presence on the municipal roster of a handful of single-ended steamboats over the years – *Welfare*, of 1930; *Riverside*, of 1906; and *Col. Clayton*, built in 1919, purchased by the city after military service during the First World War, and the only municipal vessel able to claim Milwaukee, Wisconsin, as the place where she was launched.

These institutional services excepted, Table IX-2 depicts the rise and fall of the municipal ferryboat empire: from one route in 1905 to over a dozen twenty years later, but then back to one again by 1955. Table IX-2 suggests an important qualification, though, to

---

1. The two were launched at the Todd Shipyard in Brooklyn, *Murray Hill* being the first. At a subsequent dinner in Brooklyn's Hotel Bossert to commemorate the event, ex-Governor Alfred E. Smith said: "The city undoubtedly operates more ferries than any other city in the world." Smith's wife had sponsored the *Washington Square*.

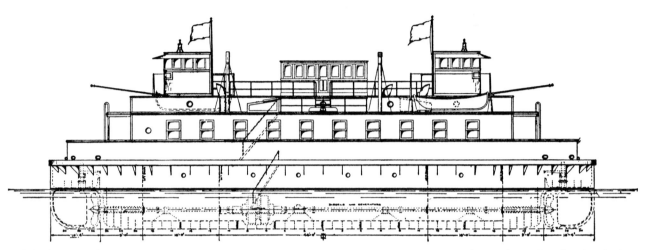

While the City of New York has run more ferryboats in the harbor over the years than any other operator, the state government was but a minor operator. In addition to a small fleet of steamboats, the state's Department of Mental Hygiene took delivery of the Tenkenas *and the* Wards Island *in 1929 for service to Wards Island, site of an East River hospital. [author's collection]*

the claim that Whitehall Street–Saint George was the *only* general-purpose ferryboat operation under municipal operation in 1955 with the very important stipulation that for a decade onward from 1954 the 69 Street/Brooklyn–Saint George service was municipally owned, vessels and all; it was operated on the city's behalf, however, by a private company. Details of this arrangement will be discussed later in this chapter.

Another important point to make is that the phase-out of mu-nicipal ferryboat services between 1925 and 1955 was not *only* the result of Depression-induced budget constraints. Several routes were rendered unnecessary because the public sector kept right on building new bridges and tunnels across previously open waterways. The East 92 Street–Astoria line across the East River, for instance, was abandoned on July 31, 1936; it had been municipally operated since 1920.[2] Captain Levi Brodhead navigated the ferryboat *Rockaway* on the route's last run, a last run that came to pass because earlier in the month the Triborough Bridge had been completed and opened for traffic, linking Astoria with the upper East Side of Manhattan. Likewise, in April 1939 the city discontinued service between Clason's Point in the Bronx and College Point in Queens because the Bronx–Whitestone Bridge had

_____

2. In 1918 the New York and East River Fy. Co. abandoned service on this route; it reopened under municipal auspices in 1920.

been built to connect the same two points and, suddenly, the 151-footers were no longer needed there, either.[3]

There's yet another consideration worthy of mention when discussing the demise of ferryboats, and that is the degree to which the area's commerce was relying less and less on horse-powered vehicles for its vitality. The bridge grades were especially hard on horses, their slow speed restricted the flow of other traffic, and so one must add to the reasons for retaining ferryboat service across the East River in the 1925–1955 period a desire to provide an option that was oriented toward the needs of horse-drawn traffic. But as animal-powered carts and wagons decreased in numbers, one more rationale for ferryboats faded away.

The 1925–1955 era, though, was not totally one of retrenchment on the ferryboat front. On the morning of Monday, November 9, 1926, a brand-new ferryboat line opened for business. It was unique in many ways. For one thing, it was a wholly corporate and for-profit effort at the end of a ten-year period that had seen the municipal government emerge as the largest operator of ferryboats in the harbor. But this wasn't all; its boats were quite different, too. Designed and built especially for the new service, they eschewed foot passengers entirely, carrying only autos, trucks, and wagons. Drivers and passengers were accommodated, but no cabin was provided for their comfort. If the weather was favorable, fine – get out and walk around the deck. But if it was cold or rainy? Well, better stay in the car and hope that the windows don't fog up.

Most unusual of all, though, were the engines that powered the new company's brand-new ferryboats. They were a new kind of internal-combustion engine called a diesel. (In the year 1926 the word "diesel" was universally capitalized, incidentally.) Propulsion was not effected, though, by the diesel engines' being directly and

---

3. Prior to the initiation of municipal ferryboat service between Clason's Point, The Bronx, and College Point, Queens, in 1921, there were two different private companies operating in the area. From 1886 to 1918 the New York & College Point Fy. Co. ran from the foot of E. 99 St. in Manhattan to College Point, with intermediate stops at E. 134 St., Manhattan, and at North Beach in Queens, then the site of an amusement park owned by the ferry company and today the location of LaGuardia Airport. The New York & College Point Fy. Co. faded from the scene in 1918 when its assets were confiscated by the U.S. Government because they were owned by an alien, one George Ehret. Between 1910 and 1917 the Twin City Fy. Co. ran a Clason's Point–College Point service. The completion of the Bronx–Whitestone Bridge and the abandonment of the municipal ferry between Clason's Point and College Point was also coincident with the opening of the 1939–1940 World's Fair in Flushing Meadows.

On Friday, December 13, 1901, the N.Y. & C. P. Fy. Co.'s *College Point* had a strange accident. En route to College Point that foggy morning she ran aground off North Brother Island. Passengers waiting at College Point for her next trip were understandably surprised when out of the fog came, not the ferryboat, but two lifeboats full of passengers. The lifeboats made more trips out to the stricken vessel, and eventually all were safely evacuated.

mechanically connected to the propellers. In a manner not at all unlike the municipal turbo-electric ferryboats described in chapter 8, the diesel engines ran electric generators and the screws were then turned by electric motors. This very same "diesel-electric" principle, a decade or so later, would be applied to railroad locomotives. It quickly banished steam engines entirely, and it remains conventional practice to this day on railways the world wide.

Electric power for ships was a fascinating and captivating subject for marine architects in the years after the First World War. The trade press was continually featuring articles arguing the greater efficiencies, not to mention reduced costs, that electric power would bring, and, despite interest in turbo-electric installations, the primary way vessels came to be powered by electricity was with diesel systems. Furthermore, in the specialized world of double-ended ferryboats there was also the prospect that diesel-electric propulsion would permit the adoption of "split-shaft" designs and allow vessels to get away from the conventional post-*Bergen* arrange-

ment where both the forward and the aft propellers rotate at the same speed.[4]

The company that initiated this new service in 1926 was not an old-line operator, but a brand-new enterprise, one with its roots in Hudson County, N.J., real-estate interests, as well as the Erie R.R. In fact, it was the company's link with the Erie that provided facilities for landing on both sides of the river. The service crossed the Hudson from the foot of Manhattan's West 23 Street to Baldwin Avenue in Weehawken, a site just a little less than a mile south of the New York Central Railroad's Weehawken depot. Baldwin Avenue was a place where the Erie R.R. had freight yards and other

waterfront facilities, while West 23 Street was a "union station," so to speak, where four of the Hudson River railroad ferryboat operators maintained service at one time or another, and the new company leased slip space there from the Erie.

On Sunday, November 8, 1926, the company demonstrated one of its new vessels for the press, and at a few minutes after eleven o'clock the next morning the *Governor Moore* – or the M.V. *Governor Moore*, to be a bit more precise – pulled out of Baldwin Avenue for the line's formal inaugural. Aboard was the incumbent governor of the Garden State, enjoying a ride on a vessel named in his honor: the new company followed Red Mike Hy-

---

4. See, for example, S. M. Robinson, "Diesel-Electric Drive for Double Ended Ferry Boats and Low Powered Cargo Vessels," *Marine Engineering*, 25 (December 1920), 974ff. Diesel-electric ferryboats were deployed in San Francisco Bay earlier than in New York: see W. H. Wild, "Electric Drive Adopted in a New Field," *Marine Engineering*, 7 (October 1922), 626–29. There was even a diesel-electric ferryboat operating on a trans-Hudson route in the Poughkeepsie, N.Y. area before such vessels appeared in New York Harbor. She was the *Poughkeepsie*, built in 1922 in Mill Basin, Brooklyn, and claimed by her owners, the Poughkeepsie & Highland Fy. Co., Ltd., to be the first commercial vessel in the world to be operated by electricity. See William H. Easton, "The Electric Ferryboat Poughkeepsie," *Marine Engineering*, 28 (March 1923), 159ff.

The original 1926 vessels that introduced diesel-electric power as a propulsion option for New York ferryboats were built as single-deck vessels with no passenger cabin. In later years, to make the vessels adaptable to routes where foot traffic was important, an enclosed passenger cabin was added on the second deck. [*author's collection*] [*Steamship Historical Society of America*]

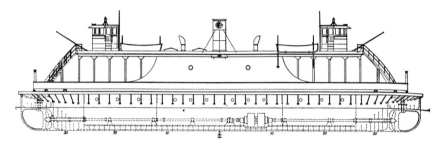

lan's lead and didn't hesitate at all in naming its ferryboats after human beings who were still among the living. As the 155-foot all-steel ferryboat navigated its way across the Hudson and angled southward toward West 23 Street it received whistle greetings from passing vessels large and small – appropriate for a maiden voyage – and, following proper maritime protocol, *Governor Moore* returned all the greetings. Coming up the Hudson at the end of an Atlantic crossing at the time was the pride of the American merchant marine, the S.S. *Leviathan* of the United States Lines, and she let out three deep reverberating salutes from her steam whistle to greet the new *Governor Moore*, blasts that

rattled windows several blocks inland in Manhattan. The new ferryboat acknowledged the welcome, but with "three strident blasts like sounds from a battered old harmonica," in the words of a newspaper report the next day.

Governor Moore's fleetmates were five sister ships, all built in Camden, N.J., to identical specifications by the American Brown Boveri Electric Corporation.[5] They were designed by a New York

5. The six were *Governor Moore, Charles W. Culkin, Grenville Kane, W. A. Baldwin, Frederick Pierce,* and *Frank E. Gannett.* See Appendix C for further details. Also see "Diesel Electric Automobile Ferry Boats," *Marine Engineering,* 31 (December 1926), 677–79.

naval architect by the name of Eads Johnson, a man who will put his hand to many novel ferryboat designs over the next quarter-century and help to make the twilight of ferryboat operations in New York a truly golden one.[6] Each boat's power plant included a pair of 6-cylinder diesels built by the New London Ship and Engine Company following a design engineered by the M.A.N. Corporation of Augsburg, Germany. Each die-

6. Johnson's name (and work) will crop up many times from here on in our story. In 1934 Mayor Fiorello LaGuardia hired him to shape-up the whole municipal ferry operation, but his principal contribution was as an independent naval architect turning out imaginative ferryboat designs for ves-

sels in New York and elsewhere. I see two things as characteristic of Johnson: the first is an abiding faith in the principal of diesel-electric power for ferryboats, and the second is total impatience with the plodding ways of public-sector bureaucracy. In 1936 he wrote a stinging article for *Marine* *Engineering* (see "Shipbuilding Nonsense – 1937 Variety," 41 [1936], 301, 308), complaining about a U.S. Navy requirement that imposed formal deep-water sea trials such as those that might be appropriate for a battleship on the ferryboat *Aquidneck*, which he had designed for service wholly within the limits of Newport, R.I. harbor. ". . . this trial should go down in the archives of nonsensical achievements we've witnessed these hectic years since March 4, 1933" (301). As this was the first day Franklin D. Roosevelt served as president of the United States, it seems

sel was rated at 350 h.p. when turning at 280 r.p.m., and each drove an electric generator; these were products of American Brown Boveri.

Power was transmitted to the propellers on these early "electric ferries" by a single electric motor, also a Brown Boveri product, which was located deep in the hull. The motor was attached to a single end-to-end propeller shaft, and so on this early deployment of the diesel-electric principle, the theoretically ideal arrangement for a double-ended ferryboat of a "split shaft" and separate motors for each screw was not adopted; it would have to await another day. Eads Johnson felt that it was better to move in the direction the theoreticians were suggesting, but take only a few steps now and more later.

All in all, everything worked out rather splendidly. The boats performed well, and traffic on the new route grew quickly to the range of a million-and-a-half vehicles a year,

reasonable to conclude that Johnson was not among F.D.R.'s stronger supporters. Johnson died in Morristown, N.J. in 1964.

a very respectable performance. Even the opening of the George Washington Bridge across the Hudson in 1931 didn't deter the Electric Ferries—the new corporation's formal title. More cars were carried across the Hudson on its boats in certain years after the bridge opened than in 1930, the last full year before the span was ready. Flushed with success, the company became aggressive in seeking out new routes and services.

At first Electric Ferries did not meet with much luck in its efforts to expand its business. Early plans envisioned operating one or more of the failing East River municipal services under contract to the city, but using its own diesel-electric vessels – East 92 Street–Astoria was discussed; nothing doing. A suggested second trans-Hudson route from the foot of fashionable West 77 Street in Manhattan brought out the kind of community opposition one might have felt appropriate had the proposal called for the construction of a rendering plant on the banks of the Hudson.

The new company was also aggressive in ways other than attempting to find new routes and services. One day in early 1927 the company's president was looking out his office window at automobiles getting in line for the several ferryboat routes operating from the West 23 Street complex. (Again thanks to the Erie, the company maintained its headquarters at this location.) And, by heavens, the president felt he detected a bias on the part of the New York City police officer directing traffic at the ferry slip. Why, the man in blue seemed to be directing autos away from the Electric Ferries line and toward the services of the competition. *Look! There goes another one. That car wants to go to Weehawken, not Hoboken. Why doesn't the cop leave it alone?*

Down the stairs flew President Carroll D. Winslow, and when Patrolman John Dilworth denied the charge and sought to back up his claim of innocence by eliciting confirming information from the very automobile drivers Winslow claimed had been directed away from the West 23 Street–Weehawken boats, Winslow took over and started directing traffic himself – with, one might assume, a corrective for the bias he felt Dilworth had earlier shown.

It was all resolved nice and peacefully the next day in the Jefferson Market Court, Magistrate Harry Goodman presiding. Charges dropped by the police; an apology from Winslow; and a sincere hope voiced by Officer Dilworth that he would never again be assigned to direct traffic at the West 23 Street ferry terminal.

Winslow's company did eventually expand. For several seasons in the 1930s it operated a New Rochelle–Port Washington service across Long Island Sound. Two of the original six boats were renamed *Westchester* and *Nassau* for this service and passenger cabins were added to their upper decks, as well. (Beginning in 1936, such newly-installed upper-deck cabins on all or most of the fleet enabled the company to carry pedestrians on its original West 23 Street–Weehawken run.) Electric Ferries also handled the Port Richmond–Bayonne, N.J. run across the Kill Van Kull from 1937 through 1945, and in a development that will be examined presently, Electric Ferries in 1939 became the operator of the 69 Street/Brooklyn–Saint George service across the Narrows, perhaps the route for which the company is best remembered in New York.

The original West 23 Street–Weehawken route came to an unusual end in July 1943, seventeen years after its opening. By this time the Port of New York Authority had opened the first tube of the Lincoln Tunnel, the Hudson River's third vehicular crossing

During the Second World War, many New York harbor ferryboats were needed for both long-term and short-term military assignments. Here the New York Central R.R.'s Stony Point has brought a boat-full of soldiers from the Brooklyn Army Base to a deepwater pier and embarcation aboard a trans-Atlantic troopship. [Library of Congress]

out of New York City, and while Electric Ferries had been able to hold its market despite the earlier opening of the George Washington Bridge, the tunnel proved a bit too much. Additionally, wartime gasoline rationing was now cutting into private automobile usage, and this also had a negative effect on business. Service on the line was severely reduced in January 1943, and eliminated entirely on July 31 of the same year. Clarence W. Walker, the company's vice-president, claimed that vehicular traffic on the line had fallen off by fifty per cent.

But the cessation of service had this unusual twist. Upriver from Electric Ferries' West 23 Street–Weehawken line, another ferry company was also having its problems and starting to feel the pinch – the Riverside and Fort Lee Ferry Company, a ferryboat-operating subsidiary of New Jersey's giant Public Service Gas and Electric Company, a utility that also operated an extensive system of trolley cars. Its fleet of ferryboats was becoming very uneconomical to operate, and on the same day Electric Ferries quit running to Baldwin Avenue,

Weehawken, Public Service did the same thing on the West 125 Street–Edgewater route. Here's the unusual twist: the very next day, August 1, 1943, Electric Ferries moved its diesel-powered fleet north and took over the Edgewater route. It was all planned and negotiated, of course; Electric Ferries didn't just start running out of West 125 Street by accident or coincidence.

The ex–Public Service route was more oriented toward the carriage of pedestrians than West 23 Street–Weehawken had been (where, in fact, pedestrians originally weren't carried at all), and so the West 125 Street service had a certain immunity from gasoline rationing. There was also a good number of "war plants" on the New Jersey side of the Hudson River, which were convenient to the Edgewater ferry slip, and this helped to maintain traffic volume, at least for the duration. With its 1926-built ferries now rigged with top-deck passenger cabins, plus a second generation of newer and larger vessels starting to arrive from various shipyards, Electric Ferries managed to keep the service going. The company felt that

operating expenses with its more efficient diesels would be lower than they had been for Public Service with its older steamers and, for a while at least, it all worked.

With the arrival of a new operator on the West 125 Street–Edgewater line in 1943, Riverside and Fort Lee's fleet of six steam-powered ferryboats was scattered.[7] One of its vessels, though, is worth tracking for a moment – *Hackensack*, a vessel that began life in 1906 as the Long Island R.R.'s *Hempstead*. Without going into all the details: she migrated to New England after the war and, following some alterations, was put to work, in something of a desperation move since new tonnage was difficult to obtain, between Woods Hole, Massachusetts, and Martha's Vineyard. Her new

---

7. Newspaper accounts of the demise of the Riverside & Fort Lee Fy. Co. in 1943 suggest that the company's vessels were to be used by the military in war-related work. It's quite likely that all or some of them were so used, but if so it was under a lease or contract arrangement. None of them was ever formally transferred to the U.S. Government. See Appendix C for details.

When the Riverside & Fort Lee Ferry Company quit running its trans-Hudson service from the foot of 125 St. in 1943, this is an advertisement the company placed in the trade press in an effort to liquidate its fleet of steam-powered double-enders. [author's collection]

FIVE FERRY BOATS FOR SALE!

	Fort Lee (Illustrated)	Hackensack	Tenafly	Edgewater	Leonia
Vehicle Capacity	39	40	40	32	29
Hull	Steel	Steel	Steel	Steel	Steel
Length	177 ft. 4 in.	185 ft.	185 ft.	146 ft. 6 in.	145 ft.
Tonnage (Gross)	923	1310	1310	687	604
H.P.	1600	1600	1600	850	500
Boiler	Scotch	Water Tube	Water Tube	Scotch	Scotch

For prices and other information inquire:

M. R. BOYLAN
Vice President in Charge of Operation

80 PARK PLACE
NEWARK, N. J.

RIVERSIDE AND FORT LEE FERRY COMPANY

owner was the Massachusetts Steamship Lines and her home port was New Bedford. And there were a couple of nice touches to it all, too. Sailing under the new name *Islander*, she was done up in a fine coat of white paint with buff-colored funnels, the tints Nature always intended for inland and coastal steamboats. (New York ferryboat operators had long since turned their backs on Mother Nature, of course, for the obvious reason that white vessels were just too hard to keep clean.[8]) Further, an upper-deck passenger cabin that Riverside and Fort Lee had installed on the vessel was removed, so in her final days she reverted to her original L.I.R.R. profile.

---

8. Hear the words of *The New York Times* on April 25, 1926, when the Walker administration announced that it was abandoning white as the color of the municipal ferryboat fleet: "The municipal ferryboats are to have their color scheme changed. For a long time they have been plying across the rivers and to and fro between the Battery and Staten Island in a more or less virgin white. Unfortunately, it was not always an immaculate, bride-like white, because the white soon lost its pristine lustre. These craft have had to run the gauntlet of many a daily smoke screen, particularly during the bituminous period from which the metropolis is just emerging, and

Islander took it all in stride and served on the 'Vineyard run for several seasons. When finally mustered out of active ferryboat service she was a veteran vessel almost 50 years old. Furthermore, *Islander*'s performance was such that her owners became sold on the utility of a double-ended ferryboat for the Woods Hole–Martha's Vineyard service, and her Eads Johnson–designed replacement in 1950, the new diesel-powered *Islander* (ii), represents a genuine milestone in the concept pioneered by Robert Fulton's *Jersey* in 1812. *Islander* (ii) is a double-ended ferryboat with a fully-enclosed main deck, including sea gates at each end to keep the rough water of Vineyard Sound from giving passengers and vehicles an unwelcome salt-water dousing on the trip over to Martha's Vineyard. This was one feature *Islander* (i) didn't have, and it made crossing the sound aboard her in any but the calmest of sea conditions something of a wet and wild adventure.

One final note: given the contemporary popularity of Martha's Vineyard and the current paucity of ferryboats in the New York area, there are many men, women, and children who live in the five boroughs today whose only experience with a true ferryboat has been aboard *Islander* (ii). That such people have had *any* ferryboat experience, though, is yet another part of the legacy of *Islander*, *a) Hempstead, b) Hackensack.*

But enough of the latter-day doings of this double-stack veteran. More needs to be said about the service on which she spent her middle years before venturing northeast to the land of Cabots, cods, Lodges, and Red Sox, the trans-Hudson service between West 125 Street, Manhattan, and Edgewater, N.J.

The Hudson River in the 125 Street area had long been an important transfer point for passengers heading in many different directions. Hudson River Day Line and Hudson River Night Line passenger steamers bound upriver to Newburgh, Poughkeepsie, and Albany paused there, as did paddlewheel vessels of the Iron Steamboat Company bound down the bay, seasonally, for Coney Island and the Rockaways. Crosstown streetcars of the Third Avenue Railway were also available to provide service inland from the river's edge to various subway and el stations, as well as to the New York Central R.R. passenger depot at Park Avenue and East 125 Street. Here passengers from northern New Jersey, after crossing the Hudson on a Riverside and Fort Lee ferryboat and then continuing crosstown on a Third Avenue car, had the convenience of catching a train without having to head "downtown" to Grand Central Terminal on East 42 Street.

their once glistening apparel of white soon degenerated to a soiled, nondescript grey, disfigured with unsightly blotches laid on by a compound of carbon and salt spray." So much for the problem; as to the solution: ". . . a deep maroon color which . . . if it does not actually keep clean longer, certainly does not advertise its uncleanliness so blatantly in a critical world." Unfortunately, the newspaper's flowing prose account was not matched with journalistic accuracy in identifying the first vessel to receive the new paint scheme. The *Times* said it was the "*Saint George.*" There was no such ferryboat in 1926, or in any year remotely close to it.

But the importance of the ferry service waned in the post-war period, and catching trains at 125 Street – or anyplace else, for that matter – just wasn't that critical any more. Early on the morning of Sunday, December 17, 1950, the ferryboat *Palisades*, one of Electric Ferries' original boats from 1926, made the final crossing.

The newer, or second-generation, ferryboats that Electric Ferries began building right before the Second World War were a wonderfully appropriate evolution from the original 1926 vessels. Again designed by the talented Eads Johnson, the newcomers were bigger than the initial six – 184 feet long *vs.* 146; 565 gross tons *vs.* 405 – had upper-deck passenger cabins from the outset, and incorporated that final element of electric ferryboat design the 1926 vessels had not, "split shaft" propulsion – i.e., a separate motor powering the screw on each end of the boat.

Eventually Electric Ferries would buy seven of these Art Deco gems, and their delivery dates stretched from 1940 to 1947. Of interest is the location of the shipyards the company retained for their construction. Three were built in relatively nearby Oyster Bay, Long Island – *Gotham* (ii) of 1941, *The Narrows* of 1946, and *The Tides* of 1947. Two were built in Boston, Massachusetts, though, and two more in far-away Texas. Indeed, the very first of the second-generation boats was launched in Orange, Texas on November 25, 1939, at the Levingston Shipyard there. She arrived in New York Harbor on March 5, 1940, and of her voyage from south to north there is a "Texas tale."

The maritime trade press gave the new ferryboat's construction more than passing interest. The years 1939 and 1940 were a time when new naval tonnage was the more common news in the industry and, once hostilities began, photographs routinely appeared of sea-going merchant ships of non-belligerent nations with huge flags painted on the sides of their hulls, lest U-boat commanders draw incorrect conclusions about their status as friend or foe. Understandably, then, construction of a vessel for such a peaceful pursuit as harbor ferry work provided a respite from the more ominous news of the day.

Much was said of the technical details of the newcomer: engines, electrical system, deck construction, carrying capacity. But also (and here's the "Texas tale"), great pains were taken to point out that the passage of the new electric-powered ferryboat from Orange, Texas to the Hudson River was, in the words of the trade publication *Marine Engineering*, the "second longest ocean voyage ever made by an American ferryboat." (The presumed longest? An earlier voyage of an ex–Chesapeake Bay vessel to Rio de Janeiro after her sale to Brazilian interests.)

But hold on a minute! When Electric Ferries' new vessel sailed from Texas to New York, there may have been a non-stop character to the trip that made it the "second longest ocean voyage ever made by an American ferryboat." But to get from Orange, Texas to open water, you must navigate Sabine Pass, and long before anybody ever thought of powering ferryboats with diesel engines and electric motors, the New York ferryboat *Clifton* (i) was steaming through the Sabine, serving with the Union Navy in the war against the Confederacy, and other New

A bright sunny day in East Boston, Massachusetts. The year is 1941 and flags are flying from an about-to-be-launched ferryboat; the 569-ton Hudson *will soon join the growing fleet of Electric Ferries, Inc. [Steamship Historical Society of America]*

York ferryboats ventured even farther west along the Texas Gulf Coast. *Marine Engineering*'s claim in 1940 may have been valid; but it's just as likely their staff was completely unaware of the role *Clifton* (i), *John P. Jackson*, *Hunchback*, et al. played during the Civil War.

The new vessel bore the name of Electric Ferries' president at the time of her launch; as a result, generations of New Yorkers who patronized the company's various services would come to regard the vessel's namesake as a true household word, even though the man's identity remained largely unknown. The Texas-built ferryboat was the *E. G. Diefenbach*, named after Elmer Diefenbach, a man in the Hudson County, New Jersey real-estate investment business and one of the movers and shakers behind Electric Ferries, Inc., but a man whom thousands of people from the 1940s to the 1960s came to know only as a name painted on a ferryboat – a pretty nice ferryboat, at that.

The route on which the *E. G. Diefenbach* would do the most to memorialize old E. G.'s name was the one across the Narrows from the foot of 69 Street in Brooklyn to Saint George in Staten Island. The original operator of this route from its inception in 1912 was the Brooklyn and Richmond Ferry Company. But in 1939 age finally caught up with its fleet of second-hand, turn-of-the-century beam-engine paddlewheelers.

Brooklyn and Richmond was in a self-perpetuating downward spiral; old and creaky vessels meant service and schedule irregularities, undependable service meant loss of patronage, and an inadequate and unpredictable revenue base ruled out the purchase of new vessels. Travelers between Brooklyn and Staten Island after 1924 also had an option – the municipally-operated line between Brooklyn's 39 Street and Saint George, which was not beset with Brooklyn and Richmond's problems. Then came the final blow: on February 2, 1939, the U.S. Department of Commerce ordered the company to halt all its service. One of its 40-year-old sidewheelers was found to be in extremely poor condition and, pending inspection of the whole fleet, service was to cease. Police officers were dispatched to the 69 Street ferry slip to enforce the order and direct traffic.

The City of New York came to the line's rescue. Two 151-footers that by 1939 were used only during summertime periods of heavy traffic were taken out of winter quarters and leased to the Brooklyn and Richmond Ferry Company. But this was an admittedly temporary move, and the city's Commissioner of Docks, John McKenzie, said so quite emphatically when he announced that *Astoria* and *Flushing* were the vessels he planned to make available.[9] And, indeed, it was temporary. On March 1, 1939, Electric Ferries, Inc., took over the operation with its newer ferryboats.

Assuming this additional route put quite a strain on the company's fleet resources, and while new vessels continued to be pur-

---

9. Curiously, it was the second time in this line's short history that a leased vessel by the name of *Flushing* worked the route. Back in 1912, when the company inaugurated service with borrowed Long Island R.R. vessels, that company's *Flushing* and *Garden City* inaugurated service on the 69 St.–St. George run.

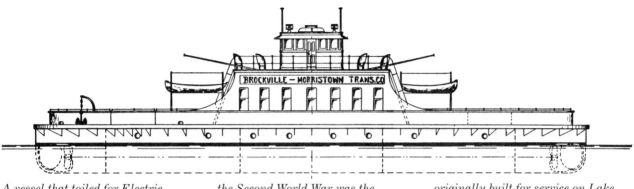

A vessel that toiled for Electric Ferries, Inc., for a short time during the Second World War was the Elmer W. Jones, *a small ferryboat* *originally built for service on Lake Ontario.* [author's collection]

chased—sister ships of *E. G. Diefenbach* – the Federal Government also requisitioned several of the company's ferryboats for war-related work. (See Appendix C for details.) Electric Ferries needed all the boats it could get, and so on three different occasions it tapped the second-hand market for relief.

The smallest of the trio of second-hand vessels that joined the Electric Ferries fleet between 1939 and 1943 was the Eads Johnson–designed *Elmer W. Jones*. She was a mere 117 feet long and 277 gross tons. Diesel-powered, but not diesel-electric, she was built in Groton, Connecticut in 1926 by the New England Ship and Engine Company. (In the same year this same company built the diesel engines for Electric Ferries' initial fleet of vessels.) The '*Jones* ran for the Brockville and Morristown Transportation Company on Lake Ontario until 1942 when she joined Electric Ferries. Her tenure with Mr. Diefenbach's company was brief, however; she was sold to the U.S. Government after about a year's service in New York. Following the war, *Elmer W. Jones* was back with the Brockville and Morristown Transportation Company.

Next came *Chelsea*. Steam-powered, she was built in 1923 for Reading R.R. service across the Delaware River at Philadelphia. She was purchased by Electric Ferries in 1939; sometime around 1943 she was sold and later turned up running for the State of Virginia as *Warwick*, but with her steam engine replaced by a diesel. Last heard, she had been sold to South American interests.

The third wartime vessel Electric Ferries bought on the second-hand market is one of the more interesting ferryboats to sail New York waters. Like *Elmer W. Jones* she began her career on fresh water in upstate New York. Built in 1937 in Burlington, Vermont for service across Lake

Champlain as *City of Plattsburgh*, she was rechristened *Richmond* and joined Electric Ferries in 1942. During the hurricane of 1944, *Richmond* was tied up at the 69 Street ferry slip riding out the storm when extra-high tides brought on by the heavy weather caused her to get snagged on the slip in such a way that when the tide ebbed she was flipped over on her side.

Righted with some difficulty, *Richmond* was sold in 1947 as new boats of the *'Diefenbach* class began to arrive on the property. Then she became *George Clinton* and ran on trans-Hudson routes north of New York City under ownership of the State of New York. In 1958 she was sold to South American interests.

But a word about *Richmond*. For if Eads Johnson's *E. G. Diefenbach* was stylish Art Deco, then *Richmond* was World's Fair futuristic. Her main deck was autos only, expectedly enough, and her passenger cabin was topside, just like on the newest "electric ferries." Indeed, vehicles below / passengers above had become a common ferryboat design by this time. Before *Richmond*, though,

designers felt compelled to include full side "walls" on the main deck of such boats, in imitation of more conventional vessels with main-deck passenger cabins. After all, that's how a ferryboat *looked*. From a purely engineering perspective such "walls" were not necessary; the weight of the upper deck could easily be accommodated by a few thin steel columns at the extremities of the vessel, with principal support coming from a center trunk, so called, an enclosure along the vessel's centerline that provided access to the engine room, space for the ducting of exhaust, and so forth. And that's the way *Richmond* was built; the automobiles she carried on her main deck were quite visible, somewhat as if they were all parked in a giant carport. *Richmond* had twin wheelhouses, and they were built into either end of a long streamlined slab placed atop the second-deck passenger cabin. Poor old *Richmond*: she may have been as modern looking as tomorrow; but she was also as ugly as sin.

In the post–Second World War years the *'Diefenbach* class was rounded out to the full seven boats.

The earlier 1926 vessels were sold, although three of them managed to enjoy brief careers with other operators in New York Harbor. (See Appendix C for details.) One of the trio, the vessel that was originally *Grenville Kane*, sits rusting away in a Staten Island junkyard to this very day. Another, *Frank E. Gannett*, b) *Nassau*, migrated to the Panama Canal in 1942, and later moved down the west coast of South America to service under Chilean registry.[10]

By 1954, Electric Ferries felt that it was no longer able to sustain operations on the 69 Street–Saint George route. The ferryboat service across the Narrows, though, was more necessary than ever. It was carrying over 2 million vehicles a year, and plans

---

10. In 1929, *Frank E. Gannett* sailed north from New York City and was chartered to the New England Steamship Company, then the operator of the Woods Hole–Martha's Vineyard service to which *Hackensack*, a) *Hempstead*, later migrated. It was a short charter, just to help the company with its late-summer traffic peak.

Bulging with Staten Island–bound cars on her broad main deck, Hamilton maneuvers into one of the Saint George ferry slips used by the ferryboat service across the Narrows to and from the foot of 69 St., Brooklyn. [author]

were proceeding, after years of talk and indecision, to bridge the entrance to New York Harbor and link Brooklyn with Staten Island.[11]

But despite the traffic volume the profit-and-loss statement had become bleak, and so for one last time the City of New York stepped

in and bought itself a ferryboat operation, vessels and all. This time municipal operation didn't eventuate, though, and the city-owned service was leased out for operation – subsidized operation – to a private corporation. The seven ferryboats remained in a variation of the olive-green paint scheme they wore for Electric Ferries and were not decorated to resemble the rest of the municipal fleet. Many regular riders, for that

11. In 1954, 2.4 million vehicles were carried on the 69 St.–St. George ferryboat line, *vs.* 1.6 million on the municipal service between Whitehall St. and St. George. The latter, on the other hand, carried far more pedestrian passengers – 22.5 million *vs.* 2.0 million in 1954. It wasn't until after the Second World War that 69 St.–St. George began to outperform Whitehall St.–St. George in the carriage of vehicles. In 1936, for example, Whitehall St.–St. George carried 857,500 vehicles; 69 St.–St. George, only 340,000. In 1940 the score was 962,900 *vs.* 534,700 in favor of Whitehall St.–St. George.

Here's the classic Art Deco look that New Yorkers knew for many years. The Narrows, *one of the second-generation ferryboats operated by Electric Ferries, Inc., makes her way across the body of water after which she was named.* [author]

matter, remained blissfully unaware that their service had shifted from the private to the public sector. Then the Verrazano–Narrows Bridge was built and on Wednesday, November 25, 1964, the newest boat in the fleet, the 1947-built *The Tides*, left Brooklyn at 11:23 P.M. with Captain George Summerville in the pilot house, on the line's very last trip. A reporter from *The New York Times* thought he'd get a

clever angle for his story of the shut-down, and he interviewed a 74-year-old passenger by the name of Blanche McQueeney, who told him about the time in 1912 when she rode the ferryboat *John Englis* on what she remembered as the first day of service between Brooklyn and Staten Island.

Then there was "Whitey": poor "Whitey," an old mixed-breed dog that wandered up to the Brooklyn terminal of the 69 Street–Saint

George ferry line during the Second World War and just adopted the whole company. When the private sector faded from the scene and the municipal government took over and leased out the service to a new corporation, it all made no difference to "Whitey." On the day before the line was to quit entirely in 1964 they called the A.S.P.C.A. and a truck was sent down to the ferry slip, and "Whitey" wasn't there when *The*

Tides left for Staten Island for the last time.

OVER AND ABOVE absorbing the seven "electric ferries" in 1954, the city's ferryboat fleet looked like this during the 1925 – 1955 era: steady construction of new state-of-the-art vessels for the Whitehall Street–Saint George service, to replace aging tonnage as well as to expand capacity; construction of a few new specialized vessels for East River institutional services; purging from the roster of older second-hand paddlewheelers purchased as various East River routes were taken over by the city during the Hylan era; and, soon enough, far more 151-footers than anyone knew what to do with as the routes for which they were built were cut back and eliminated.

Before continuing with a discussion of how ferryboat design evolved on the Whitehall Street–Saint George service, though, a story from 1936 involving one of the 151-foot class of vessels is in order. It tells how the City of New York – and the nation – celebrated the fiftieth anniversary of the dedication of the Statue of Liberty. It was, to be sure, far less

extravagant than the centenary celebration in 1986 – no "tall ships," no 200 Elvis Presley look-alikes.

President Franklin Roosevelt was in the midst of his first bid for re-election in the fall of 1936, and it is worth recounting some details of his day's schedule in New York on Wednesday, October 28 of that year.

Early in the morning, wearing a three-piece suit, a striped tie, and a light-colored fedora with the brim turned back in typical F. D. R. style, the president stepped from his private railroad car, the "Magellan," at the Bayonne station of the Jersey Central R.R. (The 1936 version of "Air Force One" normally saw the "Magellan" running as the last car of a special train called a P.O.T.U.S. Special: *President of the United States*.) A motorcade was formed and proceeded across the 1931-built Bayonne Bridge to the Port Richmond section of Staten Island – no Port Richmond–Bergen Point ferry for F. D. R. With crowds lining the streets and lights flashing from dark-maroon N.Y.P.D. motorcycles, many with side-cars, which

were providing escort, the motorcade made its way to Saint George and there boarded a municipal ferryboat (identity unknown) for a trip across the Narrows to the Brooklyn and Richmond Ferry Company's slip at the foot of 69 Street in Bay Ridge. First major stop on the day's schedule was the new Midwood campus of Brooklyn College where Roosevelt helped lay the cornerstone of a gym there – built, partially, with assistance from the Works Progress Administration. (In 1947 the president's son Franklin Delano Roosevelt, Jr. visited Brooklyn College for a ceremony that renamed the gymnasium in honor of his late father.)

Then off again and through the heart of Brooklyn to the Williamsburg Bridge; the motorcade reached Manhattan at 12:28 P.M. Down Park Row to Broadway and through the teeming financial district during the high peak of the noontime lunch hour. At the foot of Whitehall Street Roosevelt and his party boarded the city's 151-foot ferryboat *Murray Hill* for a short trip over to Governors Island; landfall at what was then a U.S. Army installation was at

The days of olive-drab vessels with the designation "Electric Ferries" painted on their flanks are over. But two survivors of the fleet remain in domestic service, one on a New York ferryboat route. The Tides *is shown at Governors Island in the spring of 1988 in U.S. Coast Guard service;* Jamestown, *once* St. George *of Electric Ferries, Inc., works a James River crossing for the Commonwealth of Virginia. [author]*

1:05, and here the president had lunch. It was hardly a leisurely meal, though, for at 1:45 he was back aboard *Murray Hill*, and the little 5-year-old ferryboat set out for Bedloe's Island and the day's principal activity. Twenty-one–gun salutes were fired both from shore batteries and from visiting warships, and Roosevelt put aside his fedora and donned a fine silk hat – this was serious business. *Murray Hill* landed at Bedloe's Island, then the name of today's Liberty Island, at 2:10 P.M.

Mayor Fiorello LaGuardia presided, and preliminary speeches by lesser dignitaries were cut short as the president was running late. At 3:45, *Murray Hill* deposited the campaigning president back on Manhattan Island. That night there was a banquet at the Waldorf-Astoria Hotel, and at 10:53 President Roosevelt reboarded the "Magellan." His train had been shuttled around to New York's Pennsylvania Station during the day and at 2:30 A.M. it quietly slipped away from the

platform and into the Hudson River tunnels, the Pennsylvania R.R. engineman being especially careful to operate his electric locomotive as smoothly as he could to avoid disturbing a presumably sleeping President of the United States back in the last car. Later that morning there was to be more campaigning—in New Jersey, Delaware, and Pennsylvania. Five days later Roosevelt out-polled Alf Landon 523 electoral votes to 8.

And that was the president's participation in the celebration of the Statue of Liberty's fiftieth anniversary. There were U.S. warships in the harbor for the occasion – the destroyer U.S.S. *Taylor* (DD-94), which would go to the ship breakers in two years, the new gunboat U.S.S. *Erie* (PG-50), and a heavy cruiser that fate would later treat most cruelly, U.S.S. *Indianapolis* (CA-35). In 1945 the *Indianapolis* transported the first atomic bomb to Tinian Island in the Marianas chain, whence it was later flown to Hiroshima aboard an airplane called the *Enola Gay*, and the world was introduced to something very new. In late July of that year, after its mission to Tinian but before the

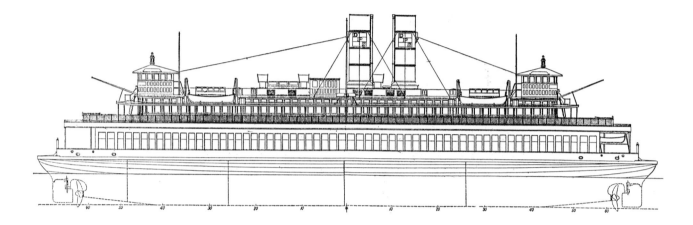

bombing of Hiroshima, the *In-dianapolis* was torpedoed in the Philippine Sea; she sank on July 30, but in the frantic pace of wartime communications her status as "overdue" was never noted and large numbers of her crew per-ished, even though they had suc-cessfully evacuated the sinking vessel. Proper search and rescue efforts were not launched in a timely fashion.

But all this horror was still in the future on October 28, 1936, and the fiftieth anniversary of the Statue of Liberty, it is suggested, marks the first, last, and only time that a President of the United States took four separate rides on a New York ferryboat in a single day's time. It also may be the only time – at very least one of the few times – that a double-ended ferry-boat landed at Bedloe's/Liberty Island. A review of President Grover Cleveland's activities in October 1886 when the Statue of Liberty was dedicated fails to turn up any direct participation by a harbor ferryboat at that time, al-though many ferryboats were used by various groups to view the ceremony from points off Bed-loe's Island. An official delegation of Brooklyn civic leaders set out from the foot of Hamilton Avenue aboard *Union*, of the Union Ferry Company, and while this 1862-

built sidewheeler *might* have dropped her party on Bedloe's Island, more likely she didn't. Cleveland's day, incidentally, concluded in much the same way as Roosevelt's fifty years later: a steamboat took him from the ceremony on the afternoon of Thursday, October 28 to the Exchange Place Depot of the Pennsylvania R.R., and at 5:37 his special train pulled out. Unlike Roosevelt in 1936, though, Grover Cleveland in 1886 wasn't days away from a bid for re-election, it being the mid-point of his four-year term. (Like Cleveland, Ronald Reagan wasn't up for re-election either on the occasion of the statue's centenary in 1986;

unlike either Cleveland's or Roosevelt's, his departure from New York after those ceremonies involved no Pennsylvania R.R. trains. City ferryboats, though, were extensively used to carry dignitaries out to the aircraft carrier U.S.S. *John F. Kennedy* anchored in the bay, the platform from which the president delivered a major address.)

REFOCUSING, now, away from Roosevelt's visit to the harbor in 1936 and looking again at the city's overall fleet policies during the 1925–1955 time period: two orders for three vessels each produced six mechanically-similar craft for

service between Manhattan and Staten Island; but, while having compatible specifications below decks, the two orders brought forth classes of vessels that were quite different-looking on the outside. The three-boat *Dongan Hills* class of 1929–1931 was, perhaps, the epitome of New York ferryboat design – two tall stacks toward one end of midships, twin compound engines, double-decked with a full around-the-boat outdoor promenade on the second deck. The three were but marginally different from earlier Whitehall Street–Saint George boats, but they were classic in that they proved to be the last of their

The Great Depression was upon the country when the City of New York built Mary Murray, Gold Star Mother, *and* Miss New York, *the last-named shown here at the city's maintenance base in Tompkinsville, Staten Island in 1954. Although mechanically similar to earlier vessels built for the demanding Whitehall St.–Saint George service, the trio included a good deal of stylish treatment in the design of their upper works that made them quite different looking from their predecessors. [Roger J. Cudahy]*

kind. They also had oil-fired boilers, something new for the larger Upper Bay boats, and when the three-boat *Mary Murray* class arrived in 1937–1938 the implications of oil fuel had a major impact on external appearance – no more tall stacks. Oil fires in the boilers don't require the same kind of draft as does coal, and while each of the twin boilers on the *Mary Murray* class had its own separate exhaust vent, these were ducted together into a short, squat housing that looked, for all the world, like a single stack.

The *Mary Murray*–class boats were also pioneers in the use of aluminum for cabin construction, and since it was a time when the word "streamlining" was used as a synonym for anything that moved and was modern, efforts were made to soften the lines of the typical harbor ferryboat with curved aluminum overlays. They were, to be sure, different-looking, although whether pleasantly so or not remains a matter of some contention. At the launching of one of the three, a reporter is said to have asked Mayor LaGuardia if this was really what he meant by streamlining, and the "little flower"

remarked that you can't really expect to streamline a big, fat thing like a ferryboat.

Another distinction of the *Mary Murray* class is that they were the first municipal ferryboats to be named after women. Mary Murray herself, the wife of a Quaker merchant, was a heroine of the Revolutionary War who successfully delayed a group of British officers at a tea party in 1776, thereby allowing General Israel Putnam's command of 4000 troops to join forces with General Washington's army for the Battle of Harlem Heights. The other two vessels of the class were not named after real, flesh-and-blood women, but were of the feminine gender – *Miss New York* and *Gold Star Mother*. (One can sometimes find the trio called the *Miss New York* class.)[12]

Despite John Hylan's unre-

---

12. Launch dates of the three vessels are *Gold Star Mother*, May 7, 1937; *Mary Murray*, June 3, 1937; *Miss New York*, December 20, 1937. In the "you've-come-a-long-way-baby" department, the *Mary Murray*–class ferryboats were the first municipal vessels to feature smoking areas designated for women.

strained proclivity for naming vessels after people, these three Depression-era ferryboats were the first city vessels to be named for non-males, real or generic. One can find a few nineteenth-century ferryboats that can be called "she" for more than one reason – e.g., *Louise*, *Ellen*, *Agnes*, and *Lydia* of the Union Ferry Company – but none built for any New York service at all since the Civil War save the *Mary Murray* class, and, more recently, the city's 1986-built *Alice Austen*.

One other novelty brought to the New York ferryboat story by these three aluminum-sheathed vessels was this: they were funded, in part, by grants and loans from the Federal Government, specifically the Public Works Administration. The price tag of each vessel was $912,000, and all were built at the United Shipyards in Mariner's Harbor, Staten Island.

After the Second World War the City of New York purchased another trio of vessels for the Staten Island service, and they represent a near-total break from the design that was exemplified, and perfected, in all the Whitehall Street–

Two vessels of a bygone era navigate southward in the waters of Upper New York Bay. To the right is R.M.S. Queen Elizabeth *of the Cunard Line, outbound for the channel ports of Europe, and to the left is* Gold Star Mother, *en route from Whitehall St. to Saint George. The ferryboat is maneuvering to allow the larger vessel to get in the clear before she swings behind her and then runs parallel to the big Cunarder off the liner's starboard side.* Queen Elizabeth *is running at slow speed, and the chances are very good that after coming around,* Gold Star Mother *overtook and passed the ocean liner before herself having to slow down for the approach to Saint George. The photographer's vantage point is Battery Park; Governors Island is off to the left, New Jersey to the right. [author]*

Saint George boats from the Borough class to the *Mary Murray* class, with an exception acknowledged and noted for the admittedly experimental turbo-electrics of 1923.

All three vessels were named after individuals with Staten Island backgrounds – men, this time – the class being identified by the first of the three to be delivered, the *Pvt. Joseph F. Merrell*, named after a Staten Island winner of the Congressional Medal of Honor. Another bore the name of Staten Island activist Cornelius G. Kolff, who had recently died, while the third was christened *Verrazzano* in honor of the six-teenth-century Italian explorer, Giovanni da Verrazzano, whose early voyages to the New World are said to have pre-dated those of Henry Hudson and therefore make him and his crew the first Europeans to lay eyes on Staten Island.

From the outset, these boats were going to be different. Four noted marine architects were given the task of preparing specifications for the vessels. The city's Department of Marine and Aviation – by then the municipal agency responsible for ferryboat operations – selected the design prepared by the firm of Kindlund and Drake, and the most notable external difference from earlier designs was the inclusion of *three* passenger decks, not two.[13] The main deck mimicked the 151-footers with three vehicle gangways, and there were reasonably-sized passenger cabins outboard of these. The second deck, where ferryboats on the Whitehall Street–Saint George run traditionally carry the bulk of their passengers, had a feature that many criticized – no outdoor promenade at all. For that matter, the promenade that was incorporated into the third deck was not of the full around-the-boat variety; rather, there were two separate end-to-end promenades on either side of the vessel, but they lacked any overhead covering and were thus useless in rainy weather.

Obviously the *Merrell* class were big boats. Their statutory dimensions exceeded those of any earlier boats that operated in New York Harbor; they were 17 feet longer than the *Mary Murray* class and exceeded them in gross tonnage by 2285 to 2126. But despite all the modernity and despite almost a quarter-century of quite favorable experience in New York and elsewhere with diesel and diesel-electric power for ferryboats, the new three-deckers were powered by steam engines.

They were not, though, ordinary steam engines. In all reciprocating steam engines, steam floods into a cylinder and expands, thus forcing the piston into motion. Power is generated on both strokes of a piston because steam is introduced, alternately, from both the top of the cylinder and its bottom and pushes the piston, alternately, on each of its two sides. In this general concept the *Merrell*-class vessels were no different from their many predecessors. But in conventional steam engines, exhausted steam is expelled by the power of the following half-stroke; "back pressure" is thus generated, and overcoming this back pressure is inefficient to the extent that it absorbs energy and produces no useful work in so doing. Each half-stroke in a cylinder's cycle after the first one, in other words, must spend some of its energy expelling used steam on the opposite side of the piston from the previous half-stroke; the steam used on that earlier half-stroke has to be "turned around" and expelled through ports in the cylinder back whence it came.

The steam engine that was selected for the *Merrell* class was produced by the Skinner Engine Company of Erie, Pennsylvania; it was called the Unaflow, and each of the three ferryboats was outfitted with a large 6-cylinder, 4800-h.p. instance of the design. The Unaflow engine eliminates the very concept of back pressure because of the way its exhaust system works: steam never has to be "turned around," but rather exits a cylinder at the conclusion of a half-stroke through exhaust ports that are "down stroke" from the entry ports. The subsequent half-stroke is then a full-power stroke, with none of its energy having to be used to exhaust steam used on the previous half-stroke. The steam flows in but one direction – hence the name, Unaflow.

A characteristic of the Unaflow is an ability to respond to "reverse

---

13. The plans submitted by three of the four architects included a third deck, as increased carrying capacity was a major goal for the new vessels. The four firms were Kindlund and Drake, whose design was selected; George C. Sharp; Gielow, Inc.; and Eads Johnson.

After the Second World War the City of New York threw away the basic ferryboat design that had evolved for vessels assigned to the Whitehall St.–Saint George service since 1905 and built a trio of 3-deck ferryboats that were different from their predecessors in virtually all respects. Lead boat in the class was the Pvt. Joseph F. Merrell, *shown under construction at Bethlehem Steel's Staten Island yard, and under way off the Battery in 1953. [Staten Island Historical Society] [author]*

engine" commands more quickly than a conventional "up and down" steam engine, and thus ferryboat applications seemed to be its strong suit.

Was the decision to specify steam engines for ferryboats built ca. 1950 a wise one, in retrospect? Perhaps not; diesel power was just a decade or two away from so totally overwhelming steam that in their latter days of operation in the 1980s the *Merrell*-class ferryboats were the only harbor vessels at work in New York still powered by reciprocating steam engines. But whether wise from an efficiency point of view or not, the decision resulted in some nice symbolism. When the Whitehall Street–Saint George service survived to become the only ordinary ferryboat line operating in New York Harbor in the late 1960s, satisfaction could be taken from the fact that until the mid-1980s its active fleet would include vessels powered by the same style of engine that had driven *Jersey, Nassau, Hunchback, Clinton,* and so many others.

Now as to price. The *Merrell* class weren't cheap ferryboats. Back before the war, the *Mary Murray* class cost the city just a little under a million dollars a boat. The *Merrell* class was over twice that.

Bids were first advertised in 1949, but when city officials opened the sealed envelopes they didn't like what they found. Low bidder, at $6,093,637.00 for three boats, was the Maryland Dry Dock Company. The two other bidders were in the mid-to-high seven-million-dollar range.

The municipal administration – then headed by Mayor William O'Dwyer – wanted very much to be able to award the work to a local shipyard, not one in Maryland. So all the bids were rejected and new bids sought, with invitations to bid mailed to 20 shipyards. Nothing like 20 responded, only two did. Maryland Dry Dock came in low again, but at a much higher $6,437,000.00. The earlier second-lowest bidder, Bethlehem Steel's Staten Island yard, was again second, but at $6,453,000.00 was just a whisper over Maryland. It was a differential the city could easily balance against travel costs to Baltimore and such, and so a contract was signed with Bethlehem, and the trio was built on Staten Island.

The three were constructed quickly and entered service in 1951. There was a modest ceremony to mark the introduction into regular service of the *Cornelius G. Kolff* on March 2, 1951. Kolff's daughter Emily was on hand at the Saint George terminal that morning when Deputy Commissioner of Marine and Aviation Sydney Baron signed a piece of paper formally accepting the big ferryboat from Bethlehem Steel, and at 10:20 she left on her first revenue trip to Whitehall Street. Kolff himself had died in February 1950. There was much discussion of his general civic activism on behalf of various Staten Island interests and causes, but there was no mention on the day *Cornelius G. Kolff* entered revenue service of the man's critical role in having the City of New York assume operation of the Whitehall Street–Saint George service in the first decade of the twentieth century.

The post-war vessel construction program was just one phase of a major improvement to the whole Whitehall Street–Saint George service. The city had planned, for instance, to replace the aging Saint George ferry terminal soon after V-J Day, a half-century-old facility dating to the time of George McClellan. Indeed,

the Board of Estimate had begun to consider the matter as early as 1936, but the war put a lid on such spending proposals. In the early afternoon of June 25, 1946, the city's timetable for action was suddenly accelerated.

A Staten Island Rapid Transit midday local train from Tottenville had just let off a large crowd of passengers, and they quickly boarded *Miss New York*, one of the pre-war boats of the *Mary Murray* class. It was 2:03 P.M. when *Miss New York* cleared her slip en route to Manhattan. Exactly what happened next, not to mention the precise timing and sequence, admits of some dispute. It must first be noted, though, that the Staten Island Rapid Transit, still under the ownership of the Baltimore and Ohio R.R., had replaced its steam-powered local trains in 1925 with modern electric cars similar in appearance and performance to city subway equipment.[14]

---

14. With $5-million advanced by the Baltimore & Ohio, S.I.R.T. installed third-rail–style electrification on three lines: the main line from Saint George to Tottenville; the North Shore line from Saint George to Arlington; and a branch line to South Beach, a spur

One account holds that a flash erupted from under a four-car S.I.R.T. train laid up on Track No. One in the rail portion of the terminal complex, and that this happened just *after Miss New York* departed. This was not the train recently inbound from Tottenville; it was out of service awaiting the onset of the evening rush hour. Such trains routinely retain contact with the 600-volt third rail, equipment like air compressors continue to operate to keep the train ready for service, and the train is by no means inert.

A conflicting account says that the fire didn't begin under an S.I.R.T. train at all but elsewhere in the terminal, that the alarm was turned in at 1:58 P.M., and what happened just after *Miss New York* departed at 2:03 is that the entire terminal virtually exploded in flames.

In any event the very next inbound ferryboat from Whitehall

Street was unable to land, as the fire spread with all the rapidity and intensity a wind-fanned blaze can so easily manage in an old and largely wooden structure. It was a clear, fresh day, too: the 2:00 o'clock temperature at Central Park was eighty degrees and the humidity a dry forty-one per cent.

The New York City Fire Department eventually had to transmit something called a "borough alarm" – the equivalent of a nine-alarm fire – and sixty-one pieces of apparatus were called to the scene. Units from Manhattan used the Holland Tunnel to New Jersey and doubled back to Staten Island over the Bayonne Bridge; Brooklyn fire engines made use of the 69 Street–Saint George ferry, whose slips in Staten Island were sufficiently removed from the fire scene to permit their use. Three city fireboats, plus U.S. Navy and private tugboats, all turned their efforts to the mighty fire.

There were two major problems firefighters faced: containing the fire to the terminal while keeping it away from the Baltimore and Ohio's near-by freight yard, and getting at burning piles and timbers that were underneath layers of concrete flooring and decking.

The fire would burn for several days.

Loss of life was miraculously low; had the several hundred people who boarded *Miss New York* still been in the terminal, perhaps just getting off their Tottenville train, it might have been far more tragic. One especially horrible tale, though, was that of a 43-year-old woman who worked as a ticket seller for the S.I.R.T. It is thought that she tried to return to her booth to save tickets and money when the fire came bursting into the terminal concourse. In all, three people lost their lives and 289 were hurt, the latter mostly firemen who would battle for *67 hours* before the fire was declared extinguished.

Ferry operations, of course, were a shambles. That evening it was thought that service might be resumed, and *Knickerbocker*, a boat of the *Dongan Hills* class, left Whitehall Street at 6:13 for Saint George, and a boat from 39 Street did the same slightly earlier; both landed in Saint George at the slips normally used by the 39 Street boats, but this was before it was realized that flames were spreading unseen below the concrete flooring. Service from 69

---

that connected with the main line to Tottenville at Clifton. A total of 21½ route miles were involved. To serve on the new electrified network, S.I.R.T. purchased 100 67-foot, all-steel, electric multiple-unit cars from the Standard Steel Car Company.

Street/Brooklyn by Electric Ferries was able to continue through most of June 25, but in the early morning hours of June 26 it, too, was annulled.

It wasn't until Friday afternoon, June 28, that normal service could be resumed from the few undamaged slips. In the interim, boats attempted to provide a passengers-only service to a conventional pier in nearby Tompkinsville; for that matter, when service was resumed out of Saint George the only available slips were those normally assigned to the 39 Street/Brooklyn service. The Whitehall Street service was considerably more important, and so the 39 Street operation was temporarily discontinued. It has yet to be restored.

Government at all levels has often been characterized as being unwieldly and slow, but let it be said that on Wednesday, June 26, 1946, while the fire in the Saint George ferry terminal *was still spreading* under all that concrete, the New York City Board of Estimate, meeting in regular session, approved the expenditure of the first $3 million to build a new Saint George terminal. Its eventual cost

was $12 million. Of course, it must also be said that plans to replace the older structure were moving along even before the June 25 fire.

The replacement terminal was formally dedicated on June 8, 1951, although portions of it were phased into service earlier. By the time it was completed the city had also purchased the three new triple-deck ferryboats of the *Merrell* class, all of which prompted *The New York Times* to opine, editorially, that all these expenditures should serve to quiet talk of secession on the part of Staten Island that was apparently being noised about – secession presumably from the city, but maybe from the nation.

Thus was a brand-new terminal built on the site of the old, S.I.R.T. trains were provided with new tracks and platforms in an area that was largely protected from the elements by a big, looping bus terminal, and the whole facility was – and is – rather marvelous, all things considered. The Electric Ferries to Bay Ridge were also accorded access to the new terminal, but on a decidedly lesser scale than the city's own vessels. Passengers could board Manhattan-

bound ferries both under cover and on either of two decks. Persons heading for Brooklyn had to go aboard on the main deck, exposed to all the elements.

WHILE THE City of New York was making major investments in the Saint George terminal, and buying new boats to use it, the Hudson River railroad ferryboat operators were moving into a very different mode. After 1925 the five railroads designed and built but one new ferryboat. Not one each: just one – o-n-e.[15] She was the Erie Railroad's *Meadville* of 1936, about which more will be said in a moment. But while none of the others saw fit to build any new boats during this period, two railroads did some out-of-the-ordinary rebuilding on older vessels – Jersey Central's *Elizabeth* (iii) and

---

15. The last new ferryboat purchased by each of the five Hudson River railroads, and its date of construction, is as follows: New York Central – *Albany* of 1925; Delaware, Lackawanna & Western – *Hoboken* (v) and *Buffalo* of 1922; Erie – *Meadville* of 1936; Pennsylvania – *Newark* (ii) of 1902; Jersey Central – *Bayonne* of 1913.

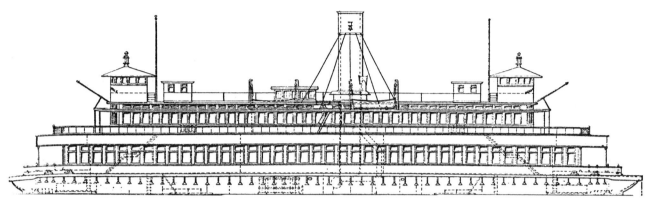

What looks like a rather conventional ferryboat is, in fact, an unusual craft. Built with a steel superstructure and powered by a Skinner Unaflow steam engine, she's the 1936-built Meadville *of the Erie R.R., the very last ferryboat to be built for trans-Hudson service by any of the railroads that operated such service. [author's collection]*

D. L. & W.'s *Lackawanna* (iii). The three represent the final efforts at vessel design on the part of the railroads.

There was nothing to *Meadville*'s looks or lines that said she was exceptional. She looked like any of the railroad's other propeller ferries – two decks, single stack, same general shape and layout, same Erie color scheme of green and white, with touches of black and touches of gold. But *Meadville* wasn't just another Hudson River ferryboat. For one thing she was big – the largest vessel ever to run for any of the railroads with statutory dimensions of 221.1 × 45.1 × 16.3 feet and gross tonnage of 1599. Her upper works were fabricated from steel, not the traditional wood, and below decks she was powered by a 1700-h.p. 5-cylinder Skinner Unaflow steam engine, the first New York ferryboat to be so powered, and, excepting the city's *Merrell* class, the only one.

Meadville, together with her more conventional fleetmate *Youngstown*, was sold to the Delaware, Lackawanna and Western R.R. in 1957 when the Erie moved its passenger trains into the D. L. & W.'s Hoboken terminal, and additional ferryboats were needed to handle the increased traffic there. The pair were renamed, respectively, *Maplewood* and *Chatham* (ii) by their new owner, and three years later, in 1960, they reverted in a sense to their original owner when the D. L. & W. and the Erie merged to form the Erie–Lackawanna R.R.

Jersey Central's *Elizabeth* (iii) was a rebuild of the fire-gutted *Lakewood*. *Lakewood* was built in

New York ferryboats have always provided an excellent vantage point for watching the big ocean liners entering and leaving port. In 1959 this is the way the superliner S.S. United States looked from a New York Central ferryboat as she was being eased away from North River Pier 86 for a trans-Atlantic crossing to Le Havre and Southampton. [author]

Wilmington, Delaware by Harlan and Hollingsworth in 1901 – of the twelve steel-hull propeller ferries built by the C.N.J., all but one were turned out by Harlan and Hollingsworth – and powered by what was conventional for this operator, a 4-cylinder triple-expansion steam engine. In 1949 *Lakewood* was extensively damaged by fire, but instead of rebuilding the vessel with a wooden superstructure in imitation of her original design, the railroad had the vessel restyled with an all-steel upper works that had a distinctive and modern look to it. *Meadville*'s steel superstructure retained the lines of earlier ferryboats; when *Lakewood* was rebuilt as *Elizabeth* (iii) she looked like nothing else on the Hudson River. Indeed, C.N.J. even used *Elizabeth* (iii) to introduce a bright new two-tone green paint scheme for its vessels.

The rebuilding in 1947–1948 that produced *Lackawanna* (iii) out of *Chatham* (i) for the Delaware, Lackawanna and Western R.R. did little to change the vessel's external appearance, although she did emerge with a short, squat stack in place of her older tall stack. The big difference was below decks in the engine room, where her original twin compound steam engines were removed and in their place a 16-cylinder General Motors diesel installed. *Lackawanna* (iii) thus became the first – and only – diesel-powered ferryboat to join the fleet of the Hudson River railroads. There will be a case, in 1967, when the Jersey Central R.R. will *lease* two diesel-powered ferries, and that will be reviewed in chapter 10. But *Lackawanna* (iii) stands as the only diesel ferryboat ever owned by any of the Hudson River railroads. She made her first revenue trip with her new power plant on September 6, 1949.

The general state of the railroad ferries during the 1925–1955 era can be seen in many ways: reduced patronage, service cutbacks, the popularity of the new bridges and tunnels. Maybe this paucity of investment over a 35-year period – one new vessel and two rebuilds – is the surest falling barometer to indicate that good sailing weather was no longer in the forecast.

FINALLY, to wrap up the 1925–1955 interval in the story of the ferryboats of New York Harbor, a word about a group of services that quietly defied long odds and kept on operating – well, kept on operating longer than they had any right to. Maybe it had something to do with their out-of-the-way location, but the fact is that three lines connecting Staten Island with the New Jersey mainland across the narrow straits called the Kill Van Kull and the Arthur Kill were still very much in business at the end of 1955; in business as private companies, too.

At one time there were four such lines. Oddly enough, the one that quit first, in 1929, was the one farthest removed from the three bridges the Port of New York Authority built between Staten Island and New Jersey in the pre–Second World War period. This was the Carteret Ferry Company connecting Carteret, N.J., with a spot in Staten Island today called Rossville, but known for many years by the marvelous name of Linoleumville.

Here the American Linoleum Company built a factory in 1873, but it wasn't until 1916 that a bona fide ferryboat company – the Carteret Ferry Company – set up shop. Prior to its arrival there had been a kind of waterborne carpooling, with employees of the linoleum company sharing the expenses of a motorboat. Even earlier, going back to Colonial times, the Carteret–Rossville crossing was the site of a ferry that bore what might well be the most evocative name of any route in the entire New York area. It was called the New Blazing Star Ferry, and if that doesn't generate a sense of mystery and wonder and poetry, nothing will.[16]

During its short time, 1916 through 1929, the Carteret Ferry Company fielded a wonderful assortment of second-hand vessels. Its inaugural trip on May 1, 1916 was run with the 1885-built sidewheeler *Carteret*, formerly *Colorado* of the Williamsburg ferries. Also on the company's roster was the crusty old *Clinton*, ex–Union Ferry Company, and ex–Union Navy in the war against the Con-

10. Staten Island–New Jersey Services

<hr />

16. For further discussion of the New Blazing Star Ferry, as well as the later doings of the Carteret Ferry Company, see Herbert H. Reed, "The New Blazing Star Ferry," *The Staten Island Historian*, 22 (October–December 1961), 30–32; 23 (January–March 1962), 7–8.

federacy. The Carteret company was also a corporate kin of the Brooklyn and Richmond Ferry Company, and vessels were used on both the Linoleumville–Carteret route and the 69 Street/Brooklyn–Saint George service. Old *Clinton* had the honor of making the last run on the Arthur Kill service to Carteret on August 1, 1929, and that was the end of it.

But the other three Staten Is-

land–New Jersey services lasted another quarter-century or more, and each of them operated literally in the shadow of one of the Port Authority's three bridges. The Port Richmond, S.I.–Bergen Point, N.J. ferry line was overshadowed by the Bayonne Bridge (at least after the latter was built in 1931). Howland Hook–Elizabethport traced the course of the 1928-built Goethals Bridge, and the ferry from the end of the S.I.R.T.'s Tottenville line across the Arthur Kill to Perth Amboy provided its passengers with a marvelous panoramic view of the Outerbridge Crossing, also a 1928 addition to the area's bridge and highway network.[17]

Each of these lines had its share of more-or-less conventional ferryboats over the years – some old, some new; some paddlewheel, some screw-propeller; some diesel, most steam – but the vessels that allowed them to beat the odds and keep running despite the Port Authority's bridges were a fleet of look-alike mini-ferries turned out by that latter-day master boat-designer, Eads Johnson.

The three lines had complex cor-

17. Reed has written of all of these services; see "The Port Richmond–Bergen Point Ferry," *The Staten Island Historian*, 20 (April–June 1959), 15–16; 20 (July–September 1959), 23–24; "The Howland Hook–Elizabethport Ferry," *The Staten Island Historian*, 23 (October–December 1962), 31–32; 24 (January–March 1963), 7–8; "The Tottenville–Perth Amboy Ferry," *The Staten Island Historian*, 21 (October–December 1960), 33–34.

porate evolutions, including relationships with operators on the upper Hudson River. Port Richmond–Bergen Point was even owned by Public Service of New Jersey for a number of years (1897 through 1937), making it a kin of the Riverside and Fort Lee Ferry Company and explaining the fact that vessels were often moved between this line and the West 125 Street–Edgewater service. Like West 125 Street–Edgewater, Port Richmond–Bergen Point passed over to Electric Ferries, Inc., after P.S.N.J. called it quits.

But the key to survival turned out to be Johnson's ferry, a vessel that was actually smaller than Robert Fulton's *Jersey*. The design was executed on nine more-or-less similar vessels built between 1932 and 1955, and Table IX-3 lists them all by name and vital statistics.

Irvington and *Piermont* were the first two, and they were initially deployed on a cross-Hudson route north of New York City where they replaced earlier steam sidewheelers of the same names, thus making them *Irvington* (ii) and *Piermont* (ii). *Irvington* (i) and *Piermont* (i) are of interest,

though; they both began their careers with the Union Ferry Company of Brooklyn, and ran for a number of years in the municipal ferryboat fleet after Union passed from the scene in 1922. *Irvington* (i) was Union's *Brooklyn* (iii), and *Piermont* (i) was called *Pierrepont* during her days on the East River, named after the former director of the Union Ferry Company, Henry Pierrepont, whose book on the company's early days is so helpful in understanding the nineteenth-century development of ferryboating in New York. But this is to digress.

Irvington (ii) and *Piermont* (ii) were simplicity itself. Said *Scientific American* of their Eads Johnson design: "Built with the square lines of a barge, braced like a bridge, powered with a Diesel engine, and designed for complete operation by a single man, a strange little ferryboat recently slid from the Staten Island ways of the United Dry Docks. It was the first of two vehicular ferryboats which have since shown such surprising service in their runs across the wide breadth of the Hudson River between Irvington and Piermont."

One of the two prototype vessels for the Sunrise Ferries' fleet that retained waterborne linkages between Staten Island and the New Jersey mainland into the 1960s. Piermont, *built in 1932, celebrated her fiftieth anniversary as an active ferryboat working a route to Shelter Island on the eastern end of Long Island.* [author]

Orion, *built in 1955, was the final ferryboat to join the Sunrise fleet; vessel was also the final New York double-ender to be built in a Staten Island shipyard. Shown here on the Tottenville–Perth Amboy route in 1956, she was sold to Mexican interests in 1961.* [author]

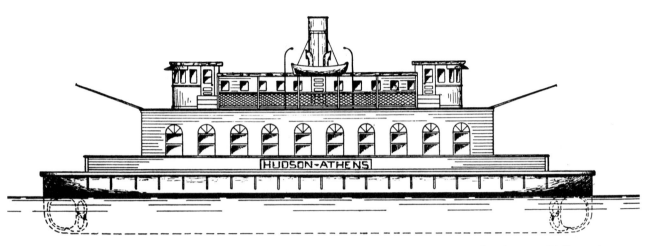

Designed by the talented Eads Johnson, this ferryboat was built in Washburn, Wisconsin in 1921 and is thought to be the world's first *direct-drive diesel-powered ferryboat. Called the* Hudson–Athens *when she worked a trans-Hudson route north of New York City, her New York City tenure was under the name* Reliance *in the fleet of the New York & Englewood Ferry Company.* [author's collection]

Actually, the new boats looked more like floating saucers than anything else. The prototypes were *54 feet long* and *29 feet wide*, making their beam 55% of their length. The same ratio, by contrast, on *E. G. Diefenbach* of the Electric Ferries fleet works out to 22%.

The wheelhouse on both *Irvington* (ii) and *Piermont* (ii) was amidships and elevated, but to one side of the vessel. Initially the main deck was fully open, but in later years small passenger compartments were installed on either side, outboard of the open deck area where the vehicles were carried. Carrying capacity of the vessels was in the range of eight or nine automobiles and a little under three-dozen passengers.

Thus using a "no frills" approach long before that term had any popular coinage, three private ferryboat lines on the far side of Staten Island survived into the 1960s. Eventually, though, they were unable to sustain themselves. Howland Hook–Elizabethport closed shop in 1961, Port Richmond–Bergen Point the following year, and on October 16, 1963 the last of the lines, Tottenville–Perth Amboy, gave up the ghost. This service had been operated by the Staten Island Rapid Transit until 1948 and was taken over by Sunrise Ferries at that time, the new diesel-powered mini-ferries in this case replacing the very last beam-engine side-

Many old New York ferryboats languished in various ships' graveyards long after their service *days were over. Seawells Point, one of the original six vessels in the fleet of* *Electric Ferries, rusts away next to the passenger steamer* New Bedford,

wheel ferryboats to operate in the harbor, S.I.R.T.'s *Charles W. Galloway* and *Perth Amboy*. It is a credit to the Eads Johnson design of the little diesels, which made all this possible, that in the 1981 edition of *Merchant Vessels of the United States*, four of them are still to be found among the nation's active merchant ships, engaged in ferryboat work in ports far from their Staten Island birthplace. *Orion*, the newest of the fleet, also represents the very last New York ferryboat to be built in a Staten Island shipyard.

Finally, to close out this chapter, let it be noted that there is an ever-so-slight imprecision in saying that the pre-1948 ferryboat service across the Arthur Kill between Tottenville and Perth Amboy was operated by the Staten Island *Rapid Transit*. Onward

a vessel that once linked Cape Cod with Martha's Vineyard and

Nantucket. In the other photo a portion of the trans-Hudson ferryboat

Lackawanna *(iii) creates a mournful still-life study. [Howard W. Serig, Jr.]*

from the Wiman–Pendleton–Garrett amalgamation of 1884, the entire island railway was *called* the Staten Island Rapid Transit. Rolling stock and certain sections of right-of-way were, in fact, owned by the S.I.R.T., but the old and original Clifton–Tottenville line remained in the hands of a subsidiary of the S.I.R.T., and it retained the old name, Staten Island Railway. This was a distinction that prevailed more in the world of stocks and bonds than anywhere else, but among the subsidiary's tangible assets were the Arthur Kill ferryboats, and up to their very last day they bore the name "Staten Island Railway" across their paddleboxes.

10. ... But Doesn't Die   1955 and onward

After the year 1955 the pattern continued to be more cutbacks and abandonments on ferryboat services throughout New York Harbor. There was one exception among the general-purpose routes, but only one – the Whitehall Street–Saint George line, where new vessels remained the order of the day.

The three-boat *Kennedy* class arrived in 1965, turned out by the same Levingston Shipyard in Orange, Texas that had built the *E. G. Diefenbach*. They were visually quite similar to the 1951 *Merrell* class and were designed by the same firm of naval architects, Kindlund and Drake. But there were important differences: diesel-electric power, not steam; a most welcome covering over the outdoor promenades on the third deck; and a much more attractive pilot house in a classic steamboat mold (the *Merrell* boats had a simply awful-looking angular pilot house, like something out of a 1950s yachting magazine). The *Kennedy* class also have their funnel housing dead in the center of the boat, giving them a perfectly symmetrical appearance. The members of the three-boat class are *John F. Kennedy*, *American Legion* (ii), and *The Gov. Herbert H. Lehman*.

The opening of the Verrazano–Narrows Bridge in 1964 affected patronage on the Whitehall Street–Saint George run. (It also allowed the city to discontinue service entirely on the 69 Street/Brooklyn–Saint George line, as described in chapter 9.) Patronage on the city's first municipally-operated ferry had grown to well over 25 million passengers a year in the early 1960s, but registered a drop in the range of 20% as commuters took advantage of flexibilities presented by the new bridge, including express bus service to Manhattan points from residential neighborhoods in Staten Island. But patronage on the ferryboats never dropped much below 20 million riders a year, and Staten Island's population has grown substantially since the bridge opened: 221,991 in the pre-bridge 1960 census and 352,029 in 1980 – an increase of 60%; utilization of the Whitehall Street–Saint George ferry is now regarded as stable in the 20-million-passengers-a-year range, and city officials feel that modest increases above that would not be surprising. The South Ferry area of Manhattan is within walking distance of an immense (and growing) concentration of

Ellis Island, *U.S. Dept. of Immigration & Naturalization, 1904–1954*

American Legion *(ii), one of the three-boat* Kennedy *class of 1965, heads out from Whitehall St. bound for Saint George.* [*author*]

business and commercial activity – i.e., jobs – and even the convenience of direct bus service to Manhattan is not always more convenient than making one's way to Saint George and taking the ferry. The Staten Island Rapid Transit, incidentally, always a major carrier for getting people to the ferry slips in Saint George, itself managed to shift from private ownership by the Baltimore and Ohio R.R. in 1971 to public ownership

and operation as an arm of the Metropolitan Transportation Authority of New York State, the umbrella agency that operates the city subway, the Long Island R.R., and other transit services. In a world of acronyms, it is known as S.I.R.T.O.A. – Staten Island Rapid Transit Operating Authority. Of the three ex-B. & O. lines that were electrified in 1925, passenger service continues only on the Saint George–Tottenville line.

Current equipment is a fleet of 52 cars that the parent authority purchased from the Saint Louis Car Company in the early 1970s as an add-on to a larger order of city subway equipment.[1]

---

1. At first, after shifting its passenger service to the S.I.R.T.O.A., the B. & O. continued to operate freight service on Staten Island. Later this was transferred to the New York, Susquehanna & Western R.R. and the

Another Kennedy-*class ferryboat,* The Gov. Herbert H. Lehman, *approaches Saint George on a foggy morning in 1967.*

opposite:

"Ghost of a Bygone Ferry": this 1972 John Noble lithograph shows a Dongan Hills-*class ferryboat approaching a Manhattan skyline dominated by the World Trade Center. The twin-stack ferryboats had departed the scene before the "twin towers" were built, but that was exactly the artist's point. "The two stacks and the twin towers may echo each other in the composition," Noble wrote, "but in life they are antagonists unto death. The victor is obvious."*
[© The John A. Noble Collection]

Within this context the two-boat *Barberi* class arrived in the early 1980s – monster vessels with an all-passenger configuration and license authority to sail the bay with as many as 6000 persons aboard (with such a full house, 4850 passengers would be able to find a seat for themselves; the other 1150 wouldn't). One has to

———

B. & O. withdrew entirely, thus writing the final chapter in the story of the enterprise Erastus Wiman and Robert Garrett once tried to create.

go back to wartime troop movements to find instances when more human beings were placed aboard a single vessel in America.

Because the *Barberi* class do not carry vehicular traffic, the second deck is positioned somewhat lower than was the case on earlier vessels. With both the *Merrell* class and the *Kennedy* class, passengers boarded on either the main deck or the second deck; the third deck was reached by interior stairways from the second deck. (The third deck could even be

closed off at times of light traffic as an economy measure.) The *Barberi* class have main-deck boarding similar to their predecessors. But the boarding area for either the second or third deck is located at a point midway between those two decks, not unlike the concept of a split-level or, more precisely, a split-entry house. From this upper boarding station one can proceed up to the third deck or down to the second.

The *Barberi* class handles the matter of an outdoor promenade

Municipal ferryboats in New York were originally operated by the Department of Docks and Ferries, then by the Department of Plant and Structures. In recent years the agency that houses the ferry bureaucracy has been the Department of Marine and Aviation, whose insignia adorn everything from ferryboat funnels to executives' business cards. [author]

This contemporary sign hangs from the ceiling inside the Saint George terminal and directs passengers to Whitehall St.–bound ferryboats. Over the years there have been fifty

different over and back routes worked by double-ended ferryboats whose far terminal could have benefited from such a sign; all carried passengers to a Manhattan landfall. [author]

with efficiency. There are outdoor promenades along the sides of the third deck. So as not to lose this carrying capacity during foul weather, however, securing windows in place converts the outdoor promenade to an indoor one.

It's difficult to say that any one feature of these new boats is the *most* novel, but surely a good case can be made for their system of propulsion. The world of ferryboat propulsion, thus far, has been a

rigid "either–or" alternative: paddlewheel or screw propeller. The *Barberi* class introduces a new concept that is neither, really. On the underside of each vessel at each end, roughly where a propeller and rudder would be on an ordinary ferryboat, there's a large revolving circular plate built flush with the hull. From each plate a number of variable-pitch paddles extend down into the water, paddles that are each about six

feet long and two feet wide. The plate revolves, and by a change in the pitch of the paddles and the speed of revolution of the plate the vessel is made to go forward or backward, slower or faster, to port or starboard. This German-designed innovation is called a Voith-Schneider cycloidal propeller, or sometimes, more simply, an "egg beater" drive; the system gives the *Barberi* class extraordinary maneuverability, including an

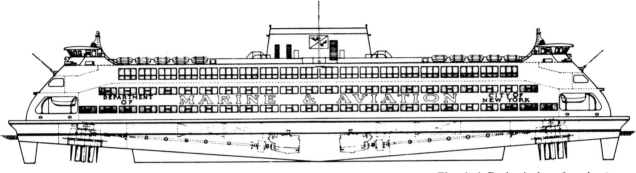

The city's Barberi-*class ferryboats.*
[*author's collection*]

ability to turn 360 degrees in little more than their own length.[2]

Andrew J. Barberi made her first trip from Saint George to Whitehall Street on October 5, 1981, and her sister ship, the *Samuel I. Newhouse*, was introduced with a luncheon cruise for the press and invited guests on October 9, 1982. Shortly thereafter came the inevitable – the retirement from service of the steam-powered *Merrell*-class boats, and thereby the end of a tradition begun by Robert Ful-

---

2. I had read of this ability of the *Barberi* class and tended to feel it was something of an exaggeration. Then one evening in the summer of 1986 I was riding back to Manhattan aboard a *Kennedy*-class boat just after the evening rush hour. One of the *Barberi* class had left St. George just before us, deadheading to Whitehall St. for some reason or other. I was impressed at the way the two vessels seemed to be maintaining exactly the same speed, with the newer vessel a thousand yards or so ahead and to our right. I didn't see the whole maneuver, but when I looked up just south of Governors Island the *Barberi* class was . . . well, it was spinning. It wasn't "turning"; it was "spinning," on an imaginary axis right through the middle of the vessel. It had finished its 360-degree pirouette when the *Kennedy* class I was on caught up and we both then continued to Whitehall St.

Summer 1987; the Andrew J. Barberi *is approaching Saint George on a rush-hour trip from Manhattan just as the* Samuel I. Newhouse *is leaving on a return trip to Whitehall St.* [*author*]

ton's *Jersey* in July 1812. Any sadness over the demise of steam propulsion on New York ferryboats was surely lessened, though, by the realization that the *Merrell* class with their Skinner Unaflow

engines delayed the inevitable as long as possible. Electric Ferries introduced diesel power to the world of New York ferryboating with the maiden voyage of *Governor Moore* on November 8, 1926.

Steam wasn't banished from the scene for another six decades!

Few would deny that the *Barberi*-class boats earn high marks when it comes to functional categories. Even fewer, though, can sustain any kind of an argument when it comes to defending the aesthetic merits of the new vessels, and some would even maintain they're downright ugly. All such arguments, of course, must not overlook the fact that, whatever else the *Barberi*-class ferryboats are, there are two very important things they're not: neither of them is a bridge and neither of them is a tunnel!

---

perfectly abreast of each other. For further discussion of these interesting ferryboats, see Theodore M. Scull, *The Staten Island Ferry* (New York: Quadrant Press, 1982), esp. pp. 81–91. For a thorough technical description of the propulsion system, see Ulrich Sturmhoefel, "The Cycloidal Propeller and Its Significance For the Propulsion of Special-Purpose Vessels," *Proceedings of the Second Inter-*

national Waterborne Transportation Conference (New York, 1978), pp. 323–57. While the '*Barberi* and the '*Newhouse* were the first U.S.-owned vessels to feature the new propulsion system, there was an earlier North American application on a pair of Canadian ferryboats, C. N. Marine's twin double-enders *Holiday Island* and *Vacationland*, vessels that link Prince Edward Island with the mainland.

Steam power has been specified for a handful of recent U.S. short-haul passenger vessels in an effort to recapture the atmosphere of an earlier era. But on the Pvt. Joseph F. Merrell, *shown here approaching Whitehall St. in 1972, as well as her two sister ships, the decision to utilize steam power had nothing to do with nostalgia; it was one of the final cases in the United States when reciprocating steam engines were selected for an inland passenger vessel for their own sake.* [author]

The *Andrew J. Barberi* and the *Samuel I. Newhouse* weren't cheap, either. The pair cost the city over $30 million, with most of the money for their purchase coming from Federal grants. One could purchase over 40 Borough-class boats (at $340,800.00) for the price of one *Barberi* class. (One could also purchase a lot of stale 1905 bread with the inflated price of a single loaf in the 1980s.)

While attention was being drawn to the large *Barberi*-class vessels, the city quietly added yet another two-boat class of ferries to its roster in the mid-1980s that are even more unusual than their larger running mates. Built by the Robert Derecktor shipyards in Middletown, Rhode Island, the 500-gross-ton *Alice Austen* and *John A. Noble* are smaller vessels designed to work the Whitehall Street–Saint George run at night when larger-capacity boats are not required. "Smaller" is, of course, relative; the 207-foot-long and two-deck *Austen*-class boats are licensed to carry 1200 passengers. Like the *Barberi* class they're passenger-only; attractively angular and also driven by Voith–Schneider cycloidal propellers, one of the newcomers now works the midnight-to-dawn stint on the Whitehall Street–Saint George run, and one of them can usually be found working during daylight hours on weekends, as well. (New York's Mayor Edward I. Koch has even said that the *Austen*-class boats could be made available for rush-hour service elsewhere in the harbor – say, a new trans-Hudson run, were one to be established.)

A bit of a short-term flap developed when it was learned that a number of officials from the city's Department of Transportation saw fit to draw expense-account money and travel to the shores of Lake Constance in Switzerland to inspect ferryboats there whose de-

The 1981-built Andrew J. Barberi.
[*author*]

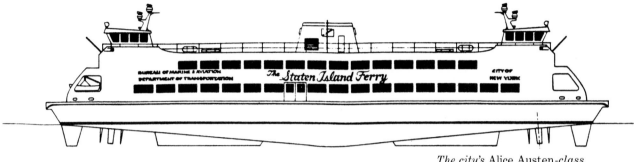

The city's Alice Austen-*class ferryboats. [author's collection]*

sign the *Austen* class imitated, but the matter, having been raised by an ever-vigilant press, was quickly forgotten.

Alice Austen and *John A. Noble* were both launched at the Derecktor yard on the same day, January 3, 1986; the '*Austen* was formally delivered to the City of New York on June 5 of the same year, and the '*Noble* a month later on July 11.

Alice Austen, the person, was a Staten Island resident who died in 1952 at the age of 86. She was an eminent photographer, specializing in local subjects, and, given Staten Island's insular character, she devoted considerable attention to things maritime. The picture on

page 305 of passengers relaxing aboard a Staten Island–bound ferryboat is her work; another of her poignant photographs shows the ill-fated Cunard Line steamship R.M.S. *Lusitania* heading out to sea through the Narrows.

John A. Noble also distinguished himself in the visual arts. Born in Paris in 1913 and brought to the United States in 1919, he began painting in 1929, although it would be 17 more years before he could devote himself to his art on a full-time basis. Meanwhile he earned his living as a seaman, and it was the sea that gave his work its principal themes. He also had a special love for the port of New York, and was very interested in

the various ferryboat lines that he continually saw being cut back and abandoned. "We are a city of bygone ferries indeed," he once wrote. John A. Noble died in 1983, but the ferryboat that bears his name is also a floating gallery of his work and will allow ferry passengers between Whitehall Street and Saint George to enjoy his legacy for many years.

This, then, is the "good news." The "bad news" is that there isn't any other news. All the rest of the harbor's general-purpose ferryboat operations fade from the scene after 1955, and a good lot of the special-purpose routes, as well. The city's institutional services, as they were called, to Wel-

The John A. Noble *at Whitehall St. in the spring of 1988.* [*author*]

Alice Austen has just cleared Whitehall St. en route to Staten Island. [*author*]

fare (*née* Blackwell's, and now Roosevelt), Randalls, North Brother, and Rikers islands have all been replaced by bridges or causeways, and only the municipal ferry to Hart Island, site of the city's Potter's Field for the burial of the indigent dead, remains.[3] The Hart Island service operates from City Island, itself linked to the mainland by bridge, and the

3. Per a report prepared by Eads Johnson in 1933, the institutional services, and their assigned vessels, were as follows:

City Island–Hart Island	*Fordham*
E. 25 St./Manhattan, to Hart Island via Welfare and Riker's islands	*Riverside; Col. Clayton*
E. 25 St./Manhattan, to Welfare & Randall's islands	*Riverside; Col. Clayton*
E. 134 St./Bronx–North Brother Island	*Mott Haven; Greenwich Village*
E. 135 St./Bronx–Riker's Island	*Mott Haven; Greenwich Village*
E. 125 St.–Randall's Island	*Chelsea*
E. 86 St.–Welfare Island	*Welfare*

See Eads Johnson, "A Report on the Operation of the Municipal and Institutional Ferries and Auxiliary Equipment of the Department of Plant and Structures of the City of New York for the City Budget Commission" (New York, 1933), pp. 5, 7.

Interior view of the lower cabin on the Alice Austen. [*author*]

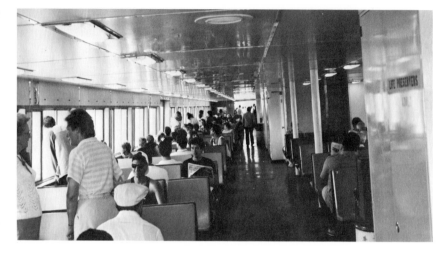

route is worked by the diminutive *Michael Cosgrove*, a vessel built by Blount Marine in Warren, Rhode Island in 1961 in rough imitation of the saucer-shaped vessels that worked various Staten Island–New Jersey routes. This City Island–Hart Island service is *not* accessible to the general public. It's occasionally the subject of a feature story in a magazine or newspaper, though, such as a September 1986 piece in *The Washington Post* that began: "If you die in New York and no one claims your body, it is nailed in a coffin made of white New England pine and sent to Potter's Field aboard a small red ferry. The ferry ties up at a tumbledown dock in the Bronx. Potter's Field lies half a mile off, on a small wind-swept island. . . . At the dock there's a shack where the ferrymen fry sausage and eggs. The morgue wagon arrives around 9. The gangway bustles with guards from the city Department of Corrections who review their manifests, and with prisoners from the city jail who bury the dead."

In past years there were more institutional services landing at Hart Island. It's been only recently that there's been a "morgue wagon," for instance. In years past bodies for burial on Hart Island came all the way up from the city morgue at Bellevue Hospital by boat, and the prisoners from Rikers Island arrived the same way. These craft were single-ended steamboats, though, not double-ended ferryboats, although the latter were known to fill in for the former from time to time.

Another special-purpose ferryboat line survives in New York, and it is anything but confined to an off-the-beaten-track location like Hart Island. It boldly operates out of the same Whitehall Street terminal as does the city's service to Saint George, although

*November 17, 1890. Alice Austen
turned her camera toward a group of
passengers relaxing in the bracing
outdoors aboard a Manhattan–Staten
Island ferryboat and created this
memorable scene. [E. Alice Austen/
Staten Island Historical Society]*

Pilot houses on Austen-*class ferryboats are angular and sharp, but they blend attractively with the overall design of the vessels.* [author]

from a ferry slip – usually slip no. 7 – that in past years had been used by municipal ferryboats on various routes to Brooklyn, and up until 1954 by the Federal Government's *Ellis Island* plying back and forth to the immigration station of the same name out in the Upper Bay.[4] This service is, of

course, the U.S. Coast Guard's operation to and from Governors Island, and while its passengers are restricted to those having business at the U.S.C.G. facility there, a word or two is in order about the service. (Governors Island was previously a U.S. Army installation, and during those days

the Army's Quartermaster Corps ran the ferry. Since 1964 Governors Island has been a Coast Guard installation.)

What's interesting about the Whitehall Street–Governors Island operation is that it represents – in fantasy, almost – what any of the older harbor routes might look like today had they survived into the 1980s. A fleet of marvelously diverse vessels works the line, some designed and built solely for the Governors Island service, others purchased after service with other operators – including the first New York fer-

---

4. The current Whitehall St. ferry terminal was built in stages during the early years of the twentieth century, although major portions of it were rebuilt in the mid-1950s. It was at the time of this rebuilding that the service to and from Governors Island had its Manhattan terminal shifted into the

municipal terminal from an open slip between the municipal terminal and Battery Park. This change serves the interests of safety, as boats sailing to and from Governors Island no longer have to cross the path of vessels on the Whitehall St.–St. George route.

Pvt. Nicholas Minue *on the Whitehall St.–Governors Island run in 1986.* [*author*]

On a dark and overcast morning in October 1986 The Tides *heads for Whitehall St. from Governors Island. Later in the day, many New Yorkers rejoiced as the New York Mets defeated the Boston Red Sox in the final game of the World Series.* [author]

ryboat to be built on the West Coast.[5] Why, the Governors Island ferryboats are even painted

in classic steamboat/ferryboat white. Not to keep alive that old tradition, though, but because the Coast Guard paints most all of its vessels white.

The service features frequent departures, with boats leaving each terminal every 15 minutes during the day, passing in mid-

---

5. She's *Governor,* built in Oakland, California in 1954 for service in San Diego and owned by the Washington (state) Toll Bridge Authority as *Kulshan* before coming east ca. 1985.

stream, and making fast to the other slip less than five minutes later – a modern-day replica, really, of Grand Street – Broadway/ Brooklyn, or Fulton Street – Fulton Street. Every trip is crowded with passengers in all shapes and sizes, for while Governors Island is headquarters for the business end of Coast Guard operations, it's also home for the families and dependents of large numbers of Coast Guard personnel. Blue-uniformed admirals, ensigns, and seamen are regular riders of the ferry, but so too are kids with school books and Mets hats, trucks delivering washing machines, and station wagons heading off to Jones Beach on a summer Sunday.

The only thing "wrong" with the Whitehall Street – Governors Island ferry today is that it's not available to the general public. Of course, if it were, and if Governors Island then became an ordinary destination for large numbers of New Yorkers, some idiot would decide that the ferryboats ought to be replaced by a bridge.

These three services excepted, then, one general-purpose and two serving quite restricted mar-

kets – and an ever-more-important exception accorded the fact that New York at the end of the 1980s is seeing what could be the beginnings of a true renaissance of waterborne transportation, albeit using single-ended vessels and not ferryboats – the news from the post-1955 era is universally negative. On January 1, 1955 there were six ferryboat routes operating across the Hudson River in New York City, two Upper Bay services to Staten Island, and three routes connecting Staten Island with the mainland of New Jersey: eleven services in all. Before the end of 1967 ten of the eleven had been abandoned. For that matter, the fate and fortune of ferryboats in waters beyond the limits of New York City were equally unfortunate. Up river from New York City, for example, a number of cross-Hudson services were phased out as new bridges diverted traffic away from the waterfronts of the old Hudson River towns. Many of these routes are of interest to the story of New York ferryboats in that they provided additional years of work for a number of vessels whose original owners were the likes of the Dela-

ware, Lackawanna and Western R.R., or the Union Ferry Company. *Weehawk, a) W. A. Baldwin*, one of the 1926-built vessels that initiated service out of West 23 Street for Electric Ferries, worked a Yonkers – Alpine service for the Westchester Ferry Corporation from 1947 through 1958. That's when the company abandoned its operation entirely, hopelessly outgunned by the new Tappan Zee Bridge of the New York State Thruway.[6]

---

6. The Yonkers – Alpine service permits a few interesting glimpses into pre – Second World War social mores. In 1935 the company provided a dressing room at its ferry terminal for young women heading for a day's outing at Palisades Interstate Park on the New Jersey side of the Hudson. Why? Because the city of Yonkers was arresting any such people who dared walk its streets wearing shorts, that's why. And during the same general time-frame, with its rates of fare subject to all the formality of the U.S. Interstate Commerce Commission and its attendant regulatory apparatus, the company's workers were flexible enough to allow a family of gypsies to cross the Hudson for the price of one live chicken.

*Newest ferryboat on the Governors
Island run is* Governor, *shown here
about to depart Whitehall St. in 1988.*
[*author*]

The Hoboken Ferry Company and its successors turned to double-deck ferryboats in the late nineteenth century to ensure maximum passenger capacity. Strangely, though, the final two vessels built for the company's service, Hoboken *(v) and* Buffalo, *shown here in 1954, were both single-deckers. The pair were turned out in 1922 to work the 14 St. –14 St. run, a service that lacked upper-deck boarding facilities. [author]*

As was discussed in chapter 9, the Pennsylvania R.R. was the first of the five overland railroad companies operating trans-Hudson ferryboats to abandon such service entirely, and that happened in 1949. Next was the Erie R.R.; here the rationale was that the company had moved all its passenger trains into the Delaware, Lackawanna and Western's nearby Hoboken Terminal in 1957, so the Chambers Street–Pavonia service was abandoned the next year. In 1959 the New York Central phased out at first its two Hudson River ferryboat lines (West 42 Street–Weehawken and Cortlandt Street–Weehawken), and its entire rail passenger service they connected with, later. Where in earlier years this West Shore operation had been an alternate route to the west for the N.Y.C.R.R., by the late 1950s it had developed into simply a suburban commuter operation out of Weehawken, and, taking advantage of new Federal legislation passed in 1958 that permitted railroads to abandon money-losing services with less regulatory review than had previously been the case, the 'Central did away with the entire operation – trains as well as boats.

The year 1967 saw the two remaining railroads give up the ghost. Early in the year it was the Jersey Central's turn. The immediate cause of the abandonment of the ferryboats was an operational improvement that had been effected on the whole C.N.J. commuter operation, something called the Aldene Plan.

The premise of the Aldene Plan was that northern New Jersey no longer had individual private railroads independently serving various markets, but rather a regional rail network serving a unified public purpose. Thus the Jersey Central's waterfront terminal at Communipaw on the banks of the Hudson was rendered unnecessary by rerouting that company's trains into the Newark station of the Pennsylvania R.R., where passengers bound for Manhattan could transfer either to Pennsy trains or to PATH rapid transit trains. PATH (i.e., Port Authority Trans-Hudson) is an arm of the Port Authority of New York and New Jersey formed in 1962 to take over the routes and services of the old Hudson and Manhattan R.R., begun by William Gibbs McAdoo back in 1908.

The Jersey Central was hardly a model of robust financial health in the years leading up to the implementation of the Aldene Plan. (Eventually, in 1976, C.N.J. would be absorbed by Conrail, the Federally-created entity designed to

rescue a number of failing railroads in the northeast, particularly the Penn Central.) Through the 1960s the C.N.J.'s fleet of turn-of-the-century ferryboats was starting to fall into serious disrepair; lacking money for major rehabilitation, and anxiously awaiting the Aldene Plan, the railroad retired one vessel after another. In fact, the only company boat that survived up until the end was *Elizabeth* (iii), the rebuilt vessel with the snappy steel superstructure, discussed in chapter 9. *Elizabeth* (iii) was supplemented during the C.N.J.'s final days of service to Communipaw by two vessels chartered from the City of New York, the diesel-electric ferryboats *The Tides* and *The Narrows*, late of Electric Ferries and owned by the city since 1954. It was *The Tides* that made the last crossing on the Liberty Street–Communipaw route in the early morning hours of Sunday, April 30, 1967. This same vessel had also run the finale on the 69 Street–Saint George line in 1964 when the Verrazano–Narrows Bridge opened, and she's still in service in 1989 on the Coast Guard's run to Governors Island.[7]

Last to go was old Colonel John Stevens' Barclay Street–Hoboken line. The Delaware, Lackawanna and Western R.R. had eliminated the Christopher Street–Hoboken line in 1955, but by 1967 what was then the Erie Lackawanna R.R. was losing money hand over fist on its passenger train operations in general, and the ferryboat connection in particular. The Erie Lackawanna was another company that would eventually become part of Conrail; its suburban passenger train operations were later spun off and are now handled – and subsidized – by an independent public agency known as N. J. Transit. (Suburban passenger services of the former Jersey Central R.R. and the Pennsylvania R.R. are now part of the N. J. Transit operation, as well.) Had N. J. Transit been around in 1967 with public subsidies to underwrite the cost of retaining the Barclay Street–Hoboken service, perhaps

7. *E. G. Diefenbach* lives! Although *The Tides* is not built to exactly the same specifications as the first of Electric Ferries' second-generation ferryboats, smartly posted under glass in her passenger cabin is an official U.S. Coast Guard affidavit specifying her

allowable carrying capacity, and referencing a stability test conducted at Orange, Texas in early 1940 on the 'Diefenbach as the basis of the findings. There's also a subtle change in the lines of *The Tides* from her Elec-

tric Ferries days. Originally she and her sister ships were equipped with two covered stairways between main and upper deck, one at each starboard/forward end. The two stairways were at opposite ends of the boat and

on opposite sides as well. The U.S.C.G. has revamped *The Tides* and both stairways are now on the same side of the vessel – the side that's always to the south as she runs between Whitehall St. and Governors Island.

This is not *the final night of Hudson River ferryboat service in 1967; it was taken several days earlier. But when Lackawanna (iii) made the last crossing – several minutes after the final scheduled and official trip – the finale must have looked just like this as she got away from Barclay St. bound for Hoboken for the very last time! [Howard W. Serig, Jr.]*

the story might have played out differently. But it wasn't. Public funds had been heavily invested in the PATH System since its take-over by the Port Authority in 1962, and as Erie Lackawanna kept moving steadily in the direction of abandoning its ferryboats, some kind of a consensus developed that

PATH was up to the task of taking on the ferry traffic. It came to pass in late November 1967.

As the evening rush hour on Wednesday, November 23 was ending, Captain Cornelius Steeval was bringing the 1460-ton *Elmira* across from Barclay Street. She had been built at Newport News,

Virginia, in 1905 – three years before the Hudson and Manhattan ran its first rapid transit train under the river – and this was the scheduled "last run" on the line. The Hoboken High School Band gave a spirited rendition of "Hello, Dolly," and the crossing was well covered by the media – "electronic

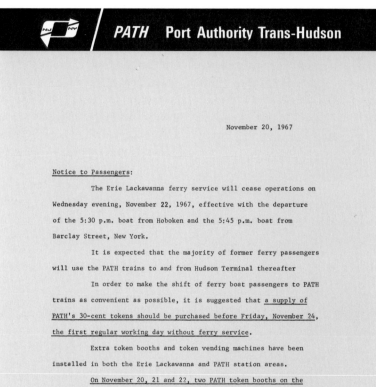

and print," as people were then starting to say.

But there's a footnote to the whole business. While *Elmira* was making the official last run, old *Lackawanna* (iii) was dispatched on one post-finale trip for the benefit of any stragglers who may have been left at Barclay Street in all the hubbub. Ironic in the extreme is the only way to describe the fact that the one and only diesel-powered ferryboat ever owned by one of the Hudson River rail-road ferryboat operators made the actual last trip. It is also ironic that *Lackawanna* (iii), built in 1891 for the railroad's predecessor company, to this day stands as the longest-lived ferryboat to work in New York.[8] Most of all, though,

---

8. Uneasy, it must be said once again, lies the head that wears the crown! See "The Oldest New York Ferryboats" for information on a still-active ex-New York ferryboat that may soon wrest this title from *Lackawanna* (iii).

it's worth noting that there was a sense of pride and professionalism about the ferry operation right up to the end, and if confusion surrounding *Elmira*'s ceremonial crossing had stranded some homeward-bound commuters on the Manhattan side of the Hudson, "The Hoboken Ferry Company" would take care of it.

The next morning, Thursday, November 24, 1967, there was a strange quiet over the Hudson River.

Epilogue

he quiet that settled over the Hudson River in November 1967 was broken – perhaps irrevocably – on the blustery afternoon of December 3, 1986. Said one local newspaper: "Thirty years after the last old-fashioned fat ferryboat waddled across the Hudson River, a sleek new craft is to carry a crowd of dignitaries from New Jersey to New York today."

Well, "thirty years" is a little on the imprecise side; it was 19 years and ten days earlier when the Erie Lackawanna R.R. abandoned the last of the Hudson River routes in the New York area, but there was certainly a "sleek new craft," and after the ceremonial inaugural on December 3, the good ship *Port Imperial* went to work the next morning hauling commuters between Weehawken and the foot of West 38 Street.

Port Imperial is hardly a double-ended ferryboat. She's a 77-foot diesel-powered speedster that can make the crossing in four minutes. But if waterborne transportation is to play a renewed role on the local New York scene in the years ahead, it will be thanks to fast new vessels like *Port Imperial*, not re-creations from an older era.

Port Imperial is owned by Arcorp Ferries, which in turn is a subsidiary of Arcorp Properties, an enterprise that is out to turn the deteriorated riverfront area in and around Weehawken into fancy new real estate development – offices, shops, restaurants, housing. The idea is to give the new development alternative access to Manhattan by water since existing bridges and tunnels operate at virtual capacity during peak hours, and so the ferry service has been established even before the new buildings are constructed.

Port Imperial's first Jerseyside terminal has been constructed on the very spot where the New York Central's most downriver ferry slip was located when the railroad ran double-enders between Manhattan and Weehawken, and the distinctive shape of that old slip can still be seen amid the pilings of the new landing. Of extreme interest is the fact that, more than three-quarters of a century after the concept of public-sector ferryboat operation was inaugurated in New York, *Port Imperial* is owned and operated by a private company.

Nassau *(i), New York & Brooklyn Steam Ferry Boat Company, 1814–n/a*

TV cameras, festivities, celebrities, and a brand-new boat! Trans-Hudson passenger service resumes in December 1986 aboard the diesel-powered speedster Port Imperial. *Circle Line vessel in the background was chartered by a news agency so its photographers would have adequate elbow room!* [author]

Port Imperial was built in Warren, Rhode Island, by Blount Marine, builder of the city's *Michael Cosgrove* as well as any number of other contemporary coastal passenger vessels, and, not long after the December 1987 inaugural between Weehawken and West 38 Street, Arcorp added a second route out of Weehawken, this one to one of the empty slips in the big municipal terminal at the foot of Whitehall Street.

Arcorp seems to be deadly serious about restoring waterborne transportation in New York. It submitted the winning proposal when the Port Authority of New York and New Jersey sought an operator to restore ferry service between the World Trade Center in Manhattan and the very same Hoboken railroad depot that was long the western terminal of so many routes of the Hoboken Ferry Company. It would certainly seem,

HOBOKEN TO LOWER MANHATTAN FERRY TRANSPORTATION SYSTEM

Request for Proposals

THE PORT AUTHORITY OF NY & NJ

In the months and years and even decades after the New York Central R.R. gave up the ghost on its Weehawken ferry services in 1959, this would have been a most improbable sign to have encountered along the Manhattan waterfront. But it's there today, by gosh, directing passengers to a new service. [author]

When the Port Authority of New York and New Jersey recently elicited proposals for the operation of a new Manhattan–Hoboken waterborne service, their informational brochure featured renditions of earlier vessels that linked Hoboken with Manhattan. [Port Authority of NY & NJ]

It wasn't the advent of a new age in ferryboat transportation; it was just a temporary effort to ease congestion while the Williamsburg Bridge was closed for emergency repairs in the spring of 1988. But double-ended ferryboats were back on the East River, even if it only lasted a few weeks. [author]

If you're going to do it, do it right! The city's Bureau of Ferries took considerable pains to ensure that passengers were properly informed about the temporary ferry service between Whitehall St. and Williamsburg in the spring of 1988, including tri-lingual signs appropriate for the ethnic neighborhood served by the new line. [author]

then, that *Port Imperial* will one day have to be called the first vessel in a major New York ferry rebirth, not a one-time aberration.

Of course, neither Arcorp nor any of the other new ferry companies that have recently emerged on the New York scene operate true *ferryboats*, as that term has been used in this book. That is to say, they do not operate over and back service with double-ended vessels. Maybe that's why what

happened on April 18, 1988 was so remarkable. Because on that day a brand-new service was inaugurated using real ferryboats.

"The Williamsburg Express Ferry" was a child of necessity, and a temporary one at that. When inspectors discovered previously undetected deterioration in the 1903-built Williamsburg Bridge, the span whose opening had caused the old Williamsburg ferries to shut down was itself closed to all

traffic. Thousands of daily commuters had to find new ways to get across the East River.

The whole business was quite short-lived, and several weeks later the Williamsburg Bridge was repaired and reopened. But during the interval when it was closed, the City of New York operated a ferryboat service between Whitehall Street and a temporary landing just downriver from the site of the old Williamsburg Ferry termi-

Old. *The* Ralph J. Palumbo *makes her way across Boston Harbor ca. 1940 on a since-abandoned municipal ferryboat route.* [*Massachusetts Bay Transportation Authority*]

nal. The vessels used were the two new smaller ferryboats recently purchased for late-night service on the Whitehall Street–Saint George route, *Alice Austen* and *John A. Noble.*

"The Williamsburg Express Ferry" was an expedient to help the city survive a shutdown of a major East River crossing. But for several weeks in the spring of 1988 double-ended ferryboats were back on the East River. Couple this purely symbolic development with the bona-fide accomplishments and promise that *Port Imperial* represents, and one can start to believe that in the years ahead passengers in New York will have more waterborne alternatives, rather than fewer. And that's a pretty good note to end on, isn't it?

Not Quite As Old. Islander *(ii) leaves Woods Hole, Massachusetts for Martha's Vineyard in 1972. Vessel is still in operation in 1989;* Islander *(i) was an ex-Long Island R.R. double-ender that migrated to Cape Cod when her New York days were over.* [author]

Ferryboats Elsewhere

Over the years there have been more double-ended ferryboats enrolled with New York as their home port than anywhere else, but New York has by no means been the exclusive home of such vessels. Today, for example, Seattle, Washington is where the largest North American concentration of the species can be found. San Francisco was a popular port where double-enders played an important role, including a service that was a parallel of Hudson River operations; ferryboats provided the cross-bay finale for railroad passengers destined for San Francisco.

There are no double-ended ferryboats active in San Francisco today, although modern single-ended vessels work several of the old routes. Indeed, there are very few bona-fide ferryboats still working over and back routes anyplace.

Herewith some photography of ferryboats from places other

New. *A fleet of bona-fide double-enders carries large crowds of people each day in, of all places, Walt Disney* *World in Florida.* Magic Kingdom II *and her three fleetmates aren't amusement-park rides, either; they* *provide basic transportation between the Magic Kingdom and surrounding parking lots.* [author]

Really Old. *San Francisco Bay was second only to New York for the number of ferryboat routes and vessels one could ride. Sidewheeler* Encinal *was built in 1888, scrapped in 1930. Alas, double-enders no longer serve San Francisco. [author's collection]*

than New York, some currently in service, others not so; some are old, some are even older; some are new; none of them are borrowed; but one of them, believe it or not, is blue!

The Oldest New York Ferryboats

Of all the hundreds of ferryboats that have carried passengers and vehicles across New York rivers and bays, one of them must have done so longer than any of the others. Herewith an accounting of not only the single oldest, but the top three vessels in this category. And watch out; "number two" is still active in 1989 and may well move into the top spot before she's finished.

First some "ground rules": a vessel's age is that period of time from the issuance of its first permanent enrollment certificate to the surrender of its last. Some might argue that this fails to account for periods of inactivity, or, for that matter, proper ferryboat service outside the limits of enrollment as a U.S. merchant vessel. But it does permit use of rather reliable and consistent statistics. Eligibility is broad in another category: a vessel merely has to have been permanently enrolled by a New York operator for some time of its career, not its entirety. The quest is for the oldest ferryboat that worked in New York, not necessarily the ferryboat that worked in New York for the longest time.

The hands-down, all-time winner turns out to be *Lackawanna* (iii), the once steam, and later diesel, ferryboat that made the final Barclay Street–Hoboken crossing for the Erie Lackawanna R.R. in 1967, and whose permanent enrollment

Old, too. Sam McBride *is one of a fleet of small double-enders that connect downtown Toronto with island parklands.* [*author*]

Blue. Holiday Island, *built in 1971, carries automobiles between the Canadian mainland and Prince Edward Island on two different decks, loads both simultaneously, and uses 2-lane ramps for each deck.* [author]

wasn't surrendered until September 20, 1971. (She's actually still around, after a fashion, rusting away in a Staten Island junkyard.)

Third place goes to a rather unassuming iron-hull sidewheeler that began work in New York for the Nassau Ferry Company in 1878 as *James M. Waterbury.* Waterbury, the man, was active in nineteenth-

century East River ferryboating, and his namesake vessel migrated to Bridgeport, Connecticut when her days in New York were over, and finally to Virginia waters where, as *City of Norfolk,* her certificate wasn't surrendered until 1953, giving her 75 years of service – actually 75 years, 4 months, and 4 days.

Number two on the all-time

list proves to be a real sleeper. Her career in New York was brief: from 1927 through 1936 she toiled as *Mount Holly* for the East 34 Street Vehicular Ferry Company, and this was the third of her six owners. Built as *South Jacksonville* for the Jacksonville Ferry and Land Company in 1913, she worked a St. Johns River crossing there for some years. Steam-

Adirondack *approaches Port Kent,*
New York on a run across Lake
Champlain from Burlington, Vermont
in June 1987. Vessel may soon become
the longest-running New York
ferryboat of all time. [author]

James M. Waterbury *worked an East River crossing for the Houston Street Ferry Company. Built in 1878, she wasn't removed from documentation until 1953, and thus stands as the third-oldest ferryboat of the hundreds that ran in New York over the years.* [Mariners Museum]

powered, of course, she was next owned by the Tacony–Palmyra Ferry Company on the Delaware River, who re-christened her *Mount Holly* to honor a community in their service area. Oddly enough, she not only retained this "Phila-delphia-sounding" name during her East River days, but her New York owners christened their other two second-hand vessels *Mount Hood* and *Mount Hope* to achieve some allitera-tive similarity in their three-boat fleet.

After New York one might have thought her days were numbered. A small (i.e., 130-foot) steam-powered ferryboat almost a quarter-century old was hardly a piece of desirable property in the depths of the Great Depression as routes were being steadily abandoned all over the place in the face of hard economic times. But a Chesapeake Bay operator snatched her up, later replaced her original reciprocating steam engine with a pair of direct-drive diesels (one engine turns the forward screw, one the aft), and as *Gov. Emerson C. Har-*

rington II she found a new home in Maryland waters until the mid-1950s. Then with the opening of the Chesapeake Bay Bridge she was again rendered surplus.

But again fate was to treat the *'Harrington* kindly. In 1954 she was purchased by the Lake Champlain Transportation Company for seasonal service between Burlington, Vermont and Port Kent, New York, and there she continues to toil faith-fully as *Adirondack* – or "Adi," as the Lake Champlain people affectionately call her.

Her passage to Lake Cham-plain was a little tricky; to clear the low fixed bridges on the New York State Barge Canal that connects Lake Champlain with tidewater and the Hudson River, she entered a shipyard in Troy, New York. There her top deck was first jacked up a bit; then, once all supporting work was removed, the deck was lowered to a position just above the main deck. In such a "squatting" posture she was towed up to Burlington, and there restored to a more normal profile.

Adirondack has changed over the years. Her pilot houses have been rebuilt, and it's uncertain if any of her wooden upper works are original construction from Jacksonville days. The Lake Champlain Transportation Com-pany is acutely aware of the his-toric gem they own in *Adiron-dack*. In the summer of 1988 a ceremony was held to mark her seventy-fifth anniversary. A special cruise was run with an-tique automobiles aboard, in-cluding a Stevens–Duryea touring car that, like *Adiron-dack*, was built in 1913. But the auto is a pure antique, used only on special occasions; *Adi-rondack* had run several regu-lar Burlington–Port Kent crossings on the day of the ceremony and was back to work again the next morning!

And what of *Adirondack*'s fu-ture? Well, during the seventy-fifth anniversary ceremony, Ray Pecor, the president of Lake Champlain Transporta-tion, was presented with a sealed bottle that contained water from all the places *Adirondack* has run over the years—*with instructions to*

The sidewheel ferryboat Brinkerhoff *at the Mystic Seaport.* [*author's collection*]

save it to re-christen the vessel when she celebrates her centennial in the year 2013.

A hundred years of service is quite a goal, but *Adirondack* has another mark to shoot for that's not all that far into the future. For if she's still an active ferryboat on the morning of November 26, 1992 she will have exceeded the service life of *Lackawanna* (iii) and earned the title of the oldest New York ferryboat of all time.

A Sad Story

For most of her life the ferryboat *Brinkerhoff* toiled outside the boundaries of New York Harbor, so she's not really part of the New York ferryboat story. But she was leased at one time or another by at least two New York operators, and so she has some legitimate claim for attention.

Brinkerhoff was built in 1899 and toiled on a trans-Hudson route for the Poughkeepsie & Highland Ferry Company until 1941. For some of her years there the walking-beam veteran was a fleetmate of the 1922-built *Poughkeepsie*, the world's first diesel-electric ferryboat. Odd assignments were *Brinkerhoff*'s lot after that, and finally in 1950 arrangements were made to tow what had by then become the last beam-engine ferryboat on the Atlantic Coast to permanent sanctuary at Mystic Seaport in Connecticut.

The voyage from Kingston, N.Y., where *Brinkerhoff* was laid up, to the museum was not without its moments; under tow of the tugboat *Joseph Meseck, Jr.*, she managed to get lost in the fog on Long Island Sound, and when heavy weather later developed and no word had been received – the *'Meseck* lacked a two-way radio in 1950, something that in the 1980s seems more dated than the notion of a ferryboat powered by a vertical-beam engine – genuine concern developed over the safety of both tug and ferry, and Coast Guard rescue vessels were sent out in search of the

pair. This part of the story had a happy ending, though. The *'Meseck*'s skipper had sought refuge first at New Haven and later at Old Saybrook, and soon enough the old *Brinkerhoff* was part of the seafaring exhibits at the Mystic Seaport.

But somehow it didn't quite work out. Maybe it was just that an over and back ferryboat felt out of place with sailing ships like the *Joseph Conrad* and the *Charles Morgan*. Funds failed to materialize for her restoration, deterioration of her upper works continued, and finally the Mystic Seaport people felt she had to go. Poor old *Brinkerhoff* was dismantled, the last link with the era of walking-beam ferryboats in New York.

One brief note about the photograph. *Brinkerhoff* represents a less popular design for a vertical-beam ferryboat in that her walking beam is enclosed in a cupola-like structure atop her upper deck. The more common arrangement placed the walking beam "outdoors" where its captivating up-and-down rocking motion was visible to all.

Vox Populi

New Yorkers are known as an outspoken lot who never hesitate to speak their mind when they see things as being substandard, and no better forum has ever been provided for such expression than the letters-to-the-editor columns that the city's newspapers have long provided. Local transportation has always been a popular subject for such letters, although to this day few subway train, bus, or ferryboat operators ever find themselves praised in print. It's usually when a passenger has a beef that he or she takes pen in hand and lets the world (i.e., one's fellow New Yorkers) know of some particularly annoying problem. Readers of *The New York Times* on Thursday, February 6, 1873, for instance, had a chance to learn of one passenger's problems with the Hudson River ferryboat service that the Pennsylvania R.R. had recently taken over from the New Jersey Railroad and Transportation Company.

You have kindly given audience to the woman who depicted the miseries of car-riding in New York, and I hope you will be equally patient with a Jersey woman while she makes you acquainted with her special grievance. My husband is not rich and we are, therefore, obliged to live in Jersey City, which, in itself, would be no great hardship were I not obliged to go daily to New York. I am, therefore, obliged to cross the Cortlandt-street ferry. The so-called "Ladies' Cabins" of these boats are not, as a rule, as cleanly kept as a well-regulated pig-pen. Apparently, the floors are never scrubbed, certainly they are never cleaned; at various hours during the day women are seen with brooms in their hands, but I have never seen the floors "broom-clean." The side moldings are covered with undisturbed dust, the backs of the seats are only cleaned by the garments of passengers rubbing against them.

But the dirt, all-pervading as it is, forms but a small part of the annoyance of women who are obliged to cross these ferries. At all hours of the day the cabins are overrun with beggars, hawkers and peddlers. Some days there are three or four kinds of nuisances on a boat at the same time. The impudent cough-drop man keeps up a continuous cry about his "Great remedy for coughs, colds, sore throats, and all diseases of the throat, chest, and lungs." There are various grades of disgustingly dirty blind men and boys; also players on all sorts of musical and unmusical instruments. These boats are literally overrun by vermin of this kind. I think the alms-houses in New York must be emptied daily into these ferry-boats. I find other ferry-boats quite clean and free from all such annoyances. Won't you, Mr. Editor, take up cudgels for the poor women who are daily obliged to endure these very disgusting nuisances?

GERTRUDE

Circle Line's Miss Liberty *heads for the Battery Park sea wall with passengers en route back to Manhattan from Liberty Island.* [author]

Single-Enders

Over the years New York Harbor has been served by many passenger-carrying vessels that operated in short-haul services very much *like* over and back ferryboat routes. Except they weren't double-ended ferryboats; they were single-ended steamboats. There still are several such services in operation today, although the vessels are now powered by diesel engines, not steam. We're not talking here about vessels that connect New York with distant points, but locally-oriented operations with one-way trips measured in minutes, not hours.

Of the contemporary services, one is an old and venerable operation, while the rest are rather new. The old service links Battery Park with the Statue of Liberty out on Liberty Island, and is run by the Circle Line, also the operator of seasonal sightseeing cruises around Manhattan island. For the service out to Liberty Island, Circle Line relies on two near-sister ships, *Miss Liberty* and *Miss Circle Line*; both are three-deck diesel-powered craft that have become fixtures on the lower Manhattan scene.

Many new ferry-type services have recently been inaugurated in New York linking downtown Manhattan with various residential communities in New

Views at the Sheepshead Bay terminal of Rockaway Boat Lines, a company whose small single-enders provided service to bungalow colonies across Jamaica Bay on the Rockaway peninsula. Columbia's *wheelhouse was down low on her main deck. [author]*

This woodcut from Frank Leslie's Illustrated Newspaper *depicts a connecting steamboat and excursion railroad service between Manhattan and Coney Island over which the* newspaper *was running a promotional special. Steamer* Sylvan Dell *also ran from lower Manhattan to points on the Harlem River. Sea* Beach Railway *has evolved into a major rapid transit line of the New York City Transit Authority, the N train. [author's collection]*

Jersey, and elsewhere, are largely commuter in nature, and represent a minor growth industry in the area. The typical vessels used on these services are crew boats, so called, designed for fast passage of workers to and from off-shore oil rigs, and modified for the convenience of briefcase-toting Wall Streeters. The largest of these new operators is a company called Direct Line.

Another new service operates between Battery Park, Ellis Island, Liberty Island, and Liberty Park in New Jersey. This operation is geared toward the needs of tourists; like the direct service to the Statue of Liberty, it, too, is run by Circle Line.

Over the years there have been many other waterborne services in and around New York that were akin to ferry-boat services, often operated under the provision of ferry leases issued by the municipal government, but worked with single-ended vessels: downtown Manhattan to Harlem, Whitehall Street to north shore points on Staten Island, across the Narrows, around the rim of Jamaica Bay.

The City of New York even owned several single-ended passenger vessels over the years that complemented its ferry-boat fleet. The last of these was the 1930-built *Welfare* whose principal assignment was an East River route between Manhattan and Welfare (now Roosevelt) Island.

To the extent that the newly-formed waterborne passenger services now appearing all over the New York area rely primarily, if not universally, on single-ended boats, the future would seem to be bright for this style of vessel.

Tables

Table II-1

1812–1860: Years of Growth

	1824	1860	% Growth
United States – population	8,500,000	63,000,000	641%
– immigration	150,000 (per decade)	2,812,000 (per decade)	1770%
– railroad mileage	0	30,000	∞
– number of states	24	33	38%
New York City – population	200,000	1,176,000	488%
– imports (tons per year)	100,000 ±	1,973,000	1873%
– exports (tons per year)	100,000 ±	1,678,000	1578%
Operating Ferryboats	6 ±	70 +	1066%

Table III-1

Ferryboats of the Union Ferry Company, 1853

VESSEL	OFF. NO.	BUILT	TONNAGE	COMMENTS/ NOTES
New York (i)	18557	1836, New York	304	1
Fulton (i)	—	1838, New York	184	
Union (i)	25077	1844, New York	296	
Montauk	50379	1846, New York	403	
Wyandank	—	1847, New York	399	
Transit	—	1847, New York	404	
Bedford	31136	1848, New York	424	
Manhattan	50370	1849, Brooklyn	326	
Gowanus	—	1851, Brooklyn	417	
Whitehall (i)	—	1850, Brooklyn	323	
Fulton (ii)	9051	1852, Brooklyn	410	
Brooklyn (ii)	2315	1853, New York	427	
Louise	—	1853, Greenpoint	341	2
Ellen	—	1853, Greenpoint	341	2
Agnes	—	1852, Greenpoint	299	2
Lydia	14938	1852, Greenpoint	299	2
Abbie	1819	1852, Greenpoint	299	2
Osprey	19040	1853, Williamsburg	468	3
Eagle	2306	1852, Greenpoint	392	3
Curlew	22804	1853, Williamsburg	366	3
Montague (i)	—	1852, Williamsburg	410	4
Exchange	7714	1853, Brooklyn	438	4
Metropolis	16302	1852, Greenpoint	433	4

1. Originally owned by Whitehall St.–Atlantic Ave. line; became part of Union fleet through merger in 1839.
2. Originally owned by Catharine St.–Main St. line; became part of Union fleet through merger in 1853.
3. Originally owned by Roosevelt St.–Bridge St. line; became part of Union fleet through merger in 1853.
4. Originally owned by Wall St.–Montague St. line; became part of Union fleet through merger in 1853.

For more details on Union's fleet, see Appendix C.

Table III-2

New York Ferryboat Routes – 1860

Manhattan Terminal	Opposite Terminal	Established	Operator
W. 42 St.	Slough's Meadow	1859	Weehawken Fy. Co.
Christopher St.	Hoboken	1838	Hoboken Land & Improvement Co.
Barclay St.	Hoboken	1821	Hoboken Land & Improvement Co.
Cortlandt St.	Paulus Hook	1812	New Jersey R.R.
Whitehall St.	Staten Island	1816	Staten Island & New York Fy. Co.
Whitehall St.	Hamilton Av.	1856	Union Fy. Co.
Whitehall St.	Atlantic Av.	1836	Union Fy. Co.
Wall St.	Montague St.	1852	Union Fy. Co.
Fulton St.	Fulton St.	1814	Union Fy. Co.
Catharine St.	Main St.	ca. 1850	Union Fy. Co.
Jackson St.	Hudson Av.	ca. 1825	Navy Yard Fy. Co.
Roosevelt St.	Broadway	1836	Williamsburg ferries
Grand St.	Broadway	1851	Williamsburg ferries
Grand St.	Grand St.	ca. 1859	Williamsburg ferries
Houston St.	Grand St.	1842	Nassau Fy. Co.
E. 10 St.	Greenpoint	1853	Greenpoint Fy. Co.
E. 23 St.	Greenpoint	1853 (see text)	Greenpoint Fy. Co.
James Slip	Hunter's Point	1859	East River Fy. Co.
E. 34 St.	Hunter's Point	1859	East River Fy. Co.
E. 86 St.	Astoria	1843 (see text)	Astoria Fy. Co.

See Appendix B for further information.

Table IV-1

New York Ferryboats in the Union Navy

Vessel	Pre-war Name and Owner	Built (Date)	Sold to U.S.N. (Price)	Civil War Assignment	Post-war Disposition
U.S.S. Commodore Read	*Atlantic*, #22095 Union Ferry Co.	Brooklyn (1857)	Aug. '63 ($91,000)	Potomac flotilla	sold to Washington, D.C. interests
U.S.S. Clifton	*Clifton* (i) Staten Island & New York Ferry Co.	Brooklyn (1861)	Dec. '61 ($90,000)	West Gulf Block-ading Squadron	None; see note A
U.S.S. Shokokon	*Clifton* (ii), #15434 Staten Island & New York Ferry Co.	Greenpoint (1862)	April '63 ($100,000)	No. Atlantic Block-ading Squadron	sold to New Orleans interests
U.S.S. Commodore Jones	None; purchased by U.S.N. before entering commercial service. Union Ferry Co.	n/a (1863?)	May '63 ($83,000)	No. Atlantic Block-ading Squadron	n/a
U.S.S. Commodore Morris	None; purchased by U.S.N. before entering commercial service. Union Ferry Co.	New York (1862)	1862 ($42,409)	No. Atlantic Block-ading Squadron	sold to Union Ferry Co.; see note B
U.S.S. Commodore McDonough	None; purchased by U.S.N. before entering commercial service. Union Ferry Co.		($42,409)	So. Atlantic Block-ading Squadron	None; see note C
U.S.S. Fort Henry	None; purchased by U.S.N. before entering commercial service. Union Ferry Co.	New York (1862)	Mar. '62 ($69,690)	East Gulf Block-ading Squadron	sold to East River Ferry Co. (i.e., L.I.R.R.); became *Huntington*, #11460

U.S.S. *John P. Jackson*	*John P. Jackson,* #12982 New Jersey Railroad & Transportation Co.	Brooklyn (1860)	Nov. '61 ($60,000)	West Gulf Blockading Squadron	sold to New Orleans interests
U.S.S. *Morse*	*Marion,* #14647 Williamsburg ferries	New York (1859)	Nov. '61 ($40,000)	No. Atlantic Blockading Squadron; Potomac Squadron	sold to Boston interests
U.S.S. *Commodore Perry*	*Commodore Perry,* #4869 Williamsburg ferries	Brooklyn (1859)	Oct. '61 ($38,000)	No. Atlantic Blockading Squadron	sold to Williamsburg ferries
U.S.S. *Ellen* (?)	*Ellen* Union Ferry Co.	Greenpoint (1853)	Oct. '61 ($23,100)	So. Atlantic Blockading Squadron	sold to South Carolina interests
U.S.S. *Wyandank*	*Wyandank* Union Ferry Co.	New York (1847)	Sept. '61 ($19,000)	Potomac Flotilla	remained in U.S. Govt. service; scrapped 1880
U.S.S. *Commodore Barney*	*Ethan Allen* Williamsburg ferries	Brooklyn (1859)	Nov. '61 ($38,000)	No. Atlantic Blockading Squadron; Potomac Flotilla	sold to Williamsburg ferries
U.S.S. *Hunchback*	*Hunchback,* #10135 Staten Island & New York Ferry Co.	New York (1852)	Dec. '61 ($45,000)	No. Atlantic Blockading Squadron	sold to Boston interests; see note D
U.S.S. *Commodore Hull*	See note E	Brooklyn (1861)	Sept. '62 ($25,000)	No. Atlantic Blockading Squadron	sold to North Carolina interests
U.S.S. *Somerset*	*Somerset,* #22876 Union Ferry Co.	Brooklyn (1862)	Mar. '62 ($69,690)	East Gulf Blockading Squadron	sold to Union Ferry Co.
U.S.S. *Southfield*	*Southfield* (i) Staten Island & New York Ferry Co.	Brooklyn (1857)	Dec. '61 ($65,000)	No. Atlantic Blockading Squadron	None; see note F

U.S.S. *Stepping Stones*	*Stepping Stones* see note J	New York (1861)	Sept. '61 ($20,000)	No. Atlantic Blockading Squadron	sold to Boston interests
U.S.S. *Westfield*	*Westfield* Staten Island & New York Ferry Co.	Brooklyn (1861)	Nov. '61 ($90,000)	West Gulf Blockading Squadron	None; see note G
U.S.S. *Whitehall*	*Whitehall* Union Ferry Co.	Brooklyn (1850)	Oct. '61 ($24,150)	No. Atlantic Blockading Squadron	None; see note H

A. Captured by Confederate forces near Sabine Pass, Texas, in September 1863; used as a blockade runner; went aground, also near Sabine Pass, in March 1864. Set afire to avoid recapture by Union forces.

B. Vessel became *Clinton* for Union Ferry Company. Was requisitioned for use by the U.S. Army during World War I. Returned to the status of civilian merchant ship and worked for the Carteret Ferry Corporation until 1931.

C. Lost off the New Jersey coast in August 1865, while being towed back to New York.

D. Actually sold to Williamsburg ferries after Civil War service, but quickly resold to Boston interests where she operated until ca. 1880 as *General Grant*.

E. Although Minick includes this vessel in her list of New York ferryboats that served in the Union Navy, the claim is subject to qualification. Built in New York, she ran in Havana, Cuba, before the war as *Nuestra Señora del Regla*.

F. Sunk at the mouth of the Roanoke River in April 1864, by the Confederate steamer *Albemarle*.

G. Blown up in Galveston Bay in January 1863, to avoid capture.

H. Lost off Fort Monroe, Virginia, in March 1862, during the same encounter made famous by the clash of the *Monitor* and the *Merrimack* (i.e., C.S.S. *Virginia*).

J. Purchased by the Union Navy from one Edward Haight. Minick speculates vessel likely ran Whitestone Landing–Throggs Neck prior to war service, but this is uncertain. Lacking further information, I have not included this vessel in the roster in Appendix C.

General Note: Many additional New York ferryboats saw military service during the Civil War under the auspices of the U.S. Army; cf. Appendix C for some details. Minick particularly mentions two of these, both of which served as troop transports and both of which were leased by the Army from the Hoboken Land and Improvement Company. They are *Chancellor Livingston* and *Hoboken* (ii). The former returned to Hoboken service after the war but the latter was lost while serving with the Coast Division of the Army of the Potomac under General Burnside in 1862 – the Burnside Expedition, so called.

Table VII-1

New York Ferryboats by Year

Year	No. boats	Est. average gross tonnage per boat	Est. total gross tonnage
1866	70	463.8	32,469
1904	147	718.2	105,587
1919	100	892.7	89,270
1936	117	991.8	116,040
1945	88	983.7	86,565
1955	57	1088.0	62,016
1975	9	1736.1	15,625

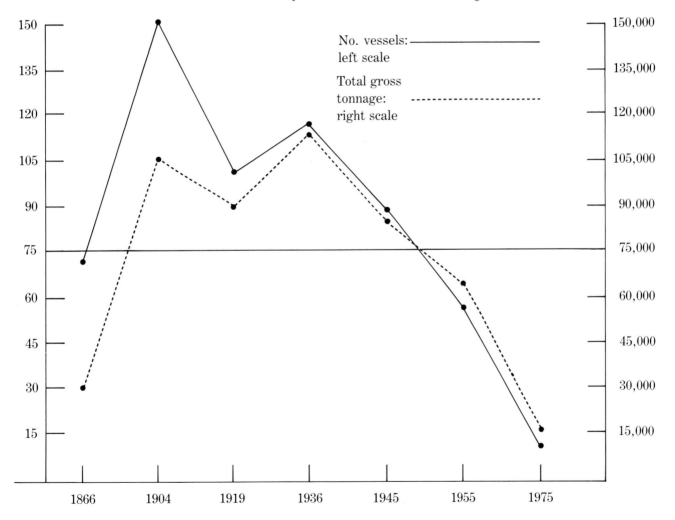

Table VII-2

Number of Vessels vs. *Total Gross Tonnage*

Table VII-3
Average Gross Tonnage per New York Ferryboat

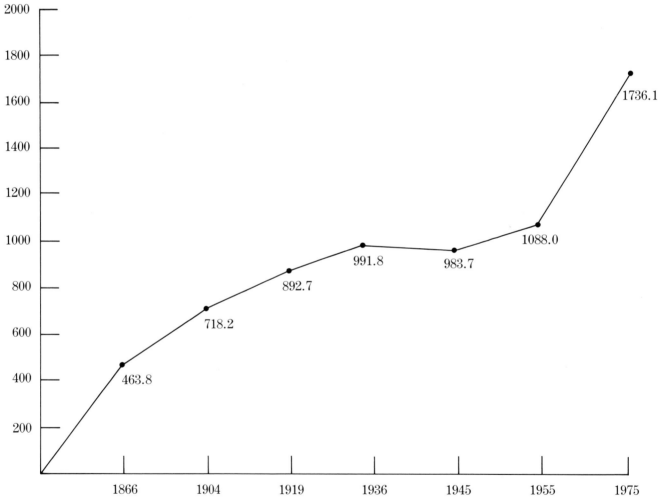

Table VII-4

Residential Population of the Territory that is Today the City of New York

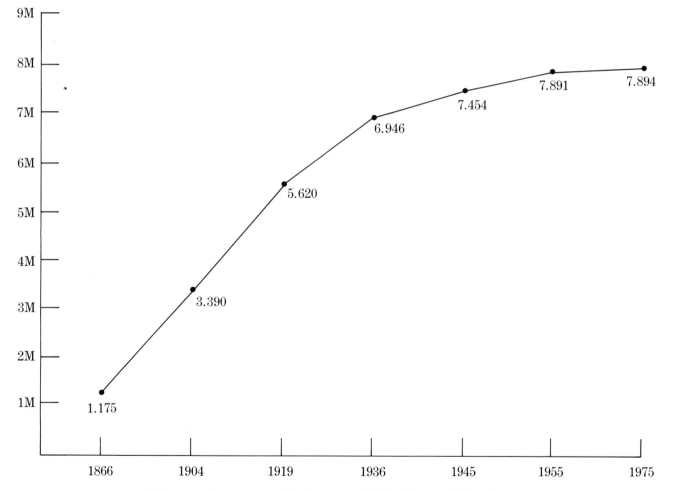

All figures are from previous U.S. Census except 1919, which uses 1920 numbers.

Table VII-5

"Impact" or "Importance" of New York Ferryboat Services

See text: 1975 is base year; index is derived by dividing total ferryboat gross tonnage by city's population.

1975	1.0
1955	+ 3.9
1945	+ 5.8
1936	+ 8.4
1919	+ 7.8
1904	+ 7.9
1866	+14.7

Table VII-6

Ferryboat Patronage (in millions)

Year	1866	1904	1908	1919	1936	1945	1955	1975
Total passengers	n/a	n/a	201.3	124.3	112.6	81.5	46.9	20.0±
% reduction	—	—	—	38%	10%	28%	46%	55%
% reduction from 1908	—	—	—	38%	45%	60%	77%	90%
Total vehicles	n/a	n/a	n/a	n/a	10.6	7.9	6.5	0.6±
Annual passenger trips per capita	—	—	54.4	22.2	15.8	10.2	6.0	2.5±

Table VII-7

New York Ferryboat Operators

Year	1866	1904	1919	1936	1945	1955	1975
No. boats	70	147	100	117	88	57	9
Railroads or railroad-related	30%	39%	48%	47%	49%	47%	0
Independent companies	70%	61%	42%	17%	21%	10%	0
The City of New York	0	0	10%	36%	30%	43%	100%

Table VII-8

Where New York Ferryboats Were Built

Year	1866	1904	1919	1936	1945	1955	1975
No. boats	70	147	100	117	88	57	9
New York City, ex. Staten Island	84%	34%	14%	10%	9%	7%	0
New Jersey; Hudson River	9%	3%	1%	0	0	0	0
L.I. Sound and New England	0	1%	3%	1%	4%	7%	23%
Upper Hudson River	4%	23%	22%	13%	12%	12%	0
Staten Island	0	4%	8%	18%	26%	40%	44%
New Jersey shore: Elizabethport, Keyport, etc.	1%	1%	2%	2%	5%	5%	0
Delaware River	1%	32%	40%	44%	32%	18%	0
Chesapeake Bay, incl. Norfolk area	0	2%	9%	10%	7%	7%	0
All others: Florida, Texas, etc.	0	0	1%	1%	4%	4%	33%

Table VII-9

New York Ferryboats: Construction and Propulsion

Year	1866	1904	1919	1936	1945	1955	1975
No. boats	70	147	100	117	88	57	9
Hull material:							
wood	100%	43%	23%	2%	1%	—	—
iron	—	29%	20%	5%	1%	—	—
steel	—	28%	57%	93%	98%	100%	100%
Engines:							
steam	100%	100%	100%	91%	86%	74%	44%
diesel	—	—	—	9%	14%	26%	56%
Propulsion:							
sidewheel	100%	77%	53%	11%	2%	—	—
propeller	—	23%	47%	89%	98%	100%	100%

Table VII-10

New York Ferryboat Safety Performance: 1899–1910

	1899	1900	1901	1902	1903	1904	1905	1906	1907	1908	1909	1910	Totals	Average per year
Collisions with another vessel	23	28	34	44	35	49	30	49	51	35	32	27	437	36.4
Ferryboat–ferryboat collisions	4	3	8	7	5	6	11	15	11	7	4	6	84	8.0
Groundings	0	0	1	0	0	1	0	1	0	2	1	1	7	0.6
Fires	0	0	1	0	0	0	2	1	2	2	1	1	10	0.8
Passengers/crew overboard	3	3	2	1	4	4	3	6	3	2	5	3	39	3.3
(drownings)	(3)	(3)	(2)	(1)	(4)	(4)	(3)	(6)	(3)	(2)	(3)	(2)	(36)	(3.0)
No. ferryboats	143	140	141	143	146	132	155	152	133	137	139	123	—	140.3
Incidents per ferryboat	0.21	0.24	0.33	0.36	0.30	0.45	0.30	0.50	0.50	0.35	0.31	0.31	—	0.346

Table VIII-1

Patronage – Hudson River Railroad Ferries
1910 vs. *1925*

	1910	*1925*
Jersey Central R.R.	14,400,400	16,524,700
Pennsylvania R.R.	24,482,500	3,542,700 (A)
Erie R.R.	10,691,600	11,498,600
Delaware, Lackawanna and Western R.R.	37,900,000	36,134,500
New York Central R.R.	10,110,100	24,276,900
Totals	97,584,600	91,877,400

(A) P.R.R.'s Hudson River tunnels opened in November 1910.

Table IX-1

Routes and Patronage – Hudson River Railroad Ferries
1925 vs. *1955*

ROUTES

1925	*1955*
Liberty St.–Communipaw	Liberty St.–Communipaw
W. 23 St.–Communipaw (Jersey Central R.R.)	—
Cortlandt St.–Exchange Place	—
Desbrosses St.–Exchange Place (Pennsylvania R.R.)	—
Chambers St.–Jersey City/Pavonia	Chambers St.–Jersey City/Pavonia
W. 23 St.–Jersey City/Pavonia (Erie R.R.)	—

ROUTES

1925	1955
Barclay St. – Hoboken	Barclay St. – Hoboken
Christopher St. – Hoboken	Christopher St. – Hoboken (A)
W. 23 St. – Hoboken	—
W. 23 St. – Hoboken/14 St. (Delaware, Lackawanna & Western R.R.)	—
W. 42 St. – Weehawken	West 42 St. – Weehawken
Cortlandt St. – Weehawken (New York Central R.R.)	Cortlandt St. – Weehawken

PATRONAGE	1925	1955
Jersey Central R.R.	16,524,700	7,549,600
Pennsylvania R.R.	3,542,700	—
Erie R.R.	11,498,600	4,130,300
Delaware, Lackawanna & Western R.R.	36,134,500	5,811,500 (A)
New York Central R.R.	24,176,900	3,889,800
Totals	91,877,400	21,381,200

(A) The D. L. & W.'s Christopher St. – Hoboken service was discontinued on March 30, 1955

Table IX-2

The Rise and Fall of the Municipal Ferry System

Route	Service Begun Under Municipal Auspices	Service Abandoned	Notes
Whitehall St. – St. George	1905	still in operation	

Whitehall St.– 39 St./Brooklyn	1906	1938	
Whitehall St.– Stapleton	1909	1913	
Roosevelt St.– Broadway/Brooklyn	1911	1918	1
E. 23 St.– Broadway/Brooklyn	1911	1918	1
E. 92 St.–Astoria	1920	1936	
College Point– Clason's Point	1921	1939	
E. 23 St.–Greenpoint	1921	1933	
Grand St.– Broadway/Brooklyn	1921	1931	
Whitehall St.– Hamilton Ave.	1922	1942	
Whitehall St.– Atlantic Ave.	1922	1933	
Fulton St.– Fulton St.	1922	1924	
Flatbush Ave.– Beach 169 St.	1925	1937	
69 St./Brooklyn– St. George	1954	1964	2

Note 1: These services were operated by the Brooklyn and Manhattan Fy. Co. and were subsidized by the city; they were not municipally owned or operated, as such. In a meeting of the Sinking Fund Commission of December 31, 1919, when the matter of municipal take-over of the E. 92 St.–Astoria ferry was under discussion, Grover Whalen referred to this earlier subsidy arrangement as "one sad experience."

Note 2: This route was fully municipally-owned during the noted period; however, it was operated for the city by a private contractor.

N.B.: Institutional services to East River health, welfare, and penal institutions are not included. See Appendix B for details.

Table IX-3

Later-day Ferryboats of the Staten Island–New Jersey Routes

Name	Built	Gross Tonnage	Statutory Dimensions
Irvington	Mariners Harbor, S.I. (1932)	113	54.2 × 29 × 8.5
Piermont	Mariners Harbor, S.I. (1932)	113	54.2 × 29 × 8.5
Altair	Port Richmond, S.I. (1946)	84	61.9 × 38.9 × 8
Deneb	Port Richmond, S.I. (1946)	84	61.9 × 38.9 × 8
Vega	Port Richmond, S.I. (1946)	84	61.9 × 38.9 × 8
Capella	Staten Island (1947)	97	58.2 × 32 × 5.1
Spica	Staten Island (1949)	99	60.3 × 36.1 × 6.2
Sirius	Port Richmond, S.I. (1950)	97	60.1 × 36.1 × 6.2
Orion	Port Richmond, S.I. (1955)	48	60 × 35 × 6

See Appendix C for further details.

Appendix A
Annotated Bibliography

A. Primary documents, indices, bibliographies, vessel registers, etc.

Albion, Robert Greenhalgh. *Naval and Maritime History: An Annotated Bibliography*, 4th ed. rev. Mystic, Conn.: Marine Historical Association, 1972.

Anyone who attempts serious maritime research without use of this work is a fool.

American Bureau of Shipping (ABS), *Record of American and Foreign Shipping*. An annual published since 1867 under various titles.

Used by insurance underwriters, etc.; ABS classifies vessels and provides considerable construction details of vessels it classifies. But ferryboat operators did not necessarily have all their boats classified by ABS, especially in the age of wooden-hull vessels.

Annual Report of the Supervising Inspector-General, Steamboat-Inspection Service. Issued by the U.S. Government at Washington, D.C. under various titles and in various formats.

Usefulness varies since kind and level of information also vary; emphasizes safety-related information.

The City of New York. *Annual Report of the Department of Docks and Ferries*. New York: irregularly published.

Particularly useful for the period of municipal take-over of the Whitehall St.–St. George service ca. 1905.

——. *Proceedings of the Commission of the Sinking Fund*. New York: irregularly published.

Contains working papers and formal documents from the meetings of the city agency responsible for executing ferry leases and making capital investment in the municipal ferry system.

——. *A Compilation of the Existing Ferry Leases and Railroad Grants Made by the Corporation of the City of New York*, compiled by David T. Valentine. New York: Jones, 1866.

Very useful, as is anything on which David Valentine's name appears. However, it is merely a catalogue of leases; operation of a ferryboat line and the existence of a lease were not the same thing.

Johnson, Eads. *Steam Vessels of the Atlantic Coast* [as well as various other titles]. New York: Eads Johnson Publishing Company, ca. 1915 through ca. 1940.

Johnson was a naval architect who designed many New York ferryboats during the first half of the twentieth century. He also pub-lished this annual directory of vessels that is especially helpful for the pre-1926 era, since prior to 1926 *MVUS* does not supply information on the owner of enrolled vessels; Johnson's format arranges vessels by owner.

Marine Transit Operations in the Tri-state Region: Interim Technical Report 4535–2129. New York: Tri-State Regional Planning Commission, 1975.

An important report that has provided basic planning data for the development of new waterborne passenger services in New York; also includes a wealth of historical information such as listings of ferryboat services, patronage statistics, etc.

Merchant Vessels of the United States (*MVUS*). Published more or less annually, 1867–1981, by various Federal agencies – e.g., Dept. of Commerce, Dept. of the Treasury, U.S. Coast Guard.

Definitive roster of U.S. flag merchant vessels; publication scheduled to resume under a new format ca. 1989.

National Archives of the United States, Washington D.C.

Original enrollment certificates are to be found in the Fiscal and Social Division of the Archives for vessels removed from documentation prior to 1955; currently operating vessels, as well as those removed from documentation after 1955, are in the custody of the U.S. Coast Guard, Washington, D.C.

The New York Times Index. New York: The New York Times, ca. 1860–current.

Keyed specifically to stories as they appear in *The New York Times*, but useful in a much broader way for gaining knowledge of events, personalities, etc.; the newspaper also publishes extensive indices containing solely obituary citations.

Stanton, Samuel Ward. *American Steam Vessels.* New York: Smith & Stanton, 1895.

A venerable work that contains excellent line drawings and brief (i.e., one-page) descriptive materials about many nineteenth-century vessels; hardly definitive with respect to New York ferryboats, but no less delightful.

Steamship Historical Society of America, *Merchant Steam Vessels of the United States, 1790–1868.* Staten Island: The Steamship Historical Society of America, 1975.

This is the latest version of a work generally known as The Lytle–Holdcamper List, an invaluable aid for work on nineteenth-century steamboating; supplements have been issued in 1978, 1982, and 1984.

Valentine, David T. *Manual of the Corporation of the City of New York for 1851.* New York: The Common Council, ca. 1850–67.

Issued annually; contain lists of all active ferry leases in a given year, often including excellent drawings of such facilities as ferry slips.

B. Books

Adams, Arthur G. *The Hudson Through the Years* (Westwood, N.J.: Lind Publications, 1983).

Study of the Hudson River from several perspectives; includes several chapters, as well as appendix material, specifically dealing with ferryboats.

——, and Raymond J. Baxter. *Railroad Ferries of the Hudson River.* Woodcliff Lake, N.J.: Lind Publications, 1987.

Historical treatments of each of the Hudson River railroad ferryboat operators, plus a first-person account by Baxter of his life as a deckhand on Erie R.R. ferries. Many excellent photographs, plus fleet rosters, etc.

Albion, Robert Greenhalgh. *The Rise of New York Port, 1815–1860.* New York: Scribners, 1939.

Albion is a most astute, scholarly, and prolific maritime historian, and this work is a tour de force. Has

been re-published many times, the most recent being New York: South Street Seaport, 1984.

Condit, Carl W. *The Port of New York*, 2 vols. Chicago: University of Chicago Press, 1980 and 1981.

Title can be misleading; deals with the *railroads* of New York, not maritime matters per se. Scholarly, with a good assemblage of facts, data and source materials; provides treatment of the Hudson River passenger terminals, plans for Hudson River bridges and tunnels, etc.

Harlan, George H. *San Francisco Bay Ferryboats.* Berkeley: Howell-North, 1967.

An excellent history of ferryboat service on San Francisco Bay that allows one to see contrasts with New York operations; good narrative text, fine photographs, roster, bibliography, etc.

Heyl, Erik. *Early American Steamers*, 5 vols. Buffalo: Erik Heyl, 1956–67.

Contains individual treatments of individual vessels, each including a line drawing by the author; a dozen or so New York ferryboats to be found throughout the various volumes.

Hilton, George W. *The Staten Island Ferry.* Berkeley: Howell-North, 1964.

Small book that traces the history of the Whitehall St.–St. George service, provides a 1964 perspective on operations, and sets a very high standard for quality; but one expects as much from this author.

Johnson, Harry, and Frederick S. Lightfoot. *Maritime New York in Nineteenth-Century Photographs.* New York: Dover, 1980.

While not overburdened with ferryboat photography, this volume provides a marvelous look at the city's waterfront between the Civil War and the turn of the century; captions are quite complete and the book has an excellent index.

Minick, Rachel. *New York Ferryboats in the Union Navy.*

This is a book-length monograph that was published serially in *The New-York Historical Society Quarterly* as follows:

"Introduction," 46 (October 1962), 422–36;

"The Potomac Flotilla; the North Atlantic Blockading Squadron," 47 (April 1963), 172–219;

"The North Atlantic Blockading Squadron," 47 (July 1963), 288–327;

"The North Atlantic Blockading Squadron, concluded; The South Atlantic Blockading Squadron," 48 (October 1963) 421–62 [421–36 not included];

"The East Gulf Blockading Squadron," 48 (January 1964), 51–80;

"The North Atlantic Blockading Squadron" [missing section per above], 49 (January 1965), 52–87. Clearly deserves to be reprinted in book form; scholarly, extensive references and citations, a major work on the subject of New York ferryboating.

Morrison, John H. *History of American Steam Navigation*, rev. ed. New York: Stephen Daye, 1958.

Originally published in 1903; contains more information than Preble on early ferryboat development.

Perry, John. *American Ferryboats.* New York: Wilfred Funk, 1957.

General treatment of U.S. ferryboating that contains chapters on *Gibbons vs. Ogden*, New York ferryboats during the Civil War, pre-steam technology, etc.

Pierrepont, Henry E. *Historical Sketch of the Fulton Ferry and Its Associated Ferries.* Brooklyn: Union Ferry Company, 1879.

An extremely valuable work. Includes an historical narrative as well as extensive statistical and informational appendices; author was a director of the company for many years.

Preble, George Henry. *A Chronological History of the Origin and Development of Steam Navigation* (Philadelphia: Hamersley, 1883).

Important study from a late nineteenth-century perspective.

Roberts, Franklin B., and John Gillespie. *The Boats We Rode.* New York: Quadrant, 1974.

Hardly scholarly, but a rare gem; a treatment of ferryboats and excursion boats in and around New York Harbor between 1950 and 1975, roughly. Each page contains a photograph and a short narrative description of a particular vessel or class of vessels.

Scull, Theodore W. *The Staten Island Ferry.* New York: Quadrant, 1982.

Popular treatment of the contemporary Whitehall St.–St. George service.

Smith, Harry J. *Romance of the Hoboken Ferry.* New York: Prentice-Hall, 1931.

A minor classic that lovingly tells the story of one of the more famous and important ferry operations in New York.

Turnbull, Archibald Douglas. *John Stevens, an American Record.* New York: Century, 1923.

Biography of Col. John Stevens, the man who initiated steamboat service between New York and Hoboken, and whose sons perfected ferryboating into an industrial art form in the early nineteenth century.

Writers Program of the Work Projects Administration. *A Maritime History of New York*. Garden City: Doubleday, 1941.

Not the best of the WPA Writers Program efforts, but a decent general history of the port of New York; complements Albion's *Rise of New York Port* in a chronological sense, but is not in the same league in terms of substance.

C. Five Important Periodicals

Marine Engineering Log. Current name of a venerable maritime industry trade publication that began in 1897 as *Marine Engineering*.

Early issues coincide with the final era of large-scale ferryboat experimentation, technical innovation, etc.

Seaport. Published bi-monthly by the South Street Seaport.

Has helped to launch a current renaissance of interest in New York's maritime heritage.

The Staten Island Historian. Quarterly journal of the Staten Island Historical Society.

Because of the important role ferryboat transportation has played in the history of this island borough, there is considerably more ferryboat coverage in this journal than in the periodicals of other area historical societies.

Steamboat Bill. The quarterly journal of the Steamship Historical Society of America that has been published regularly since 1941. Formerly called *Steamboat Bill of Facts*.

An excellent source of historical articles as well as news of ferryboat developments, reported by enthusiastic steamship buffs; stranded on the proverbial desert island with the equally proverbial single choice, this is the one to take—back issues plus a subscription.

Via the Port of New York. Published monthly by the Port Authority of New York and New Jersey.

Primarily geared to the interests of shippers; this will be the magazine to watch for news of new ferry services in New York.

D. Selected Articles

[Many articles are cited in footnotes throughout the book and its appendices; the following are largely supplementary to those.]

Harry J. Cotterell, Jr., "Double-ended Diggins," *Steamboat Bill*, No. 147 (Fall 1978), 135–41.

No single human being ever has known, ever will, or even ever could, know as much about double-ended ferryboats as Harry Cotterell. Period.

Sigurd Grava, "Water Mode to the

Rescue: Past and Future Ferry Service in New York City," *Transportation Quarterly*, 40 (July 1986), 333–57.

Contains listings and maps of all ferry services ever operated in New York.

"Our Ferries," *The New York Times*, April 23, 1856, pg. 2; "New-Jersey Ferries," *The New York Times*, September 3, 1870, pg. 6; "The East River Ferries," *The New York Times*, September 4, 1870, pg. 6.

Three extremely interesting newspaper articles that provide a broad historical perspective on the development of local ferryboat transportation from a mid- to late nineteenth-century point of view.

E. A. Stevens, "The Origin and Development of the Ferryboat," *Marine Engineering*, 1 (April–May 1897), 14–15, 18–19; 2 (June 1897), 14–17.

Another little gem that deserves reprinting; a past, present, and future assessment of New York ferryboating by a descendant of Col. John Stevens.

Graham T. Wilson, "The Hoboken Ferries," *Steamboat Bill*, No. 149 (Spring 1979), 3–10; No. 150 (Summer 1979); 91–99.

An excellent overall treatment of this important line; closes the gap between the publication of Smith's book in 1939 and the abandonment of service in 1967.

Appendix B
The Routes

Attempting to catalogue all the ferryboat services that operated to or from at least one landing in what is today the City of New York runs certain risks. Information from the early days is not always the best; there are reasons to suspect that services were begun, altered, sold, traded, consolidated, and abandoned by various companies with minimum, or no, adherence to established procedures. "Leases" issued by the City of New York were the common instrument used to authorize the operation of ferry services. Yet there are cases of leases formally entered into between the municipal government and a seemingly bona-fide operator that never saw any ferryboats actually run, as well as ferry lines that blissfully went about their over and back business totally absent the formality of an official lease.

The following listing of routes begins with the northernmost service across the Hudson River, works south to the Battery, then proceeds back north along the East River. Other operations that do not touch Manhattan Island are included after this.

The Manhattan terminal is listed in the so-indicated left-hand column. For the relatively few lines that did not serve Manhattan, the left-hand column displays the "non-Manhattan" terminal inside parentheses.

One matter that requires some pre-liminary discussion is the identity of the various ferryboat operators. While an effort has been made to trace in a general way whatever corporate evolution took place over the years on a given line or service, each and every change, such as a minor alteration in a corporate title, is not shown. Ferryboat services that were operated by railroads often proved to be especially troublesome in this regard, as American railroads themselves were notorious for the practice of constructing their empires on a bewildering foundation of underlying companies, wholly-owned subsidiaries, dummy corporations, and so forth.

Distinctions between predecessor and succeeding organizations have been made when they were felt to be important. But every little change whereby the hypothetical XYZ Ferry Company quietly became the XYZ Ferry and Transportation Company for a year or two, and then just as quietly shifted again and became the XYZ Ferry Corporation for the rest of its days is not shown. It is assumed that the users of these tables are interested in ferryboat operations in a general sort of way and are not investigative journalists, members of the anti-trust division of the Department of Justice, auditors from the Internal Revenue Service, or attorneys out to litigate some subtle point in civil court.

The sources from which this listing has been compiled are identified in the Bibliography (Appendix A); the following symbols are used throughout this appendix:

(*) service known to have operated seasonally: i.e., did not run during winter months

(+) service not continuous over the time span shown

(#) substitute landings in the general vicinity of the shown landing known to have been used at various times.

NOTES

1. Begun as independent company and taken over by the New Jersey & Hudson River Railway and Fy. Co., "the Hudson River Line," in 1900; ferry and railway taken over by Public Service of New Jersey in 1911.
2. Railroad service out of Weehawken often called "the West Shore line"; see text, chapter 5, for details of its complex corporate evolution.
3. Manhattan terminal at a number of different sites over the years: Jay St., 1885–ca. 1893; Franklin St., ca. 1893–1909; Desbrosses St., 1909–1930; Cortlandt St. thereafter.
4. The name "Hoboken Ferry Company" was commonly used over the years, despite various mergers, acquisitions, etc.; see text, chapter 6, note 6, for details. Ferry

operation acquired by the Delaware, Lackawanna & Western R.R., by lease, in 1903.

5. Manhattan terminal was W. 14 St., 1886–1903; W. 23 St., 1903–1942. Roswell and Louis Eldridge, owners of the E. 92 St.–Astoria line on the East River, owned the Hoboken Ferry Company in the years leading up to the lease to the D. L. & W. in 1903. They purchased this W. 14 St.–14 St. line first on January 1, 1896; the rest of the company a year later.

6. First ferryboat route in the harbor – and the world; initiated by Robert Fulton. See text for corporate evolution from the Associates of the New Jersey Company, an independent company, through operation by the New Jersey Railroad & Transportation Co., to final operation by the Pennsylvania R.R.

7. Between 1877 and 1898 operated for the P.R.R. by an independent entity, the Brooklyn Annex Fy. Co. Taken over by the railroad in 1898, although service always required separate fleet of vessels from railroad's Manhattan routes; see Appendix C.

8. Temporary operation to compensate for closing of the Williamsburg Bridge: service began on April 18, 1988; ended on June 13, 1988 when *John A. Noble* made the final run.

9. Some evidence of early affiliation with the S.I.R.T.; details uncertain.

10. Operated by independent company prior to 1853; taken over by Union Fy. Co. at that time.

11. Use of the name Union Ferry Company did not begin until 1839 when Fulton St.–Fulton St. and Whitehall St.–Hamilton Ave. services were merged. See text, chapter 3, for details.

12. Apparently the company was popularly called the Williamsburgh Fy. Co. throughout its history, and there is some evidence that this was its formal corporate name at some time, perhaps at its very beginnings. By the 1860s the names Brooklyn Fy. Co. and Long Island Fy. Co. appear as the owners of the line's vessels; next comes the New York & Brooklyn Fy. Co., and it lasted until 1873. From then until 1886, the company was formally called the New York Fy. Co. From 1886 through 1898 the title Brooklyn & New York Fy. Co. is found on official records, and for the company's final era, 1898–1908, the name Brooklyn Fy. Co. was again used. The full corporate history of the various East River companies, including relationships through common directors and holding companies, as well as sale of ferry leases from one company to another, remains to be told.

13. Company's original name was Houston Street Fy. Co.

14. Apparently the service from the foot of E. 23 St. began under auspices of the Roman Catholic Church (i.e., "Trustees of St. Patrick's Cathedral") for the benefit of persons heading for Calvary Cemetery in Long Island City. The name Gideon Lee Knapp appears in early leases as the agent of the trustees. The same man was also a

principal in the Greenpoint Fy. Co., and the service and lease are thought to have been conveyed by Knapp to the secular company. Records are confusing here, especially David Valentine's *Manuals*. There may have been some period of operation from E. 23 St. to *both* Penny Bridge and Greenpoint Ave.

15. In 1889, company's name changed to East Tenth and Twenty-third St. Fy. Co.; unclear if service on the E. 23 St.–Greenpoint line was continuous from private ownership through public ownership.

16. See text, chapter 3, for details of corporate evolution; railroad's ferryboats were operated by a subsidiary, the New York & East River Fy. Co.

17. Company known as Astoria Fy. Co. prior to 1892. Originally operated from the foot of E. 86 St., Manhattan; shifted to E. 92 St. in 1866.

18. Special-purpose service; not open to the general public.

19. For some period of time, details uncertain, this was a four-terminal service: E. 99 St., Manhattan to E. 134 St., The Bronx, to North Beach, Queens (the site of today's LaGuardia Airport), and then on to College Point.

20. Dates are for service with double-ended ferryboats only; earlier steamboat service was also provided.

Manhattan Terminal (Non-Manhattan Terminal)	Opposite Terminal	Dates Of Operation	Popular Name(s)	Operator	Notes
Dyckman St.	Englewood, N.J.	1915–1942	Englewood Ferry	New York and Englewood Ferry Corp.	(*)
W. 125 St.	Edgewater, N.J.	1888–1950	Edgewater Ferry	Riverside and Fort Lee Ferry Co., 1888–1943; Electric Ferries, Inc., 1943–1950	1
W. 42 St.	Slough's Meadow, N.J.	1859–1902	North Weehawken Ferry	Weehawken Ferry Co., 1859–1872; New York Central R.R., 1872–1902	2
W. 42 St.	West New York, N.J.	1902–1922	West New York Ferry	New York Central R.R.	2
W. 42 St.	Weehawken, N.J., West Shore Depot	1884–1959	Weehawken Ferry	New York Central R.R.	2
Cortlandt St. (#)	Weehawken, N.J., West Shore Depot	1885–1959	West Shore Ferry	New York Central R.R.	2, 3
W. 23 St.	Weehawken, N.J., Baldwin Ave.	1926–1943	Electric Ferry	Electric Ferries, Inc.	
W. 23 St.	Hoboken, N.J., D. L. & W. Depot	1905–1947	Lackawanna Ferry	Hoboken Ferry Co.	4
W. 14 St.	Hoboken, N.J., 14 Street (#)	1886–1942	Upper Ferry	Hoboken Ferry Co.	4, 5
Christopher St.	Hoboken, N.J., D. L. & W. Depot	1838–1955	Christopher Street Ferry	Hoboken Ferry Co.	4
Barclay St. (#)	Hoboken, N.J., D. L. & W. Depot	1821–1967	Hoboken Ferry	Hoboken Ferry Co.	4
W. 23 St.	Jersey City, N.J., Erie Depot	1868–1942	Erie Ferry	Erie R.R.	
Chambers St.	Jersey City, N.J., Erie Depot	1861–1958	Pavonia Ferry	Erie R.R.	

Manhattan Terminal (Non-Manhattan Terminal)	Opposite Terminal	Dates Of Operation	Popular Name(s)	Operator	Notes
(Fulton St., Brooklyn)	Jersey City, N.J., Erie Depot	1885–ca. 1900	Annex Ferry	Erie R.R.	
(Port Morris, The Bronx)	Jersey City, N.J., Harsimus Cove	1876–1912	Steamer Maryland Ferry	New York, New Haven and Hartford R.R.	
W. 34 St.	Jersey City, N.J., Exchange Pl.	1880–1883	34 Street Ferry	Pennsylvania R.R.	
W. 23 St.	Jersey City, N.J., Exchange Pl.	1897–1910	Pennsylvania Ferry	Pennsylvania R.R.	
W. 13 St.	Jersey City, N.J., Harsimus Cove	1891–1901	West 13 St. Ferry	Pennsylvania R.R.	
Desbrosses St.	Jersey City, N.J., Exchange Pl.	1862–1930	Desbrosses St. Ferry	Pennsylvania R.R.	
Cortlandt St.	Jersey City, N.J., Exchange Pl.	1812–1949	Paulus Hook Ferry	Pennsylvania R.R.	6
(Fulton St., Brooklyn)	Jersey City, N.J., Exchange Pl.	1877–1910	Brooklyn Annex Ferry	Pennsylvania R.R.	7
(Atlantic Ave., Brooklyn)	Jersey City, N.J., Exchange Pl.	1929–1935	Atlantic Annex Ferry	Pennsylvania R.R.	
W. 23 St.	Jersey City, N.J., C.N.J. Depot	1905–1941	Jersey Central Ferry	Jersey Central R.R.	
Liberty St.	Jersey City, N.J., C.N.J. Depot	1864–1967	Communipaw Ferry	Jersey Central R.R.	
Whitehall St.	Jersey City, N.J., C.N.J. Depot	1897–1905	Royal Blue Line Ferry	Jersey Central R.R.	
Whitehall St.	St. George, Staten Island	1816–current	Staten Island Ferry	Staten Island Rapid Transit, 1816–1905; City of New York, 1905–current	
Whitehall St.	Stapleton, Staten Island	1909–1913	Stapleton Ferry	City of New York	

Manhattan Terminal (Non-Manhattan Terminal)	Opposite Terminal	Dates Of Operation	Popular Name(s)	Operator	Notes
(39 St., Brooklyn)	St. George, Staten Island	1924–1926	New York Bay Ferry	City of New York	
(69 St., Brooklyn)	St. George, Staten Island	1912–1964	Brooklyn and Richmond Ferry; 69 Street Ferry	Brooklyn and Richmond Ferry Co., 1912–1939; Electric Ferries, Inc., 1939–1954; City of New York, 1954–1964	
Whitehall St.	Kent Ave., Brooklyn	1988–1988	Williamsburg Express Ferry	City of New York	8
Whitehall St.	39 St., Brooklyn	1887–1938	South Brooklyn Ferry	New York and South Brooklyn Ferry and Transportation Co., 1887–1906; City of New York, 1906–1938	9
Whitehall St.	Hamilton Ave., Brooklyn	1856–1942	Hamilton Ferry	Union Ferry Co., 1856–1922; City of New York, 1922–1942	11
Whitehall St.	Atlantic Ave., Brooklyn	1836–1933	South Ferry	Union Ferry Co., 1836–1922; City of New York, 1922–1933	10
Wall St.	Montague St., Brooklyn	1852–1912	Wall St. Ferry	Union Ferry Co.	10
Fulton St.	Fulton St., Brooklyn	1814–1924	Fulton Ferry	Union Ferry Co., 1814–1922; City of New York, 1922–1924	11
Roosevelt St.	Bridge St., Brooklyn	1853–1859	n/a	Union Ferry Co.	10
Catharine St.	Main St., Brooklyn	ca. 1850–1912	Catharine St. Ferry	Union Ferry Co.	10
Gouverneur St.	Bridge St., Brooklyn	ca. 1850–1857	n/a	Union Ferry Co.	
Roosevelt St.	Broadway, Brooklyn	1836–1909(+) 1911–1918	Broadway Ferry	Williamsburg Ferries, 1836–1909; Brooklyn and Manhattan Ferry Co., 1911–1918	12

Manhattan Terminal (Non-Manhattan Terminal)	Opposite Terminal	Dates Of Operation	Popular Name(s)	Operator	Notes
Grand St.	Broadway, Brooklyn	1851–1909(+) 1921–1931	Broadway Ferry	Williamsburg Ferries, 1851–1909; City of New York, 1921–1931	12
Grand St.	Grand St., Brooklyn	1859(?)–1909	Williamsburg Ferry	Williamsburg Ferries	12
E. 23 St.	Broadway, Brooklyn	1885–1909(+) 1911–1918	Broadway– 23 Street Ferry	Williamsburg Ferries, 1885–1909; Brooklyn and Manhattan Ferry Co., 1911–1918	12
E. 42 St.	Broadway, Brooklyn	1901–1909	Uptown Ferry	Williamsburg Ferries	12
Jackson St.	Hudson Ave., Brooklyn	1825(?)–1868	Navy Yard Ferry (?)	Navy Yard Ferry Co.	
Houston St.	Grand St., Brooklyn	1842–1918	Houston Street Ferry	Nassau Ferry Company	13
E. 23 St.	Penny Bridge, Long Island City	1851–1853	Calvary Cemetery Ferry	Trustees of Saint Patrick's Cathedral	14
E. 23 St.	Greenpoint Ave., Brooklyn	1853–1933	Greenpoint Ferry	Greenpoint Ferry Co., 1853–1921; City of New York, 1921–1933	15
E. 10 St.	Greenpoint Ave., Brooklyn	1853–1914	10 Street Ferry	Greenpoint Ferry Co.	15
James Slip	Hunter's Point, Long Island City	1859–1907	Annex Ferry	Long Island R.R.	16
E. 34 St.	Hunter's Point, Long Island City	1859–1925	Hunter's Point Ferry	Long Island R.R.	16
E. 34 St.	Borden Ave., Long Island City	1927–1936	n/a	East 34 Street Vehicular Ferry Co.	
E. 92 St. (#)	Astoria	1843–1918(+) 1920–1936	Astoria Ferry	New York and East River Ferry Co., 1843–1918; City of New York, 1920–1936	17
E. 99 St.	College Point, Queens	1886–1918	n/a	New York and College Point Ferry Co.	19 (*)

Manhattan Terminal (Non-Manhattan Terminal)	Opposite Terminal	Dates Of Operation	Popular Name(s)	Operator	Notes
(Clason's Point, The Bronx)	College Point, Queens	1910–1917	n/a	Twin City Ferry Co.	
(Clason's Point, The Bronx)	College Point, Queens	1921–1939	n/a	City of New York	
(Flatbush Ave., Brooklyn)	Riis Park, Rockaway	1925–1937	Rockaway Ferry	City of New York	
(Tottenville, Staten Island)	Perth Amboy, N.J.	1867–1963	Perth Amboy Ferry	Staten Island Railway, 1867–1948; Sunrise Ferries, 1948–1963	
(Linoleumville, Staten Island)	Carteret, N.J.	1916–1929	Carteret Ferry	Carteret Ferry Co.	(*)
(Howland Hook, Staten Island)	Elizabethport, N.J.	1896–1961	Howland Hook Ferry	New Jersey and Staten Island Ferry Co., 1896–ca. 1932; Sunrise Ferries, ca. 1932–1961	
(Port Richmond, Staten Island)	Bayonne, N.J.	1876–1962	Bergen Point Ferry	Port Richmond and Bergen Point Ferry Co., 1876–1937; Electric Ferries, Inc., 1937–1945; Port Richmond Ferry Co., ca. 1946–1948; Kill Van Kull Ferry Corp., et al., ca. 1948–1962	
Whitehall St.	Ellis Island	1892–1954	Ellis Island Ferry	U.S. Immigration and Naturalization Service	18
Whitehall St.	Governors Island	ca. 1870–current	Governors Island Ferry	U.S. Army, ca. 1870–1965; U.S. Coast Guard, 1965–current	18
(City Island, The Bronx)	Hart Island	1923–current	Hart Island Ferry	City of New York	18
E. 134 St., The Bronx)	North Brother Island	1923–1969(?)	n/a	City of New York	
(E. 134 St., The Bronx)	Riker's Island	1923–1969	Rikers Island Ferry	City of New York	
E. 116 St.	Ward's Island	1929–ca. 1936	n/a	Dept. of Mental Hygiene, State of New York	20

Appendix C
The Vessels

Herewith, an effort to identify and classify *every single ferryboat* that was ever owned by a New York Harbor ferryboat operator from 1812 to the present day.

As much as possible, official records have been used to compile this roster, and these are identified in both the Introduction and the Bibliography (Appendix A). Unfortunately, the mere fact that a record is "official" does not automatically make it accurate. Errors, misprints, and so forth are not unknown. The diesel-powered ferryboat *Hudson*, as just one example, that ran for many years in the fleet of Electric Ferries, Inc., is identified in a quite reputable and very official record in one year, but one year only, as being *steam*-powered, an obvious mistake.

Errors of this sort are almost humorous and easily correctable. It gives one pause, though, to realize that errors in the various source materials that are not so obvious are not as easily corrected.

Every vessel here listed has been cross-checked to official records; assignment of a vessel to a particular fleet, however, especially for nineteenth-century vessels, has frequently been on the basis of secondary information. In many cases these secondary sources have been identified in notes; in many more cases, however, a mere mention of a vessel in a newspaper or magazine article was the basis of assigning it to a certain fleet and owner, and all of these citations have not been provided.

As was mentioned earlier, in the Introduction, the principal sources and records deal in terms of vessel ownership and are quite indifferent to leasing arrangements. Leasing of ferryboats does not appear to be a *terribly* common arrangement over the years, but from the instances discovered it is certainly reasonable to assume that it more likely happened, and of these arrangements this roster remains largely ignorant. Another irritation is the not infrequent practice of enrolling the various vessels in a given operational fleet under separate owners, even though all are painted in similar colors and carry a common fleet identification. The reasons for this have to do with business purposes of one sort or another – liability, insurance, taxes, and such. But it is frustrating to know that the hypothetical ferryboats *Ajax*, *Baker*, and *Charlie* all ran for the equally hypothetical Red White and Blue Ferry Company, but find them, on official registers, as owned by, respectively, John Smith, Harry Brown, and Fred Jones.

Efforts have not been scrupulous in identifying every mortgage holder, ship broker, holding company, or scrap merchant who might appear as the official owner of a ferryboat for a year or so, especially at the end of a vessel's life.

As to symbols and abbreviations used in the roster: under the heading "type" is to be found an abbreviation that tells a vessel's power plant and the style of its propulsion system. The abbreviations are a variation on the system used in *Merchant Vessels of the United States*, but are not identical with it:

st.p. = steam powered, paddlewheel propelled
st.s. = steam powered, screw propelled/direct drive
st.el. = steam powered, screw propelled/electric drive
ol.p. = oil engine, paddlewheel
ol.s. = oil engine, screw/direct drive
ol.el. = oil engine, screw/electric drive.

The term "oil engine" refers to an internal-combustion engine, not a steam engine with oil-fired boilers. (*MVUS* uses "ol." only to designate diesel engines, "ga." being the abbreviation for gasoline-powered engines.) While there have yet to be any New York Harbor ferryboats that merit classification as "ol.p.," the designation is included for balance. Besides, you can just never tell what tomorrow might bring!

Under "hull" are to be found abbreviations of the principal materials used in hull construction over the years:

W = wood
I = iron
S = steel
O = other; see note for details

"Engine" is a description of a vessel's power plant, with most notations being self-evident – i.e., a 12-cylinder diesel is rendered "12-cyl diesel," a pair of 2-cylinder compound steam engines is "2 2-cyl comp." Other abbreviations used in this column are: VB = vertical-beam engine; TE = triple-expansion engine.

"Built" means the city where a vessel was constructed; "Wilm." is an abbreviation of Wilmington, Delaware. "Year" normally is when the first permanent certificate of enrollment was issued, and "Yard" is the shipbuilding company – i.e., ship*yard* – that constructed the vessel.

If available, cylinder measurements have been supplied, a common way for understanding the relative size of the power plant. The initial number (or numbers) tells the diameter of the cylinder(s) in inches; the number following the "×" gives the length of the stroke, and this is also in inches. Thus a triple-expansion steam engine with three successively-larger-diameter cylinders might be characterized 16, 23, 36 × 28; a 6-cylinder diesel engine could be described 9 × 18.

Engine information has not been supplied unless it has been confirmed from some official source document. In the early years, while most vessels were powered by single-cylinder vertical-beam engines, unless this could be confirmed as a fact for a particular boat, it has not been included. The Union Ferry Company, as an instance, operated many vessels that were powered by single-cylinder inclined engines during the nineteenth century.

Vessel dimensions should be cut-and-dried enough. Waterline length, overall width, and draft amidships are expressed in feet, with any and all fractions simply not shown. These numbers have not been "rounded," in other words. Over the years one finds such measurements expressed as a decimal, other times as a fraction, and still other times in inches. To avoid confusion a "good enough" rule has been adopted, and decimals, fractions, and inches are ignored entirely.

A vessel's statutory dimensions occasionally change over its lifetime; it might be lengthened, for instance. Changes in gross tonnage are far more common, as the calculation of this figure is itself as much an artistic exercise as an engineering one. (Gross tonnage is a single number measurement of a merchant vessel's overall size and carrying capacity, with 100 cubic feet of permanently enclosed space being held to equal one gross ton.) There have been no attempts made to show the history of "remeasurements" (i.e., changes in gross tonnage) a vessel might have undergone, save in a few cases; about the only certainty that can be guaranteed for any number shown as gross tonnage is that it was taken from an official record from some period in the vessel's service life.

The other roster items are reasonably self-explanatory. The last entry under "disposition" refers to a vessel's departure from the list of enrolled vessels. More often than not this will be the expression "out of documentation," since that is the official explanation one often finds in *MVUS*. From time to time, either through *MVUS*, examination of a certificate of enrollment, or some other source, it has been possible to ascertain further details, perhaps that a vessel was scrapped, or lost through fire. In such cases that information is also included.

As a practical matter, removal from documentation often follows a protracted lay-up, and thus the year when a vessel last ran in actual service need not be the same as the date shown in the disposition column. For that matter, operators frequently retained physical possession of a vessel after removing it from documentation, perhaps awaiting an upturn in the scrap market. The City of New York, from time to time, also seems to have retained vessels in documentation after they had been physically reduced to scrap and ashes, a practice that must be decried as maddening. It must also be noted that sale of a vessel to the U.S. Government constitutes removal from the roster of documented merchant vessels, as does sale to a foreign-flag owner, even though such vessels may have continued to operate as ferryboats. Once in a while a vessel will return to the domain of documented U.S. merchant vessels

after it earlier departed that realm; that's when the "disposition" column can get complicated.

All names a given vessel bore in its lifetime are also listed, and these are identified with lower-case sequential letters. More often than not, additional names imply different owners for a vessel, and these are usually identified in the disposition column or in footnotes. Occasionally, though, a ferryboat bore two (or more) names for the same owner; when this is the

case, the symbol (#) is used to indicate such names. Names that a vessel bore operating in some status other than as a documented U.S. merchant vessel – e.g., for a foreign-flag owner, for the U.S. Government – are designated after the name by the symbol (+). The symbol (*) after one or another of a vessel's names indicates that it appears elsewhere in the roster as owned by another operator under that name.

VESSEL ROSTER

FLEET: New York and Englewood Ferry Company
SERVICE: Hudson River (seasonal)
DATES: 1915–1942

Off. No. Name(s) [Notes]	Type Hull Gross Tons	Built Year Yard	Engines Cylinder size (in inches)	Dimensions (in feet)	Disposition
106860 *George W. Loft* a) *Annex 5* (*) c) *Casablanca* (+) [1]	st.p. W 507	Wilm. 1891 Jackson & Sharp	1-cyl VB 40 × 108	136 × 31 × 11	to Cuban registry, 1916
161750 *Henry L. Joyce* (*) a) *Vermont* (*) b) *Alexandria* [2]	st.p. I 810	Chester, Pa. 1895 Delaware River Iron SB	1-cyl VB 46 × 120	156 × 36 × 13	dismantled, 1935

Florida (*)	st.p.	Chester, Pa.	1-cyl VB	156 × 36 × 13	abandoned, 1946
	I	1896	42 × 120		
[3]	818				

107140					
America (*)	st.p.	Chester, Pa.	1-cyl VB	156 × 36 × 13	lost (fire), 2-15-'37, in winter
	I	1895	42 × 120		lay-up at foot of Dyckman
	818	Delaware River			St., Manhattan
[4]		Iron SB			

221726					
Reliance	ol.s.	Washburn, Wis.	2 diesels	102 × 33 × 11	sold to Florida interests, ca.
a) *Hudson–Athens*	S	1921			1949; out of documentation,
c) *Jean Lafitte*	556				1979
[5]					

127167					
Englewood (*)	st.p.	Wilm.	1-cyl VB		scrapped, 1941
a) *City of Englewood* (*)	W	1896			
[6]	347	Jackson & Sharp			

80870					
Dyckman	st.p.	Wilm.	1-cyl. VB		abandoned, 1935
a) *Wenonah*	I	1882	44 × 120		
[7]	326				

145539					
George W. Perkins	st.p.	Wilm.	1-cyl VB		abandoned, 1935
a) *Texas* (*)	I	1890	46 × 120		
b) *Harry B. James*	896				
[8]					

[1] Purchased from Delaware River interests (i.e., Kensington & New Jersey Fy. Co.) in 1914; previously operated in "Pennsylvania annex" service. Vessel is also the source of a minor mystery: when the City of New York built three turbo-electric ferryboats in 1923 it named one of them after George W. Loft. There was a flap touched off in City Hall, though, because it was felt there should not be two ferryboats operating in the harbor with the same name, this one plus the newcomer. But this *George W. Loft* shows in offi-

cial U.S. Government records as having been sold to Cuban interests in 1916.

[2] Purchased from the Brooklyn & Manhattan Fy. Co. in 1924; owned by Potomac River interests (i.e., Washington & Alexandria Fy. Co.), 1911–1912; owned by the Williamsburg ferries, 1895–1911.

[3] Purchased from the City of New York in 1934; earlier owned by the East Tenth and Twenty-third St. Fy. Co.; originally owned by the Williamsburg ferries.

[4] Purchased from the Brooklyn & Manhattan Fy. Co. in 1918; owned by Williamsburg ferries, 1895–1911.

[5] Purchased from upper Hudson River interests (i.e., Hudson–Athens Fy. Co.) ca. 1937. Vessel was designed by Eads Johnson and is claimed to be the world's first direct-drive diesel ferryboat. (See *Steamboat Bill*, No. 73 [Spring 1960], 26.) Built in Wisconsin and brought east via the New York State Barge Canal; final U.S. owner was the Fernandia (Florida) Port Authority where she worked a Mayport–Fort George service. After being removed from documentation was sold to interests in the Bahamas. Vessel may have been leased to Electric Ferries, Inc., at some time during her New York tenure.

[6] Purchased from Riverside & Ft. Lee Fy. Co. in 1939, and leased from that company in earlier years. Vessel was owned, at various times, by the two ferryboat subsidiaries of Public Service of New Jersey, the Riverside & Ft. Lee Fy. Co. and the Port Richmond & Bergen Point Fy. Co.

[7] Purchased from Philadelphia interests in 1926. Owned by Gotham Assets during New York service, and not N.Y. & Englewood Fy. Co.

[8] Owned by Williamsburg ferries through 1913. Between 1913 and ca. 1925, under the name *Harry B. James*, is listed in *MVUS* as a freight boat, not a ferryboat. Owned by Gotham Assets during final phase of career, and not N.Y. & Englewood Fy. Co.

Special Note: The N.Y. & Englewood Fy. Co. was also associated with a firm called the Ferry Holding Co. Some vessels used on the Dyckman St.–Englewood line were formally owned by Ferry Holding Co., as well as other "third party" corporations, during all or part of their tenure with N.Y. & Englewood, and not by the ferry company proper. Ferry Holding was likely associated with Gotham Assets, as well.

FLEET: Riverside and Fort Lee Ferry Company
SERVICE: Hudson River
DATES: 1888(?)–1943
COMMENTS/REFERENCES: In 1911 became a subsidiary of Public Service of New Jersey; see note 2 for further details.

Off. No. Name(s) [Notes]	Type Hull Gross Tons	Built Year Yard	Engines Cylinder size (in inches)	Dimensions (in feet)	Disposition
17012 *Fort Lee* (i) a) *Maspeth* (*) [1]	st.p. W 431	New York 1866 Laurence & Foulks	n/a	137 × 29 × 10	abandoned, 1898

127167 *Englewood* (*) a) *City of Englewood* (#) [2]	st.p. W 484	Wilm. 1896 Jackson & Sharp	1-cyl VB	135 × 31 × 12	sold, 1922; scrapped, 1941
136971 *Edgewater*	st.s. S 709	Wilm. 1902 Harlan & Hollingsworth	3-cyl comp 22, 30, 30 × 24	146 × 39 × 15	sold, 1945; scrapped, 1948
136350 *Leonia* a) *Easton* (*) [3]	st.s. S 406	Wilm. 1893 Harlan & Hollingsworth	2 2-cyl comp 16, 30 × 22	145 × 32 × 14	sold to Westchester Fy. Corp., 1945; scrapped, 1947
207961 *Paterson* a) *Governor Russel* [4, 8]	st.s. W 579	Boston 1898	2 2-cyl comp 14, 28 × 24	160 × 37 × 13	abandoned, 1938
150931 *Ridgefield* a) *Port Morris* (*) b) *Nathan Hale* c) *Governor King* [5, 8]	st.p. W 534	Brooklyn 1901 Devine Burtis	1-cyl 40 × 96 (?)	143 × 37 × 13	dismantled, 1934
205363 *Hackensack* a) *Hempstead* (*) b) *Islander* [6]	st.s. S 1310	Wilm. 1906 Harlan & Hollingsworth	2 2-cyl comp 18, 38 × 28	188 × 45 × 16	sold to New England interests, 1945; dismantled, 1957

Off. No. Name(s) [Notes]	Type Hull Gross Tons	Built Year Yard	Engines Cylinder size (in inches)	Dimensions (in feet)	Disposition
203468 *Tenafly* a) *Babylon* (*) [6]	st.s. S 1310	Wilm. 1906 Harlan & Hollingsworth	2 2-cyl comp 18, 38 × 28	188 × 45 × 16	dismantled, 1946
213656 *Fort Lee* (ii)	st.s. S 923	Wilm. 1915 Harlan & Hollingsworth	2 2-cyl comp 17, 34 × 26	177 × 39 × 16	sold to Norfolk interests, 1944; scrapped, ca. 1950
225813 *Thomas N. McCarter* a) *Philadelphia* c) *Newport News* [7]	st.s. S 822	Wilm. 1926 Bethlehem SB	2 2-cyl comp 17, 34 × 24	189 × 36 × 14	sold to Virginia interests, 1943; out of documentation, 1959

[1] Purchased from Houston St. Fy. Co. in 1882.

[2] In 1922, sold to Port Richmond & Bergen Point Fy. Co., like R. & F.L., a subsidiary of Public Service of New Jersey, the largest operator of streetcars in New Jersey. Other vessels were known to have been leased from the one company to the other over the years. *Englewood* was resold to Riverside & Ft. Lee in 1937 and later sold to the New York & Englewood Fy. Co. in 1939. May have been leased back to Riverside & Ft. Lee after 1939.

[3] Purchased from Jersey Central R.R. in 1906.

[4] Purchased from the City of Boston ca. 1925.

[5] Purchased from the State of Maine in 1928. As *Port Morris* worked in New York for the New York & College Point Fy. Co. from 1901 through 1918. Worked briefly at New London, Conn. from 1918 through 1920 before being sold to the State of Maine.

[6] Purchased from the Long Island R.R. in 1921. See chapter 9 for details of *Hackensack*'s later career in Massachusetts on the Woods Hole–Martha's Vineyard service.

[7] Purchased from Reading R.R. ca. 1938. After career as a ferryboat, converted to (and redocumented as) a luxury houseboat.

[8] Known to have been leased to Port Richmond & Bergen Point Fy. Co.

FLEET: New York Central R.R. and predecessor companies.
SERVICE: Hudson River
DATES: 1859–1959
COMMENTS/REFERENCES: See Harry Cotterell, Jr., "The Weehawken and West Shore Ferries," *Steamboat Bill*, No. 70 (Summer 1959), 38–42.

Off. No. Name(s) [Notes]	Type Hull Gross Tons	Built Year Yard	Engines Cylinder size (in inches)	Dimensions (in feet)	Disposition
1819 *Abbie* (*) [1]	st.p. W 299	Greenpoint 1852 Eckford Webb	n/a	120 × 27 × 10	sold to Albany interests, ca. 1870; abandoned, 1884
14938 *Lydia* (*) [1]	st.p. W 331	Greenpoint 1852 Eckford Webb	n/a	121 × 27 × 9	abandoned, 1872
21440 *Rosyln* (*) [2]	st.p. W 462	New York 1860	n/a	139 × 32 × 11	abandoned, 1888
20729 *Midland*	st.p. W 402	Greenpoint (1872) Laurence & Foulkes	n/a	132 × 27 × 10	sold to New London interests, 1903; out of documentation, ca. 1910
106246 *Albany* (i)	st.p. I 1059	Newburgh 1883 Ward, Stanton	1-cyl VB 50 × 120	195 × 36 × 13	sold to Carteret Fy. Co., 1917; scrapped, 1939

Off. No. Name(s) [Notes]	Type Hull Gross Tons	Built Year Yard	Engines Cylinder size (in inches)	Dimensions (in feet)	Disposition
130262 *Newburgh* (*) b) *Gov. Albert C.* *Ritchie* [3]	st.p. I 1053	Newburgh 1883 Ward, Stanton	1-cyl VB 50 × 120	193 × 36 × 13	sold to Erie R.R., ca. 1916; later ran for Annapolis interests; to Canadian registry, 1947
14420 *Kingston* b) *Newport News*	st.p. I 1064	Newburgh 1883 Ward, Stanton	1-cyl VB 50 × 120 (?)	193 × 36 × 13	sold to Norfolk interests, 1917; out of documentation, ca. 1925
130644 *Oswego* b) *Passaic* (*)	st.p. I 1055	Newburgh 1883 Ward, Stanton	1-cyl VB 50 × 120	193 × 36 × 13	sold to Erie R.R., ca. 1916; abandoned, 1935
125456 *Chester W. Chapin* (*) [4]	st.p. W 428	Rondout, NY 1875 McCausland	n/a	163 × 55 × 9	sold to Staten Island Ry., 1901; out of documentation, ca. 1910
3704 *Buffalo* b) *Chesapeake*	st.p. S 1021	Wilm. 1897 Harlan & Hollingsworth	1-cyl VB 50 × 120	192 × 36 × 15	sold to Norfolk interests, 1925; dismantled, 1951
81737 *West Point*	st.s. S 1328	Newburgh 1900 Marvel	2 2-cyl comp 18, 38 × 16	192 × 40 × 16	sold to Norfolk interests, 1941; dismantled, 1948
117261 *Syracuse* [5]	st.s. S 1344	Newburgh 1903 Marvel	2 2-cyl comp 18, 38 × 28	194 × 40 × 16	dismantled, 1959

202712
Rochester

[5]

st.s.	Newburgh	2 2-cyl comp	194 × 40 × 16	dismantled, 1959
S	1905	18, 38 × 28		
1328	Marvel			

207842
Utica

[5, 6]

st.s.	Newburgh	2 2-cyl comp	181 × 40 × 15	out of documentation, 1962
S	1910	19, 38 × 28		
1351	Marvel			

210464
Niagara

[5]

st.s.	Newburgh	2 2-cyl comp	183 × 40 × 16	out of documentation, 1959
S	1912	19, 38 × 28		
1250	Marvel			

212802
Weehawken

[5, 6]

st.s.	Wilm.	4-cyl comp	187 × 38 × 16	out of documentation, 1962
S	1914	19, 19, 38		
1402	Harlan &	38 × 28		
	Hollingsworth			

212027
Catskill

st.s.	Newburgh	2 2-cyl comp	183 × 38 × 16	lost (fire), 1952
S	1914	19, 38 × 28		
1400	Marvel			

215069
Stony Point

[5]

st.s.	Wilm.	2 2-cyl comp	196 × 38 × 16	sold to Florida interests,
S	1917	19, 38 × 28		ca. 1960; dismantled, 1963
1391	Harlan &			
	Hollingsworth			

225146
Albany (ii)

[5]

st.s.	Mariners Harbor	2 2-cyl comp	203 × 44 × 16	out of documentation, 1964
S	1925			
1389	Staten Island S.B.			

---

[1] Purchased from the Union Fy. Co. in 1859.

[2] Purchased from the Union Fy. Co. in 1871.

[3] Prior to service with Maryland interests (i.e., Clairborne–Annapolis Fy. Co.) in 1926, steam engine and paddlewheels were removed and replaced by direct-drive diesel engines and screw propellers.

[4] Purchased from the Boston & Albany R.R. in 1881.

[5] These vessels were reportedly sold ca. 1959 for use in South Florida in conjunction with a land development project. While some kind of preliminary contracts may have been drawn up, all vessels save *Stony Point* were removed from documentation by the New York Central R.R. and do not show as ever having been owned by the development company. *Stony Point* was sold, and actually did reach Florida, but never sailed there in any kind of ferry service. Her final owner was the Tampa Ship Repair & Dry Dock Co.; she eventually sank in the Caloosahatchee River near Ft. Myers. Later raised, she was supposedly towed to deep water in the Gulf of Mexico and there permanently sunk. *MVUS* cites her disposition as "dismantled."

[6] One or more of these New York Central vessels were also used to satisfy the whims of bureaucracy. A Federal subsidy program for the construction of new ocean-going ships in the mid-1960s required that an old vessel – *any* vessel – be "traded in" as part of the deal. Both *Weehawken* and *Utica* were likely involved in such arrangements, *Utica* actually returning to the 1968 issue of *MVUS* and listed there as owned by the U.S. Secretary of Commerce.

FLEET: Electric Ferries, Inc.
SERVICE: Hudson River, Upper N. Y. Bay, Kill Van Kull, misc.
DATES: 1926–1954

Off. No. Name(s) [Notes]	Type Hull Gross Tons	Built Year Yard	Engines Cylinder size (in inches)	Dimensions (in feet)	Disposition
226087 *Governor Moore* [1]	ol.el. S 405	Camden 1926 American Brown Boveri	2 6-cyl diesels 12½ × 18	145 × 37 × 12	sold to U.S. Govt., 1941
226088 *Charles W. Culkin* b) *Gotham* (i) (#) c) *Jamestown* (*) [2]	ol.el. S 405	Camden 1926 American Brown Boveri	2 6-cyl diesels 12½ × 18	145 × 37 × 12	sold, ca. 1941; see note for details on later owners; out of documentation, 1966

226132
Grenville Kane   ol.el.   Camden   2 6-cyl diesels   145 × 37 × 12   sold to Virginia interests,
b) Palisades (#)   S   1926   12½ × 18   ca. 1951; later ran for City
c) Seawells Point (*)   405   American Brown   of New York; out of
                                   Boveri   documentation, 1967

226166
W. A. Baldwin   ol. el. Camden   2 6-cyl diesels   145 × 37 × 12   sold, 1948; see note for
b) Weehawk (#)   S   1926   12½ × 18   details on later owners; out
                          405   American Brown   of documentation, 1968
[3]   Boveri

226194
Frederick Peirce   ol.el.   Camden   2 6-cyl diesels   145 × 37 × 12   sold to U.S. Govt., 1943; see
b) Westchester (#)   S   1926   12½ × 18   note for details on later
c) North Jersey (*)   405   American Brown   civilian owners; out of
d) Eastern Bay   Boveri   documentation, 1968
e) B. Frank Sherman
f) Chesapeake
[4]

226234
Frank E. Gannett   ol.el.   Camden   2 6-cyl diesels   145 × 37 × 12   sold to U.S. Govt., 1942;
b) Nassau (#)   S   1927   12½ × 18   later ran for Chilean
c) Presidente Porras   405   American Brown   interests
   (+)   Boveri
d) Alonzo de Ercilla (+)
[1]

223222
Chelsea   st.s.   Wilm.   2 2-cyl comp   189 × 36 × 14   sold to Virginia interests,
b) Warwick   S   1923   17, 34 × 24   1943; out of documentation,
[5]   1028   Pusey & Jones   1964

239258
E. G. Diefenbach (*)   ol.el.   Orange, Texas   12-cyl diesel   184 × 45 × 13   sold to City of New York,
b) Fonseca (+)   S   1940   8½ × 10   1954; to Nicaraguan registry,
                          565   Levingston   1970

Off. No. Name(s) [Notes]	Type Hull Gross Tons	Built Year Yard	Engines Cylinder size (in inches)	Dimensions (in feet)	Disposition
239632 *Hamilton* (*) b) *Nicoyano* (+)	ol.el. S 565	Orange, Texas 1940 Levingston	12-cyl diesel 8½ × 10	184 × 45 × 13	sold to City of New York, 1954; out of documentation, 1970; to Costa Rican registry
240384 *Gotham* (ii) b) *Asquith* (+) c) *Gotham* (ii) (#) (*) d) *Delaware*	ol.el. S 565	Oyster Bay, N.Y. 1941 Jakobson	12-cyl diesel 8½ × 10½	178 × 45 × 13	sold to U.S. Govt., 1945; returned to Electric Ferries, 1947; sold to City of New York, 1954; later sold to Delaware River interests; out of documentation, 1978
240877 *Hudson* b) *Gould Island* (+) c) *Hudson* (#) (*) d) *Chester*	ol.el S 569	Boston 1941 General Ship & Engine	12-cyl diesel 8½ × 10½	177 × 45 × 13	sold to U.S. Govt., 1943; returned to Electric Ferries, 1946; sold to City of New York, 1954; later sold to Delaware River interests; out of documentation, 1978
225543 *Elmer W. Jones* b) *Colington* (+) c) *Elmer W. Jones* [6]	ol.s. S 277	Groton, Conn. 1926 New London Ship & Engine	diesel powered	117 × 37 × 9	sold to U.S. Govt., 1943; returned to civilian registry, 1946; to Canadian registry, 1953
242176 *St. George* (*) b) *Bridgeport* c) *Jamestown*	ol.el. S 569	Boston 1942 General Ship & Engine	12-cyl diesel 8½ × 10½	177 × 45 × 13	sold to City of New York, 1954; later ran for Delaware River interests; in service for the Commonwealth of Virginia, 1989
236530 *Richmond* a) *City of Plattsburgh*	ol.s. S	Burlington, Vt. 1937	8-cyl diesel	152 × 39 × 10	sold to New York State Bridge Authority, 1946; to

c) *George Clinton* [7]	373	General Ship & Engine			Panamanian registry, 1958

250214 *The Narrows* (*) [8]	ol.el. S 545	Oyster Bay, N.Y. 1946 Jakobson	2 8-cyl diesels 8¾ × 10½	178 × 45 × 13	sold to City of New York, 1954; to U.S. Govt., 1970

251539 *The Tides* (*) [8]	ol.el. S 545	Oyster Bay, N.Y. 1947 Jacobson	2 8-cyl diesels 8¾ × 10½	178 × 45 × 13	sold to City of New York, 1954; to U.S. Govt., 1970

[1] Both *Governor Moore* and *Nassau* were sold to the U.S. Government early in World War II for service in the Panama Canal Zone. Both vessels continued to be listed in *ABS* through 1955 as so owned. *Nassau* thought to have later been transferred to Chilean registry. It has also been claimed that *Governor Moore* never operated in the Canal Zone and was lost at sea en route to Panama in 1942. See Harry Cotterell, Jr., "Across the Canal," *Steamboat Bill*, No. 89 (Spring 1964), 17–18.

[2] As *Gotham*, owned by Kass Fy. Corp. of Camden, N.J. from ca. 1941 through ca. 1950 and known to have run on various Delaware River services. As *Jamestown*, owned by the Commonwealth of Virginia from ca. 1951 through 1960; was last vessel to operate on the Willoughby–Old Point Comfort line in the Hampton Roads area. Owned by the City of New York, 1960–1966.

[3] Sold to Westchester Fy. Corp., 1948. After that company's Yonkers–Alpine service was abandoned in 1958, sold to St. Lawrence Seaway Development Corp.

[4] After government service operated as *North Jersey* for the Pt. Richmond Fy. Co., ca. 1947–1948; operated for the State of Maryland as both *Eastern Bay* and *B. Frank Sherman* through ca. 1954. Final owner was the Commonwealth of Virginia.

[5] Purchased from the Reading R.R. in 1938. As *Warwick*, was converted to diesel power during service in Virginia. May have operated in U.S. Government service ca. 1941.

[6] Designed by Eads Johnson and purchased from the Brockville & Morristown Fy. Co., an operator on Lake Ontario, in 1942. Returned to that company after government service during World War II.

[7] Purchased from the Champlain Transportation Company of Burlington, Vermont in 1942. *MVUS* shows "place built" as Burlington; *ABS* claims *built* in Boston and *assembled* at Burlington. Sister ship *City of Burlington* later sold by Champlain Transportation to Commonwealth of Virginia for James River service as b) *Virginia*, where she runs as a fleetmate with the ex-Electric Ferry *St. George*, b) *Bridgeport*, c) *Jamestown*.

[8] *The Tides* continues to operate, in 1989, for the U.S. Coast Guard on the Whitehall St.–Governors Island service. *The Narrows* was also purchased by the Coast Guard; stripped of parts for *The Tides* she was sold to Rhode Island interests for use as a shoreside facility in Jamestown, R.I. In 1967 both vessels leased to the Central R.R. of N.J. for service on that company's Liberty St.–Communipaw service.

FLEET: Hoboken Ferry Company, and successor
companies
SERVICE: Hudson River
DATES: 1821–1967
COMMENTS/REFERENCES: See Harry J. Smith, *The
Romance of the Hoboken Ferry* (New York: Prentice-Hall,
1931).

Off. No. Name(s) [Notes]	Type Hull Gross Tons	Built Year Yard	Engines Cylinder size (in inches)	Dimensions (in feet)	Disposition
n/a *Hoboken* (i)	st.p. W 207	Hoboken 1822	n/a	98 × 26 × 3	abandoned, 1856
n/a *Pioneer*	st.p. W 143	New York 1824	n/a	n/a	abandoned, 1860
n/a *Fairy Queen* b) *Phoenix* (#)	st.p. W 161	New York 1826 Capes & Ellison	1-cyl VB	149 × 16 × 6	abandoned, 1855
13164 *John Fitch* [1]	st.p. W 125	Hoboken 1845	n/a	n/a	abandoned, 1878
n/a *James Rumsey* (i) [1]	st.p. W 341	Hoboken 1851	n/a	153 × 27 × 9	lost (fire), 1853

13165					
James Watt	st.p. W 372	Hoboken 1851	n/a	153 × 27 × 9	lost (fire), 1870

4863					
Chancellor Livingston [2]	st.p. W 457	Hoboken 1852 Capes & Ellison	n/a	169 × 27 × 10	sold, 1880; abandoned, 1886

19907					
Paterson	st.p. W 360	Hoboken 1854	n/a	158 × 28 × 10	abandoned, 1874

n/a					
Hoboken (ii) [3]	st.p. W 530	Hoboken 1861	n/a	n/a	chartered to U.S. Govt., 1862; lost, 1862

11468					
Hoboken (iii)	st.p. W 551	Hoboken 1864	n/a	n/a	abandoned, 1880

16988					
Morristown	st.p. W 682	Hoboken 1865 John Stuart	n/a	198 × 44 × 12	abandoned, 1898

13828					
James Rumsey (ii) (*)	st.p. W 671	Hoboken 1867 John Stuart	n/a	206 × 44 × 11	sold to N.Y. & College Point Fy. Co., 1887; dismantled, 1907

95143					
Hackensack (*)	st.p. W 917	Hoboken 1871 John Stuart	n/a	215 × 50 × 12	sold to N.Y. & College Point Fy. Co., 1893; out of documentation, 1912 (?)

Off. No. Name(s) [Notes]	Type Hull Gross Tons	Built Year Yard	Engines Cylinder size (in inches)	Dimensions (in feet)	Disposition
26900 *Wiehawken* b) *College Point* (*) [4]	st.p. W 724	Hoboken 1868	n/a	214 × 45 × 11	sold to N.Y. & College Point Fy. Co., 1887; dismantled, 1907
115313 *Secaucus* (*) [5]	st.p. W 971	Hoboken 1868	1-cyl VB 46 × 120	214 × 46 × 12	see note; sold to Carteret Fy. Co., 1926; lost (fire), 11-3-'35, foot of Bay Ridge Ave. (i.e., 69 St.), Brooklyn
91015 *Moonachie* b) *Queens* (*)	st.p. W 810	Hoboken 1877 John Stuart	1-cyl VB 46 × 120	197 × 45 × 13	sold to N.Y. & College Point Fy. Co., 1907; lost (fire), 11-9-'18, at New York
140419 *Lackawanna* (i)	st.p. I 822	Newburgh 1881 Ward, Stanton	n/a	200 × 35 × 12	sold to Washington, D.C. interests, 1907; out of documentation, ca. 1910 (?)
95667 *Hoboken* (iv) b) *Tottenville* (*)	st.p. I 831	Newburgh 1881 Ward, Stanton	1-cyl VB 44 × 120	198 × 35 × 12	sold to S.I. Ry., 1910; abandoned, 1936
150267 *Paunpeck*	st.p. I 820	Newburgh 1882	1-cyl VB 44 × 120	199 × 35 × 12	sold to Westchester Fy. Corp., 1923; abandoned, 1938
95860 *Hopatcong* (i) [6]	st.p. I 854	Newburgh 1885 John Bigler	1-cyl VB 44 × 120	197 × 35 × 13	lost (fire), 8-7-'05, at Hoboken

91813
Musconetcong   st.p.   Newburgh   1-cyl VB   197 × 35 × 13   sold to Westchester Fy.
b) *F. R. Pierson*   I   1885   44 × 120   Corp., 1923; scrapped, 1947
[6]   846   John Bigler

155132
Orange   st.p.   Newburgh   1-cyl VB   218 × 35 × 13   dismantled, 1944
                        S   1886   46 × 120
                        1096   T. S. Marvel

91903
Montclair   st.p.   Newburgh   1-cyl VB   218 × 35 × 13   dismantled, 1944
                        S   1886   46 × 120
                        1095   T. S. Marvel

3418
Bergen   st.s.   Newburgh   3-cyl TE   220 × 37 × 16   scrapped, 1953
                        S   1888   18½, 27,
                        1120   Delamater   42 × 24
[7]   Iron

3523
Bremen   st.s.   Newburgh   2 2-cyl comp   219 × 40 × 16   dismantled, 1947
b) *Maplewood* (ii) (#) S   1891   20, 36 × 38
                        1252   T. S. Marvel

96148
Hamburg   st.s.   Newburgh   2 2-cyl comp   219 × 40 × 16   out of documentation, 1971
b) *Chatham* (i) (#)   S   1891   20, 36 × 38
c) *Lackawanna* (iii) (#) 1266 T. S. Marvel
[8, 9]

Off. No. Name(s) [Notes]	Type Hull Gross Tons	Built Year Yard	Engines Cylinder size (in inches)	Dimensions (in feet)	Disposition
130644 *Netherlands* b) *Oswego* (#)	st.s. S 1129	Newburgh 1893 T. S. Marvel	2 2-cyl comp 18, 38 × 28	190 × 42 × 16	dismantled, 1956
201628 *Scranton*	st.s. S 1462	Newport News 1904 Newport News S.B. & Dry Dock	2 2-cyl comp 18, 36 × 26	187 × 43 × 16	out of documentation, 1968
201816 *Scandinavia* b) *Pocono* (#) [8]	st.s. S 1462	Newport News 1905 Newport News S.B. & Dry Dock	2 2-cyl comp 18, 36 × 28	187 × 43 × 16	out of documentation, 1971
201684 *Elmira* [8]	st.s. S 1460	Newport News 1905 Newport News S.B. & Dry Dock	2 2-cyl comp 18, 36 × 28	187 × 43 × 16	out of documentation, 1970
201734 *Binghampton* [8, 11]	st.s. S 1462	Newport News 1905 Newport News S.B. & Dry Dock	2 2-cyl comp 18, 36 × 28	187 × 43 × 16	out of documentation, 1970
203492 *Ithaca*	st.s. S 1462	Newport News 1906 Newport News S.B. & Dry Dock	2 2-cyl comp 19, 38 × 28	187 × 43 × 16	lost (fire), August 1946

202552					
Lackawanna (ii)	st.s.	Wilm.	3-cyl TE	206 × 39 × 14	sold to Delaware River
a) *Woodbury*	S	1905	19, 30,		interests, 1948; scrapped,
	1079	Harlan &	35 × 35		1954
[10]		Hollingsworth			
203025					
Hopatcong (ii)	st.s.	Wilm.	4-cyl TE	206 × 39 × 14	scrapped, 1949
a) *Callahan*	S	1905	19, 30, 35,		
	1079	Harlan &	35 × 30		
[10]		Hollingsworth			
222638					
Hoboken (v)	st.s.	Elizabethport	2 2-cyl comp	220 × 43 × 18	dismantled, 1955
	S	1922	18, 38 × 28		
	1292	John W. Sullivan			
222703					
Buffalo	st.s.	Elizabethport	2 2-cyl comp	220 × 43 × 18	dismantled, 1955
	S	1922	18, 38 × 28		
	1292	John W. Sullivan			
222704					
Chatham (ii)	st.s.	Mariners Harbor	2 2-cyl comp	206 × 44 ×	out of documentation, 1963
a) *Youngstown* (*)	S	1922	18, 36 × 28		
[12]	1553	Staten Island S.B.			
234618					
Maplewood (ii)	st.s.	Chester, Pa.	5-cyl Unaflow	221 × 45 × 16	retired, 1965
a) *Meadville* (*)	S	1936			
[12]	1599	Sun S.B.			

[1] Various secondary sources claim these were sister ships with identical tonnage and dimensions; numbers shown taken from enrollment certificates in the National Archives. *James Rumsey*'s engine used in the construction of *Paterson* in 1854.

[2] Chartered to U.S. Government in 1861 for Civil War service as a troop transport.

[3] Lost while serving as a troop transport with the Coast Division of the Army of the Potomac under General Burnside in 1862.

[4] Vessel often appears in secondary literature as *Weehawken*. All certificates issued prior to name change to *College Point* use *Wiehawken*.

[5] Permanent enrollment certificate surrendered at New York on May 10, 1923, and vessel removed from documentation; written on the certificate are the words, "abandoned, as unfit for use." Sold to Carteret Fy. Co. and redocumented in 1926.

[6] Both vessels ordered from the Newburgh shipyard of Ward, Stanton. In 1884, while they were under construction, Ward, Stanton went bankrupt. John Bigler arranged to complete their construction and delivery. T. S. Marvel, who would later emerge as Newburgh's principal latter-day shipbuilder, was a superintendent in the Ward, Stanton yard.

The fire that destroyed *Hopatcong* (i) on August 7, 1905 also destroyed the entire Hoboken ferry terminal and railroad depot. The replacement terminal opened on February 25, 1907 and remains in service as a commuter railroad facility to this day.

[7] World's first successful double-ended ferryboat propelled by screw propellers.

[8] Ended career as a "box top." A Federal maritime subsidy program in the late 1960s required that ocean-going steamship companies participating in the program surrender and "trade in" an old vessel before taking delivery of a new one. Many ferryboats and excursion steamers were purchased from their former owners before heading to the scrap yard and used for this purpose, as the Federal government was indifferent to what kind of vessel be traded-in on the new tonnage. Traded-in vessels came to be called "box tops."

[9] Converted from steam to diesel-electric power in 1949. New engine characterized as follows: 16-cyl diesel; 8½ × 10. First certificate of enrollment issued on February 17, 1892; final certificate surrendered, at Wilmington, Delaware, on September 29, 1971. "Sold for non-transportation use" noted in U.S. Coast Guard files. Vessel's documented life of 79 years, 7 months, and 12 days is the longest achieved by a New York ferryboat thus far. See *Mount Holly*, listed with the East 34 Street Vehicular Ferry Co., for a potential challenger.

[10] Purchased from Potomac River interests (i.e., Norfolk & Washington Steamboat Co.) in 1907. Each vessel was lengthened 20 feet to the dimensions shown in 1926.

[11] Serves as an undocumented floating restaurant on the Hudson River at Englewood, N.J.

[12] Purchased from the Erie R.R. in 1957 when Erie's Jersey City passenger terminal was closed and Erie trains rerouted into the D. L. & W. Hoboken terminal.

FLEET: Erie R.R.
SERVICE: Hudson River
DATES: 1861–1958
COMMENTS/REFERENCES: See Raymond J. Baxter and Arthur G. Adams, *Railroad Ferries of the Hudson* (Woodcliff Lake, N.J.: Lind, 1987), pp. 82–116.

Off. No. Name(s) [Notes]	Type Hull Gross Tons	Built Year Yard	Engines Cylinder size (in inches)	Dimensions (in feet)	Disposition

18182 *Niagara* (*) [1]	st.p. W 409	New York 1849 Perrine, Patterson & Stack	n/a	128 × 32 × 10	lost (fire), 1-26-'68, at Jersey City
19037 *Onalaska* (*) [1]	st.p. W 409	New York 1849 Perrine, Patterson & Stack	n/a	128 × 32 × 10	out of documentation and converted to barge, 1873
19903 *Pavonia* b) *Rutherford* (i) (#)	st.p. W 864	Brooklyn 1861 Devine Burtis	1-cyl VB 48 × 132	192 × 34 × 13	abandoned, 1911
22797 *Susquehanna* b) *Arden* (#)	st.p. W 921	New York 1865 Simonson(?)	1-cyl VB 50 × 120	196 × 35 × 12	abandoned, 1924
6634 *Delaware* b) *Sterlington* (#) c) *Suffern* (#)	st.p. W 985	New York 1868	1-cyl VB 50 × 120	198 × 35 × 13	abandoned, 1925
75118 Jay Gould b) *Chautauqua* (i) (#)	st.p. W 498	Brooklyn 1868 John Englis	n/a	158 × 34 × 12	sold to Camden interests, ca. 1904; out of documentation, ca. 1911
75120 James *Fisk, Jr.* b) *Passaic* (i) (#) c) *Broadway* (#)	st.p. W 755	New York 1869 Charles Sneeden	1-cyl VB 50 × 120	170 × 34 × 12	sold to Bklyn & Manhattan Fy. Co., 1910; out of documentation, ca. 1918

Off. No. Name(s) [Notes]	Type Hull Gross Tons	Built Year Yard	Engines Cylinder size (in inches)	Dimensions (in feet)	Disposition
8930 *Erie* b) *Ridgewood* (#)	st.p. W 981	Chester, Pa. 1873 Delaware River Iron S.B.	1-cyl VB 46 × 132	136 × 40 × 14	out of documentation, ca. 1915
155090 *Passaic* (ii) a) *Oswego* (*) [2]	st.p. I 1055	Newburgh 1883 Ward, Stanton	1-cyl VB 50 × 120	193 × 36 × 13	abandoned, 1935
130262 *Newburgh* (*) b) *Gov. Albert C.* *Ritchie* [2, 3]	st.p. I 1053	Newburgh 1883 Ward, Stanton	1-cyl VB 50 × 120	193 × 36 × 13	sold to Annapolis interests, 1925; to Canadian registry, 1947
76632 *John King* b) *Paterson* (#)	st.p. I 1057	Phila. 1886 Cramp & Sons	1-cyl VB 50 × 120	190 × 36 × 13	lost (sunk), 12-29-'06, Hudson River off Christopher St.; see text, chapter 7
76922 *John G. McCullough* b) *Rutherford* (ii) (#) c) *Chautauqua* (ii) (#) d) YFB-48 (+) [4, 5]	st.s. S 1372	Phila. 1891 Neafie & Levy	2 2-cyl comp 26, 50 × 30	200 × 45 × 15	sold to U.S. Govt., ca. 1943
200661 *Arlington*	st.s. S 1446	Port Richmond 1903 Burlee	2 2-cyl comp 18, 38 × 28	206 × 43 × 16	dismantled, 1962
202685 *Goshen*	st.s.	Wilm.	2 2-cyl comp	205 × 43 × 16	sold to U.S. Govt., ca. 1943

b) YFB-47 (+) [5]	S 1459	1905 Harlan & Hollingsworth	18, 38 × 28		
200636 *Tuxedo*	st.s. S 1483	Wilm. 1904 Harlan & Hollingsworth	2 2-cyl comp 18, 38 × 28	205 × 43 × 16	out of documentation, 1955
204817 *Jamestown*	st.s. S 1538	Port Richmond 1907 Burlee	2 2-cyl comp 18, 38 × 28	206 × 44 × 17	dismantled, 1962
222704 *Youngstown* *b) Chatham* (*)	st.s. S 1553	Mariners Harbor 1922 Staten Island S.B.	2 2-cyl comp 18, 38 × 28	206 × 44 × 17	sold to D.L. & W., 1957; out of documentation, 1963
234618 *Meadville* *b) Maplewood* (*) [6]	st.s. S 1599	Chester, Pa. 1936 Sun S.B.	5-cyl Unaflow 25 × 24	221 × 45 × 16	sold to D.L. & W., 1957; retired, 1965

[1] Purchased from Williamsburg ferries, ca. 1860.

[2] Purchased from New York Central R.R. in 1911.

[3] Retired by Erie in 1925, presumably for scrapping; thought to be of no further value. Purchased by Maryland interests (i.e., Clairborne–Annapolis Fy. Co.); steam engine and paddlewheels replaced by diesel engines and screw propellers.

[4] Second New York ferryboat with screw propellers.

[5] Government service was in Pensacola, Florida.

[6] First New York ferryboat to be equipped with Skinner Unaflow engine; last (and largest) ferryboat built for Hudson River railroad service.

FLEET: New York, New Haven & Hartford R.R. and
predecessor company
SERVICE: Exchange Place, Jersey City–Port Morris, The
Bronx
DATES: 1876–1912
COMMENTS/REFERENCES: See George W. Hilton,
"The Steamer Maryland Route," *Steamboat Bill*, No. 95
(Fall 1965), 87–93.

Off. No. Name(s) [Notes]	Type Hull Gross Tons	Built Year Yard	Engines Cylinder size (in inches)	Dimensions (in feet)	Disposition
17794 *Maryland* (i) [1]	st.p. I 1150	Wilm. 1854 Harlan & Hollingsworth	2 horizontal engines 40 × 96	294 × 36 × 10	lost (fire), 12-8-'88 at Port Morris, The Bronx
92156 *Maryland* (ii)	st.p. I 859	Wilm. 1890	2 horizontal comp	238 × 38 × 13	converted to barge, 1913

[1] Operated across Susquehanna River by Phila., Wilm. & Balt.
R.R., 1854–1866; out of service, 1866–1876.

FLEET: Pennsylvania R.R. and predecessor companies
SERVICE: Hudson River
DATES: 1812–1949
COMMENTS/REFERENCES: See Baxter and Adams,
Railroad Ferries of the Hudson, pp. 63–81; see also
separate listing, "Pennsylvania Annex," for service between
Jersey City and Fulton St., Brooklyn.

Off. No. Name(s) [Notes]	Type Hull Gross Tons	Built Year Yard	Engines Cylinder size (in inches)	Dimensions (in feet)	Disposition
n/a *Jersey* [1, 2]	st.p. W 118	New York 1812 Charles Brown	n/a	80 × 30 × 5	abandoned, 1818
n/a *York* [2]	st.p. W 118	New York 1813 Charles Brown	n/a	80 × 30 × 5	n/a
n/a *Richard Varick* [2]	st.p. W n/a	New York 1826	n/a	n/a	abandoned, 1834 (?)
n/a *Washington* (i) [3]	st.p. W 258	Newburgh 1833	n/a	n/a	converted to barge, 1859
n/a *Sussex*	st.p. W 290	New York 1834	n/a	150 × 22 × 9	abandoned, 1849

Off. No. Name(s) [Notes]	Type Hull Gross Tons	Built Year Yard	Engines Cylinder size (in inches)	Dimensions (in feet)	Disposition
n/a *Essex*	st.p. W 243	New York 1835	n/a	119 × 24 × 9	sold to Albany interests, early 1850s; abandoned, 1859
n/a *New Jersey*	st.p. W 288	New York 1836	n/a	n/a	abandoned, 1862
n/a *Washington* (ii)	st.p. W 117	New York 1843	n/a	71 × 21 × 8	abandoned, 1868
4857 *Colden*	st.p. W 577	Brooklyn 1851 Burtis & Morgan	n/a	168 × 32 × 11	converted to barge, 1891
20295 *Philadelphia* (i)	st.p. W 341	Hoboken 1852 Capes & Allison	n/a	125 × 35 × 9	sold to U.S. Govt., 1863; redocumented at New Orleans, 1866; abandoned, 1869
6266 *D. S. Gregory*	st.p. W 578	Brooklyn 1853	n/a	187 × 25 × 11	abandoned, 1890
17867 *Mechanic* [4]	st.p. W 229	Camden 1856	n/a	124 × 28 × 7	sold to Florida interests, 1884; lost (stranded), 8-15-'91, at Jacksonville

13192					
John S. Darcy	st.p. W 614	Brooklyn 1857 Devine Burtis	1-cyl VB 42 × 132	191 × 33 × 11	out of documentation, 1903
12982					
John P. Jackson *b)* U.S.S. *John P.* *Jackson* (+) *c) J. P. Jackson* [5]	st.p. W 777	Brooklyn 1860 Devine Burtis	1-cyl VB 45 × 132	192 × 32 × 12	sold to U.S. Govt., 1861; redocumented at New Orleans, 1865; abandoned, 1871
13158					
Jersey City [6]	st.p. W 982	Brooklyn 1862 Devine Burtis	1-cyl VB 46 × 132	192 × 34 × 13	dismantled, 1917
18277					
New York	st.p. W 881	Brooklyn 1863 Devine Burtis	n/a	192 × 34 × 13	dismantled, 1905
18278					
Newark (i) *b) Amenia* [7]	st.p. W 661	Brooklyn 1864 Devine Burtis	n/a	166 × 33 × 13	sold to Central Stockyard & Transit Co. of New York, 1879; out of documentation, 1903
5602					
Camden [8]	st.p. W 598	Camden 1865	n/a	129 × 29 × 8	sold to Albany interests, ca. 1887; abandoned, 1900

Off. No. Name(s) [Notes]	Type Hull Gross Tons	Built Year Yard	Engines Cylinder size (in inches)	Dimensions (in feet)	Disposition
18295 *New Brunswick* (i)	st.p. W 909	Brooklyn 1866 Devine Burtis	1-cyl VB 46 × 132	193 × 36 × 13	lost (fire), 12-28-'96, at Jersey City
11927 *Hudson City* (*)	st.p. W 1008	Brooklyn 1867	1-cyl VB 46 × 132	203 × 35 × 12	sold to Long Island R.R., 1904; abandoned, 1913
18785 *New Jersey* (ii)	st.p. W 1062	Brooklyn 1873 New York Iron Wks	1-cyl VB 50 × 144	212 × 36 × 12	dismantled, 1912
150187 *Princeton*	st.p. W 888	Brooklyn 1879 Devine Burtis	1-cyl VB 46 × 132	192 × 36 × 12	dismantled, 1909
3207 *Baltimore*	st.p. I 1080	Wilm. 1882 Harlan & Hollingsworth	1-cyl VB 46 × 132	192 × 36 × 12	converted to barge, 1916
126102 *Chicago* (i)	st.p. I 1006	Wilm. 1882 Harlan & Hollingsworth	1-cyl VB	192 × 36 × 12	lost (sunk), 10-31-'99, at New York

126803 *Cincinnati* [11]	st.s. S 1255	Elizabeth 1891 Samuel Moore & Sons	2 2-cyl comp 18, 36 × 26	192 × 46 × 15	sold to Delaware River interests, 1929; scrapped, 1952
81386 *Washington* (iii) [11]	st.s. I 1247	Chester, Pa. 1891 Delaware River Iron Wks	2 2-cyl comp 18, 36 × 26	193 × 46 × 15	sold to Delaware River interests, 1937; out of documentation, 1952
116755 *St. Louis* [9]	st.s. S 1273	Phila. 1896 Charles Hillman	2 3-cyl comp 20, 32, 32 × 24	200 × 46 × 15	out of documentation, 1954
150741 *Pittsburgh* [9, 11]	st.s. S 794	Phila. 1896 Wm. Cramp & Sons	2 3-cyl comp 20, 32, 32 × 24	200 × 46 × 15	sold to Delaware River interests, 1939; scrapped, 1952
130757 *New Brunswick* (ii) [9, 10]	st.s. S 1273	Phila. 1897 Charles Hillman	2 3-cyl comp 20, 30, 30 × 24	200 × 46 × 15	scrapped, 1951
150806 *Philadelphia* (ii) [9, 10, 11]	st.s. S 1306	Chester, Pa. 1899 Delaware River Iron Wks	2 3-cyl comp 20, 32, 32 × 24	191 × 45 × 15	sold to Delaware River interests, 1948; out of documentation, 1952

Off. No. Name(s) [Notes]	Type Hull Gross Tons	Built Year Yard	Engines Cylinder size (in inches)	Dimensions (in feet)	Disposition
127509 *Chicago* (ii) [11]	st.s. S 1334	Port Richmond 1901 Burlee	3-cyl comp 22, 32, 32 × 24	193 × 46 × 15	sold to Delaware River interests, 1949; scrapped, 1952
130994 *Newark* (ii)	st.s. S 1308	Newburgh 1902 Marvel	3-cyl comp 22, 32, 32 × 24	192 × 46 × 15	out of documentation, 1950

[1] The very first steam-powered, double-ended ferryboat to operate in New York Harbor – or the world.

[2] *Jersey* and *York* known to be, and *Richard Varick* thought to be, twin-hull vessels propelled by a single paddlewheel situated between the hulls.

[3] Considerable uncertainty about this vessel, including whether it existed or not.

[4] Owned by New Jersey Fy. Co. of Camden, N.J. through 1884 when title was tranferred to the Pennsylvania R.R. at New York. Original owner was the West Jersey Fy. Co., also of Camden. Both of these Delaware River companies were subsidiaries of the Pennsylvania R.R. and/or its predecessors.

[5] Carried president-elect Abraham Lincoln across the Hudson River on February 21, 1861, en route to his inauguration in Washington; see chapter 4.

[6] Thought to have carried the Lincoln funeral cortège across the Hudson River on April 24, 1865; see chapter 4.

[7] Vessel's service for the Central Stockyard & Transit Co. between 1879 and 1903 was not bona-fide ferryboat work.

[8] Originally worked for the P.R.R. in Delaware River service at Philadelphia; transferred to New York in 1881.

[9] Equipped with dual propeller shafts and twin screws at each end.

[10] Primarily New York boats, but known to have worked P.R.R.'s Baltimore–Love Point (Maryland) service for some time before that route was abandoned in 1944.

[11] Delaware River service was for the Delaware & New Jersey Fy. Co. between Deepwater, N.J. and New Castle, Delaware.

Special Note: more so than with other operators, the Pennsylvania R.R. frequently remeasured its vessels and altered their gross tonnage. Whenever possible, original gross tonnage is shown. The Pennsylvania R.R. also operated a sizable ferryboat fleet in trans-Delaware service between Philadelphia and Camden, and some of these vessels may have been used on the Hudson from time to time, in addition to the two cases of formal transfer noted in the roster. At the time of World War I, for example, the following vessels were operating for the railroad at Philadelphia: *Coopers Point, Baltic, Wenonah, Beverly, Camden, Hammonton, Wildwood, Bridgeton,* and *Salem.*

FLEET: The Pennsylvania Annex
SERVICE: Brooklyn – Jersey City
DATES: 1877–1910
COMMENTS/REFERENCES: Connected Pennsylvania
R.R.'s Exchange Place Terminal in Jersey City with the
foot of Fulton Street in Brooklyn; independent company
until 1897, then taken over by P.R.R.

Off. No. Name(s) [Notes]	Type Hull Gross Tons	Built Year Yard	Engines Cylinder size (in inches)	Dimensions (in feet)	Disposition
105751 *Annex* (i)	st.p. W 324	New Baltimore, N.Y. 1877	n/a	127 × 26 × 8	out of documentation, ca. 1895
105800 *Annex No. 2*	st.p. W 298	Baltimore, Md. 1878	n/a	117 × 38 × 10	out of documentation, ca. 1890
105841 *Annex No. 3* [1]	st.p. W 367	Wilm. 1879	1-cyl VB	128 × 29 × 9	out of documentation, ca. 1895
106789 *Annex No. 4*	st.p. W 501	Wilm. 1890 Jackson & Sharp	1 cyl VB 40 × 108	138 × 31 × 11	dismantled, 1911
106860 *Annex No. 5* b) *George W. Loft* (*) c) *Casablanca* (+)	st.p. W 406	Wilm. 1891 Jackson & Sharp	1 cyl VB 40 × 108	136 × 31 × 11	sold to Delaware River interests, 1911; later ran for N.Y. & Englewood Fy. Co.; to Cuban registry, 1916

107187					
Annex (ii)	st.p.	Tompkins Cove,	1-cyl VB	139 × 31 × 12	sold to Virginia interests,
b) *Warwick*	W	N.Y.	42 × 108		ca. 1911; abandoned, 1920
	529	1895			

[1] Engine removed from *Annex No. 3* ca. 1895 and used in the construction of the steamboat *John G. Carlisle* in 1896. The *'Carlisle* operated between Manhattan and Ellis Island until the arrival of the ferryboat *Ellis Island* in 1904.

FLEET: Central Railroad of New Jersey
SERVICE: Hudson River
DATES: 1864–1967
COMMENTS/REFERENCES: See Harry Cotterell, Jr.,
"Jersey Central Ferries," *Steamboat Bill*, No. 13 (April
1944), 225–28; *addenda*, No. 14 (August 1944), 263.

Off. No. Name(s) [Notes]	Type Hull Gross Tons	Built Year Yard	Engines Cylinder size (in inches)	Dimensions (in feet)	Disposition
14101					
Kill Van Kull	st.p. W	New York 1858	n/a	252 × 35 × 14	lost (fire), 1889
[1]	1463				
4876					
Communipaw	st.p. W 1028	Brooklyn 1863 Devine Burtis	1-cyl VB	217 × 33 × 12	out of documentation, 1905

4877 *Central*	st.p. W 4877	Brooklyn 1863 Devine Burtis	1-cyl VB	$217 \times 33 \times 12$	out of documentation, 1903
8281 *Elizabeth* (i)	st.p. W 1082	Brooklyn 1867 Devine Burtis	1-cyl VB	$215 \times 35 \times 12$	lost (fire), 11-22-'01, at New York
20296 *Plainfield* (i)	st.p. W 1051	Brooklyn 1869 Devine Burtis	1-cyl VB	$213 \times 35 \times 12$	lost (fire), 9-18-'00, at Jersey City
120265 *Fanwood*	st.p. W 1092	Brooklyn 1876	1-cyl VB	$213 \times 36 \times 13$	out of documentation, 1904
92944 *Mauch Chunk* b) *Margate* c) *Mount Hood* (*)	st.s. S 642	Wilm. 1893 Harlan & Hollingsworth	2 2-cyl comp 16, 30 $\times$ 22	$145 \times 32 \times 14$	sold to Delaware River interests, 1906; later ran in New York for E. 34 St. Veh. Fy. Co.; abandoned, 1935
136350 *Easton* a) *Leonia* (*)	st.s. S 634	Wilm. 1893 Harlan & Hollingsworth	2 2-cyl comp 16, 30 $\times$ 22	$145 \times 32 \times 14$	sold to Riverside & Ft. Lee Fy. Co., 1905; scrapped, 1947

Off. No. Name(s) [Notes]	Type Hull Gross Tons	Built Year Yard	Engines Cylinder size (in inches)	Dimensions (in feet)	Disposition
3909 *Bound Brook*	st.s. S 1016	Wilm. 1901 Harlan & Hollingsworth	4-cyl TE 19, 30, 35, 35 × 30	200 × 44 × 17	dismantled, 1948
141723 *Lakewood* b) *Elizabeth* (iii) (#) c) *Second Sun* (+) [2]	st.s. S 1016	Wilm. 1901 Harlan & Hollingsworth	4-cyl TE 19, 30, 35, 35 × 30	200 × 43 × 17	out of documentation, 1967
111411 *Red Bank*	st.s. S 1016	Wilm. 1904 Harlan & Hollingsworth	4-cyl TE 19, 30, 35, 35 × 30	200 × 44 × 17	scrapped, 1964
201355 *Wilkes-Barre* [3, 4]	st.s. S 1197	Wilm. 1904 Harlan & Hollingsworth	4-cyl TE 19, 30, 35, 35 × 30	191 × 44 × 15	scrapped, 1965
200879 *Plainfield* (ii)	st.s. S 1225	Elizabethport 1904 Crescent	4-cyl TE 19, 30, 35, 35 × 30	200 × 43 × 15	dismantled, 1956
202704 *Cranford*	st.s. S 1197	Wilm. 1905 Harlan & Hollingsworth	4-cyl TE 19, 30, 35, 35 × 30	191 × 44 × 15	out of documentation, 1967

202713 *Somerville*	st.s. S 1197	Wilm. 1905 Harlan & Hollingsworth	4-cyl TE 19, 30, 35, 35 × 30	191 × 44 × 15	scrapped, 1964
201490 *Elizabeth* (ii)	st.s. S 1197	Wilm. 1904 Harlan & Hollingsworth	4-cyl TE 19, 30, 35, 35 × 30	191 × 44 × 15	dismantled, 1947
208674 *Westfield*	st.s. S 1238	Wilm. 1911 Harlan & Hollingsworth	4-cyl TE 19, 30, 35, 35 × 30	191 × 46 × 17	dismantled, 1956
211559 *Bayonne*	st.s. S 1334	Wilm. 1913 Harlan & Hollingsworth	3-cyl TE 20, 32, 35 × 30	182 × 46 × 17	dismantled, 1948

[1] The Lytle–Holdcamper List shows as *Kill Von Kull*; certificates in the National Archives show, at different times, *Kill Von Kull* and *Kill Van Kull*. The waterway between Staten Island and New Jersey after which she is named is officially called the Kill Van Kull. Vessel had many remeasurings and shows with at least these three gross-tonnage ratings at different times: 1463, 1191, and 1125. Not known to have run on the railroad's trans-Hudson ferry services; see text, chapter 4.

[2] Rebuilt with steel superstructure as *Elizabeth* (iii) after serious fire damage to *Lakewood* ca. 1949. Last company-owned ferryboat to remain in service; see text, chapter 10, for details.

Sold to Public Service of New Jersey for use as a floating exhibition hall to promote nuclear generation of electricity. Called *Second Sun* by Public Service; exempt from formal documentation.

[3] Converted to undocumented floating restaurant in Brielle, N.J.

[4] A Federal subsidy program for the construction of new seagoing merchant tonnage in the 1960s required the owners of such new vessels to "trade in" an older vessel – *any* vessel. Many ferryboats and excursion steamers were thus purchased by ocean shipping companies en route, really, to the scrapyard so they might be used as the mandated trade-in. *Wilkes-Barre* was such a vessel; the industry called these trade-in old-timers "box tops."

FLEET: Staten Island Rapid Transit
SERVICE: Upper New York Bay
DATES: 1852–1905
COMMENTS/REFERENCES: Service begun ca. 1817
using single-ended steamboats; see text for details. For this
company's Arthur Kill service, see separate listing under
Staten Island Railway. See Appendix A for references.

Off. No. Name(s) [Notes]	Type Hull Gross Tons	Built Year Yard	Engines Cylinder size (in inches)	Dimensions (in feet)	Disposition
10135 *Hunchback* b) U.S.S. *Hunchback* (+) c) *General Grant* [1]	st.p. W 517	New York 1852 Jeremiah Simonson	1-cyl VB 40 × 96	179 × 29 × 10	sold to U.S. Govt., 1861; redocumented, 1866, and sold to Boston interests; abandoned, 1880
n/a *Southfield* (i) b) U.S.S. *Southfield* (+) [1]	st.p. W 751	Brooklyn 1857 John Englis	1-cyl VB	200 × 34 × 11	sold to U.S. Govt., 1861; lost in combat, 4-19-'64
n/a *Westfield* (i) b) U.S.S. *Westfield* (+) [1]	st.p. W 891	Brooklyn 1861 Jeremiah Simonson	1-cyl VB 50 × 120	213 × 34 × 12	sold to U.S. Govt., 1861; lost in combat, 3-21-'64
n/a *Clifton* (i) b) U.S.S. *Clifton* (+)	st.p. W 892	Brooklyn 1861 Jeremiah Simonson	1-cyl VB 50 × 120	210 × 40 × 13	sold to U.S. Govt., 1861; lost in combat, 3-21-'64

15434 *Clifton* (ii) b) U.S.S. *Smokokon* (+) c) *Lone Star* [1, 2]	st.p. W 700	Greenpoint 1862	1-cyl VB 43 × 120	n/a	sold to U.S. Govt., 1863; redocumented, 1865; lost, 3-31-'68
26504 *Westfield* (ii) (*)	st.p. W 609	Brooklyn 1862 Jeremiah Simonson	1-cyl VB 50 × 120	202 × 32 × 13	sold to City of New York, 1906; out of documentation, 1912
18276 *Northfield* [3]	st.p. W 600	Brooklyn 1863 Jeremiah Simonson	1-cyl VB 50 × 120	202 × 34 × 13	out of documentation, 1902
16981 *Middletown* (*)	st.p. W 641	Brooklyn 1864	1-cyl VB	201 × 33 × 14	sold to City of New York, 1906; abandoned, 1912
115831 *Southfield* (ii) (*)	st.p. W 758	Clifton, N.Y. 1882 Lawler	1-cyl VB 50 × 120	209 × 35 × 13	sold to City of New York, 1906; out of documentation, 1912
110780 *Robert Garrett* b) *Stapleton* (*) c) *Express* d) *York River* [4]	st.p. S 1592	Baltimore 1888 Columbian Iron Wks	inclined compound 39, 70 × 60	225 × 61 × 14	sold to City of New York, 1906; later ran for Baltimore interests; converted to barge, 1940; dismantled, 1956

136019

Erastus Wiman	st.p.	Baltimore	inclined	225 × 61 × 14	sold to City of New York,
b) *Castleton* (#) (*)	S	1888	compound		1906; later ran for Norfolk
	1587	Columbian	39, 70 × 60		interests; lost (fire), 2-2-'18,
[5]		Iron Wks			at Norfolk

[1] Served with U.S. Navy during Civil War; see text, chapter 4.
[2] Service after the Civil War was under the ownership of New York Mail Steamship Company, likely not in ferryboat service; configuration of vessel after Civil War not known.
[3] Involved in major collision with Jersey Central R.R.'s *Mauch Chunk* on June 14, 1901; see chapter 6 for details.
[4] Owned by the City of New York through 1922; owned by T. H. Franklin, 1922–1925; owned by Tolchester Beach Improvement Co., of Maryland, 1925–1940; owned by Chesapeake Corp., 1940–1956. Renamed *Stapleton* by the City of New York on December 8, 1906.
[5] Owned by City of New York through 1915; owned by Charles L. Dimon of Mt. Vernon, N.Y., 1915–1917; owned by Chesapeake Fy. Co., 1917–1918. Renamed *Castleton* by S.I.R.T. on October 14, 1894.

FLEET: The City of New York
SERVICE: Upper New York Bay, East River, etc.
DATES: 1905–current
COMMENTS/REFERENCES: City-owned ferryboats displayed in three categories: A) New vessels for Upper New York Bay services; B) Other new vessels; and, C) Second-hand vessels.

Off. No. Name(s) [Notes]	Type Hull Gross Tons	Built Year Yard	Engines Cylinder size (in inches)	Dimensions (in feet)	Disposition

Category A: New vessels for Upper New York Bay services

202346

Manhattan	st.s.	Baltimore	2 2-cyl comp	246 × 46 × 18	out of documentation, 1944
	S	1905	22½, 50 × 30		
	1954	Maryland Steel			

202349 *Brooklyn* (i)	st.s. S 1954	Baltimore 1905 Maryland Steel	2 2-cyl comp 22½, 50 × 30	246 × 46 × 18	scrapped, 1947
202347 *Queens*	st.s. S 1954	Baltimore 1905 Maryland Steel	2 2-cyl comp 22½, 50 × 30	246 × 46 × 18	scrapped, 1947
202348 *Bronx*	st.s. S 1954	Baltimore 1905 Maryland Steel	2 2-cyl comp 22½, 50 × 30	246 × 46 × 18	abandoned, 1941
201898 *Richmond* [1]	st.s. S 2006	Port Richmond 1905 Burlee	2 2-cyl comp 22½, 50 × 39	232 × 46 × 18	converted to barge, 1944; scrapped, 1947
204213 *Bay Ridge* b) *Rappahannock River* [2]	st.s. S 862	Wilm. (1907) Harlan & Hollingsworth	2 2-cyl comp 18, 38 × 28	182 × 45 × 16	sold and converted to barge, 1940
204339 *Gowanus* [2]	st.s. S 862	Wilm. (1907) Harlan & Hollingsworth	2 2-cyl comp 18, 38 × 28	182 × 45 × 16	sold for scrap, 1940
204561 *Nassau* [2]	st.s. S 862	Wilm. 1907 Harlan & Hollingsworth	2 2-cyl comp 18, 38 × 28	182 × 45 × 16	sold for scrap, 1940

Off. No. Name(s) [Notes]	Type Hull Gross Tons	Built Year Yard	Engines Cylinder size (in inches)	Dimensions (in feet)	Disposition
212028 *Mayor Gaynor* [3]	st.s. S 1634	Camden 1914 New York S.B.	4-cyl TE 21½, 33, 39, 39 × 30	210 × 45 × 17	dismantled, ca. 1951
221732 *President Roosevelt*	st.s. S 1907	Port Richmond 1921 Staten Island S.B.	2 2-cyl comp 22½, 50 × 30	241 × 46 × 18	scrapped, 1956
223001 *William Randolph Hearst* b) *Whitehall* (ii) (#) [2]	st.el. S 875	Port Richmond 1923 Staten Island S.B.	steam turbine	209 × 45 × 16	out of documentation, 1954
223021 *Rodman Wanamaker* [2]	st.el. S 875	Port Richmond 1923 Staten Island S.B.	steam turbine	209 × 45 × 16	out of documentation, 1954
223020 *George W. Loft* b) *West Brighton* (#) [2]	st.el. S 875	Port Richmond 1923 Staten Island S.B.	steam turbine	209 × 45 × 16	out of documentation, 1954
226106 *American Legion* (i)	st.s. S 2089	Port Richmond 1926 Staten Island S.B.	2 2-cyl comp 22½, 50 × 30	251 × × 17	scrapped, 1963
228307 *Dongan Hills*	st.s. S 2029	Port Richmond 1929 Staten Island S.B.	2 2-cyl comp 22½, 50 × 30	251 × 46 × 18	out of documentation, 1968

230240 *Tompkinsville*	st.s. S 2045	Mariners Harbor 1930 United	2 2-cyl comp 22½, 50 × 30	251 × 46 × 18	out of documentation, 1967
231148 *Knickerbocker*	st.s. S 2045	Mariners Harbor 1931 United	2 2-cyl comp 22½, 50 × 30	252 × 47 × 18	sold for scrap, 1965
236871 *Gold Star Mother*	st.s. S 2126	Mariners Harbor 1937 United	2 2-cyl comp 22½, 50 × 30	252 × 47 × 18	out of documentation, 1972
237022 *Mary Murray*	st.s. S 2126	Mariners Harbor 1937 United	2 2-cyl comp 22½, 50 × 30.	252 × 47 × 18	out of documentation, ca. 1982
237080 *Miss New York*	st.s. S 2126	Mariners Harbor 1938 United	2 2-cyl comp 22½, 50 × 30	252 × 47 × 15	out of documentation, 1979
261133 *Pvt. Joseph F. Merrell* *b) Vernon C. Bain* [4, 5]	st.s. S 2285	Staten Island 1950 Bethlehem Steel	6-cyl Unaflow 23 × 26	269 × 69 × 19	converted to dormitory at Rikers Isl., 1987
261463 *Cornelius G. Kolff* [4, 5]	st.s. S 2285	Staten Island 1950 Bethlehem Steel	6-cyl Unaflow 23 × 26	269 × 69 × 19	converted to dormitory at Rikers Isl., 1987

Off. No. Name(s) [Notes]	Type Hull Gross Tons	Built Year Yard	Engines Cylinder size (in inches)	Dimensions (in feet)	Disposition
261917 *Verrazzano* [4, 6]	st.s. S 2285	Staten Island 1951 Bethlehem Steel	6-cyl Unaflow	269 × 69 × 19	see note 6
298241 *John F. Kennedy*	ol.el. S 2109	Orange, Texas 1965 Levingston	4 16-cyl diesels 8.5 × 10	277 × 69 × 19	in service, 1989
298830 *American Legion* (ii) [7]	ol.el. S 2109	Orange, Texas 1965 Levingston	4 16-cyl diesels 8.5 × 10	277 × 69 × 19	in service, 1989
298821 *The Gov. Herbert H. Lehman*	ol.el. S 2109	Orange, Texas 1965 Levingston	4 16-cyl diesels 8.5 × 10	277 × 69 × 19	in service, 1989
629314 *Andrew J. Barberi* [8]	ol.el. S 3335	New Orleans 1981 Equitable	4 16-cyl diesels 9.06 × 10	300 × 70 × 20	in service, 1989
629315 *Samuel I. Newhouse* [8]	ol.el. S 3335	New Orleans 1982 Equitable	4 16-cyl diesels	300 × 70 × 20	in service, 1989
696013 *Alice Austen* [8]	ol.s. S 499	Middletown, R.I. 1986 Derecktor	16-cyl diesel 6.7 × 7.5	207 × 41 × 15	in service, 1989

696014					
John A. Noble	ol.s.	Middletown, R.I.	16-cyl diesel	$207 \times 41 \times 15$	in service, 1989
	S	1986	6.7×7.5		
[8]	499	Derecktor			

Category B: New vessels for other municipal services

224506					
Murray Hulbert	st.s.	Brooklyn	2 2-cyl comp	$142 \times 37 \times 13$	out of documentation, 1967
b) *Rockaway* (#)	S	1925	12, 26 $\times$ 18		
c) YFB-59 (+)	593	Todd			
d) *Rockaway* (#)					
[9]					

224504					
Edward Riegelmann	st.s.	Brooklyn	2 2-cyl comp	$142 \times 37 \times 13$	dismantled, ca. 1948
b) *Bushwick* (#)	S	1925	12, 26 $\times$ 18		
[9]	593	Todd			

224505					
Julius Miller	st.s.	Brooklyn	2 2-cyl comp	$142 \times 37 \times 13$	dismantled, ca. 1948
b) *Stuyvesant* (#)	S	1925	12, 26 $\times$ 18		
[9]	593	Todd			

224986					
Maurice E. Connolly	st.s.	Brooklyn	2 2-cyl comp	$142 \times 37 \times 13$	out of documentation, 1963
b) *Elmhurst* (#)	S	1925	12, 26 $\times$ 18		
[9]	593	Todd			

224984					
John H. McCooey	st.s.	Brooklyn	2 2-cyl comp	$142 \times 37 \times 13$	dismantled, ca. 1948
b) *Sea Gate* (#)	S	1925	12, 26 $\times$ 18		
[9]	593	Todd			

224899					
William T. Collins	st.s.	Mariners Harbor	2 2-cyl comp	$142 \times 37 \times 13$	out of documentation,
b) *Astoria* (#)	S	1925	12, 26 $\times$ 18		ca. 1966
[9]	593	Staten Island S.B.			

Off. No. Name(s) [Notes]	Type Hull Gross Tons	Built Year Yard	Engines Cylinder size (in inches)	Dimensions (in feet)	Disposition
225171 *Henry A. Meyer* b) *Williamsburg* (#) [9]	st.s. S 593	Mariners Harbor 1925 Staten Island S.B.	2 2-cyl comp 12, 26 × 18	142 × 37 × 13	out of documentation, 1963
225235 *Joseph A. Guider* b) *Flushing* (#) c) USFB-84 (+) d) *Sgt. Cornelius H.* *Charlton* (+) (*) [9, 10]	st.s. S 593	New York 1925 Sullivan	2 2-cyl comp 12, 26 × 18	142 × 37 × 13	sold to U.S. Govt., 1943
225176 *Frank A. Cunningham* b) *Flatbush* (#) [9]	st.s. S 593	Mariners Harbor 1925 Staten Island S.B.	2 2-cyl comp 12, 26 × 18	142 × 37 × 13	out of documentation, 1954
224521 *Henry Bruckner* b) *Tremont* (#) [9]	st.s. S 593	Mariners Harbor 1925 Staten Island SB	2 2-cyl comp 12, 26 × 18	142 × 37 × 13	out of documentation, ca. 1954
224522 *John A. Lynch* b) *Harlem* (#) c) *Maj. Gen. Wm. H.* *Hart* (+) (*) [9, 10]	st.s. S 593	Mariners Harbor 1925 Staten Island S.B.	2 2-cyl comp 12, 26 × 18	142 × 37 × 13	sold to U.S. Govt., 1941
225151 *Joseph J. O'Brien* b) *Jamaica* (#) [9]	st.s. S 593	New York 1925 Sullivan	2 2-cyl comp 12, 26 × 18	142 × 37 × 13	out of documentation, 1954

229173 *Melrose* b) *Col. Robert E.* *Shannon* (+) (*) [9, 10]	st.s. S 593	Brooklyn 1929 Todd	2 2-cyl comp 12, 26 × 18	142 × 37 × 13	sold to U.S. Govt., 1941
228264 *Yorkville* [9]	st.s. S 593	Brooklyn 1929 Todd	2 2-cyl comp 12, 26 × 18	142 × 37 × 13	out of documentation, 1960
230778 *Murray Hill* [9]	st.s. S 593	Brooklyn 1931 Todd	2 2-cyl comp 12, 26 × 18	141 × 37 × 13	out of documentation, 1954
230782 *Washington Square* b) *Staten* [9]	st.s. S 593	Brooklyn 1931 Todd	2 2-cyl comp 12, 26 × 18	141 × 37 × 13	sold to U.S. Govt., 1943
222622 *Bird S. Coler* b) *Fordham* (#) [11]	st.s. S 190	City Island, N.Y. 1922 Kyle & Purdy	2 2-cyl comp 9, 20 × 14	84 × 26 × 10	out of documentation, 1982
227200 *Mott Haven*	ol.s. S 245	Brooklyn 1927 Todd	6-cyl diesel 12½ × 18	99 × 29 × 10	sold to Lake Champlain interests, 1945; to British registry, 1961
229949 *Chelsea*	ol.el. S 245	Brooklyn 1930 Todd	2 6-cyl diesels 10½ × 15	99 × 29 × 10	sold and converted to yacht, 1968

Off. No. Name(s) [Notes]	Type Hull Gross Tons	Built Year Yard	Engines Cylinder size (in inches)	Dimensions (in feet)	Disposition
227201 *Greenwich Village*	ol.s. S 245	Brooklyn 1927 Todd	6-cyl diesel	99 × 29 × 10	out of documentation, ca. 1967
287626 *Michael Cosgrove*	ol.s. S 139	Warren, R.I. 1961 Blount	2 diesels	60 × 35 × 9	in service, 1989

Category C: Second-hand vessels

Off. No. Name(s) [Notes]	Type Hull Gross Tons	Built Year Yard	Engines Cylinder size (in inches)	Dimensions (in feet)	Disposition
26504 *Westfield* (*) [12]	st.p. W 609	Brooklyn 1862 Jeremiah Simonson	1-cyl VB 50 × 120	202 × 32 × 13	out of documentation, 1912
16981 *Middletown* (*) [12]	st.p. W 641	Brooklyn 1864 Jeremiah Simonson	1-cyl VB	201 × 33 × 14	abandoned, 1912
115831 *Southfield* (*) [12]	st.p. W 758	Clifton, S.I. 1882 Lawler	1-cyl VB 50 × 120	209 × 35 × 13	out of documentation, 1912
110780 *Robert Garrett* (*) *b) Stapleton* (#) *c) Express* *d) York River* [13]	st.p. S 1592	Baltimore 1888 Columbian Iron	2-cyl inclined comp 39, 70 × 60	225 × 61 × 14	sold to Baltimore interests, 1922; converted to barge, ca. 1940; dismantled, 1956

136019 *Castleton* (*) a) *Erastus Wiman* (*) [14]	st.p. S 1587	Baltimore 1888 Columbian Iron	2-cyl inclined comp 39, 70 × 60	225 × 61 × 14	sold to Norfolk interests, 1915; lost (fire), 2-2-'18, at Norfolk
106348 *Atlantic* (*) [15]	st.p. S 930	Brooklyn 1885	1-cyl 48 × 120	190 × 36 × 13	scrapped, 1939
150477 *Pierrepont* (*) b) *Piermont* [15]	st.p. S 1095	Newburgh 1889	1-cyl VB 50 × 120	196 × 37 × 14	sold to Hudson River interests, 1929; abandoned, 1935
92259 *Montauk* (*) b) *Pennsville* [15]	st.p. S 1087	Newburgh 1890	1-cyl VB 50 × 120	196 × 37 × 14	sold to Delaware River interests, 1926; out of documentation, 1940
25076 *Union* (*) [15]	st.p. W 502	Greenpoint 1862	1-cyl 38 × 120	153 × 33 × 11	sold, ca. 1924; lost (fire), 7-17-'29 at Port Richmond
17016 Shinnecock (*) a) *Monticello* [15]	st.p. W 650	Brooklyn 1866	1-cyl 40 × 120	160 × 33 × 13	abandoned, 1928
3313 *Brooklyn* (ii) (*) b) *Irvington* [15]	st.p. S 930	Brooklyn 1885	1-cyl VB 48 × 120	190 × 36 × 13	sold to Hudson River interests, 1928; abandoned, 1935

Off. No. Name(s) [Notes]	Type Hull Gross Tons	Built Year Yard	Engines Cylinder size (in inches)	Dimensions (in feet)	Disposition
5497 *Columbia* (*) [15]	st.p. W 586	Brooklyn 1867	1-cyl 40 × 120	154 × 31 × 12	abandoned, 1928
17928 *Mineola* (*) [15]	st.p. W 620	Brooklyn 1868	1-cyl	156 × 33 × 12	abandoned, 1926
116026 *Steinway* (*) [16]	st.p. W 354	Brooklyn 1884	1-cyl VB 32 × 108	125 × 32 × 10	sold, 1924; out of documentation, 1939
81086 *Wyoming* (*) [17]	st.p. I 833	Wilm. 1885 Harlan & Hollingsworth	1-cyl VB 46 × 120	171 × 36 × 13	abandoned, 1943
121032 *Florida* (*) [17]	st.p. I 818	Chester 1896	1-cyl VB 42 × 120	156 × 36 × 13	sold to N.Y. & Englewood Fy. Co., 1934; abandoned, 1946
77284 *Greenpoint* (*) a) *Joseph J. O'Donahue* (*) [17]	st.p. S 901	Chester, Pa. 1898 Delaware River Iron Works	1-cyl VB 48 × 120	174 × 36 × 13	scrapped, 1941
3485 *Bowery Bay* (*) a) *Bouwery Bay* (*) [16]	st.p. W 432	Greenpoint 1890	1-cyl VB 34 × 96	130 × 32 × 11	sold, 1926; abandoned, 1931

Whitehall (i) (*) [15]	st.p. S 1088	Newburgh 1890	1-cyl 50 × 120	196 × 37 × 14	out of documentation, ca. 1943
96029 *Harlem* (*) a) *Haarlaem* (*) [16]	st.p. W 382	Greenpoint 1889	1-cyl VB 34 × 96	130 × 31 × 10	abandoned, 1926
239258 *E. G. Diefenbach* (*) b) *Fonseca* (+) [18]	ol.el. S 565	Orange, Texas 1940 Levingston	12-cyl diesel 8½ × 10	184 × 45 × 13	to Nicaraguan registry, 1970
239632 *Hamilton* b) *Nicoyano* (+) [18]	ol.el. S 565	Orange, Texas 1940 Levingston	12-cyl diesel 8½ × 10	184 × 45 × 13	out of documentation, 1970
240384 *Gotham* (*) a) *Gotham* (*) b) *Asquith* (+) d) *Delaware* [18]	ol.el. S 565	Oyster Bay, NY 1941 Jakobson	12-cyl diesel 8½ × 10½	178 × 45 × 13	sold to Delaware River interests, ca. 1966; out of documentation, 1978
240877 *Hudson* (*) a) *Hudson* (*) b) *Gould Island* (+) d) *Chester* [18]	ol.el. S 569	Boston 1941 General Ship & Engine	12-cyl diesel 8½ × 10½	177 × 45 × 13	sold to Delaware River interests, ca. 1966; out of documentation, 1978

Off. No. Name(s) [Notes]	Type Hull Gross Tons	Built Year Yard	Engines Cylinder size (in inches)	Dimensions (in feet)	Disposition
242176 *St. George* (*) *b) Bridgeport* *c) Jamestown* [18]	ol.el. S 569	Boston 1942 General Ship & Engine	12-cyl diesel 8½ × 10½	177 × 45 × 13	sold to Delaware River interests, ca. 1966; later sold to Commonwealth of Virginia, and still in service in 1989
250214 *The Narrows* (*) [18]	ol.el. S 545	Oyster Bay, N.Y. 1946 Jakobson	2 8-cyl diesels 8¾ × 10½	178 × 45 × 13	sold to U.S. Govt., 1971
241539 *The Tides* (*) [18]	ol.el. S 545	Oyster Bay, N.Y. 1947 Jakobson	2 8-cyl diesels 8¾ × 10½	178 × 45 × 13	sold to U.S. Govt., 1970; still in service in New York in 1989 on U.S.C.G. route to Governors Island
226132 *Seawells Point* *a) Grenville Kane* (*) *b) Palisades* (*) [19]	ol.el. S 405	Camden 1926 American Brown Boveri	2 6-cyl diesels 12½ × 18	145 × 37 × 12	out of documentation, 1967
226099 *Jamestown* *a) Charles W. Culkin* (*) *b) Gotham* (*) [19]	ol.el. S 405	Camden 1926 American Brown Boveri	2 6-cyl diesels 12½ × 18	145 × 37 × 12	out of documentation, 1966

[1] The five Borough-class ferryboats were all built for the city under the terms of a contract with Maryland Steel. Four vessels were built by the prime contractor at its Sparrows Point, Md. shipyard, but the company subcontracted the construction of *Richmond* to the Burlee Dry Dock Co. of Port Richmond.

[2] Designed to accommodate only vehicles on the main deck, passengers on the second deck.

[3] Rebuilt ca. 1930 to accommodate only vehicles on the main deck, with passengers on the second deck.

[4] Last steam-powered ferryboats built for service in New York;

last steam-powered ferryboats to operate in New York.

[5] Converted to a prison dormitory at Rikers Island in 1987; uncertain if vessels retain status of documented U.S. merchant vessel.

[6] Out of service and in lay-up status in 1989; future uncertain and return to service most unlikely.

[7] Chartered in December 1986 for use in the Hollywood film *Love You to Death*. Ever the hard-luck boat, *American Legion* (ii) managed to get stranded on a mud flat near Buttermilk Channel during the filming, throwing shooting schedules totally out of whack. The production company then hastily chartered *The Gov. Herbert H. Lehman* and, with the name *American Legion* hastily affixed to one of her nameboards, she filled in for several hours of movie work, and even made a few revenue trips out of Whitehall St. with different names on either end of the vessel. *American Legion* (ii)'s reputation for bad luck stems from being hit in 1981 by a Norwegian freighter, and from ramming into the Battery Park seawall several years later.

[8] Equipped with Voith Schneider cycloidal propellers; see chapter 10 for further details.

[9] These are the 16 "151-foot" ferryboats, the largest single class of ferryboats in the harbor's history—*so far*!

[10] Later worked the Whitehall St.–Governors Island service for the U.S. Army. The '*Hart* and '*Charlton* were equipped with upper-deck passenger cabins by the Army, and the '*Hart* survives, the sole member of the class to do so, as an exhibit at the South Street Seaport in New York. See roster heading U.S. Army; U.S. Coast Guard for further details.

[11] Later dieselized; 4 6-cylinder engines, $4.25'' \times 5''$.

[12] All purchased from S.I.R.T. on April 21, 1906, but saw little if any service under municipal auspices. *Southfield* (and perhaps *Westfield*) transferred to Bellevue and Allied Hospitals after being removed from documentation for use as floating health-care facility. Hospital trustees attempted to sell *Southfield* for $575.00 in 1920 to an operator on the lower Hudson River who intended to reapply for Federal enrollment and use her in some kind of service there. Sale never materialized and *Southfield* eventually sank at her berth between piers 26 and 28 in the East River. Sinking Fund Commission voted in 1922 to accept the hulk of *Southfield* from Bellevue and see to its disposition.

[13] Purchased from Rapid Transit Fy. Co., a subsidiary of the S.I.R.T., in 1906. Renamed *Stapleton* on December 8, 1906. Sold to one T. H. Franklin in 1922; owned by the Tolchester Beach Improvement Co., of Kent County (Maryland), from 1925 through 1940.

[14] Purchased from the Rapid Transit Fy. Co. on April 21, 1906.

[15] Purchased from the Union Fy. Co. in 1922.

[16] Purchased from the New York & East River Fy. Co. in 1922.

[17] Purchased from the E. 10 & 23 St. Fy. Co. ca. 1920; earlier owned by the Williamsburg ferries.

[18] Purchased from Electric Ferries, Inc., in 1954.

[19] Purchased from the Commonwealth of Virginia, *Seawells Point* in 1959, *Jamestown* in 1960. Both earlier ran in New York for Electric Ferries, Inc.

FLEET: U.S. Army; U.S. Coast Guard
SERVICE: Governors Island
DATES: ca. 1870–1964, U.S. Army; 1964–current, U.S.
Coast Guard
COMMENTS/REFERENCES: All vessels shown during
ca. 1917–1920 are not known to have worked Whitehall
St.–Governors Island service, but are found in various
records as ferryboats owned by the U.S. Army in the Port
of New York.

Off. No. Name(s) [Notes]	Type Hull Gross Tons	Built Year Yard	Engines Cylinder size (in inches)	Dimensions (in feet)	Disposition
[Official numbers shown inside brackets were assigned during civilian service before or after government ownership.]					
[80056] *General George E. Pond* [+] a) *Winona* (*) c) *Winona* (*) [1]	st.p. W 649	New York 1868 Webb & Bell	1-cyl 42 × 120	115 × 54 × 14	sold to Carteret Fy. Co., ca. 1922; out of documentation, 1925
[228755] *General Hancock* (+) b) *General Hancock*	st.s. S 309	Wilm. 1898	2-cyl comp 14¼, 32 × 18	102 × 23 × 10	sold to Alexandria Bay, N.Y. interests, 1928; abandoned, 1941
[4870] *General John Simpson* (+) a) *Clinton* (*) b) U.S.S. *Commodore Morris* (+) c) *Clinton* (*) e) *Clinton* (*) [2]	st.p. W	New York 1862	1-cyl 38 × 120	152 × 32 × 11	sold to Carteret Fy. Co., 1920; abandoned, 1931

[130942] *General John F. Weston* (+) *a) North Beach* (*)	st.p. I 833	Shooter's Island, N.Y. (1901) Townsend & Downey	1-cyl VB 44 × 108	164 × 37 × 15	n/a
[235027] *General Otis* (+) *b) Nancy Helen* (*) *c) Resolute* (*) [8]	st.s. S 389	Wilm. 1910 Pusey & Jones	3-cyl comp 16, 24, 24 × 18	114 × 32 × 12	sold to Sunrise Ferries, ca. 1940; dismantled, 1957
General Charles F. *Humphrey* (+) [3]	ol.s. S 593	Portsmouth, Va. 1928 Spear Engineering	6-cyl diesel 14 × 17	128 × 44 × 15	n/a
[224522] *Major General Wil-* *liam H. Hart* (+) *a) John A Lynch* (*) *b) Harlem* (*) [4]	st.s. S 593	Mariners Harbor 1925 Staten Island S.B.	2 2-cyl comp 12, 26 × 18	142 × 37 × 13	out of service, ca. 1970; preserved at South Street Seaport, New York
[229173] *Colonel Robert E.* *Shannon* (+) *a) Melrose* (*) *b) Lieut. Robert E.* 　*Shannon* (+) (#) [4]	st.s. S 593	Brooklyn 1925 Todd	2 2-cyl comp 12, 26 × 18	142 × 37 × 13	scrapped, 1964
[225235] *Sgt. Cornelius H.* *Charlton* (+) *a) Joseph A. Guider* (*) *b) Flushing* (*) *c) USFB-84* (+) [4]	st.s. S 593	New York 1925 John W. Sullivan	2 2-cyl comp 12, 26 × 18	142 × 37 × 13	scrapped, 1964

Off. No. Name(s) [Notes]	Type Hull Gross Tons	Built Year Yard	Engines Cylinder size (in inches)	Dimensions (in feet)	Disposition
Lieut. Samuel S. *Coursen* (+) [7]	ol.el. S 869	Camden 1956 John H. Mathias	diesel	180 × 48 × 16	in service, 1989
Pvt. Nicholas Minue (+)	ol.el. S 869	Camden 1956 John H. Mathias	diesel	180 × 48 × 16	in service, 1989
[251539] *The Tides* (+) (*) [5]	ol.el. S 545	Oyster Bay, N.Y. 1947 Jakobson	2 8-cyl diesels 8¾ × 10½	178 × 45 × 13	in service, 1989
[267527] *Governor* (+) a) *Crown City* b) *Kulshan* [6]	ol.el. S 678	Oakland, Calif. 1954 Moore	3 6-cyl diesels 6¼ × 8	230 × 46 × 17	in service, 1989

[1] Purchased from Union Fy. Co. in 1917.

[2] Purchased from Union Fy. Co. ca. 1917. Vessel was built in 1862 for the Union Fy. Co. but sold to the U.S. Navy for Civil War duty before entering civilian service. See chapter 4 for details. After the Civil War was resold to the Union Fy. Co. where she operated until purchased by the U.S. Army for service in New York Harbor during the First World War. After this tour of duty she was sold to the Carteret Fy. Co. and operated on the Linoleumville–Carteret service until she was retired in 1931.

[3] First diesel-powered ferryboat on the Whitehall St.–Governors Island run. Not regarded as a successful venture; tended to ship water in dead-calm sea conditions. Disposition uncertain.

[4] Three ferryboats purchased from the City of New York: 'Hart and 'Shannon ca. 1941, 'Charlton in 1943. All had been members of the City's 16-boat 151-foot class. Both the 'Hart and the 'Shannon rebuilt by the U.S. Army with an upper-deck passenger cabin, while the 'Charlton retained her original profile. The 'Shannon and 'Charlton were scrapped with the arrival of the 'Coursen and 'Minue ca. 1956, while the 'Hart was retained as a spare, or relief, boat until *The Tides* was purchased in 1970. She is now being preserved at the South Street Seaport in New York.

[5] Purchased from the City of New York in 1970; earlier owned by Electric Ferries, Inc.

[6] Purchased from the Washington (state) Ferries ca. 1984; earlier owned by San Diego interests. First New York Harbor ferryboat to be built on the West Coast.

[7] A true celebrity boat! On October 21, 1957, used to bring Queen Elizabeth II and Prince Philip ashore from their royal yacht during a visit to New York. On December 7, 1988, carried Soviet premier Mikhail S. Gorbachev from Manhattan to Governors Island (and back) for a luncheon meeting with President Ronald Reagan and Vice-President George Bush. The two U.S. leaders traveled to Governors Island by helicopter. Together, the 'Minue and the 'Coursen cost $2,222,373.00 when they were constructed in 1956.

[8] Later dieselized.

FLEET: U.S. Immigration and Naturalization Service
SERVICE: Upper New York Bay (Ellis Island)
DATES: 1904–1954
COMMENTS/REFERENCES: Vessel owned by the United
States Government; not a registered U.S. merchant vessel.

Off. No. Name(s) [Notes]	Type Hull Gross Tons	Built Year Yard	Engines Cylinder size (in inches)	Dimensions (in feet)	Disposition
(none) *Ellis Island* (+) [1]	st.s. S 802	Wilm. 1904 Harlan & Hollingsworth	2-cyl comp 18, 36 × 24	144 × 37 × 12	out of service, 1954; allowed to decay at Ellis Island

[1] While vessel had almost totally deteriorated at her Ellis Island slip between 1954 and ca. 1986, an effort is now underway to restore this fine ferryboat as part of a larger effort to turn Ellis Island into a museum of immigration.

FLEET: New York & South Brooklyn Ferry &
Transportation Co.
SERVICE: Upper New York Bay
DATES: 1887–1906

Off. No. Name(s) [Notes]	Type Hull Gross Tons	Built Year Yard	Engines Cylinder size (in inches)	Dimensions (in feet)	Disposition
81161 *West Brooklyn* b) *Havana* (+) [1]	st.p. I 740	Newburgh 1887	1-cyl VB	174 × 34 × 12	to Cuban registry, 1910

116146 *South Brooklyn* b) *Fordham* (*)	st.p. I 728	Newburgh 1887	1-cyl VB	173 × 34 × 12	sold to Twin City Fy. Co., 1910; lost (fire), 4-17-'13, at Shooter's Isl.

[1] Sold by N. Y. & S. B. in 1907, presumably upon completion of charter to City of New York. (See text, chapter 6.) Owned by various individuals until transfer to Cuban registry on January 31, 1910. One of these was Francis Weeks, a man who was president of the Twin City Fy. Co., the firm that purchased *West Brooklyn*'s sister ship, *South Brooklyn*, b) *Fordham.* Thus it is quite possible that *West Brooklyn* also worked for the Twin City Fy. Co., although never formally owned by the firm itself.

FLEET: The Union Ferry Company and predecessor companies
SERVICE: Lower East River
DATES: 1814–1922
COMMENTS/REFERENCES: See Henry E. Pierrepont, *Historical Sketch of the Fulton Ferry* (Brooklyn, N.Y.: The Union Ferry Company of Brooklyn, 1879).

Off. No. Name(s) [Notes]	Type Hull Gross Tons	Built Year Yard	Engines Cylinder size (in inches)	Dimensions (in feet)	Disposition
n/a *Nassau* (i) [1]	st.p. W 118	New York 1814 Charles Brown	n/a	80 × 30 × 5	converted to shoreside chapel, 18??
n/a *William Cutting* [1]	st.p. W 85	New York 1828	n/a	100 × ×	abandoned, 1840
n/a *Brooklyn* (i) [2]	st.p. W 304	New York 1836	n/a	155 × ×	to Canadian registry, 1853

18557 *New York* (i) [2, 3]	st.p. W 304	New York 1836	n/a	151 × 23 × 9	sold to Hoboken Fy. Co., 18?? abandoned, 1867
n/a *Olive Branch*	st.p. W 159	Brooklyn 1836	1-cyl VB	89 × 23 × 8	sold, 1852; abandoned, 1858
n/a *Relief* b) *Nassau* (ii) (#) [4]	st.p. W 145	New York 1836	n/a	100 × ×	see note
n/a *Jamaica* [2]	st.p. W 173	New York 1837	n/a	125 × ×	sold 1849; abandoned, 1868
n/a *Fulton* (i)	st.p. W 184	New York 1838	n/a	110 × ×	sold, 18??; abandoned, 1859
n/a *Suffolk* [5]	st.p. W 266	New York 1842	n/a	130 × ×	sold and converted to barge, 1846
25077 *Union* (i) [6]	st.p. W 296	New York 1844	n/a	130 × ×	sold to upper Hudson River interests, 1861; lost (fire), 12-15-'78

Off. No. Name(s) [Notes]	Type Hull Gross Tons	Built Year Yard	Engines Cylinder size (in inches)	Dimensions (in feet)	Disposition
50379 *Montauk* (i) [7]	st.p. W 403	New York	n/a	140 × ×	sold and converted to barge, 1866
n/a *Wyandank* b) U.S.S. *Wyandank* (+) [8, 15]	st.p. W 399	New York 1847	n/a	132 × 31 × 10	sold to U.S. Govt., 1861; scrapped, 1880
n/a *Transit* [9]	st.p. W 404	New York 1847	n/a	140 × ×	abandoned, 1856
31136 *Bedford* [10]	st.p. W 425	New York 1848	n/a	142 × ×	sold to Jersey Central R.R., 1862; converted to barge, 1866
50370 *Manhattan* [11]	st.p. W 326	Brooklyn 1849	n/a	135 × ×	sold to Philadelphia interests, 1863; sold to U.S. Govt., 1864; converted to barge, 1867
n/a *Gowanus* [12]	st.p. W 417	Brooklyn 1851 Burtis & Morgan	n/a	132 × 32 × 10	abandoned, 1857
n/a *Whitehall* (i) [8]	st.p. W 323	Brooklyn 1850 Burtis & Morgan	n/a	126 × 28 × 10	sold to U.S. Govt., 1861; lost in combat, 1862

9051 *Fulton* (ii)	st.p. W 410	Brooklyn 1852 Burtis & Morgan	n/a	145 × ×	sold, 1863; abandoned, 1867
2315 *Brooklyn* (ii)	st.p. W 427	Brooklyn 1853	n/a	136 × 31 × 11	sold to Camden interests, 1868; abandoned, 1873
n/a *Louise* (*) [13]	st.p. W 341	Greenpoint 1853	n/a	125 × 28 × 10	sold to East River Fy. Co., 1860; abandoned, 1866
n/a *Ellen* b) U.S.S. *Ellen* (+) [8, 13]	st.p. W 341	Greenpoint 1853 Eckford Webb	1-cyl inclined	125 × 28 × 10	sold to U.S. Govt., 1861
1819 *Agnes* [13]	st.p. W 299	Greenpoint 1852 Eckford Webb	n/a	135 × ×	sold to New Bedford interests, 1859; lost (fire), 6-19-'62
14938 *Lydia* (*) [13]	st.p. W 299	Greenpoint 1852 Eckford Webb	n/a	120 × 26 × 10	sold to Weehawken Fy. Co., 1859; abandoned, 1872
1819 *Abbie* (*) [13]	st.p. W 392	Greenpoint (1852) Eckford Webb	n/a	120 × 27 × 10	sold to Weehawken Fy. Co., 1859; later sold to Albany interests; abandoned, 1884

Off. No. Name(s) [Notes]	Type Hull Gross Tons	Built Year Yard	Engines Cylinder size (in inches)	Dimensions (in feet)	Disposition
19040 *Osprey* (*) [14]	st.p. W 468	Williamsburg 1853	n/a	125 × 32 × 12	sold to Greenpoint Fy. Co., 1856; later sold to Camden interests; lost (fire), 10-4-'04 at Billingsport, N.J.
2306 *Eagle* (*) b) *Baltimore* [14]	st.p. W 392	Greenpoint 1852	n/a	125 × 32 × 11	sold to Williamsburg ferries, 1859; later sold to U.S. Govt.; redocumented in 1865 and sold to Maryland interests; lost, 1866, in Chesapeake Bay
22804 *Curlew* (*) b) U.S.S. *Curlew* (+) c) *South Side* (*) [8, 14]	st.p. W 366	Williamsburg 1853	n/a	126 × 21 × 12	sold to Williamsburg ferries, 1859; later sold to U.S. Govt.; redocumented, 1866; later ran for Greenpoint Fy. Co.; abandoned, 1912
n/a *Montague* [16]	st.p. W 410	Williamsburg 1852	n/a	140 × ×	lost (fire), 12-8-'53, at New York
7714 *and* 8386 *Exchange* [16]	st.p. W 438	Brooklyn 1853	n/a	131 × 30 × 11	sold, 1867; abandoned, 1878
16304 *Metropolis* [16]	st.p. W 433	Greenpoint 1852	n/a	130 × 30 × 11	sold to Boston interests, 1865; converted to barge, 1875

18280 *Nassau* (iii)	st.p. W 504	Brooklyn 1854	n/a	137 × 32 × 11	converted to barge, 1888
22095 *Atlantic* (i) b) U.S.S. *Commodore* *Read* (+) c) *State of Maryland* [8, 17]	st.p. W 650	Brooklyn 1857	n/a	179 × 33 × 11	sold to U.S. Govt., 1863; redocumented, 1865; lost (wrecked), 3-31-'76, Chesapeake Bay
16984 *Montague* (ii) [18]	st.p. W 449	New York 1859	n/a	141 × 31 × 11	sold to East River Fy. Co., 1868; abandoned, 1877
19901 *Pacific*	st.p. W 596	New York 1859	n/a	160 × 32 × 12	abandoned, 1898
16983 *Manhassett*	st.p. W 462	New York 1860	n/a	137 × 32 × 11	sold to Norfolk interests, 1874; abandoned, 1900
21440 *Roslyn*	st.p. W 462	New York 1860	n/a	139 × 32 × 11	sold to Weehawken Fy. Co., 1871; abandoned, 1888
21440 *Peconic*	st.p. W 506	Brooklyn 1860	n/a	145 × 33 × 11	sold to Camden interests; abandoned, 1897

Off. No. Name(s) [Notes]	Type Hull Gross Tons	Built Year Yard	Engines Cylinder size (in inches)	Dimensions (in feet)	Disposition
865 *America*	st.p. W 580	Greenpoint 1862 Webb & Bell	inclined engine	153 × 33 × 11	sold to Camden interests; abandoned, 1903
25076 *Union* (ii) (*)	st.p. W 562	Greenpoint 1862	1-cyl 38 × 120	153 × 33 × 11	sold to City of New York, 1922; lost (fire), 7-17-'29, at Port Richmond
11456 *Hamilton*	st.p. W 584	Brooklyn 1862	1-cyl 38 × 120	153 × 33 × 11	abandoned, 1918
n/a *Whitehall* (ii) [19]	st.p. W 555	n/a 1862	n/a	164 × ×	n/a
2570 *Baltic*	st.p. W 642	Greenpoint 1863	1-cyl 40 × 120	161 × 33 × 11	converted to barge, 1917
18279 *New York* (ii) [20]	st.p. W 642	Brooklyn 1863	1-cyl 40 × 120	161 × 33 × 12	converted to barge, 1917
21439 *Republic*	st.p. W 539	Greenpoint (1863)	n/a	146 × 33 × 11	abandoned, 1918

4870
Clinton
b) U.S.S. Commodore
  Morris (+)
c) Clinton (#)
d) General John
  Simpson (+)
e) Clinton (*)
[8, 21]
	st.p.
	W
	586
		New York
		1862
			1-cyl
			40 × 120
				152 × 32 × 11	see note

22876 *Somerset* *b) U.S.S. Somerset* (+) *c) Somerset* (#) [8]	st.p. W 538	Brooklyn 1862	n/a	149 × 34 × 11	sold to U.S. Govt., 1862; redocumented and returned to Union Fy. Co., ca. 1864; abandoned, 1914
17016 *Monticello* *b) Shinnecock* (#) (*)	st.p. W 538	Brooklyn 1862	1-cyl 40 × 120	149 × 34 × 11	sold to City of New York, 1922; abandoned, 1928
5497 *Columbia* (*)	st.p. W 586	Brooklyn 1867	1-cyl 40 × 120	154 × 31 × 12	sold to City of New York, 1922; abandoned, 1927
17928 *Mineola* (*) [22]	st.p. W 620	Brooklyn 1868	1-cyl 40 × 120	156 × 33 × 12	sold to City of New York, 1922; abandoned, 1926
80056 *Winona* (*)	st.p. W 460	New York 1869 Webb & Bell	1-cyl 42 × 120	155 × 33 × 12	sold to U.S. Govt., 1917; redocumented, ca. 1922; later ran for Carteret Fy. Co.; out of documentation, 1925

Off. No. Name(s) [Notes]	Type Hull Gross Tons	Built Year Yard	Engines Cylinder size (in inches)	Dimensions (in feet)	Disposition
9981 *Fulton* (iii)	st.p. I 647	Brooklyn 1871	1-cyl inclined 40 × 120	153 × 33 × 12	out of documentation, 1917
9982 *Farragut*	st.p. I 647	Brooklyn 1871	1-cyl inclined 40 × 120	153 × 33 × 12	out of documentation, 1914
150477 *Pierrepont* (*) b) *Piermont*	st.p. S 1095	Newburgh 1889	1-cyl VB 50 × 120	196 × 37 × 14	sold to City of New York, 1922; later ran for upper Hudson River interests; dismantled, 1935
92259 *Montauk* (*) b) *Pennsville*	st.p. S 1087	Newburgh 1890	1-cyl VB 50 × 120	196 × 37 × 14	sold to City of New York, 1922; later ran for Wilmington interests; out of documentation, 1940
106348 *Atlantic* (ii) (*)	st.p. S 930	Brooklyn 1885	1-cyl 48 × 120	190 × 36 × 13	sold to City of New York, 1922; abandoned, 1938
3313 *Brooklyn* (iii) (*) b) *Irvington*	st.p. S 930	Brooklyn 1885	1-cyl VB 48 × 120	190 × 36 × 13	sold to City of New York, 1922; later ran for upper Hudson River interests; abandoned, 1935
81299 *Whitehall* (iii) (*) b) *New Castle*	st.p. S 1088	Newburgh 1890	1-cyl VB 50 × 120	196 × 37 × 14	sold to City of New York, 1922; later ran for Wilmington interests; out of documentation, ca. 1943

[1] Twin-hull vessel with single paddlewheel between the hulls.

[2] Originally owned by company that operated Whitehall St.–Atlantic Ave. ferry; joined Union fleet through merger in 1839.

[3] No evidence vessel ever operated for Hoboken Fy. Co., and not included in that company's roster.

[4] The Lytle–Holdcamper List shows as abandoned in 1844; Pierrepont claims sold to Albany, N.Y. interests in 1852.

[5] Sold to Delaware & Hudson Canal Co. 1846–47 and converted to a barge; engine removed and used in *Wyandank*.

[6] Engine salvaged and used by the Newburgh Fy. Co. on upper Hudson River in their *City of Newburgh* of 1879.

[7] The Lytle–Holdcamper List gives date of barge conversion as 1866; Pierrepont claims 1860. Engine removed and used in *Manhassett*; hulk/barge sold to Erie R.R.

[8] Served with the U.S. Navy during the Civil War; see text, chapter 4, for further details.

[9] Engine removed and used in *Roslyn*.

[10] No evidence vessel ever ran as a ferryboat for the Jersey Central R.R.; likely used as a barge for the railroad, and not listed in the roster with C.N.J.'s vessels.

[11] Government service during Civil War with the Quartermaster Division of the U.S. Army.

[12] Engine used in *Republic*; The Lytle–Holdcamper List shows abandoned in 1857; Pierrepont claims converted to barge in 1863.

[13] Originally owned by the company that operated the Catharine St.–Main St. ferry; joined Union fleet through merger in 1853.

[14] Originally owned by the company that operated the Roosevelt St.–Bridge St. ferry; jointed Union fleet through merger in 1853.

[15] Vessel's history after U.S. Government service somewhat uncertain.

[16] Originally owned by the company that operated the Wall St.–Montague St. ferry; joined Union fleet through merger in 1853.

[17] Sold to Washington, D.C. interests following Civil War service with the Union Navy.

[18] No evidence that vessel ever operated in ferryboat service for the East River Fy. Co. (i.e., Long Island R.R.); not included in roster with that company's vessels.

[19] Pierrepont identifies this vessel as having been built in 1862. I have not been able to establish further confirmation of its existence.

[20] Sold to New York & Cuba Mail Steamship Co. as barge in 1917.

[21] Perhaps more correct to show U.S.S. *Commodore Morris* as first name; vessel was purchased from Union Fy. Co. by the U.S. Navy before being formally enrolled as *Clinton* and before entering service. Returned to Union after the Civil War and saw duty with the U.S. Army as *General John Simpson* during World War I. Concluded career with Carteret Fy. Co.

[22] Leased to City of New York and made first trip under municipal auspices on Whitehall St.–39 St./Brooklyn line in 1906. Sold to City of New York in 1922.

FLEET: Navy Yard Ferry Company
SERVICE: East River
DATES: 1825(?)–1868

Off. No. Name(s) [Notes]	Type Hull Gross Tons	Built Year Yard	Engines Cylinder size (in inches)	Dimensions (in feet)	Disposition
n/a *General Jackson*	st.p. W 174	New York 1829	n/a	n/a	out of U.S. registry (?), 1849

				111 × 30 × 5	
22815					
Seneca (*)	st.p.	New York			sold to Williamsburg ferries,
	W	1849			1867 (?); lost (fire), 1870, at
	232	John L. Brown			New York

FLEET: Williamsburg ferries
SERVICE: East River
DATES: 1826–1909
COMMENTS/REFERENCES: See Clifford S. Hawkins,
"Hey-Day of the Williamsburgh Ferries," *Steamboat Bill*,
No. 19 (April 1946), 366–69; see also Appendix B, for
various corporate names.

Off. No. Name(s) [Notes]	Type Hull Gross Tons	Built Year Yard	Engines Cylinder size (in inches)	Dimensions (in feet)	Disposition
n/a *New York* (i) (*)	st.p. W 189	New York 1842	n/a	100 × 23 × 8	sold to Trustees of St. Patrick's Cathedral, ca. 1848; abandoned, 1854
18575 *Newtown*	st.p. W 162	Williamsburg 1842	n/a	n/a	abandoned, 1876
n/a *Wallabout*	st.p. W 189	New York 1842	n/a	100 × 23 × 8	converted to barge, 1858
5498 *Cayuga*	st.p. W 318	Williamsburg 1849	n/a	110 × 30 × 10	abandoned, 1872

18282 *Niagara* (*)	st.p. W 411	New York 1849 Perrine, Patterson & Stack	n/a	130 × 32 × 11	sold to Erie R.R., ca. 1860; lost (fire), 1-26-'68, at Jersey City
19037 *Onalaska* (*)	st.p. W 411	New York 1849 Perrine, Patterson & Stack	n/a	130 × 32 × 11	sold to Erie R.R., ca. 1860; converted to barge, 1873
19036 *Oneida*	st.p. W 313	New York 1849	n/a	175 × 24 × 10	abandoned, 1876
n/a *Oneota*	st.p. W 411	Williamsburg 1849	n/a	130 × 32 × 11	sold to U.S. Govt., 1863
22815 *Seneca* [1]	st.p. W 313	New York 1849 John L. Brown	n/a	130 × 30 × 10	lost (fire), 1870, at New York
4859 *Canada*	st.p. W 338	Williamsburg 1851	n/a	115 × 30 × 11	abandoned, 1876
16985 *Minnesota*	st.p. W 355	Williamsburg 1852	n/a	115 × 30 × 11	abandoned, 1876

Off. No. Name(s) [Notes]	Type Hull Gross Tons	Built Year Yard	Engines Cylinder size (in inches)	Dimensions (in feet)	Disposition
22804 *Curlew* b) U.S.S. *Curlew* (+) c) *South Side* (*)	st.p. W 392	Williamsburg 1853	n/a	$125 \times 32 \times 11$	sold to U.S. Govt., 1862; redocumented, 1865 and sold to Greenpoint Fy. Co.; abandoned, 1912
18281 *Nebraska*	st.p. W 411	New York 1854	n/a	$130 \times 32 \times 11$	abandoned, 1875
10490 *George Washington*	st.p. W 414	Brooklyn 1856	n/a	$134 \times 32 \times 11$	abandoned, 1911
10489 *George Law*	st.p. W 414	Brooklyn 1856	n/a	$134 \times 32 \times 11$	sold to Camden interests, ca. 1888; lost (fire), 8-27-'01, at Bridgeton, N.J.
2306 *Eagle* b) *Baltimore* [2]	st.p. W 392	New York 1853	n/a	$125 \times 32 \times 11$	sold to U.S. Govt., 1862; redocumented, 1865 and sold to Maryland interests; lost, 1866, in Chesapeake Bay
4900 *Ethan Allen* b) U.S.S. *Commodore Barney* c) *Commodore Barney* (#)	st.p. W 538	Brooklyn 1859 Perrine, Patterson & Stack	1-cyl VB $38\frac{1}{2} \times 108$	$143 \times 33 \times 12$	sold to U.S. Govt., 1861; redocumented, 1865 and returned to Williamsburg ferries; sold to Florida interests, 1885; lost (stranded), 9-22-'01, off Jacksonville

14647 *Marion* b) U.S.S. *Morse* c) *Lincoln*	st.p. W 513	New York 1859	n/a	143 × 33 × 12	sold to U.S. Govt., 1861; redocumented, 1865 and sold to Boston interests; abandoned, 1865
12205 *Idaho* [3]	st.p. W 496	Brooklyn 1864	n/a	153 × 33 × 11	lost, 1895
867 *Arizona*	st.p. W 496	Brooklyn 1864	n/a	153 × 33 × 11	converted to barge, 1898
4869 *Commodore Perry* b) U.S.S. *Commodore* *Perry* (+) c) *Commodore Perry* (#)	st.p. W 513	Brooklyn 1859 Thomas Stack	1-cyl VB 38 × 108	143 × 33 × 12	sold to U.S. Govt., 1861; redocumented and sold to Williamsburg ferries, 1866; sold to Charleston interests, 1898; abandoned, 1907
26508 *Warren* (*)	st.p. W 513	Brooklyn 1859	n/a	143 × 33 × 12	sold to S.I. Ry., 1896; abandoned, 1908
22791 *Superior*	st.p. W 570	New York 1862	n/a	156 × 35 × 12	sold to Norfolk interests, ca. 1900; lost (fire), 4-20-'11, at Norfolk
18648 *Nevada*	st.p. W 666	Greenpoint 1870	n/a	168 × 35 × 12	out of documentation, 1912

Off. No. Name(s) [Notes]	Type Hull Gross Tons	Built Year Yard	Engines Cylinder size (in inches)	Dimensions (in feet)	Disposition
105162 *Alaska* [4]	st.p. W 730	Brooklyn 1872	n/a	168 × 35 × 12	out of documentation, 1912
90435 *Montana*	st.p. W 734	Brooklyn 1872	1-cyl VB	172 × 35 × 12	out of documentation, 1908
157021 *Dakota*	st.p. W 553	Brooklyn 1880	1-cyl VB	147 × 34 × 12	out of documentation, 1915
12684 *Colorado* (*) b) *Carteret* (*)	st.p. I 833	Wilm. 1885 Harlan & Hollingsworth	1-cyl VB 46 × 120	171 × 36 × 13	sold to E. 10 & 23 St. Fy. Co., 1915; later ran for Carteret Fy. Co.; out of documentation, 1943
81068 *Wyoming* (*) [5]	st.p. I 833	Wilm. 1885 Harlan & Hollingsworth	1-cyl VB 46 × 120	171 × 36 × 13	sold to E. 10 & 23 St. Fy. Co., 1914; later ran for City of New York; see note; scrapped, 1943
155121 *Oregon* b) *Eastern Shore*	st.p. I 831	Wilm. 1885 Harlan & Hollingsworth	1-cyl VB 46 × 120	171 × 36 × 13	sold to Baltimore interests, ca. 1920; lost (fire), 1-4-'28 at Bay Shore, Md.
130601 *New York* (ii)	st.p. I 896	Wilm. 1892 Harlan & Hollingsworth	1-cyl VB 46 × 120	175 × 36 × 13	sold to Norfolk interests, ca. 1920; converted to barge, ca. 1951

92049 *Maine* *b) Baltimore*	st.p. I 850	Wilm. 1888	1-cyl VB 46 × 120	174 × 36 × 13	sold to Maryland interests, ca. 1920; lost (fire), 1926
145535 *Texas* *b) Harry B. James* *c) George W. Perkins* (*) [6]	st.p. I 896	Wilm. 1890	1-cyl VB 46 × 120	175 × 36 × 13	sold, 1913; later ran for N.Y. & Englewood Fy. Co.; abandoned, 1935
155147 *Ohio* *b) Seawells Point*	st.p. I 867	Wilm. 1887 Harlan & Hollingsworth	1-cyl VB 46 × 120	174 × 36 × 13	sold to E. 10 & 23 St. Fy. Co., ca. 1911; later ran for Norfolk interests; dismantled, 1951
127069 *Columbia*	st.p. I 810	Chester, Pa. 1895	1-cyl VB 42 × 120	156 × 36 × 13	sold to Brooklyn & Manhattan Fy. Co., ca. 1911; later ran for Norfolk interests; out of documentation, 1938
161750 *Vermont* *b) Alexandria* *c) Henry L. Joyce* (*)	st.p. I 810	Chester, Pa. 1895 Delaware River Iron S.B.	1-cyl VB 46 × 120	156 × 36 × 13	sold to Washington, D.C. interests, 1911; later ran for Brooklyn & Manhattan Fy. Co. and N.Y. & Englewood Fy. Co.; abandoned, 1936
107140 *America* (*)	st.p. I 818	Chester, Pa. 1895 Delaware River Iron S.B.	1-cyl VB 46 × 120	156 × 36 × 13	sold to Brooklyn & Manhattan Fy. Co., 1911; later ran for N.Y. & Englewood Fy. Co.; lost (fire), 2-15-'37, foot of Dyckman St., Manhattan

Off. No. Name(s) [Notes]	Type Hull Gross Tons	Built Year Yard	Engines Cylinder size (in inches)	Dimensions (in feet)	Disposition
121032 *Florida* (*)	st.p. I 818	Chester, Pa. 1896	1-cyl VB 46 × 120	156 × 36 × 13	sold to E. 10 & 23 St. Fy. Co., ca. 1915; later ran for City of New York; abandoned, 1946
161775 *Virginia* b) *City of Richmond*	st.p. I 818	Chester, Pa. 1896	1-cyl VB 46 × 120	156 × 36 × 13	sold to Brooklyn & Manhattan Fy. Co., ca. 1911; later ran for Norfolk interests; scrapped, 1953
77284 *Joseph J. O'Donahue* b) *Greenpoint* (*)	st.p. S 901	Chester, Pa. 1898 Delaware River Iron S.B.	1-cyl VB 48 × 120	174 × 36 × 13	sold to E. 10 & 23 St. Fy. Co., 1911; later ran for City of New York; scrapped, 1941
96555 *Harry B. Hollins* b) *New Amsterdam* (*)	st.p. S 1019	Newburgh 1901	1-cyl VB 50 × 120	180 × 37 × 14	sold to Carteret Fy. Co., 1916; scrapped, 1940
77469 *John Englis* (*) [7]	st.p. S 1022	Newburgh 1901	1-cyl VB 50 × 129	180 × 37 × 14	sold to Carteret Fy. Co., 1916; scrapped, 1940

[1] Purchased from Navy Yard Fy. Co., possibly in 1867.

[2] Purchased from Union Fy. Co. in 1859.

[3] Vessel was involved in a near disaster when she caught fire on a trip across the East River in December 1866; see text, chapter 5. This blaze did not destroy the vessel, however; she was rebuilt and served until 1895.

[4] A ferryboat named *Alaska* seems comfortable in a fleet where many of the vessels are named after states of the union. It should be recalled, though, that Alaska didn't become a state until 1959.

[5] Following service with the City of New York between 1921 and 1928 was sold to Ferries Operating Co. for use in upper Hudson River service.

[6] Between 1913 and ca. 1925 while vessel was known as *Harry B. James* she is characterized in *MVUS* as a freight boat, not a ferryboat.

[7] Known to have been leased to Staten Island Rapid Transit in 1901 to help that company maintain schedules after the loss of their *Northfield*; see text, chapter 6.

FLEET: Brooklyn & Manhattan Ferry Company
SERVICE: East River
DATES: 1911–1918
COMMENTS/REFERENCES: This was a municipally-
subsidized company organized in 1911 to restore service on
certain abandoned routes of the Williamsburg ferries; see
text, chapter 6.

Off. No. Name(s) [Notes]	Type Hull Gross Tons	Built Year Yard	Engines Cylinder size (in inches)	Dimensions (in feet)	Disposition
92049 *Maine* (*) b) *Baltimore* [1]	st.p. I 850	Wilm. 1888	1-cyl VB 46 × 120	174 × 35 × 13	sold to Baltimore interests, ca. 1920; lost (fire), 1926
155121 *Oregon* (*) b) *Eastern Shore* [1]	st.p. I 831	Wilm. 1885 Harlan & Hollingsworth	1-cyl VB 46 × 120	171 × 36 × 13	sold to Baltimore interests, ca. 1920; lost (fire), 1-4-'28 at Bay Shore, Md.
107140 *America* (*) [1]	st.p. I 818	Chester, Pa. 1895	1-cyl VB 42 × 120	156 × 36 × 13	sold to N.Y. & Englewood Fy. Co., 1918; lost (fire), 2-15-'37 at foot of Dyckman St., Manhattan
161750 *Henry L. Joyce* (*) a) *Vermont* (*) b) *Alexandria* [2]	st.p. I 810	Chester, Pa. 1895	1-cyl VB 46 × 120	156 × 36 × 13	sold to ship broker, 1918; later ran for N.Y. & Englewood Fy. Co.; abandoned, 1936

Off. No. Name(s) [Notes]	Type Hull Gross Tons	Built Year Yard	Engines Cylinder size (in inches)	Dimensions (in feet)	Disposition
126284 *Colorado* (*) b) *Carteret* (*) [1]	st.p. W 662	Wilm. 1885 Harlan & Hollingsworth	1-cyl VB 46 × 120	171 × 36 × 13	sold to E. 10 & 23 St. Fy. Co., 1915; later ran for Carteret Fy. Co.; out of documentation, 1943
127069 *Columbia* (*) [1]	st.p. I 810	Chester, Pa. 1895	1-cyl VB 42 × 120	156 × 36 × 13	sold to Norfolk interests, ca. 1920; out of documentation, 1938
161775 *Virginia* (*) b) *City of Richmond* [1]	st.p. I 818	Chester, Pa. 1896	1-cyl VB 46 × 120	156 × 36 × 13	sold to Norfolk interests, ca. 1920; scrapped, 1953
75120 *Broadway* a) *James Fisk, Jr.* (*) b) *Passaic* (*) [3]	st.p. W 755	New York 1869 Charles Sneeden	1-cyl VB 50 × 120	170 × 34 × 12	out of documentation, 1918

[1] Purchased from Williamsburg ferries, ca. 1911.

[2] Purchased from Potomac River interests (i.e., Washington & Alexandria Fy. Co.), 1912.

[3] Purchased from Erie R.R., 1911.

FLEET: Nassau Ferry Company
SERVICE: East River
DATES: 1842–1918
COMMENTS/REFERENCES: Firm also known as the Houston Street Ferry Company.

Off. No. Name(s) [Notes]	Type Hull Gross Tons	Built Year Yard	Engines Cylinder size (in inches)	Dimensions (in feet)	Disposition
4855 *California*	st.p. W 262	New York 1851	n/a	n/a	abandoned, 1878
n/a *City of Williamsburgh*	st.p. W 323	Williamsburg 1852 Perrine, Patterson & Stack	n/a	122 × 39 × 10	dismantled, 1866
10487 *Gerald Stuyvesant*	st.p. W 316	Williamsburg 1854	n/a	126 × 30 × 10	abandoned, 1886
17012 *Maspeth* b) *Fort Lee* (*)	st.p. W 430	New York 1866 Laurence & Foulks	n/a	137 × 29 × 10	sold to Riverside & Ft. Lee Fy. Co., 1882; abandoned, 1898
75980 *James M. Waterbury* b) *Rye Beach* c) *Pleasure Beach* d) *City of Norfolk* [1]	st.p. I 412	Wilm. 1878 Harlan & Hollingsworth	1-cyl VB 38 × 108	144 × 32 × 9	sold to Long Island Sound interests, ca. 1918; later sold to Norfolk interests; dismantled, 1953
130170 *Newtown*	st.p. I 450	Wilm. 1879 Harlan & Hollingsworth	1-cyl VB 38 × 108	143 × 32 × 9	sold to Buffalo interests, 1920; abandoned, 1930

76290					
Jamaica	st.p.	Wilm.	1-cyl VB	143 × 32 × 8	sold to Buffalo interests,
	I	1882	38 × 108		ca. 1920; abandoned, 1930
	435	Harlan &			
		Hollingsworth			

[1] The first permanent enrollment certificate for the *James M. Waterbury* was issued by the U.S. Government at Wilmington, Delaware to Harlan & Hollingsworth, the vessel's builder, on January 9, 1878. Issuance of a first certificate to a builder was not unusual. This certificate was surrendered at New York on January 16, 1878, and a new certificate issued to the Nassau Ferry Company. The vessel's final certificate was surrendered by her final owner, the Chesapeake Ferry Company, at Newport News, Virginia on May 13, 1953. From issuance of first certificate to surrender of last involves an active life of 75 years, 4 months, and 4 days. This makes the *James M. Waterbury* the third-oldest New York ferryboat of all time. The oldest is currently *Hamburg*, b) *Lackawanna* (ii) of the Hoboken Ferry Company, a vessel whose service life entailed 79 years, 7 months, and 12 days. The vessel in second place is still active, and may yet claim the top spot. She's *Mount Holly*, a) *South Jacksonville*, c) *Gov. Emerson C. Harrington II*, d) *Adirondack*, currently working for the Lake Champlain Transportation Company.

FLEET: Trustees of St. Patrick's Cathedral
SERVICE: East River (to Calvary Cemetery)
DATES: 1851–1853

Off. No. Name(s) [Notes]	Type Hull Gross Tons	Built Year Yard	Engines Cylinder size (in inches)	Dimensions (in feet)	Disposition
n/a *New York* (*) [1]	st.p. W 189	New York 1842	n/a	100 × 23 × 8	abandoned, 1854
16990 *Martha* (*) b) *West Side* (*)	st.p. W 447	Williamsburg 1852 Perrini, Patterson & Stack	n/a	145 × 29 × 11	sold to Greenpoint Fy. Co., 1853; lost (fire), 10-4-'04, at Billingsport, N.J.

[1] Purchased from Williamsburg ferries, ca. 1850.

FLEET: Greenpoint Ferry Company
SERVICE: East River
DATES: 1853–1921
COMMENTS/REFERENCES: After 1889 company was known as the East Tenth and Twenty-third Street Ferry Company.

Off. No. Name(s) [Notes]	Type Hull Gross Tons	Built Year Yard	Engines Cylinder size (in inches)	Dimensions (in feet)	Disposition
10495 *Greenpoint* (i)	st.p. W 460	Williamsburg 1852 Perine, Paterson & Stack	n/a	126 × 31 × 12	abandoned, 1912
16990 *Martha* (*) b) *West Side* (#) [1]	st.p. W 570	Williamsburg 1852	n/a	144 × 30 × 12	sold to Camden interests; lost (fire), 10-4-'04, at Billingsport, N.J.
19040 *Osprey* (*) [2]	st.p. W 392	Williamsburg 1853	n/a	125 × 32 × 12	sold to Camden interests; lost (fire), 10-4-'04, at Billingsport, N.J.
n/a *Iola*	st.p. W 248	New York 1853	n/a	131 × 24 × 8	broken up, 1866
22804 *South Side* a) *Curlew* (*) b) U.S.S. *Curlew* (+) [3]	st.p. W 366	Williamsburg 1853	n/a	123 × 32 × 8	abandoned, 1912

Off. No. Name(s) [Notes]	Type Hull Gross Tons	Built Year Yard	Engines Cylinder size (in inches)	Dimensions (in feet)	Disposition
18702 *North Side* b) *Kentucky* (#)	st.p. W 567	Greenpoint 1871	n/a	150 × 33 × 12	out of documentation, 1913
135707 *East Side* b) *Tennessee* (#)	st.p. W 547	Greenpoint 1883	n/a	150 × 33 × 12	out of documentation, 1913
126284 *Colorado* (*) b) *Carteret* (*) [4]	st.p. W 833	Wilm. 1885 Harlan & Hollingsworth	1-cyl VB 46 × 120	171 × 36 × 13	sold to Carteret Fy. Co., 1916; out of documentation, 1943
77284 *Greenpoint* (ii) (*) a) *Joseph J. O'Donahue* (*) (#) [5]	st.p. S 901	Chester, Pa. 1898 Delaware River Iron Works	1-cyl VB 48 × 120	174 × 36 × 13	sold to City of New York, 1921; scrapped, 1941
121032 *Florida* (*) [4]	st.p. I 818	Chester, Pa. 1896	1-cyl VB 42 × 120	156 × 36 × 13	sold to City of New York, ca. 1920; abandoned, 1946
81068 *Wyoming* (*) [6]	st.p. I 833	Wilm. 1885 Harlan & Hollingsworth	1-cyl VB 46 × 120	171 × 36 × 13	sold to City of New York, ca. 1920; later ran for upper Hudson River interests; scrapped, 1943
155147 *Ohio* (*) b) *Seawells Point* [7]	st.p. I 867	Wilm. 1887 Harlan & Hollingsworth	1-cyl VB 46 × 120	174 × 36 × 13	sold to Norfolk interests, ca. 1920; dismantled, 1951

[1] Obtained when service previously operated by the Trustees of St. Patrick's Cathedral was absorbed by Greenpoint Fy. Co. ca. 1853.
[2] Purchased from Union Fy. Co. in 1856.
[3] Purchased from U.S. Government at Baltimore on November 1, 1865; vessel owned by Williamsburg ferries before Civil War service with the U.S. Navy.
[4] Purchased from Brooklyn & Manhattan Fy. Co., ca. 1915.
[5] Purchased from Williamsburg ferries, 1911.
[6] Purchased from Brooklyn & Manhattan Fy. Co., 1914.
[7] Purchased from Williamsburg ferries, ca. 1911.

FLEET: Long Island R.R. and predecessor companies
SERVICE: East River
DATES: 1859–1925
COMMENTS/REFERENCES: See Ron Ziel and George Foster, *Steel Rails to the Sunrise* (New York: Duell, Sloan and Pearce, 1965), pp. 310–11.

Off. No. Name(s) [Notes]	Type Hull Gross Tons	Built Year Yard	Engines Cylinder size (in inches)	Dimensions (in feet)	Disposition
n/a *Louise* (*) [1]	st.p. W 341	Greenpoint 1853	n/a	125 × 28 × 10	abandoned, 1866
20527 *Queens County*	st.p. W 320	New York 1859	n/a	148 × 31 × 11	converted to barge, 1887
22792 *Suffolk County*	st.p. W 512	New York 1860	n/a	140 × 31 × 11	sold to Delaware River interests, 1893; abandoned, 1901

Off. No. Name(s) [Notes]	Type Hull Gross Tons	Built Year Yard	Engines Cylinder size (in inches)	Dimensions (in feet)	Disposition
14102 *Kings County*	st.p. W 467	New York 1861	1-cyl VB 34 × 108	148 × 31 × 11	lost (fire), 11-2-'68, at Hunter's Point
11460 *Huntington* *a*) U.S.S. *Fort Henry* (+) [2]	st.p. W 552	New York 1861	n/a	148 × 32 × 11	lost (fire), 11-2-'68, at Hunter's Point
16984 *Montague* (*) [3]	st.p. W 449	New York 1859	n/a	141 × 31 × 11	abandoned, 1877
21855 *Ravenswood*	st.p. W 430	New York 1867	n/a	137 × 29 × 10	sold to Florida interests, 1886; lost (fire), 1-13-'95, at Jacksonville
11927 *Hudson City* (*) [4]	st.p. W 1008	Brooklyn 1867	1-cyl VB 46 × 132	203 × 35 × 12	abandoned, 1913
15632 *Long Island City*	st.p. W 562	Greenpoint	1-cyl VB	149 × 33 × 11	sold and converted to barge, ca. 1897
115028 *Southampton* *b*) *Southland*	st.p. I 673	Wilm. 1869 Harlan & Hollingsworth	1-cyl inclined 48 × 120	170 × 33 × 10	sold to Louisiana interests, 1925; lost (fire), 8-22-'25, at Lake Pontchartrain, La.

85425 *Garden City* [5]	st.p. I 825	Chester, Pa. 1872 Delaware River S.B.	1-cyl inclined 48 × 120	171 × 33 × 14	converted to barge, 1916
20469 *Pennsylvania* b) *Old Point Comfort* [6]	st.p. I 430	Wilm. 1874 Harlan & Hollingsworth	1-cyl VB 38 × 108	136 × 29 × 8	sold to Norfolk interests, ca. 1925; out of documentation, ca. 1940
120282 *Flushing* b) *Tarrytown* [5]	st.p. I 521	Wilm. 1877 Harlan & Hollingsworth	n/a	163 × 32 × 6	sold to upper Hudson River interests, 1912; abandoned, 1938
110389 *Rockaway*	st.p. I 520	Wilm. 1879 Harlan & Hollingsworth	1-cyl 44 × 108	150 × 32 × 10	sold to Norfolk interests, 1909; abandoned, 1938
140339 *Long Beach*	st.p. I 519	Wilm. 1880 Harlan & Hollingsworth	1-cyl inclined 44 × 108	150 × 32 × 10	sold to Wilmington interests, 1913; out of documentation, ca. 1940
91074 *Manhattan Beach* b) *Harding Highway* [7]	st.p. I 630	Newburgh 1884 Ward, Stanton	1-cyl 44 × 108	152 × 32 × 12	sold to Wilmington interests, ca. 1925; lost (foundered), 2-14-'26, at Wilmington

Off. No. Name(s) [Notes]	Type Hull Gross Tons	Built Year Yard	Engines Cylinder size (in inches)	Dimensions (in feet)	Disposition
116007 *Sag Harbor*	st.p. I 630	Newburgh 1884 Ward, Stanton	1-cyl VB 44 × 108	152 × 32 × 12	sold to Savannah interests, ca. 1911; out of documentation, 1918 (?)
203468 *Babylon* b) *Tenafly* (*) [8]	st.s. S 1310	Wilm. 1906 Harlan & Hollingsworth	2 2-cyl comp 18, 38 × 28	188 × 45 × 16	sold to Riverside & Ft. Lee Fy. Co., 1921; dismantled, 1946
205363 *Hempstead* b) *Hackensack* (*) c) *Islander* [8]	st.s. S 1310	Wilm. 1906 Harlan & Hollingsworth	2 2-cyl comp 18, 38 × 28	188 × 45 × 16	sold to Riverside & Ft. Lee Fy. Co., 1921; later ran for Cape Cod interests; dismantled, 1957

[1] Purchased from Union Fy. Co., 1860.
[2] Purchased from U.S. Govt., ca. 1865.
[3] Purchased from Union Fy. Co., 1868.
[4] Purchased from Pennsylvania R.R., 1904.
[5] Leased to Brooklyn & Richmond Fy. Co., ca. 1912.
[6] Purchased from Pennsylvania R.R.'s Philadelphia operation, 1923.

[7] Vessel foundered in the Christina River while operating for the Wilmington & Pennsgrove Fy. Co.; 18 lives were lost.
[8] Only propeller boats owned by L.I.R.R. *Hempstead* leased to City of New York in December 1911 for a short stint on the Whitehall St.–Stapleton line.

FLEET: East 34 Street Vehicular Ferry Company
SERVICE: East River
DATES: 1927–1936

Off. No. Name(s) [Notes]	Type Hull Gross Tons	Built Year Yard	Engines Cylinder size (in inches)	Dimensions (in feet)	Disposition
127157 *Mount Hope* a) *Camden* c) *Penn–Jersey* [1]	st.s. S 437	Elizabeth 1896 Lewis Nixon	2 2-cyl comp 16, 36 × 22	148 × 38 × 13	sold to Philadelphia interests, 1936; scrapped, 1952
211156 *Mount Holly* a) *South Jacksonville* c) *Gov. Emerson C. Harrington II* d) *Adirondack* [2]	st.s. S 292	Jacksonville 1913 A. D. Stevens	1-cyl 18 × 22	130 × 40 × 11	sold to State of Maryland, 1936; currently operating for Lake Champlain interests
92499 *Mount Hood* a) *Mauch Chunk* (*) b) *Margate* [3]	st.s. S 642	Wilm. 1893 Harlan & Hollingsworth	2 2-cyl comp 16, 30 × 22	145 × 32 × 14	abandoned, 1935

[1] Purchased from Delaware River interests (i.e., Phila. & Camden Fy. Co.), 1928; thought to have been leased to Norfolk interests during World War II.

[2] Purchased from Delaware River interests (i.e., Tacony–Palmyra Fy. Co.), ca. 1927; originally owned by the Jacksonville Ferry & Land Co., in Florida. Steam engine replaced by twin Atlas diesels while working for State of Maryland. First permanent enrollment certificate issued at Jacksonville on April 19, 1913. Vessel still in service in 1989 for the Lake Champlain Transportation Company, and stands as the second-oldest ferryboat ever to run in New York. Should she still be in service on November 26, 1992 she will eclipse the mark currently held by *Hamburg*, b) *Lackawanna* (iii) of the Hoboken Ferry Company as the oldest ferryboat ever to run in New York.

[3] Purchased from Philadelphia interests (i.e., Reading R.R.), ca. 1927; earlier owned at New York by Central R.R. of N.J. Was involved in 1901 collision with S.I.R.T.'s *Northfield*; see chapter 5 for details.

FLEET: Astoria Ferry Company
SERVICE: East River
DATES: ca. 1850–1918
COMMENTS/REFERENCES: Company later renamed
New York & East River Ferry Company.

Off. No. Name(s) [Notes]	Type Hull Gross Tons	Built Year Yard	Engines Cylinder size (in inches)	Dimensions (in feet)	Disposition
n/a *Astoria* (i)	st.p. W 102	New York 1840	n/a	n/a	abandoned, 1865
n/a *Bushwick* [1]	st.p. W 151	Hoboken 1848	n/a	75 × 22 × 8	converted to barge, 1872
n/a *Williamsburgh* [1]	st.p. W 255	New York 1856	n/a	119 × 40 × 9	dismantled, 1873
105398 *Astoria* (ii) b) *Public Service* (*)	st.p. W 305	Greenpoint 1872	1-cyl VB 32 × 96	102 × 30 × 9	sold to Port Richmond & Bergen Pt. Fy. Co., ca. 1891; scrapped, 1917
116026 *Steinway* (*)	st.p. W 354	Brooklyn 1884	1-cyl VB 32 × 108	125 × 32 × 10	sold to City of New York, 1922; out of documentation, 1939

96029					
Harlem (*)	st.p.	Greenpoint	1-cyl VB	123 × 31 × 10	sold to City of New York,
a) *Haarlaem* (#)	W	1889	33 × 96		ca. 1922; abandoned, 1926
	382				

3485					
Bowery Bay (*)	st.p.	Greenpoint	1-cyl VB	130 × 32 × 11	sold to City of New York,
a) *Bouwery Bay* (#)	W	1890	34 × 96		ca. 1922; abandoned, 1931
[2]					

[1] Both of these vessels have names that certainly *sound like* they might have been owned by the Williamsburg ferries at one time or another. No evidence could be found, however, linking them to any company other than the Astoria Ferry Co.

[2] A tragic event is associated with this vessel. On June 16, 1904 she was making a routine East River crossing. At about ten o'clock in the morning she passed closely astern of an excursion steamer headed out toward Long Island Sound with a boat full of people. The ferry's crew waved to children lining the rails of the big excursion boat; music from the boat's band could be heard. The vessel was the *General Slocum*, and even then fire was starting to spread through her upper works. Within a short time 1,030 persons on the excursion boat would be dead.

FLEET: State of New York, Department of Mental Hygiene
SERVICE: East River
DATES: 1929–ca. 1936
COMMENTS/REFERENCES: State operated other single-ended steamboats to East River institutions; these are the only known ferryboats.

Off. No. Name(s) [Notes]	Type Hull Gross Tons	Built Year Yard	Engines Cylinder size (in inches)	Dimensions (in feet)	Disposition
229050 *Tenkenas* [1]	ol.s. S 447	Groton, Conn. 1929 Electric Boat	2 diesels	101 × 32 × 14	abandoned, 1937

229051

Wards Island	ol.s. W	Groton, Conn. 1929	2 diesels	101 × 32 × 14	abandoned, 1937
[1]	447	Electric Boat			

[1] Both vessels designed by Eads Johnson; diesels by Winton Engine Co., of Cleveland; generators by General Electric. *MVUS* shows one with wooden hull; the other, with steel.

FLEET: New York & College Point Ferry Company
SERVICE: East River; Long Island Sound
DATES: 1886–1918

Off. No. Name(s) [Notes]	Type Hull Gross Tons	Built Year Yard	Engines Cylinder size (in inches)	Dimensions (in feet)	Disposition
13828 *James Rumsey* (*) [1]	st.p. W 671	Hoboken 1867 John Stuart	n/a	206 × 44 × 11	dismantled, 1907
91015 *Queens* a) *Moonachie* (*) [2]	st.p. W 810	Hoboken 1877 John Stuart	1-cyl VB 42 × 120	197 × 45 × 13	lost (fire), 11-9-'18, at New York
26900 *College Point* a) *Wiehawken* (*) [3]	st.p. W 724	Hoboken 1868	n/a	214 × 45 × 11	dismantled, 1907
95143 *Hackensack* (*) [4]	st.p. W 917	Hoboken 1871 John Stuart	n/a	215 × 50 × 12	out of documentation, 1912 (?)

120586					
F. P. James	st.p.	Brooklyn	n/a	141 × 29 × 9	broken up, 1917
b) Bronx (#)	W	1884			
	445				

150931					
Port Morris	st.p.	Brooklyn	1-cyl	143 × 37 × 13	see note; dismantled, 1934
b) Nathan Hale	W	1901	40 × 96		
c) Governor King	534	Devine			
d) Ridgefield (*)		Burtis			
[5]					

130943					
North Beach	st.p.	Shooter's Island,	1-cyl VB	164 × 37 × 15	sold to U.S. Govt., 1918
b) Genl. John F. Weston	I (?)	N.Y.	44 × 108		
(+) (*)	833	1901			
		Townsend &			
		Downey			

[1] Purchased from Hoboken Fy. Co., 1887.
[2] Purchased from Hoboken Fy. Co., 1907.
[3] Purchased from Hoboken Fy. Co., 1887.

[4] Purchased from Hoboken Fy. Co., 1893.
[5] Sold in 1918 to New London interests; sold to State of Maine, ca. 1920; sold to Riverside & Ft. Lee Fy. Co., 1928.

FLEET: Twin City Ferry Company
SERVICE: Long Island Sound
DATES: 1910–1917

Off. No. Name(s) [Notes]	Type Hull Gross Tons	Built Year Yard	Engines Cylinder size (in inches)	Dimensions (in feet)	Disposition
116146					
Fordham	st.p.	Newburgh	1-cyl VB	173 × 34 × 12	lost (fire), 4-17-'13 at
b) South Brooklyn (*)	I	1887			Shooter's Island, N.Y.
[1]	728				

136372
Queensboro	st.p.	Bath, Maine	1-cyl	$100 \times 26 \times 9$	lost (foundered), 2-15-'20,
a) *Elizabeth City*	W	1893	28×84		off Clason's Pt. Rd., N.Y.
[2]	254				

[1] Purchased from the New York & So. Brooklyn Fy. & Transportation Co., 1910; see note 1 under that company's vessel roster for additional speculation.

[2] Purchased from Portland, Maine interests, 1913.

FLEET: Staten Island Railway
SERVICE: Arthur Kill
DATES: 1867–1948
COMMENTS/REFERENCES: See Herbert B. Reed, "The Staten Island–Perth Amboy Ferry," *Steamboat Bill*, No. 53 (March 1955), 17–18; see also listing under Staten Island Rapid Transit for company's Upper New York Bay service.

Off. No. Name(s) [Notes]	Type Hull Gross Tons	Built Year Yard	Engines Cylinder size (in inches)	Dimensions (in feet)	Disposition
17736 *Maid of Perth*	st.p. W 148	Newburgh 1867	n/a	$82 \times 23 \times 7$	apparently sold to Albany interests; abandoned, 1905
20508 *Warren* (*) [1]	st.p. W 480	Brooklyn 1859 480	n/a	$142 \times 33 \times 12$	scrapped, 1908

125456 *Chester W. Chapin* (*) [2]	st.p. W 428	Rondout, N.Y. 1875 McCausland	n/a	163 × 55 × 9	out of documentation, ca. 1910
95667 *Tottenville* *a) Hoboken* (*) [3]	st.p. I 831	Newburgh 1891 Ward, Stanton	1-cyl VB 44 × 120	200 × 35 × 12	abandoned, 1936
204779 *Perth Amboy*	st.p. W 618	Noank, Conn. 1907 Robert Palmer & Son	1-cyl VB 42 × 108	142 × 34 × 12	scrapped, 1948
222620 *Charles W. Galloway* [4]	st.p. W 587	Wilm. 1922 Amer. Car & Foundry	1-cyl VB 42 × 108	140 × 34 × 12	scrapped, 1948

[1] Purchased from Williamsburg ferries, 1896.
[2] Purchased from New York Central R.R., 1901; earlier ran for the Boston & Albany R.R.
[3] Purchased from the Hoboken Fy. Co., 1910.

[4] Last paddlewheel ferryboat built for New York service; last paddlewheel ferryboat to operate in New York. Made final Tottenville–Perth Amboy crossing under Staten Island Ry. auspices in the early morning hours of October 16, 1948.

FLEET: Carteret Ferry Company
SERVICE: Arthur Kill (see Special Note, below)
DATES: 1916–1939
COMMENTS/REFERENCES: See Herbert B. Reed, "The
New Blazing Star Ferry," part ii, *The Staten Island
Historian*, 23 (January–March 1962), 7–8.

Off. No. Name(s) [Notes]	Type Hull Gross Tons	Built Year Yard	Engines Cylinder size (in inches)	Dimensions (in feet)	Disposition
4870 *Clinton* a) *Clinton* (*) b) U.S.S. *Commodore Morris* (+) c) *Clinton* (*) d) *General John Simpson* (+) (*) [1]	st.p. W 586	New York 1862	1-cyl 38 × 120	152 × 32 × 11	abandoned, 1931
80056 *Winona* a) *Winona* (*) b) *General George E. Pond* (+) (*) [2]	st.p. W 460	New York 1869 Webb & Bell	1-cyl 42 × 120	155 × 33 × 12	out of documentation, 1912
115323 *Secaucus* (*) [3]	st.p. W 974	Hoboken 1873	1-cyl VB 46 × 120	214 × 46 × 13	lost (fire), 11-3-'35, at foot of Bay Ridge Ave. (i.e., 69 St.), Brooklyn
106246 *Albany* (*) [4]	st.p. I 735	Newburgh 1883 Ward, Stanton	1-cyl VB 50 × 120	195 × 36 × 13	scrapped, 1939

77469					
John Englis (*)	st.p.	Newburgh	1-cyl VB		scrapped, 1940
	S	1901	50 × 120	180 × 37 × 14	
[6]	770	T. S. Marvel			

96554					
New Amsterdam (*)	st.p.	Newburgh	1-cyl VB	180 × 37 × 14	scrapped, 1940
a) *Harry B. Hollins* (*)	S	1901	50 × 120		
[6]	778	T. S. Marvel			

12684					
Carteret	st.p.	Wilm.	1-cyl VB	171 × 36 × 13	out of documentation, 1943
a) *Colorado* (*)	I	1885	46 × 120		
	833	Harlan &			
[5]		Hollingsworth			

[1] Built by the Union Fy. Co. but sold to the U.S. Navy before ever seeing service with Union; see text, chapter 4. Returned to Union Fy. Co. after the Civil War, on July 13, 1865, and ran for that company until World War I, when title transferred to the U.S. Army. Final enrollment certificate surrendered in New York on February 24, 1931, *sixty-nine years* after the vessel was built. In the space on her final certificate where it calls for the reason the certificate is being surrendered are typed these words: "Dismantled—sold for junk." The word "abandoned" is also stamped across the certificate in blue ink.

[2] Owned by Union Fy. Co., 1869–1917; owned and operated by U.S. Army, 1917–ca. 1922.

[3] Owned by Hoboken Fy. Co., 1873–1923; enrollment certificate surrendered at New York on May 10, 1923 and marked "abandoned, as unfit for use." Redocumented by Carteret ca. 1926.

[4] Purchased from New York Central R.R. in 1917; original gross tonnage reduced from 833 to 662 in 1932.

[5] Purchased from the E. 10 and 23 St. Fy. Co., 1916; originally owned by the Williamsburg ferries. Gross tonnage reduced from 833 to 662 in 1932.

[6] Purchased from Williamsburg ferries, ca. 1916; gross tonnage reduced from 1019 ('*Hollins*) and 1022 ('*Englis*) in 1930.

Special Note: The Carteret ferryboat fleet was utilized by the Brooklyn & Richmond Fy. Co. for service across the Narrows on the 69 St./Brooklyn–St. George route between 1912 and 1939.

FLEET: New Jersey and Staten Island Ferry Company
SERVICE: Arthur Kill
DATES: 1896–ca. 1932
COMMENTS/REFERENCES: See Herbert B. Reed, "The Howland Hook–Elizabethport Ferry," *The Staten Island Historian*, 23 (October–December 1962), 31–32; 24 (January–March 1963), 7–8.

Off. No. Name(s) [Notes]	Type Hull Gross Tons	Built Year Yard	Engines Cylinder size (in inches)	Dimensions (in feet)	Disposition
25196 *Uncas* [1]	st.p. W 127	Mystic, Conn. 1872	n/a	77 × 22 × 7	scrapped, ca. 1914
13161 *Arthur Kill* a) *J. C. Doughty* (#) [2]	st.p. W 147	Athens, N.Y. 1861	1-cyl VB 26 × 72	88 × 25 × 8	lost (fire), 4-22-'23, at Howland Hook
210463 *Aquehonga*	st.p. W 290	Newburgh 1912 T. S. Marvel	1-cyl VB 30 × 72	102 × 31 × 10	sold to upper Hudson River interests, 1932; lost (foundered), 12-14-'32, at Piermont, N.Y.
223196 *Manadnock* (*) [3]	st.s.	Mariners Harbor 1923 Staten Island S.B.	n/a	127 × 36 × 12	sold to Sunrise Ferries, 1932; later ran for Florida interests; to British registry, 1956

[1] Purchased from upper Hudson River interests, 1896.

[2] Purchased from Poughkeepsie & New Paltz Fy. Co., 1899.

[3] Dieselized sometime after 1932. There is also confusion over the spelling of this vessel's name, it sometimes being found as *Monadnock*. This latter is incorrect. It is likely due to a clerical error made by the company in applying to the Collector of Customs in New York for an official number in 1923 when the incorrect version was typed on the application. It was later corrected in pencil; the document is part of the vessel's file in the National Archives. Owned by Florida interests, 1949 through 1956.

FLEET: Port Richmond and Bergen Point Ferry Company
SERVICE: Arthur Kill
DATES: 1848–1937 (not continuous)
COMMENTS/REFERENCES: See Herbert B. Reed, "The Port Richmond–Bergen Point Ferry," *The Staten Island Historian*, 20 (April–June 1959), 15–16; (July–September 1959), 23–24.

Off. No. Name(s) [Notes]	Type Hull Gross Tons	Built Year Yard	Engines Cylinder size (in inches)	Dimensions (in feet)	Disposition
n/a *Harlequin* [1]	st.p. W 68	Troy, N.Y. 1841	n/a	n/a	abandoned, 1852
2255 *Bushwick* (*; see note) [2]	st.p. W 162	Williamsburg 1842	n/a	n/a	abandoned, 1880
26510 *Bergen Point* a) *West Point* [3]	st.p. W 106	Brooklyn 1857	n/a	72 × 20 × 7	abandoned, 1874

Off. No. Name(s) [Notes]	Type Hull Gross Tons	Built Year Yard	Engines Cylinder size (in inches)	Dimensions (in feet)	Disposition
14935 *Lark* [4]	st.p. W 305	Brooklyn 1860	n/a	108 × 23 × 8	abandoned, 1905
195398 *Public Service* a) *Astoria* (*) [5]	st.p. W 305	Greenpoint 1872	1-cyl VB 32 × 96	102 × 30 × 9	scrapped, 1917
3781 *B. M. Shanley* a) *Bayonne City* (#)	st.p. S 414	Wilm. 1899	1-cyl 30 × 108	125 × 30 × 9	later sold to upper Hudson River interests; abandoned, 1938
127167 *Englewood* (*) a) *City of Englewood* (*) [6]	st.p. W 484	Wilm. 1899 Jackson & Sharp	1-cyl VB	135 × 31 × 12	sold to Riverside & Ft. Lee Fy. Co., 1937; later ran for N.Y. & Englewood Fy. Co.; scrapped, 1941

[1] Purchased from Albany interests, 1849.

[2] Reed claims this was a double-ended ferryboat purchased second-hand in 1866; no other reference to her elsewhere in the roster, although clearly the name *Bushwick* suggests service on the East River. The only *Bushwick* referenced with East River operators was built in Hoboken in 1848, converted to a barge in 1872, and is shown with the New York & East River Fy. Co. (i.e., Astoria Fy. Co.).

[3] Purchased from upper Hudson River interests (i.e., Garrison & West Point Fy. Co.), 1881.

[4] Purchased from upper Hudson River interests (i.e., Rhinebeck–Kingston Fy. Co.), ca. 1883.

[5] Purchased from the New York & East River Fy. Co., ca. 1891.

[6] Purchased from the Riverside & Fort Lee Fy. Co. in 1922. Like the Port Richmond & Bergen Point Fy. Co., the R. & F. L. Fy. Co. was a subsidiary of Public Service of New Jersey, the largest operator of streetcars in the Garden State; both ferry lines served as feeders to the company's rail operations. Other vessels were leased and transferred from the one Public Service ferry company to the other from time to time, such as Riverside & Fort Lee's *Ridgefield* and *Paterson* that are known to have worked the Port Richmond & Bergen Point service in the 1920s and 1930s, but only *Englewood* was formally transferred by having her enrollment (i.e., ownership) changed.

Special Note: Reed identifies the following vessels as having worked for this company under lease or charter: *Annex* (i) of the Pennsylvania Annex service in 1890, and *J. W. Brinkerhoff* of the Poughkeepsie & New Paltz Fy. Co. in 1891.

FLEET: Port Richmond Ferry Company
SERVICE: Arthur Kill
DATES: ca. 1947–1948

Off. No. Name(s) [Notes]	Type Hull Gross Tons	Built Year Yard	Engines Cylinder size (in inches)	Dimensions (in feet)	Disposition
226194 *North Jersey* a) *Frederick Peirce* (*) b) *Westchester* (*) d) *Eastern Bay* e) *B. Frank Sherman* f) *Chesapeake* [1]	ol.el. S 405	Camden 1926 American Brown Boveri	2 6-cyl diesels 12½ × 18	145 × 37 × 12	sold to Maryland interests, ca. 1948; later ran for Virginia interests; out of documentation, 1968

[1] Purchased from U.S. Government; originally ran for Electric
Ferries, Inc.

FLEET: Sunrise Ferries and associated companies
SERVICE: Kill Van Kull; Arthur Kill
DATES: 1932–1963
COMMENTS/REFERENCES: See Special Note, below.

Off. No. Name(s) [Notes]	Type Hull Gross Tons	Built Year Yard	Engines Cylinder size (in inches)	Dimensions (in feet)	Disposition
231526 *Irvington* [1]	ol.s. S 113	Mariners Harbor 1932 United	6-cyl diesel 6 × 6½	54 × 29 × 8	out of documentation, ca. 1967

Off. No. Name(s) [Notes]	Type Hull Gross Tons	Built Year Yard	Engines Cylinder size (in inches)	Dimensions (in feet)	Disposition
231469 *Piermont* [1]	ol.s. S 113	Mariners Harbor 1932 United	6-cyl diesel 6 × 6½	54 × 29 × 8	sold to Shelter Island, N.Y. interests, ca. 1960
235027 *Nancy Helen* a) *General Otis* (+) (*) c) *Resolute* (#) [2]	ol.s. S 52	Wilm. 1910 Pusey & Jones	n/a	93 × 31 × 11	dismantled, 1957
230899 *Saugerties*	ol.s. W 48	Greenport, N.Y. 1930	n/a	57 × 28 × 4	sold to Florida interests; out of documentation, 1962
223196 *Manadnock* (*) [3]	ol.s. S 456	Mariners Harbor 1923 Staten Island S.B.	n/a	127 × 36 × 12	sold to Florida interests, 1949; to British registry, 1956
230060 *Queen Mary* a) *Coxsackie*	ol.s. W 48	Greenport, N.Y. 1930	n/a	57 × 28 × 4	sold to Michigan interests, 1957; to Canadian registry, 1957
249195 *Altair* [4, 6]	ol.s. S 84	Port Richmond 1946 Evans	n/a	61 × 38 × 8	lost (foundered), 6-3-'61, in the Yucatan Channel off Mexico
249196 *Deneb* [4]	ol.s. S 84	Port Richmond 1946 Evans	n/a	61 × 38 ×	to Mexican registry, 1961

249197 *Vega* [4, 6]	ol.s. S 84	Port Richmond 1946 Evans	n/a	61 × 38 × 8	lost (foundered), 1-11-'61, off Snake River breakwater, N.J.
254059 *Capella* b) *North Haven* [4]	ol.s. S 97	Staten Island 1947 Evans	n/a	58 × 32 × 5	sold to Shelter Isl. interests, ca. 1960
257720 *Spica* [4]	ol.s. S 99	Staten Island 1949 Evans	n/a	60 × 36 × 6	sold to Florida interests, ca. 1954
259253 *Sirius* [4]	ol.s. S 97	Port Richmond 1950 Evans	n/a	60 × 36 × 6	sold to Florida interests, ca. 1954; later sold to Mobile interests
270355 *Orion* [4, 5]	ol.s. S 48	Port Richmond 1955 Evans	n/a	60 × 35 × 6	to Mexican registry, 1961

Special Note: Under the heading Sunrise Ferries, our interest is those vessels that operated between Staten Island and New Jersey across the Kill Van Kull and the Arthur Kill in the final days of ferryboat transportation in those areas. As pointed out in the text, the general corporate name under which a fleet of small, diesel-powered vessels ran was Sunrise Ferries, Inc. Sunrise, though, proves to be a complex corporation with links to operations on the Hudson River north of New York City. Some of the Staten Island services appear in official records during certain years under names other than Sunrise, as well. This has not been fully sorted out; the roster includes a variety of ferryboats that appear in official records as owned by Sunrise at one time or another. *All may not have worked the Staten Island services.* See Appendix B for more detail on the various routes.

[1] The two prototypes, designed by Eads Johnson, which became the model for Sunrise Ferries' basic fleet. See text, chapter 9, for further details.
[2] Formerly operated by the U.S. Army and formerly steam-powered.
[3] Purchased from the New Jersey & Staten Island Fy. Co. in 1932; originally steam-powered, but date of diesel conversion uncertain.
[4] Vessels follow basic design pioneered in 1932 by *Piermont* and

Irvington. The 1932 vessels had a single diesel engine with mechanical connections to fore and aft propellers; the latter-day vessels featured twin diesels, one connected with the fore propeller, one with the aft.

[5] The last New York Harbor double-ended ferryboat to be built on Staten Island—or anyplace else in the City of New York.

[6] Neither *Altair* nor *Vega* shows in *MVUS* as having been sold by Sunrise, merely as having been lost through foundering. It would certainly seem that *Altair* was en route to a new Mexican owner. Two of her fleetmates, *Deneb* and *Orion*, were in fact sold to Mexican interests in 1961, the year she was lost, and the place of her foundering was 22° 35′ N. latitude, 86° 30′ W. longitude, a point in the Yucatan Channel between Cuba and Mexico. *Altair* was lost in the Atlantic Ocean off the New Jersey coast; perhaps she too was en route to Mexico.

Index

B. Ferryboats

Vessels that did not operate in New York Harbor, and are therefore not included in the fleet roster in Appendix C, are indicated (∗). Minimal information is supplied here to distinguish different vessels with the same name that are owned by different operators: i.e., "(City)" refers to a vessel owned by the City of New York. See Appendix C for further details. Successor vessels with the same name owned by the same operator are indicated by small sequential Roman numerals set inside parentheses.

C: Ferryboat Operators

See Appendix B on limitations associated
with tracing the corporate evolution of
ferryboat companies. In the following index, a "see also" reference indicates the
principal name used in the narrative for
identifying the service, or services, in
question. (I.e., the designation "Williamsburg ferries" has generally been used in
the text to refer to any of the various companies that succeeded the Williamsburgh
Ferry Co. in the 1860–1909 era.) Ferryboat operators not involved in New
York Harbor operations are indicated (∗).
See general index for further references
to the several railroad companies that operated ferryboat service.